Before World Literature

BEFORE WORLD LITERATURE

The Trickster Tales of al-Ḥarīrī in an Age of Commentary

Matthew L. Keegan

PENN

UNIVERSITY OF PENNSYLVANIA PRESS

PHILADELPHIA

Published by
University of Pennsylvania Press
Philadelphia 19104 USA
www.pennpress.org
EU Authorized Representative: Easy Access System Europe—Mustamäe tee 50, 10621 Tallinn, Estonia, gpsr.requests@easproject.com

Printed in the United States of America on acid-free paper
10 9 8 7 6 5 4 3 2 1
A Cataloging-in-Publication record for this book is available from the Library of Congress.
Hardcover ISBN 978-1-5128-2887-0
Ebook ISBN 978-1-5128-2888-7

For Perla. Without whom not.

Contents

A Note on Conventions

Dates are given in both the Islamic lunar calendar and the ostensibly secular and neutral Christian calendar, specifically the Julian calendar for dates before 1582 and the Gregorian calendar for those after.

Names and Arabic words are transliterated according to the *IJMES* system and, following that system, transliteration is avoided if the terms are in common usage or can be found on an English map, such as Sanaa or Baghdad. The common terms "Quran" and "hadith" are both presented without diacritics. Transliterations are occasionally offered to clarify the choices that I have made in translation or to elucidate technical terminology.

As is conventional in the study of medieval Arabic literature and Islamic studies, the first reference to a historical figure will include the death date in both calendars. When a name appears again much later in the text, the death date is repeated. Whereas it is less common to know the precise birth date of medieval scholars, the medieval Arabic biographical sources are generally fastidious about recording death dates.

Throughout the text, verbs in the present tense are used to describe what authors write or say in books. Other actions are in the past tense. (A biographer *lists* various works by an author in his biography, which he *wrote*.)

In general, I refer to the *Maqāmāt Abī Zayd al-Sarūjī*, written by al-Ḥarīrī, as the *Ḥarīriyya*, an abridgment of the way it is often described in Arabic: *al-Maqāmāt al-Ḥarīriyya*. The term *maqāma* has been variously translated as "assembly," "séance," and "imposture." In what follows, it is left untranslated.

Dramatis Personae: A Very Short History of Ḥarīrian Commentary

What follows is a list of important historical figures who appear in this book. Reading through this roughly chronological list in the order that it appears here can also provide the reader with an abridged, proleptic history of commentary on the *Ḥarīriyya* up to the Mongol conquest of Baghdad in 656/1258. Readers may wish to bookmark this page so that they can refer to these potted biographies when encountering these characters later on in the book.

Al-Hamadhānī (d. 398/1008): The "inventor" of the *maqāma* genre

His *maqāmas* are more variegated than al-Ḥarīrī's, but most feature an eloquent rogue named Abū al-Fatḥ al-Iskandarī ("The Alexandrian") and ʿĪsā b. Hishām. Al-Hamadhānī served the Buyid vizier al-Ṣāḥib b. ʿAbbād (d. 385/995) and also wrote epistles, some of which are devoted to begging for material aid in ways that echo the rogue's mendicant performances. Unlike his successor al-Ḥarīrī, he did not produce a stable, bounded collection, and his *maqāmas* circulated in various recensions. His *maqāmas* were not as celebrated as al-Ḥarīrī's up until the twentieth century, but they then quickly came to be seen as more "literary."

Al-Tibrīzī (d. 502/1109): A philologist who trained many of the *Ḥarīriyya*'s first readers

He was the professor of Arabic philology at the Niẓāmiyya madrasa in Baghdad in his day and had previously studied with al-Maʿarrī (d. 449/1058) whose intricate, edgy, and philologically complex works set the stage for the emergence of the *Ḥarīriyya*. Al-Tibrīzī taught and wrote commentaries on both pre-Islamic poetry and the poems of his elder contemporary al-Maʿarrī. In the latter case, he built on al-Maʿarrī's autocommentaries.[1]

Al-Ḥarīrī (d. 516/1122): The author of the *Ḥarīriyya* and a grammarian from Basra

He wrote autocommentaries on nine of his *maqāma*s, all of which are found in the oldest manuscripts of the text. The *Ḥarīriyya* made him famous, but he was also known for writing a work dedicated to correcting the solecisms committed by scholars.[2] He was a wealthy landowner with estates outside Basra and participant in the Abbasid imperial postal service, which also served as an intelligence apparatus.

Ibn al-Ḥarīrī (d. 556/1161): The son of the author

Known as Abū al-ʿAbbās, he did not write a discrete commentary on the *Ḥarīriyya*, but his kinship with the author and his mastery of the text made him a sought-after commentator on the text. A bureaucrat and litterateur named ʿImād al-Dīn al-Iṣfahānī (d. 597/1201) who served under Saladin once visited Ibn al-Ḥarīrī on tax business. ʿImād al-Dīn relieved some of his tax burden and, as a thank you, Ibn al-Ḥarīrī read and commented on the *Ḥarīriyya* for ʿImād al-Dīn. They only completed forty *maqāma*s before ʿImād al-Dīn fell gravely ill and had to return to Baghdad to recover. Ibn al-Ḥarīrī seems to have caught that same illness but was not so lucky and died shortly after ʿImād al-Dīn's visit.[3] Later scholars sometimes mistakenly referred to the author of the *Ḥarīriyya* as "Ibn al-Ḥarīrī (the son of al-Ḥarīrī)."

Ibn al-Khashshāb (d. 567/1172): A vociferous critic of the *Ḥarīriyya*

He wrote a series of critiques of the *Ḥarīriyya* known as the *Corrections* (*istidrākāt*), which is the name of a genre of critical commentary that focuses on philological errors. The biographical sources portray Ibn al-Khashshāb as a miserly, cantankerous scholar who would damage a book he wanted to buy just to get a cheaper price. One report says that he played chess in the street and enjoyed the entertainments of roadside magicians. This report is immediately followed by a reference to Ibn al-Khashshāb's *Corrections*. What this collocation suggests to me is that his poor reputation was, in part, conjured up as a response to his critiques of the *Ḥarīriyya*, which readers found to be "miserly" and uncharitable. An exception proves the rule: a laudatory biography of Ibn al-Khashshāb from one of his contemporaries omits any mention of his *Corrections*.[4]

Ibn Barrī (d. 582/1187): A Cairene philologist and defender of the *Ḥarīriyya*

He wrote a point-by-point rebuttal to Ibn al-Khashshāb's *Corrections* of the *Ḥarīriyya*. In fact, Ibn al-Khashshāb's *Corrections* do not seem to survive independently in manuscript; they are always accompanied by a rebuttal. This form of philological debate is one kind of commentary that grew up around the *Ḥarīriyya* and informed its reception. Ibn Barrī was an authority in lexicography and appears frequently in the massive medieval dictionary called *The Tongue of the Arabs* (*Lisān al-ʿArab*) by Ibn Manẓūr (d. 711/1311).

Al-Muṭarrizī (d. 610/1213): Author of the first programmatic commentary on the *Ḥarīriyya*

He was a philologist from Khwārazm in Central Asia and a member of the Muʿtazilī theological school. When I say that he composed a programmatic commentary, I mean that his commentary offers a holistic interpretive program. In his case, he argues that the inimitable aesthetic achievements of the *Ḥarīriyya* can be discovered if one is acquainted with the theory of poetics put forward by the Ashʿarī theologian and theorist ʿAbd al-Qāhir al-Jurjānī (d. 471/1078 or 474/1081). Many manuscripts of this commentary survive, attesting to its widespread influence. One later Yemeni commentator from the tenth/sixteenth century "cannibalized" al-Muṭarrizī's commentary, reusing much of his introductory material and reformatting his commentary so that it included the full text of the *Ḥarīriyya* instead of only the lemmas.

Al-Panjdīhī (d. 584/1188): Author of the first digressive commentary on the *Ḥarīriyya*

He was a Sufi scholar who hailed from the town of Panjdeh (Persian for "five villages"), north of Herat. His name was spelled in various ways in Arabic, including al-Bandīhī and al-Fanjdīhī. He traveled widely and eventually became a part of Saladin's retinue, serving as a tutor to the famous sultan's son. His commentary is both programmatic and digressive, by which I mean that it does not simply gloss and explicate the text. Instead, he takes even simple, philologically uninteresting words as an incitement to digress on a wide range of topics, especially the Quran and hadith. Al-Panjdīhī also included his own passionate rebuttals to Ibn al-Khashshāb's critiques, occasionally drawing on and expanding on Ibn Barrī.[5] Although al-Panjdīhī's explicitly Islamic commentary on the *Ḥarīriyya* was incredibly influential, it has remained largely overlooked in the era of print.

Al-Sharīshī (d. 619/1222): An Andalusian scholar and commentator on the *Ḥarīriyya*

He wrote three commentaries of different lengths on the *Ḥarīriyya*. The two shorter commentaries are focused on glossing difficult words and phrases. The third is a digressive commentary that cannibalizes much of al-Panjdīhī's commentary while reshaping it to be more focused on poetry and narrative material. If al-Panjdīhī digresses in the Islamic archive, al-Sharīshī focuses instead on the archive of poetry and *adab* narrative. It is interesting that al-Panjdīhī's commentary seems to have flourished up until the sixteenth century. In the Ottoman realms, al-Sharīshī came to displace al-Panjdīhī and, as a result, his commentary was printed by the Ottoman Būlāq press in the nineteenth century.

ʿAbd al-Laṭīf al-Baghdādī (d. 629/1231): A physician and philosopher

We will meet ʿAbd al-Laṭīf in the introduction, and we will encounter him again and again in the chapters of this book. Although he was not a major commentator on the *Ḥarīriyya*, his life and his encounters with the book are illustrative precisely because he was a rather unremarkable scholarly reader who, as a matter of course, participated in the Arabic philological tradition. His true intellectual passions were found in philosophy, medicine, and alchemy, but it is illustrative to see how this sort of scholar returned time and again to read, comment on, and transmit the *Ḥarīriyya*.

* * *

In some sense, al-Ḥarīrī's stories are also main characters in our story, even when they are not always central to the analysis that follows. To give readers a sense of the narratives themselves, brief summaries of two *maqāma*s follow:

The Third *Maqāma*—Known as the *Maqāma* of the Dinar

The narrator al-Ḥārith finds himself in the company of learned men holding a sophisticated conversation when a man wearing shabby garments limps toward them and explains in eloquent terms that fickle fortune has brought him low. Al-Ḥārith takes out a golden dinar and offers it to the man if he will praise the dinar in verse, which he does, and al-Ḥārith gives him the dinar. When the man is about to depart, al-Ḥārith offers him a second dinar if he will censure that same gold coin in verse, which he does. Al-Ḥārith is impressed and realizes that this man is none other than Abū Zayd, a companion of his whom he already knows. His limp is nothing more than a disguise. Al-Ḥārith tells Abū Zayd that he has been recognized and asks after his condition. Abū Zayd greets al-Ḥārith but seems sullen, saying that he moves between hardship and ease. He then disappears after extemporizing some poetry on the purpose of his feigned disability. A medieval critic would describe this *maqāma* as an ideal example of eloquent rhetoric because it demonstrates that language can be used to praise and censure the very same thing in ways that are equally elegant and beautiful.[6]

The Thirty-Second *Maqāma*—Known as the *Maqāma* of Ṭayba

The narrator al-Ḥārith is returning from the pilgrimage to Mecca and is on his way to Medina to visit the tomb of the Prophet. While on the road, he and his companions stop at a nomadic encampment where the people are flocking toward a man they call the Jurist of the Arabs. Al-Ḥārith watches as this jurist listens to one hundred different legal questions and responds to each in turn with one hundred legal opinions (*fatwās*) that are patently incorrect until one realizes that there is a crucial double-entendre in the question. It turns out that the jurist's answers are correct if one knows that he is answering each question according to its less likely meaning. Al-Ḥārith realizes that this jurist is none other than Abū Zayd, so he follows him and confronts him, asking when he had become a legal scholar. Abū Zayd explains in verse: "In every era I wear disguises and mix with both happy and unhappy conditions."[7] Finally, Abū Zayd invites al-Ḥārith to join him on a trip to Medina, but al-Ḥārith refuses unless Abū Zayd explains his *fatwās*. Once he has done so, the two travel to Medina and continue on in amicable discussion until they part ways.

Introduction

> In place of the old local and national seclusion and self-sufficiency, we have intercourse in every direction, universal interdependence of nations. And as in material, so also in intellectual production. The intellectual creations of individual nations become common property. National one-sidedness and narrow-mindedness become more and more impossible, and from the numerous national and local literatures there arises a world literature.
>
> —Karl Marx and Friedrich Engels, *The Communist Manifesto*

> It is therefore not in the name of *adab* that the *maqāma* is judged but in the name of "literature" (one knows that the word is relatively recent), which seeks to free itself from any didactic concerns.
>
> —Abdelfettah Kilito, *Les Séances*

Whatever world literature might be, it is of relatively recent vintage. For Marx and Engels, it arose in the wake of an age of national literatures and mirrors the increasing globalization of the economic realm. Under these new globalizing conditions, "literature" came to be seen as something that each culture (or language or nation) possessed. Literature was therefore becoming a universal category, even if the linguistic terrain and literary achievement of each culture might differ. Recent critics of world literature like Aamir Mufti and Michael Allan have shown that the concepts of "literature" and "literariness" exert a kind of normative force by insisting on particular modes of reading that flatten out the distinct cultures of reading and writing that existed before world literature. The title of this book, *Before World Literature*, is intended as a provocation, inviting us to think about different modes of reading that are not inflected by more recent assumptions about literature and literariness.

The emerging critiques have revealed the Eurocentrism of world literature, its roots in Orientalism, and the ways in which its secular sensibilities are maintained by conjuring the fanatical reader as literature's sinister Other. These accounts of world literature, however, generally offer brief or vague accounts of what came before world literature, focusing instead on the emergence of the new "literary" dispensation. Where more detail has been given, the accounts tend to be misleading. Consider Marx and Engels (and later Pascale Casanova), for whom what precedes world literature is local and national. As Michiel Leezenberg points out, this account does not fit well with the traditions of reading and writing in Arabic known as *adab*, which were cosmopolitan and transregional.[1] Beyond these matters of geographical scope, there remains the question of how people came to read and interpret books before literariness became the rubric through which any tradition's texts came to be evaluated. This is the question that organizes the work of this book.

The universalizing logic of world literature has led many specialists in Arabic literature writing in the past half century or so to insist that the correct approach to reading Arabic prose and poetry from the precolonial period is to read those texts "as literature."[2] The purpose of this argument was to push back against the dismissiveness of certain modes of Orientalist scholarship that disparaged Arabic literature as dry and devoid of any interest beyond the philological and historical. Paradoxically, however, these disparaging judgments emerged precisely because Arabic poetry and prose had already come to be read in the nineteenth century "as literature," thus inviting it to be judged against European literature and to be found wanting. According to the emerging logic of world literature, each "culture" (or nation or people or civilization) possesses a literary tradition, and this tradition's quality and vitality are reasonable proxies for the quality and vitality of that civilization. It was the British politician and colonial official Thomas Macaulay (d. 1276/1859) who famously stated that, although he knew neither Sanskrit nor Arabic, he had it on good authority that "a single shelf of a good European library was worth the whole native literature of India and Arabia."[3]

Reading Arabic texts "as literature," whether to disparage or to celebrate those texts, produces problematic erasures and distortions by insisting that we interpret and evaluate texts using the reading practices, interpretive methods, and aesthetic assumptions that have been fruitful for reading modern literature, especially the novel. These kinds of literary interpretations may be meaningful, delightful, and important, but they often erase or explicitly reject the philological and hermeneutical approaches that would have been familiar (and meaningful, delightful, or important) to readers who lived before colonial modernity.

The concepts and institutions of "literature" spread across the world during an era of colonial violence, often accompanied by radical reforms in education. As a result, many of the diverse forms of reading that existed across the world came to be discarded or assimilated, unevenly and in different ways, into "world literature." The conceptual hegemony that is the product of colonial modernity is now so total that it is exceedingly difficult to think without categories like "literature" and the "literary." Rather than attempting to ignore the category of literature altogether, however, this book attempts to make the lens of the literary apparent to us so its reading and interpretive practices can come into focus. The assimilationist approach of applying literary techniques to premodern Arabic texts underpins an expansionist model of world literature that seeks to bring more and more texts into the realm of the literary without interrogating the methodological flattening that this entails. These modes of reading may make some texts come "alive" to modern readers and their sensibilities, but the success of this proposition often depends very much on whether those texts are processable by literary tastes and modes of reading. To read Arabic narrative texts without assimilating them to literature, as is attempted in this book, may seem quixotic, but it is only a *demotion* of those texts if inclusion within literature is considered a *promotion*. I am skeptical of the latter proposition for reasons that this book will explain.

The subtitle of the book introduces the "trickster tales" of al-Ḥarīrī, which refers to a text known in English as *The Impostures of Abū Zayd al-Sarūjī* or in Arabic as *Maqāmāt Abī Zayd al-Sarūjī*. Its author was Abū al-Qāsim al-Ḥarīrī (d. 516/1122). That book comprises an authorial introduction and fifty episodes, called *maqāma*s, about an eloquent trickster. Each *maqāma* features an eloquent and erudite performance of Arabic and Islamic knowledge by the main character, the roguish vagabond named Abū Zayd al-Sarūjī. The word *maqāma* literally means "an instance of standing" and thus refers both to each story as a narrative unit and to the eloquent performance of Abū Zayd within each story. Translators have glossed the term *maqāma* in various ways. It has been called an assembly, a séance, and, most recently, an imposture, a term that brings together the notions of the standing posture and the trickster's ruse.[4] In each *maqāma*, the trickster encounters the story's narrator, another fictional character who is called al-Ḥārith b. Hammām. Al-Ḥarīrī's *Maqāmāt* were often called *al-Maqāmāt al-Ḥarīriyya* or sometimes simply the *Ḥarīriyya*, and it is this latter term that I will use here. This collection of stories was central to Islamic education and thrived in a culture of commentary that stretched from West Africa and Iberia to South Asia and China for centuries. The social, intellectual, and material practices of commentary described and analyzed in this book understood the *Ḥarīriyya* to be constitutive of a transregional Islamic scholarly tradition, rather than part of "literature."

Before the rise of world literature, the *Ḥarīriyya* inhabited and thrived in the world of *adab*. The Arabic term *adab* is now often deployed in modern Arabic as a calque for "literature," but it continues to be a more capacious concept, encompassing ideas of comportment and ethics. If someone in Cairo were to tell me today that I lack *adab*, it would be a comment on my manners and not my knowledge of literature. In the precolonial world, a book of *adab* might contain poetry, history, science, and philosophy, as well as observations on correct behavior or the comportment of courtiers. Behavior and eloquent performance were part of *adab*. Scholars have long recognized the incommensurability of the terms "literature" and "*adab*," and they have suggested other translations like *belles-lettres* and *paideia* (two more non-English terms).[5]

The disparity between *adab* and literature is not, however, merely conceptual. Reading the *Ḥarīriyya* as part of *adab* also requires us to appreciate the materiality of *adab*. The social, aesthetic, and historical contexts that attended the reception of a text like the *Ḥarīriyya* are not merely conceptually distinct but also materially different because they were, in the precolonial period, embedded in particular modes of textual production and circulation. The textual culture of world literature, as well as its institutions, norms, and capitalist modes of circulation are radically different, and they reconfigure the reading and interpretation of texts like the *Ḥarīriyya*. This book seeks to understand how the *Ḥarīriyya* first appeared in Baghdad in 1111 AD (504 AH), how it became a sensation from Spain to Central Asia, and why it was considered by many to be the pinnacle of *adab* prose for eight centuries. What were the institutional and material conditions underpinning the enthusiastic and energetic teaching of the *Ḥarīriyya* in mosques, madrasas, and private homes?

I contend that commentary was the crucial social, material, and intellectual practice that made the *Ḥarīriyya* such a success. Al-Ḥarīrī wrote commentaries on parts of his *Ḥarīriyya*, and later scholars followed his lead, expanding and elaborating on what had come before. Some of these commentaries contain glosses and debates about the text's recherché vocabulary or solutions to Abū Zayd's riddles. Other commentaries are more systematic, addressing the aesthetic excellence of the text as a whole or potential symbolic readings. Still others are outrageously digressive commentaries, which delve into poetry and narrative material that seem, at first glance, only tangentially related to the text. To read the *Ḥarīriyya* as *adab* was to read commentarially.

In the nineteenth century, the *Ḥarīriyya* and the commentary culture that underpinned its transmission fell swiftly and dramatically out of favor. Whereas the *Ḥarīriyya* had been a celebrated and canonical work for centuries, it now became a sign of cultural decadence to both Arab reformers and Orientalist critics. The story of literature's global triumph is also the story of the *Ḥarīriyya*'s fall from grace, which is why the story of its reception is an ideal case for exploring the practices of reading before world literature. The restructuring of material, social, and aesthetic conditions that attended the arrival of literature as a universal category reconfigured the canon of *adab*. The material and institutional shift in the conditions of reading made it possible to translate *adab* "as literature." As a result, the *Ḥarīriyya* became a text deracinated from the practices of reading and commentary that made it legible and celebrated.

To illustrate the transformation of reading practices, we can compare the autobiographies of two scholars, ʿAbd al-Laṭīf al-Baghdādī (557–629/1162–1231) and Muḥammad ʿAbduh (1266–1323/1849–1905). Precisely because autobiographies are shaped retrospectively by the ideological concerns of their authors, their depictions of early educational encounters can be extremely instructive. ʿAbd al-Laṭīf describes in his autobiography how he had memorized numerous texts in his childhood, including the *Ḥarīriyya*, the Quran, the poems of al-Mutanabbī (d. 354/965), and primers on law and grammar. When he attended his very first formal lesson, an event discussed in detail in Chapter 2, his teacher was commenting on a text that ʿAbd al-Laṭīf had already memorized. The lesson was, however, a complete disaster for the young student. ʿAbd al-Laṭīf found the commentary baffling and incomprehensible. When the teacher recognized that his other students were expressing appreciation at his commentary but that his newest student was out of his depth, he dismissed the young ʿAbd al-Laṭīf and assigned him to a disciple who could train him in the commentary tradition. Under the supervision of his new tutor, ʿAbd al-Laṭīf was made to study "all the commentaries (*jamīʿ al-shurūḥ*)," which the two then discussed. Finally, ʿAbd al-Laṭīf was required to offer his own commentary on the text.[6] As this anecdote illustrates, commentary was much more than explication. For ʿAbd al-Laṭīf to participate in scholarly discourse as a student, he needed first to be able to comprehend the kind of advanced commentary that his teacher produced. ʿAbd al-Laṭīf needed to become a walking commentary to participate in the social, material, and intellectual practices of reading.

By contrast, Muḥammad ʿAbduh describes himself as deeply disaffected with commentary culture. He was particularly frustrated by the fact that his teachers' commentaries were full of abstruse jargon.[7] In other words, his teachers (like those who taught ʿAbd al-Laṭīf) engaged in a form of commentary that assumed a high degree of familiarity with the existing scholarly tradition, its technical terms, and the topics of debate. According to his autobiography, ʿAbduh tried to abandon the scholarly path his family had chosen for him when a chance encounter with a Sufi relative changed his outlook. This scholar's commentaries conveyed the meaning of the text, eschewing the abstruse jargon that he had encountered in his schooling.[8] Later in ʿAbduh's career, he would champion a different mode of reading and attempt to recast the canons of Arabic literature and education in ways that he thought were more consistent with both modernity and the more authentic Arabic-Islamic past.[9] He sought to supplant the inconveniently persistent "postclassical" tradition of reading and commentary with a newly revived "classical" heritage, a topic that we will discuss in detail in Chapter 1.

Whereas ʿAbd al-Laṭīf memorized, studied, and commented on the *Ḥarīriyya*, ʿAbduh denigrated the *Ḥarīriyya* for its weak style, claiming that it reflected non-Arab tastes. When ʿAbduh produced an edition in 1889 of an earlier series of *maqāma*s by al-Hamadhānī (d. 398/1001), the goal seems have been not only to reconfigure the Arabic canon but also to inculcate new reading practices that were more suited for literary modernity. Rather than an elaborate commentary, his edition contained footnotes that conveyed the meaning of unusual words and the like. He also bowdlerized the text, removing sexually explicit material he found improper. When an English translation appeared in 1915, it followed ʿAbduh's expurgated edition and was lauded by an English scholarly journal as a vindication for al-Hamadhānī, "who, as to taste, is distinctly superior to Hariri."[10] The new literary tastes were underpinned by new reading practices and new expectations about translatability and legibility, and these new tastes rendered texts like the *Ḥarīriyya* unliterary.

The new literary tastes, reading practices, and editorial norms were decisive in reshaping the canon, and these days, the *Ḥarīriyya* enjoys very little of its former favor. Even where al-Ḥarīrī's name is remembered as one of the great authors in Arabic, his masterpiece is little studied and less taught. Critics in the nineteenth and twentieth centuries preferred the *maqāmas* of al-Ḥarīrī's predecessor al-Hamadhānī (d. 398/1008) because they felt that the earlier author had not "sacrificed" the story for the sake of verbal pyrotechnics.[11] The richly allusive language of the *Ḥarīriyya* thus became a mark of decadence. According to the French Orientalist Charles Pellat, the fact that the *Ḥarīriyya* had been so celebrated for centuries "must be accounted for by the decline of literary taste."[12] For both European Orientalists and the reformers of the Arab Renaissance (the *Nahḍa*), al-Ḥarīrī became a symptom of the "era of decline (*ʿaṣr al-inḥiṭāṭ*)," an era supposedly marked by the attention that literary works devoted to stylistics and verbal acrobatics at the expense of plot and other appropriately *literary* features. Naturally, the era of literary decline was thought to be accompanied by the decline of Islamic scholarship and the sciences more generally, such that each "decadent" work became less worthy of attention when compared to the supposedly more creative, more original, or more virile works that preceded it.[13] Scholars and critics in the nineteenth and twentieth centuries who sought to revive this supposedly decadent and moribund Arab culture renovated the canon in favor of al-Hamadhānī, while the *Ḥarīriyya*, at times, was banished from the precincts of the literary altogether.[14]

This book seeks to provincialize and relativize the category of literature, calling into question the becoming-universal of that category. Both ʿAbd al-Laṭīf and ʿAbduh will play central roles over the course of this book to illustrate the contrast between practices of reading before and after world literature. My account builds on the critique of world literature undertaken by scholars such as Haifa Saud Alfaisal, Michael Allan, Emily Apter, Karim Mattar, Aamir Mufti, and Muhsin al-Musawi. These emerging critiques of world literature have sought to show how limited and limiting Eurocentric accounts of literature have been while expanding the possibilities of thinking and imagination. We cannot achieve this admirable goal, however, if we restrict ourselves to reading novels or to examining the world shaped by colonial modernity. We must engage with the practices of reading that existed before world literature.

To get a flavor of the *Ḥarīriyya*, let us begin with the very first story in the collection (*maqāma* #1), which is called "The *Maqāma* of Sanaa."[15] Al-Ḥārith b. Hammām, the narrator of all fifty stories, finds himself in the city of Sanaa in the highlands of Yemen. He is hungry and weary and short on funds, so he wanders the streets in search of food until he comes upon a throng of people weeping. Making his way to the center of the crowd, he finds a man giving a rousing sermon on the certainty of death and the vanity of earthly pleasures.[16] The exhortation to asceticism inspires the crowd to shower alms on this man of pious poverty who then departs. Al-Ḥārith, still hungry for food but having feasted his ears on the preacher's words, notices that the man is attempting to sneak off and surmises that he is aiming to conceal where he dwells. Al-Ḥārith surreptitiously follows the man until he sees him slip into a cave. After waiting a few moments, al-Ḥārith charges into the cave to discover this supposed ascetic feasting on wine and meat in the company of a young confederate.

The narrator al-Ḥārith is shocked by this hypocrisy and cries out, "Is that your speech and this your reality?" The pseudoascetic extemporizes a few lines of cheeky poetry in which he confesses that the sermon was not sincere. It was a snare to catch his prey. As an excuse, he blames Fate (*dahr*), which forces worthy men like him to rely on trickery while it elevates the undeserving to positions of power.[17] Al-Ḥārith reacts indignantly to the rogue's excuse and demands to know his identity. The young companion explains that "this is Abū Zayd al-Sarūjī, the lamp of strangers and the crown of those who do *adab*."[18] The next forty-nine *maqāma*s offer variations on this theme, although al-Ḥārith is not always so upset about Abū Zayd's deceptions and hypocrisies. In the very next story, *maqāma* #2, the narrator al-Ḥārith is found enjoying the pleasant and amusing company of Abū Zayd and then longing for his presence after they part ways. Sometimes al-Ḥārith becomes Abū Zayd's confederate, and he mentions at the end of *maqāma* #33 that he became the rogue's traveling companion for two years.[19]

It is often assumed that this text, with its playful treatment of serious topics and overt fictionality, must have been offensive or problematic to medieval Islamic sensibilities.[20] However, these assumptions have overlooked the actual reception of the text, for which we have extensive evidence. The story of the book's reception began in February of the year 504 after the Hijra (1111 AD) when Abū al-Qāsim al-Ḥarīrī launched his *Maqāmāt* into Baghdad society. He did not deliver his book to a wealthy patron or begin selling his book to the merchant classes. Instead, he treated his book as a text to be studied and circulated in the same way Muslim scholars studied and circulated collections of Prophetic sayings, legal treatises, and grammatical works. That is, al-Ḥarīrī deliberately inserted his *Maqāmāt* into the infrastructure of Islamic knowledge production by having it read aloud over the course of a month to an assembly of elite Muslim scholars in Baghdad.[21] Among the scholars at this first public reading was Ibn al-Naqūr (d. 565/1170), an otherwise unremarkable scholar who became one of the early authorities in the text and oversaw authorized reading sessions to transmit the *Ḥarīriyya*. In fact, ʿAbd al-Laṭīf had first heard the text when he was six years old in the presence of Ibn al-Naqūr, for which he received a certificate attesting to his chain of transmission back to the author. By the time al-Ḥarīrī died in 516/1122, the text had already become a transregional sensation with readers from the Straits of Gibraltar to the shores of the Caspian Sea eagerly studying his masterpiece with scholars who had heard it from the now-famous author. Within the next two centuries, translations and adaptations had appeared in Persian, Hebrew, and Syriac.[22] For the next eight hundred years, the *Ḥarīriyya* was held in such high regard that some Muslim scholars compared it to the Quran itself, claiming that both possessed miraculous inimitability.[23]

This book examines reading practices in the age of commentary and in the formation of world literature to answer two fundamental questions. First, why did the *Ḥarīriyya* fall so suddenly out of favor? And second, what made it such a success in the first place? To answer the first question, we must come to grips with the ways in which the radical shifts in the social, material, and aesthetic conditions of reading and writing that attended the emergence of "world literature." It might seem odd to suggest that there could be a time "before (world) literature" because the category of literature has become so much a part of our conceptual vocabulary that its universality is taken for granted. However, as Abdelfettah Kilito points out in the epigraph above, the *maqāma* has come to be judged by the standards of literature, a recently arrived ethic of reading, rather than those of *adab*. Moreover, Kilito points out that literariness disavows didacticism—mere learning—and aspires to something more sublime, which hints at the normative edge that is always already present when literature is invoked.

The idea of literature's universality is, in fact, underpinned by an act of appropriation. In the same breath that Goethe coined the phrase *Weltliteratur* in 1827, he declared that "poetry is the universal possession of mankind."[24] This dream of global cosmopolitanism cannot be extricated from the advent of colonial modernity that subtended it and through which European powers laid claim—and took possession of—the material and intellectual production of much of the globe. The assumptions of Orientalism led to a conceptualization of the world on European terms with Europe at its center. As a result of literature's universalization, which brought with it *particular* genres and reading practices, the commentary culture that made the *Ḥarīriyya* such a success was erased or thoroughly marginalized.

To answer the second question—namely, why the *Ḥarīriyya* was so celebrated prior to the nineteenth century—we must learn to read the *Ḥarīriyya* with our young friend ʿAbd al-Laṭīf. In other words, we must learn to read commentarially. Before the nineteenth century, the *Ḥarīriyya* circulated in an "age of commentary," as the subtitle of my book suggests. Becoming a scholarly adult required more than memorization and listening. A student like ʿAbd al-Laṭīf would study both written and oral commentary to deepen their understanding of a text and make connections between different parts of the textual tradition. Without mastering the commentary tradition on Islamic law, grammar, and the *Ḥarīriyya*, ʿAbd al-Laṭīf would have been unable to participate in the upper echelons of Islamic scholarship later in life. This culture of commentary eventually came to be seen in the nineteenth and twentieth centuries as a sign of intellectual stagnation, decline, and decadence, but we cannot read with ʿAbd al-Laṭīf unless we understand what commentarial reading was like.

To read before world literature is to recognize that the transformations of the nineteenth century fundamentally reshaped the social, intellectual, and material contexts in which the *Ḥarīriyya* circulated and was read. The first chapter of my book explores this nineteenth-century transformation in order to perform an exorcism of sorts—or, perhaps better, a séance. It is not that I believe myself (or anyone) to be capable of expelling these ghosts who haunt our reading and writing. Rather, my aim in this particular séance is to make these spirits familiar to us. That is, I would like to make clear the extent to which the ways we have recently read and interpreted the *Ḥarīriyya* are haunted by something that came to be called "the literary." Then we—and this "we" refers to the heterogeneous assemblage of modern readers who encountered and have continued to encounter the text after the transformations wrought by print culture and colonialism—can begin to seek out new ways of approaching the *Ḥarīriyya* and other texts like it without immediately subjecting it to the categories and strategies shaped by literature.

I should be clear that this project is *not* an attempt to provide a new, better, or "nonliterary" *interpretation* (in the singular) of the *Ḥarīriyya*. Instead, I would eschew any attempt to reduce the *Ḥarīriyya*'s meaning to a single, coherent interpretation, preferring to proffer an encounter with the ramified and contested *interpretations* of the *Ḥarīriyya* that could be found among the readers who left traces of their diverse responses during the first centuries of the text's reception. None of this is to say that a present-day reader's direct engagement with a text is itself illegitimate, but the insistence on unmediated readings of a text abstracted from its contexts can function as an act of erasure, especially in the case of Arabic and Islamic history. Furthermore, historical claims are often unconsciously smuggled into these ostensibly abstract, literary readings, as is the case when interpreters conjure up an assemblage of medieval Islamic sensibilities against which the *Ḥarīriyya* was presumed to be subversive (see Chapter 1). Social contexts cannot be extrapolated from the formal and structural features of a text. Although texts like the *Ḥarīriyya* continue to be open to rereading and reinterpretation, how much richer would these reinterpretations become if they were aware of the many meanings that had been made with the text in the medieval past?

Part of the challenge in this book is that it requires bringing several fields of study into conversation: comparative literature, the study of classical Arabic literature, Islamic studies, and manuscript studies. There are distinct genealogies and scholarly expectations in each of these fields that some may find frustrating. Although scholars of Islamic studies and classical Arabic literature may find the first chapter's attention to the nineteenth century unfamiliar and superfluous, I argue that it is important to understand the genealogies that inform our reading practices and fields of scholarship. Similarly, scholars of comparative literature may find the methods and contexts in Chapters 2 through 7 less familiar, but my argument is that a deep understanding of these precolonial reading and interpretive practices is crucial to the project of provincializing world literature. My hope is that scholars from each of these fields will nevertheless find the interventions and arguments here useful.

For scholars of comparative literature, this book offers a way of thinking about the social, intellectual, and material conditions of reading before the advent of world literature. Too often, scholars of comparative literature have trod through the same canon of nineteenth- and twentieth-century texts in the hopes of critiquing the categories called into being through the dialectic of colonial modernity. What has been left aside is attention to what comes before world literature, which ought to shed light on the contours of how world literature is formulated.

For scholars of precolonial Arabic literature, this book offers one of the first attempts to provide an appreciative account of the social, intellectual, and aesthetic features of commentary culture. The intellectual contributions of commentary have been recognized by scholars of intellectual history, exegesis, and Islamic law, but scholars of precolonial Arabic literature continue to dismiss commentary traditions as dry, philological readings (or misreadings) of the poetry and prose of the past. The stories in the *Ḥarīriyya* can be understood differently when we understand that commentary is part and parcel of the narrative drama of the texts themselves. In a noncommentarial (or even anticommentarial) reading culture, these features appear deadening, nonliterary, and nonnarrative. But these commentaries are best understood as a vibrant engagement with the text and its contexts that authors invited through their highly referential and erudite prose. Indeed, commentaries were themselves sometimes celebrated as significant performances of scholarship and hermeneutics.

For scholars working in the field of Islamic studies, this book contends that "literary" topics should be taken seriously as Islamic. Islamic discourses were one of the primary structures through which the *Ḥarīriyya* was interpreted, but it is generally seen as a text that does not lie within the purview of Islamic studies because it is part of literature. The marginalization of *adab* within the field of Islamic studies, on both the structural and intellectual levels, has led to accounts of Islam that take for granted that it should be defined by the contours of the concept of "religion." This book draws on the methodologies associated with Islamic studies—paying attention to the social and material contexts of a text's reception—to read a text in a way that does not conform to the reading practices of world literature.

The *Ḥarīriyya* is not a well-loved text these days, at least in the realm of world literature. It is a now-obscure classic that is treated as a triumph of style over substance, pushed aside in an era of world literature in spite of the ministrations of brilliant scholars and translators in recent years. The name al-Ḥarīrī may remain as part of an abstract canon of great authors like al-Jāḥiẓ and al-Mutanabbī, but his work is no longer a central part of the "literary" heritage of Arabic literature. The context in which the *Ḥarīriyya* continues to be a celebrated feature of Islamic education is Nigeria, in which students of Arabic in Islamic educational institutions continue to study the text intensively, as Sulaiman Adewale Alagunfon has shown in his recent monograph *The Classical Arabic "Maqāma" in Yorubaland, Nigeria*.[25] The transformation of the *Ḥarīriyya*'s reception in the secularized world of literariness is therefore an ideal case study for rethinking the limitations of both the literary imagination and the institutions that shape how we read and interpret stories. The cultural configurations that underpinned the *Ḥarīriyya*'s vibrant reception across continents and centuries were bound up with different social, material, and intellectual practices in an Age of Commentary.

* * *

What follows is a brief outline of this book's argument and a word of caution about what this book is and what it is not. The first chapter focuses on the theoretical and methodological problems of reading the *Ḥarīriyya* "as literature." It examines the changing reception of the *Ḥarīriyya* in the nineteenth and twentieth centuries to shed light on what I call "the colonial economy of literature." I maintain that the introduction of "literature" as a supposedly universal category with European teleologies led to the reshaping of canons and the displacement of the *Ḥarīriyya*. Recent approaches to the nineteenth century, I contend, risk erasing crucial aspects of the texts and institutions of *adab* that preceded the nineteenth century. In the chapters that follow, I offer an alternative approach that traces the reading and interpretive practices of commentary that would have been familiar to ʿAbd al-Laṭīf al-Baghdādī. Indeed, each subsequent chapter begins with a short vignette about ʿAbd al-Laṭīf's life that sheds light on the chapter's theme and argument. Because he is a relatively minor figure in the *Ḥarīriyya*'s reception, his engagements with the *Ḥarīriyya* and with commentary culture more broadly can be illustrative of the extensive scholarly reception of the text beyond specialists in *adab*.

Chapters 2 and 3 seek to acquaint us with the reading practices that underpinned the *Ḥarīriyya*'s reception. They explore in some detail the reading and interpretive practices that informed the first century and a half of the *Ḥarīriyya*'s reception. In Chapter 2, I focus on the reading sessions in which budding scholars like ʿAbd al-Laṭīf would listen to, memorize, and eventually offer oral commentary on texts that were read aloud. To become a scholar was to become a vessel of textual knowledge that could be performed in a range of different ways. It was not simply a matter of memorization but also one of mastering the commentarial tradition. As it happens, the *Ḥarīriyya* treats this mode of reading and commentary as one of its major themes, such that the activities of reading *within* the *Ḥarīriyya* are mirrored by the activities of reading that take place *around* the *Ḥarīriyya*. Chapter 3 shifts our focus from the embodied text to the handwritten books that were part of the *Ḥarīriyya*'s transmission. Scholars carefully created and collated their copies of the text, but they also produced authenticated certificates attesting to acts of reading like the one ʿAbd al-Laṭīf carried with him throughout his life. The social and cultural logics of these material practices need to be understood if we want to understand how a reader like ʿAbd al-Laṭīf interacted with a text like the *Ḥarīriyya*. These two chapters together show that reading was not simply an abstract, interpretive activity but rather was both an embodied and a material practice.

Chapters 4 and 5 turn to the early controversies that grew up around the *Ḥarīriyya*. Chapter 4 shows that a vibrant debate over both the text and its author was carried out in both the commentaries and the biographical tradition. These kinds of philological debates have been dismissed as unliterary, atomistic, and pedantic in the era of world literature, but I argue that they can be understood as microcosms of broader interpretive commitments held by individual commentators. The scholarly audiences who read these quibbles would have understood the broader interpretive stances of the seemingly atomistic commentators. Likewise, I suggest that biographical anecdotes about al-Ḥarīrī and his critics were not intended primarily to be claims about the author's life but were rather a form of textual criticism. Chapter 5 zeroes in on one particular commentarial debate that has been understood by modern scholars as evidence for a widespread hostility toward fictional writing in the Arabo-Islamic world—that is, its hostility toward certain kinds of "literary" works. This hostility ostensibly forced al-Ḥarīrī to obfuscate and apologize for his overtly fictional characters. Chapter 5 shows that commentators developed myriad sophisticated concepts of fictionality in ways that pick apart a more reified notion of "fiction" and seek to index the relationship between textual representation and reality. The rhetoric of "lack" and "hostility" in modern scholarship are symptoms of literature's universalizing, evaluative edge, which has tended to underwrite the application of a specific literary aesthetics to diverse traditions of writing and reading.

Chapter 6 discusses the vibrant Islamic reception of the *Ḥarīriyya*. Whereas previous chapters show how the Islamic scholarly tradition of reading and commentary underpinned the text's reception, this chapter explores how scholars came to view the *Ḥarīriyya* as a quintessentially Islamic text.

For example, two major sixth/twelfth-century commentators discussed in this chapter claim that the *Ḥarīriyya* is Quran-like in its inimitability. Whereas literary reading has tended to assume that texts like the *Ḥarīriyya* should be understood as secular, with the implication that it is either separate from or opposed to religion, it is clear from these commentaries that many readers took the Islamicness of the *Ḥarīriyya* for granted. Chapter 7 makes the case that both commentary and adaptation are a form of intertextual practice that can be likened to "gate-crashing." It begins with the digressive commentary by the Andalusian scholar al-Sharīshī (d. 619/1222). Although his commentary drew heavily on an earlier commentary, he also strategically replaced some material. In doing so, he turned his digressive commentary on the *Ḥarīriyya* into a kind of *adab* anthology. A single word or a single line of the *Ḥarīriyya* could inspire excursions into the vast tradition of poetry and anecdotal prose. Al-Sharīshī describes his commentarial anthology as "running alongside" the *Ḥarīriyya.* I argue that it can also be seen as a commentary that "gatecrashes" the text. The gatecrasher (*ṭufaylī*) is a stock figure of Arabic belles-lettres and a common motif of the *Ḥarīriyya.* The conclusion of the chapter draws a parallel between al-Sharīshī's commentarial gatecrashing and the authors who adopted and adapted al-Ḥarīrī's model for their own, writing *maqāma*s in the Ḥarīrian style.

A word of caution is in order by way of a caveat: It should be kept in mind that this book focuses on a handful of the historically recoverable interpretations of the *Ḥarīriyya.* The countless readers who engaged with the *Ḥarīriyya* over the past nine centuries often left little trace of their individual interpretations, even though many of those readers would have had their interpretations structured (although not determined) by the commentary tradition. Medieval scholars were well aware of the fact that different readers had divergent interpretations of the text. This is amply demonstrated by the comments of a prominent author and devoted fan of the *Ḥarīriyya* named Khalīl b. Aybak al-Ṣafadī (d. 764/1363).[26] In one of his books, al-Ṣafadī describes the enthusiastic reception of the *Ḥarīriyya* and the intensity with which students studied the text. He also mentions some of the commentaries that are discussed later in this book and tells us that a certain commentator claimed to have discovered alchemical riddles in the text. I have not found an alchemical commentary on the *Ḥarīriyya*, but the point al-Ṣafadī is making is that the text is both the object of intense study and cannot be reduced to a single interpretation. Al-Ṣafadī thus encourages us to take note of interpretive multiplicity.

In the same passage, al-Ṣafadī points to a further, cross-cultural reception of the *Ḥarīriyya*, one that is quite different from the scholarly reception. He claims that the Franks—that is, Europeans—"recount the stories of the *Ḥarīriyya* to each other as they drink together" and that they have produced illustrated copies of the text in their language. Al-Ṣafadī claims that they did so because they enjoyed the stories. As he says, the stories are compelling because "when a person begins to be acquainted with them, his soul seeks out their resolution, longing to read the end of that story."[27] Al-Ṣafadī adds that whenever he reads certain passages of the Ḥarīriyya, he finds that they possess an "intoxicating effect like the intoxication of wine."[28] Al-Ṣafadī's comments on the Franks and on his own affective response to reading might well be seen as evidence of his "literary" appreciation of the *Ḥarīriyya*, one focused on the dynamics of plot and suspense rather than verbal pyrotechnics. However, al-Ṣafadī's point is not that Franks enjoy the *Ḥarīriyya* for its plot while Arabs enjoy it for its language and as an object of scholarly study. His point seems to be that the *Ḥarīriyya* can be enjoyed and appreciated in myriad ways.

If the *Ḥarīriyya* contains such multitudes, why *not* read it "as literature?" Might not a literary reading appeal more to a modern readership? Why not simply expand the definition of literature to encompass a broader range of reading and writing? These are all valid queries, so let me be clear: I am not denying that the *Ḥarīriyya* can be read meaningfully "as literature," and I am not of the opinion that modern theory is inapplicable to premodern texts. As Michael Cooperson has pointed out with reference to premodern Arabic biographical writing, "A full acceptance of the historicity of reception justifies reading any past writing 'as literature' if we choose to do so." He crucially adds that "this (often useful) procedure should not be confused with reconstructing the ways in which that piece of writing was understood in the past."[29] Cooperson has also recently produced a very "literary" English adaptation of the *Ḥarīriyya*, which he calls *Impostures*. The conceit of his translation is to adapt each *maqāma* in a different register or dialect of English, exploring the varieties and potentialities of the English language in a way that pays homage to the way al-Ḥarīrī plumbs the depths of Arabic. Making a text "alive" to modern readers in this way is gratifying and sometimes dizzying, but it should also catch us up short. Revivifying a text through "Englishing," as Cooperson calls it, draws attention to the fact that translations work within (or against) the linguistic and literary demands of the target language. Producing a "literary" translation that appeals to readers of English literature or offering "literary" interpretations of a text may risk becoming a kind of "rescue mission" that saves a text from nonliterary obscurity or from its earlier, nonliterary readers and translators. Many scholars in the past two hundred years have seen the philological and digressive commentaries on *adab* as deadening or superfluous to the task of truly (read: literarily) appreciating the text.[30] As we will see in Chapter 5, the idea persists that medieval readers have "failed" in some way to recognize the literariness of their texts.

To manage these potential problems, it is helpful to think of textual meaning as consisting of "three planes" or "three dimensions," as the Sanskritist Sheldon Pollock has suggested. The first dimension concerns the text's meaning at its moment of creation. Scholars who are interested in the origins of the *maqāma* genre are focused on this dimension of meaning because they are focused on how a particular *author* draws on and differentiates his own work from what went before it, but claiming to access the mind of a long-dead author is fraught with peril. The second dimension of textual meaning concerns how the text was understood by its historical readers. This book is primarily concerned with this second dimension. The third dimension concerns the text's "presence to my own subjectivity."[31] Each new reader's engagement with a text belongs to this third dimension, which is constantly slipping into the second dimension. The following questions remain: Why is it worth pursuing this second dimension in all its messy multiplicity and, presuming that this task is worthwhile, how can we gain access to it through the traces that readers have left behind? This book is, in part, an attempt to say that this "second dimension" of reception is not only of historical importance but also of ethical importance for readers in the "third dimension." This second dimension is crucial to a broader project of provincializing European literary studies and recognizing the colonial and Orientalist assumptions that underpin the study of Arabic texts. Pushing back against the flattening-out of literary cultures through an attention to the practices of reading and interpretation that attended the *Ḥarīriyya* resonates with the notion of exilic philology limned by Aamir Mufti in his reading of Edward Said and Erich Auerbach. As Mufti points out, "The 'literature' in world literature marks the plane of equivalence and comparability between historically distinct and particular practices of writing."[32] This book offers a disturbance and a few wrinkles that resist this flattening-out of literature. Its goal is to be attentive to the "worldliness of language and text" that informed the *Ḥarīriyya*'s rise and fall.[33]

Chapter 1

The Colonial Economy of Literature

A Séance

Some years ago, I gave a public lecture about the *Maqāmāt al-Ḥarīrī* (henceforth the *Ḥarīriyya*) and its commentary tradition in which I briefly addressed the tendency of scholars to deploy the work of the Russian theorist Mikhail Bakhtin to interpret medieval Arabic texts. I offered a fleeting critique of the scholarly habit of interpreting Arabic trickster stories like the *Ḥarīriyya* as a kind of "carnivalesque," one of Bakhtin's most influential terms.[1] In the past, whenever I had decided simply to ignore Bakhtin, a question from the audience would inevitably summon his ghostly presence. The suggestion implicit in these well-meaning questions was that Bakhtin, a central figure in the institution of literary studies in both the Euro-American academy and beyond in the latter half of the twentieth century, would offer a fruitful way of conceptualizing the trickster's subversive energies in the *Ḥarīriyya*. Given that my research focuses on the reading and interpretive practices in the first few centuries of the *Ḥarīriyya*'s reception, the implication seemed to be that the carnivalesque would be *more* fruitful than the medieval commentators. I explained in my talk that Bakhtin's notion of the carnivalesque comes from his monograph on Rabelais (d. 960/1553) and posits folk humor as being a form of opposition to the "intolerant, dogmatic seriousness of the Middle Ages" but not to those forms of seriousness that were free of dogmatism, which Bakhtin locates in the tragic seriousness of Antiquity and in nondogmatic, open seriousness that arrived in the wake of the Renaissance.[2] The *Ḥarīriyya*'s Islamic reception was enthusiastic, not intolerant, and the text is decidedly not part of the "folk" tradition, all of which suggested to me that this way of reading the text would obfuscate rather than illuminate the *Ḥarīriyya*'s early reception. At the end of my talk, a professor of comparative literature raised his hand. He wondered aloud if it might be better to read the *Ḥarīriyya* through other Bakhtinian concepts, such as the chronotope. I admitted that such an approach was plausible and might even be quite fruitful. "But what for?" I asked. What are the forces at work, I wondered aloud, that insist on circumventing the commentary tradition in favor of the canons of European theory. My churlish reply was, as far as I can tell, not well received.

This professor's Bakhtinian question is an example of what I call the "colonial economy of literature," a term I have coined to refer to the phenomenon through which ostensibly "local" materials like the *Ḥarīriyya* become meaningful only insofar as they are processed or become processable by the dominant reading practices of Euro-America. The assumption underpinning the professor's question and a thousand others like it is that the appropriate manner of evaluating and interpreting the texts of other cultures is through methods and theories that are based upon and have already been proven fruitful with European texts. The institutional power and presumed *generalizability* of Euro-American theory makes it the natural framework through which literary texts are made meaningful and through which scholars prove their disciplinary mastery. Modes of reading are also at work in delimiting what can be considered literature in the first place and how nonliterary texts come to be read. I should hasten to add that Bakhtin was not himself a powerful member of the Euro-American establishment. Rather, the point is that his oeuvre became, over the course of the late twentieth century, part of that powerful canon. We will return to Bakhtinian readings of the *maqāma* genre at the end of this chapter. For now, let us begin this séance to make the ghosts that haunt our readings familiar to us through an exploration of the dynamics and the genealogies of the colonial economy of literature.

The Colonial Economy of Literature

The colonial economy of literature haunts the study of *adab*. As Karim Mattar has put it in his study of the emergence of the Arabic novel, global capitalist modernity is "the unconscious" of world literature and its "repressed origin and condition of possibility."[3] Within that economy, I argue, certain interpretive possibilities of *adab*'s past are foreclosed. Imagine a reading of

Proust or Shakespeare that drew on the ideas of the fifth/eleventh-century theorist of poetry and aesthetics ʿAbd al-Qāhir al-Jurjānī. This sort of project would, I think, have no place in a comparative literature department, whereas a Bakhtinian or Genettian reading of the *maqāma* might be deemed natural and obvious. The unstated assumption persists that *all* materials must pass through the comparative lens or the theoretical apparatus that has been developed in the Euro-American world. Thus, texts like the *Ḥarīriyya* must be (or ought to be) tractable to the aptly chosen European method or through comparison with the "right" European literary work in order to become part of the conversation.[4]

The Moroccan scholar Abdelfettah Kilito describes this drive to explain Arabic texts on European terms in his 2002 study *Lan Tatakallam Lughatī* (*You Will Not Speak My Language*).[5] Kilito introduces his book by recounting the difficulties he faced when giving a lecture about the *maqāma* to a French audience who would be wholly unfamiliar with both the genre and the whole network of authors and texts within which the *maqāma* makes sense. He found himself forced to introduce the *maqāma* through a comparison with the Spanish picaresque, but he notes with dismay that his act of cultural translation is far from innocent.[6] Kilito conjures up the specter of Charles Pellat, the French Orientalist who, as we saw previously, attributed the success of the *Ḥarīriyya* to "a decline of literary taste."[7] Kilito points out that Pellat dismissed all Arabic books in a single sentence as boring, no matter what their topic, although he mustered up a degree of admiration for authors who were comparable to a desirable French equivalent. Al-Jāḥiẓ, Pellat asserts, was something akin to the European humanists. Al-Tawḥīdī becomes a satirist like La Bruyère (d. 1107/1696), and al-Shidyāq offers "a critique of Near Eastern society influenced by Rabelais."[8] In this economy of comparison, Arabic literature can only avoid being boring if it can reproduce the dynamics of the category of "literature" and thereby be "rescued" by comparability with European models.[9]

Over the course of the twentieth century, Pellat's dismissiveness became less fashionable, but the logic of literary comparison continued to serve as a way of permitting certain kinds of Arabic texts to be recognized in the colonial economy of literature while decisively excluding others. In 1980 the prominent scholar of Arabic literature Jaroslav Stetkevych published an influential essay outlining a program of how to study premodern Arabic literature. In that essay, he proposes to liberate Arabic poetry from the clutches of the philologists by reading *adab* "as literature." Stetkevych contrasts this approach with that of the philological tradition, represented by Wilhelm Ahlwardt (d. 1320/1909) and Julius Wellhausen (d. 1336/1918), whose dry, deadening discourse emphasized Arabic's alterity. Instead, Stetkevych endorses the methods of "our most modern scholars" who contend that "we must use our own critical and conceptual language if we want to understand literature—any literature."[10] The application of modern European methods like structuralism or archetypal symbolism, he argues, is analogous to the enthusiastic literary Orientalism of William Jones (d. 1208/1794). Like Goethe and others whom Edward Said identifies as part of "Romantic Orientalism," William Jones saw "Asiatick" poetry as a source of renewal for European literature, which had "subsisted too long on the perpetual repetition of the same images."[11] What Jones achieves in his literary translations is, according to Stetkevych, a transformation of the Arabian desert into the bucolic landscapes of the French neoclassicists, a move that Stetkevych sees as felicitous because it identifies the underlying pastoralism of the two poetries. Rather than treating Arabic poetry as wholly Other, these Romantics "were reading Arabic poetry within the vibrant energy field of their own national poetries."[12]

Stetkevych is rightly critical of the dismissive attitudes toward Arabic poetry and prose that were once rampant in Orientalist scholarship, but his essay is seemingly sanguine about a scholarly genealogy that leads back to a colonial official like William Jones. Reading *adab* "as literature" functions for Stetkevych as a kind of liberation, but it appears to be a qualified one. It is a mode of reading that is deeply embedded in the colonial economy of literature which extricates the text from its non-Western context to serve as a kind of raw material that can resonate with and revivify the metropole's literary industries. After all, Jones and Stetkevych are both interested in making *adab* speak to and within the concerns of European literature and European theory. In this sense, Stetkevych is more unapologetic about the Eurocentrism of his scholarly project than a more recent advocate of world literature like David Damrosch, who describes world literature as a "mode of reading," rather than as a stable canon of texts, which enables "a form of detached engagement with worlds beyond our own time and place."[13] These modes of reading are, however, embedded in evaluative epistemologies. What is permitted to join the pantheon of world literature depends very much on the tastes, temperaments, and proclivities that shape (and are shaped by) this "literary" mode of reading. There is nothing neutral about a mode of reading, informed as it is by intellectual traditions and preexisting literary canons.[14] As Kilito notes in *Les Séances*, his monograph on the *maqāma* collections of al-Hamadhānī and al-Ḥarīrī, "It is therefore not in the name of *adab* that the *maqāma* is judged but in the name of 'literature' (one knows that the word is relatively recent)."[15]

As Aamir Mufti has shown, the discourse of world literature renders texts legible *as literature* by flattening out the heterogeneous practices of reading and writing that existed elsewhere in time and space. Literature itself thus functions as a concept of exchange or a "plane of equivalence," which allows for comparison and evaluation.[16] In this sense, world literature is the true heir of Orientalism, which Edward Said likened to Jeremy Bentham's panopticon.[17] What Mufti allows us to see is that we are not simply dealing with a *conceptual* incongruity between, in our case, *adab* and literature. As an institution, literature is underpinned by universities, academic departments, professional organizations, conferences, publications, grants, agents, and curricula. The material conditions of this diffuse institution shape canons and set agendas for inquiry, and these constraints are as difficult to escape as the capitalist market. Even critics of literature's global pretensions are likely to reproduce the very structures they intend to dismantle. Trained as they are in the institutions of modern literature, their examples tend to be novels, and their theorists tend to be French and German.[18]

Critics of Orientalism and world literature like Michael Allan, Emily Apter, Baidak Bhattacharya, Karim Mattar, and Aamir Mufti have pointed out the Eurocentricity of literature and maintained that colonial modernity reshaped the interpretive world.[19] It remains a problem, however, that those scholars giving an account of this rupture tend to be specialists in the modern period who concern themselves with genres, authors, and readers who have lived in the wake of colonial modernity and have been shaped by its discourses, canons, and ideologies. These critics hailing mainly from the institutions of comparative literature are, in a sense, *our* "most modern" scholars. The various accounts of how the rupture that shapes literary modernity took place have a tendency to set aside or devote little attention to the precolonial *adab* tradition, which in turn produces misleading accounts of the nineteenth century's newness, its transformations, and its deformations. This problem is not easily solved because the *adab* produced between the twelfth century and the eighteenth was, for many years, systematically marginalized due to the presumed intellectual and literary decadence of that period.[20] There is not a robust tradition of scholarship that gives an account of this "decadent period," even as revisionists' narratives have emerged to demonstrate the richness and sophistication of cultural production in this period, which have included contributions from Thomas Bauer, Konrad Hirschler, Muhsin al-Musawi, and Elias Muhanna, among others.[21] At the same time, the polemics of nineteenth-century Orientalists and Arab reformers about the decadence of the postclassical period continue to be accepted uncritically as reliable accounts of postclassical scholarship. Most recently, Ahmed El Shamsy has given an account of the nineteenth-century "rediscovery" of the classical Islamic past in the modern period. In the process, he has revived portions of the decline narrative, particularly when it comes to commentary culture. For El Shamsy, commentaries had "encased" some texts in "layers of subsequent commentary" to the extent that the original text came to be overwhelmed. In this account, commentary culture also narrowed the canon and pushed texts from the "classical period" to the margins, if it did not forget them entirely.[22] For other recent scholars more focused on *adab* texts, the commentaries on Arabic poetry and prose are deficient because they lack the kinds of interpretations that are recognizably "literary."[23] A series of ghostly assumptions are haunting these statements, which suggest that postclassical commentary is a barrier to understanding a text "properly" and that commentary culture is at best extraneous and at worst harmful to the development of an authentic literary and intellectual culture.

This chapter responds to these strands of scholarship by drawing attention to the nineteenth-century transformations and debates in both Orientalist scholarship and Arab reformist scholarship about the *Ḥarīriyya*. These debates tell us a great deal about the role of the commentary tradition in the nineteenth century as the concept of literariness began to emerge. I argue that these nineteenth-century discourses continue to haunt scholarship both on the *Ḥarīriyya* and on commentary culture more broadly. Among the Orientalists, I focus on Silvestre de Sacy (d. 1253/1838) and Ernest Renan (d. 1310/1892), two scholars whose work Edward Said describes in *Orientalism* as more or less indistinguishable expressions of French Orientalist thought. Through their encounters with the *Ḥarīriyya*, I offer a reassessment of Said's classic treatment by focusing on their radically different approaches to Orientalist scholarship. What Said and others have overlooked is that Sacy's approach was a kind of colonial mimicry that drew heavily on the rich traditions of Arabic philology and commentary. Among the Arab reformers, I explore the works of the Muslim thinker and sometime mufti of Egypt Muḥammad ʿAbduh (d. 1323/1905) as well as the Christian scholar and novelist Jurjī Zaydān (d. 1332/1914).[24] Although hailing from different backgrounds and undertaking different forms of scholarship, both were engaged in revivalist projects, and both responded forcefully to colonial critiques while simultaneously accepting and reconfiguring their diagnoses of decline.[25] They both expressed similar views about commentary and the problems of texts like the *Ḥarīriyya*. Although the projects and approaches of all four of these figures are distinct, they shared varying degrees of distaste for the *Ḥarīriyya* that continue to haunt scholarship.

Edward Said, Silvestre de Sacy, and Ernest Renan

In the second chapter of his 1979 monograph *Orientalism*, Edward Said introduces Silvestre de Sacy as a foundational Orientalist who is implicated in colonial structures of knowledge and power, all of which is surely true. However, Said also posits that Sacy's anthology, his *Chrestomathie Arabe*, is a project that *makes visible* the Orient as a tableau, in the manner of Bentham's panopticon.[26] Insofar as the *Chrestomathie* is designed for French education, is dedicated to Napoleon, celebrates his conquests, and begs for Napoleon's protection over the "Eastern muses," the work is unquestionably colonial.[27] However, it would be misleading to see the anthology as an instrument of epistemological domination analogous to a panoptical prison because to do so would overlook the fact that Sacy's *Chrestomathie* mimics the form and structure of an established Arabic genre—namely, the *adab* anthology, variously called *tadhkira*, *majmūʿa*, among other things.[28] This vibrant tradition of anthologizing flourished in Arabic manuscript culture from the third/ninth century down to the thirteenth/nineteenth and produced notable encyclopedic anthologies, such as al-Nuwayrī's *Nihāyat al-Arab fī Funūn al-Adab*, a thirty-one volume luxury item that might be available in its entirety only to the very wealthy.[29] Like Sacy's *Chrestomathie*, some anthologies were intended to be used pedagogically, while other anthologies were made up of discarded books that were cut up, rebound, and refurbished by enterprising booksellers. One such up-cycled anthology even included a new introduction, presumably penned by the bookseller, that celebrates sexually experienced women to entice the buyer to purchase the "un-virginal" book.[30]

I do not mean to valorize Sacy's *Chrestomathie*, which also had European precursors.[31] Rather, my point is to *make visible* the fact that a rich anthologizing tradition already existed in precolonial *adab*, one that Said seems to have overlooked, and that Sacy aimed to situate his own work as a kind of European contribution to that tradition. The most obvious marker of this strategy of philological mimicry is Sacy's rhyming Arabic title: *al-Anīs al-Mufīd li-l-Ṭālib al-Mustafīd* (The Beneficial Friend for the Studious Pupil). Sacy's title draws on the long tradition of giving Arabic books rhyming titles, as was the case with al-Nuwayrī's aforementioned *Nihāyat al-Arab*. Additionally, in his French preface, Sacy justifies his strategy of collecting fragments as opposed to complete texts by citing the authority of a Persian poet. He quotes two verses of Saʿdī Shīrāzī (d. 691/1292) in both Persian and French translation to say: "Although silver and gold come from stone, not every stone contains silver and gold."[32] In other words, an *adab* anthology casts precious texts before your eyes while letting the less interesting stones fall by the wayside. If this is a Benthamite panopticon, it is one that comes dressed in Persian and Arab garb.

The *Chrestomathie* is best understood as a typical work of Orientalist philology not because it reorganized the Orient into a panopticon but because it was based on the appropriation of the Arabic manuscript collections, the adoption of Arabic scholarly genres, and their subsequent adaptation for new pedagogical and ideological ends. In Sacy's mimicry of Arabic discourses, the *Chrestomathie* is closer to Napoleon's famous proclamation to the Egyptians in 1798 as he conquered their country. The proclamation was written in a classicizing Arabic and declared the French to be "sincere Muslims" liberating the Arabs from their Mamluk overlords. Shaden Tageldin identifies this proclamation as part of colonialism's seductive self-translation, which encouraged Egyptians to see themselves on equal footing with the French who had made themselves over into sincere Muslims.[33]

When it comes to Sacy's printed edition of the *Ḥarīriyya*, published in 1822, we can see that the Frenchman's philological practice was heavily and explicitly reliant on the Arabic philological and commentarial traditions. Sacy produced an extensive commentary for his edition, which he placed in footnotes below the main text. This commentary is drawn almost entirely from the Arabic commentaries on the *Ḥarīriyya* that were available to him in manuscript. Sacy's act of commentarial appropriation was itself a common strategy in the precolonial commentarial tradition. Countless scholars of Arabic from the twelfth century through the eighteenth had composed their own commentaries on the *Ḥarīriyya* through the adaptation and reshaping of earlier commentaries (see Chapter 2).

Arab readers astutely recognized that Sacy's *Ḥarīriyya* was not so much an "edition" of the *Ḥarīriyya* as it was a "commentary (*sharḥ*)," which relied in its footnotes on earlier Arabic commentaries. The 1834 travelog of al-Ṭahṭāwī (d. 1290/1873) observes that Sacy had "made an abridged commentary on the *Ḥarīriyya*, which he called *The Selected Glosses*."[34] Around the same time, when the Lebanese author Nāṣīf al-Yāzijī (d. 1287/1871) wrote an epistle critiquing the grammar of Sacy's Arabic introduction and to correct errors in the edition of the *Ḥarīriyya*, he referred to Sacy's book as a "commentary" on the text. Al-Yāzijī's epistle, which was printed in 1848 by the German Oriental Society in Leipzig with a facing-page Latin translation, states that "had al-Ḥarīrī encountered it, he would have found that which would have not occurred to him."[35] Although it is unclear whether al-Yāzijī meant these words as a critique or an appreciation of Sacy's edition and commentary, it can be surmised that, for al-Yāzijī, the act of producing an edition and elucidation of the text was recognizable as an act of commentary. Al-Yāzijī's contemporary al-Shidyāq (d. 1305/1887) also published a biting critique of Sacy's errors in Arabic in 1855 in an appendix to his raucous work of *adab* entitled *al-Sāq ʿalā l-Sāq* (*Leg Over Leg*). He likewise refers to Sacy's edition there as a "commentary." These Arab scholars of the nineteenth century and later editors of the *Ḥarīriyya* were aware that Sacy was not imposing on them and their texts a philological frame from Europe. Rather, they viewed him as someone attempting to participate—albeit as a junior partner prone to error—in a tradition of textual transmission and philological commentary in which those Arab scholars remained the central nodes of authority.[36]

If Sacy's *philological* project of glossing the *Ḥarīriyya* was an imitation of Arabic philology, his *literary* judgments were something else entirely. He found the text to be somewhat tiresome, repetitive, and overwrought with ornament.[37] A nineteenth-century English Orientalist ascribed the French scholar's dismissive judgment to the weariness of an exhausted editor, arguing that exuberant ornamentation was precisely the point of the *Ḥarīriyya*.[38] This Englishman's position of aesthetic relativism did not call into question the underlying assumption that the *Ḥarīriyya* was a triumph of style over substance, and it did nothing to stem the tide of criticism.

In *Orientalism*, Said identifies Ernest Renan as Sacy's successor in the French academy, and it was Renan who put forward a full-throated civilizational critique of the *Ḥarīriyya*'s decadence. Whereas Said suggests that "the difference between Sacy and Renan is the difference between inauguration and continuity," their approaches to the *Ḥarīriyya* could not be more different.[39]

In an essay about the *Ḥarīriyya* published in 1859, early on in Renan's career, he claims that the text is a symptom of Oriental, Asian, and Arab moral and intellectual backwardness.[40] He attributes its popularity to the Oriental taste for extravagant style, to their mania for rare words that can only be understood with the help of a commentary, and to the "literary sleights of hand, which have no merit other than the difficulty in overcoming them."[41] These ornamental features and "beautés intraduisibles" are portrayed as necessarily unattractive to the European reader, who is by nature more interested in content than in form. Renan's essay concocts an imagined Oriental cast of mind that is more interested in verbal trivialities than in exploring the human condition.[42] He associates this superficiality with a more general "Arab decadence," of which al-Ḥarīrī is "the wittiest and most interesting author." The *Ḥarīriyya* exemplifies for Renan the fatal limitations of Muslim civilization that have hampered both its moral and intellectual development.[43] Specifically, the *Ḥarīriyya*'s protagonists inhabit a world where man must resign himself to his fate, rather than take his destiny into his own hands. It is this fatalism that prevents the Orient, in his view, from being *modern*.[44] In another essay on Islamic science, more famous than his remarks on the *Ḥarīriyya*, Renan depicts the Orient as a place of dogmatism where a "species of iron circle" surrounds the head of the believer, making them incapable of acquiring knowledge. Thus, for Renan, the *Ḥarīriyya* was merely a *literary* expression of a broader truth: that the Oriental, the Arab, and the Muslim could not be modern and that modernity's intellectual, cultural, and political future was inevitably European.[45] The civilizational stakes of literature were not part of Sacy's philological Orientalism but were rather part of an emerging logic of world literature.

Muḥammad ʿAbduh and the Reconfiguration of the Literary Canon

Renan's theories of Oriental decadence and European triumphalism became the target of rebuttals from Muslim intellectuals like the protean anticolonial activist Jamāl al-Dīn al-Afghānī (d. 1314/1897). However, these rebuttals generally admitted Renan's premise of a decadent Orient. The assertion of decadence by Arab and Muslim reformers became the impetus for bold projects of reform in the fields of ethics, education, language, politics, and religion.

Many of the resources for these modernizing projects lay in a Golden Age that preceded the ostensible decline of morality, scientific achievement, and political independence. This idea was made explicit by al-Afghānī's publishing partner and fellow Freemason Muḥammad ʿAbduh.[46] Whereas Renan had blamed the rigidity of the Orient on Islam's inherent dogmatism, ʿAbduh contends that the crime of rigidity (*jināyat al-jumūd*) was to be blamed on political circumstances. Specifically, he identifies the beginning of this decline into rigidity and stagnation as the moment that the Abbasid caliph decided to rely on foreign armies instead of Arab ones. As a result, "Islam became un-Arab and barbaric (*hunāka istaʿjama al-islām wa-inqalaba ʿajamiyyan*)."[47] The term *ʿajam* that he uses pejoratively here has a range of meanings having to do with the inability to speak or to speak clearly and thus becomes a marker of "foreignness" and, in this case, of "uncivilized" peoples. For ʿAbduh, it was when the Abbasid caliphs turned to "foreign," mostly Turkic, armies that the trouble began because, he argues, these non-Arab warriors seized power and became tyrants who saw free thought among the Arab inhabitants as a threat to their tendentious claims to authority. To protect their positions, ʿAbduh claims, they encouraged intellectual conformity, superstitions like the veneration of saints, and an apolitical fatalism.[48] ʿAbduh penned this historical inventory of failure in the early 1900s while casting his gaze backward to an earlier, glorious past. He longed for and sought to reconstruct what we might call a "classical" past that was marked by vigor, rationality, and political independence, all flourishing under enlightened Arab caliphs. A barely encoded critique of European colonial rule in nineteenth-century Egypt and beyond bubbles under the surface of ʿAbduh's historiography. His scholarly projects about language and literary reform harkened back to the spirit of that pristine past that supposedly preceded these eras of decline and despotism. In this regard, ʿAbduh echoed Renan's view that decadence had reigned ever since the "liberal spirit" of the early caliphate had been extinguished.[49]

According to ʿAbduh, the *Ḥarīriyya* was a symbol and a symptom of the now-decadent present that needed to be displaced by the construction and propagation of a "classical" past.[50] Educational reform required a newly constructed "classical" canon that could provide members of a hoped-for nation with the linguistic and moral capacities that modern society required. After ʿAbduh was exiled from Egypt for his involvement in the ʿUrābī revolt that was crushed in 1882, he moved to Paris and then to Beirut where he published an edition of *Nahj al-Balāgha* in 1885. The *Nahj al-Balāgha* is a collection of eloquent speeches and sayings attributed to ʿAlī, the cousin and son-in-law of the Prophet, and it was supposedly anthologized by the Shi'ite theologian and scholar of *adab* al-Sharīf al-Raḍī (d. 406/1015).[51] ʿAbduh had high hopes that this newly edited text would benefit "the youths of this age," introducing the text as an antidote to those who would celebrate style over substance:

> Everyone wishes to have an orator's tongue and an author's pen, but they seek what they desire through reading the *Maqāmāt* [of al-Ḥarīrī] and the books of epistles that were written by non-Arabs (*muwalladūn*) or by later authors who imitate them. In their compositions, they only pay attention to delicate speech, to congruous assonance, to the arrangement of words, and linguistic embellishments of that sort, which they call the rhetorical arts (*al-funūn al-badīʿiyya*)—even if the phrases are devoid of momentous substance (*al-maʿānī al-jalīla*) and lacking elevated style.[52]

His complaints about *maqāma*s are clearly directed at the *Ḥarīriyya*, which had been the standard of eloquence for centuries as well as a central pillar of education. For ʿAbduh, they were nothing but a triumph of style over substance. What is more, he uses a complex but, in this instance, derogatory and racialized term to describe the authors of embellished prose. He calls them *muwalladūn*, a term that has a complicated history but generally refers to those who participated in Arabic culture but were not of "pure" Arab descent.[53] The speeches of an unimpeachable linguistic and religious authority like ʿAlī seem designed to offer an antidote to *Ḥarīrian* decadence and the influence of more ornamental, "non-Arab" aesthetic values.

In 1889, a few years after editing the *Nahj al-Balāgha*, ʿAbduh published his edition of al-Hamadhānī's *maqāma*s (the *Hamadhāniyya*) with the Jesuit Press in Beirut. ʿAbduh's reasons for publishing this second text were, as with the *Nahj al-Balāgha*, tied to his ethical, linguistic, and literary projects of reform. The *Hamadhāniyya*'s vocabulary is simpler than the *Ḥarīriyya*'s, and it is devoid of certain language games (such as palindromes) found in the *Ḥarīriyya*. As the English Orientalist Thomas Chenery (d. 1301/1884) had noted in his 1867 translation of the *Ḥarīriyya*, al-Hamadhānī "has less artifice, if less genius, and in his Assemblies the story or adventure is more dwelt upon and less sacrificed to the display of style."[54] When W. J. Prendergast published his translation of the *Hamadhāniyya* in 1915, a reviewer for the Royal

Asiatic Society of Great Britain and Ireland deemed the translation a long overdue vindication of the earlier and better *maqāma* author, al-Hamadhānī.[55] Whether or not ʿAbduh knew Chenery's work and the proclivities that prompted European readers to prefer the *Hamadhāniyya*, it seems likely that he would have largely agreed with their sentiments.

ʿAbduh's ethical and literary concerns informed his edition of the *Hamadhāniyya*, which he purged of its more salacious elements. In bowdlerizing the text, ʿAbduh sought to displace both the *Ḥarīriyya* and an earlier edition of the *Hamadhāniyya* published in 1881, which had been edited by a rather different sort of scholar with his own notions about bringing the textual tradition into print. This earlier edition of the *Hamadhāniyya* was produced by a printing press in Istanbul run by the aforementioned al-Shidyāq, but the editor of the volume was a certain Yūsuf al-Nabhānī (d. 1350/1932), a scholar and a poet born in Palestine and trained in Egypt. Al-Nabhānī's edition is a fascinating example of how nineteenth-century Arabic print culture often mirrored manuscript culture, even when it was produced through moveable type rather than lithograph.[56] For one thing, al-Nabhānī's name does not appear in an editor's introduction or on the title page. This information appears instead at the end of the text in a colophon, as it would in a hand-copied manuscript. This now-unfamiliar practice has led some scholars to misattribute the edition to al-Shidyāq or to assume that it was edited anonymously, but the colophon provides extensive information about the editor and his process.[57] Al-Nabhānī calls himself a corrector (*muṣaḥḥiḥ*) and gives details in the colophon about the two manuscripts that he used and the libraries in which they could be found, the dates when those manuscripts were copied, as well as the relative merits of these manuscript witnesses.[58]

The erasure of al-Nabhānī's editorial work is part of a broader trend in scholarship on the nineteenth century in which the intellectual activities of traditional, antireformist, and conservative scholars have been sidelined in favor of those who participated in what Albert Hourani dubbed "the Liberal Age." As Amal Ghazal has shown, al-Nabhānī was a Sufi who became a vociferous critic of ʿAbduh's reform projects, which he considered an abandonment of the entire Islamic intellectual tradition in favor of European thought and the ideas of the controversial Ḥanbalī Ibn Taymiyya (d. 728/1328).[59] Al-Nabhānī rejected entirely the idea that the recent past or the Islamic intellectual heritage was a site of decadent decline. He did not see these traditions to be inadequate to the challenges of modernity. In an early twentieth-century poem, al-Nabhānī says that ʿAbduh "pretends to be an Imam on the one hand, but he imitates infidels on the other."[60] This explicit enmity between al-Nabhānī and ʿAbduh may not have existed back in the 1880s when their dueling editions of the *Hamadhāniyya* were published, but their divergent approaches to editing texts indicate different ways of adapting the textual inheritance in the age of print.

ʿAbduh's edition followed the more "modern" procedure of placing the editor's name and his methodological introduction at the beginning of the text, rather than in a colophon. In ʿAbduh's introduction, he dismisses the editor of the Istanbul edition, without naming al-Nabhānī, as a "scribe (*nassākh*)" who had introduced errors, additions, and deletions that would confuse the reader. Furthermore, ʿAbduh points out that the earlier edition lacked any glosses for difficult words, which makes it challenging or impossible to understand the text without added toil, a deficiency that ʿAbduh rectifies with a commentary (*sharḥ*) in the form of footnotes, as Sacy had done in his edition-commentary on the *Ḥarīriyya*. By adding these simple and straightforward glosses, ʿAbduh made the *Hamadhāniyya* more accessible for the new reading public that he envisioned, which would not rely on the commentarial authority of teachers.

If we take ʿAbduh's introduction to the *Hamadhāniyya* and his introduction to the *Nahj al-Balāgha* together, it is clear that ʿAbduh intended to displace the *Ḥarīriyya* with the earlier, less philologically complex collection of *maqāmas* by al-Hamadhānī so that it might serve as a tool for teaching Arabic and inculcating new literary values. He sought to reach back to an earlier age that reflected what he saw as more "pure" Arab aesthetic ideals. The success of ʿAbduh's gambit may have been partially the result of his institutional positions as part of the Administrative Council of al-Azhar and then later as the grand mufti of Egypt from 1899 until his death in 1905, platforms that he used to advocate for educational reforms that would enact an epistemic shift away from what he perceived as decadent modes of education.[61]

ʿAbduh already had a reputation for teaching outside of what was then the standard Islamic curriculum, reaching back to earlier texts or to European ones. Before his exile, he had offered lessons at the newly founded Dār al-ʿUlūm based on a translation of François Guizot's *Histoire de la Civilisation en Europe* and a treatise in philosophical ethics by al-Hamadhānī's contemporary Miskawayh (d. 421/1030), neither of which were part of the traditional curriculum.[62] When he returned from exile, ʿAbduh and other reformers sought to marginalize the teaching of commentary and of "auxiliary subjects," such as grammar, rhetoric, and prosody, so that students could focus on the essential topics, such as theology, law, and exegesis. ʿAbduh joined the newly formed Administrative Council of al-Azhar, whose recommendations, including a ban on teaching supercommentaries (*al-ḥawāshī*), became law in 1314/1896. Teaching "clear commentaries (*al-shurūḥ al-wāḍiḥa*)" was permitted, but supercommentaries could only be studied as elective texts, unless specifically permitted by the Administrative Council. Some years later, ʿAbduh complained that the professors at al-Azhar continued to teach whatever they wished, ignoring the legal limits that restricted the teaching of commentaries.[63] Commentarial texts like the *Ḥarīriyya*, with their attention to eloquence and linguistic artifice, were becoming the targets of governmental reforms, and ʿAbduh took this opportunity to reshape the social, material, and intellectual practices of reading and education. Throughout his life, ʿAbduh engaged in both editing texts and lobbying the government to reformulate the Arabic canon according to new aesthetic, ethical, and pedagogical concerns that constructed a "classical" tradition, all the while inscribing al-Ḥarīrī and his successors within a *non*-Arab, decadent tradition.

As I noted earlier, ʿAbduh refused to produce an unexpurgated edition of the *Hamadhāniyya*, as al-Nabhānī had done. He felt that some portions of the text would embarrass the educated and would be shameful to explain. In other words, there are bawdy bits in the *Hamadhāniyya*, and it is "not fitting for innocents to perceive its meaning or have their minds led to its signification," a comment that once again hints at the reading public that ʿAbduh imagined for his edition.[64] ʿAbduh therefore expurgated portions of the text—he informs his reader that an entire *maqāma* has been removed—in addition to a handful of offending passages. However, he only alerts the reader to some of his elisions. In one telling example, al-Hamadhānī's trickster figure interrupts a funeral and claims that a dead man is still alive and that he can bring him back to health. The Istanbul edition, following the manuscripts, has the trickster say that one can tell that a man is dead because his anus grows cold. The mourners rush to stick their hands in the man's anus to verify this claim. In ʿAbduh's edition, the anus (*ist*) has been transformed into a much less offensive armpit (*ibṭ*) without the slightest hint to the reader that a transformation has taken place.[65]

It is not so much that ʿAbduh was "rediscovering" the classical past, as Ahmed El Shamsy puts it.[66] Rather, he was actively producing a "classical" past by constructing a textual tradition that he believed would be suitable for modernity, its agents, and its emerging reading publics. This project required suppressing aspects of the textual tradition when necessary, so that the past could appropriately shape modern sensibilities in the present. ʿAbduh was undoubtedly aware of the use of bowdlerization in European publishing and its use to suppress certain aspects of Arabic literature for the sensibilities of a European audience. Such translational bowdlerizations were already mentioned in the early nineteenth-century Egyptian travelog of al-Ṭahṭāwī (d. 1290/1873), who notes that French translators of Arabic homoerotic poetry would transform the male beloved into a woman in order to accommodate the French reader's prejudices.[67] The homoeroticism and licentiousness of many works of *adab* came to be considered part and parcel of Oriental decadence and, it should be added, moral deviance. When the aforementioned Victorian translator Thomas Chenery came across Abū Zayd in the *Ḥarīriyya* mourning the death of his penis, he avoided producing an English translation of it. Instead, he reproduced William Jones's Latin translation.[68] These evasions by ʿAbduh and Chenery reflect anxieties about print culture in which consumers belong to a broader reading public that might include the "naive" who would be unduly influenced by "indecent" content or by the love that dare not speak its name.[69]

To sum up, ʿAbduh's construction of a classical past involved suppressing whatever he found problematic for public morality and intellectual development. It also involved promoting new kinds of texts. Already in 1881, a year before his exile, ʿAbduh had published an article condemning various categories of books that he found in the hands of his fellow Egyptians. In his article, he takes issue with "superstitious material (*khurāfāt*)" having to do with astrology, alchemy, and evil spirits as well as historical epics like Sīrat ʿAntar or the Sīrat Banī Hilāl, which he calls "lies (*akādhīb*)." He suggests that those drawn to these fantastical stories should instead busy themselves with true histories like the books of al-Masʿūdī (d. 345/956) or Ibn al-Athīr (d. 630/1233). He also recommends the translations of European literature that appeared in *al-Ahrām*, such as *al-Intiqām*, a translation of Pierre Zaccone's (d. 1312/1895) *Une Vengeance Anglaise*. ʿAbduh notes that undesirable books were being printed enthusiastically in Cairo and that the current censorship regime only blocked the publication of books that might offend religion or politics. However, ʿAbduh announces that "from now on, no press will be given permits to print these books"—namely, those books belonging to the superstitious and unedifying genres he has laid out.[70] It is true that elite Muslim scholars and rulers stretching back for centuries had taken aim at alchemists and others whom they perceived as charlatans or threats to public order, but ʿAbduh recognized that the power of the bureaucratic state to regulate the press could achieve what market inspectors and polemicists in a manuscript culture could not.[71]

It is high time now to pause amid our séance with the dead to emphasize that I am not here to bury ʿAbduh or to dispraise him. There is no use adopting al-Nabhānī's insinuations that ʿAbduh's reforms were simple mimicry of European thought, just as there is no sense in accepting ʿAbduh's account of the recent past as decadent, pedantic, and superstitious. This is a séance, not a trial of these two editors of the *Hamadhāniyya*. What the presence of these uneasy ghosts can help us realize is that reformers like ʿAbduh and his successors saw *adab* as a textual tradition in need of pruning and cultivation. There was, as Sinan Antoon puts it, a concerted effort among reformists to "cleanse the cultural past from all that is deemed unproductive and unedifying."[72] ʿAbduh's program for reconfiguring the past was incredibly successful, likely because it aligned with certain widely held (or, at least, influential and eventually triumphant) modernist views. Diagnosing the symptoms of moral, linguistic, religious, and political decadence was part of laying the groundwork for a way forward to a more liberated future. Intellectuals like ʿAbduh displaced Renan's racist civilizational polemic against an essentially decadent Orient by putting forward a discourse of reform and civilizational reclamation that similarly identified the present and the recent past as decadent and closed-minded. However, the return to a classical past, newly reconstructed and republished for the purpose of reform, was framed as the condition of possibility for renovation and liberation. Scholars like al-Nabhānī and the many others who continued to compose commentaries on the *Ḥarīriyya* ended up being dismissed by reformers as part of a backward past that was still inconveniently present. The period of the *Nahḍa* was marked by both rupture and continuity with the commentarial past, and the forces of both ambled on in uneasy awareness of the other.

Jurjī Zaydān and the Freedom of Literature

When we turn to other prominent *Nahḍa* figures from quite different backgrounds and contexts, we find arguments about literariness, decline, and revival that echo those of ʿAbduh. For instance, the prominent Lebanese Christian intellectual Jurjī Zaydān (d. 1332/1914) made the case that literature was properly understood as a realm of liberation and revival of a lost civilizational spirit. These arguments can be found in his encyclopedic work that was completed in the last years of his life entitled *Tārīkh Ādāb al-Lugha al-ʿArabiyya* (*The History of Arabic Letters*), a book that included discussions of both scientific and cultural achievements. The fourth and final volume concerns "the recent literary awakening (*al-nahḍa al-adabiyya al-akhīra*)," but it begins by surveying the marvels of "modern civilization," including medicine and journalism. Above all, Zaydān celebrates the return of "personal freedom (*ḥuriyya shakhṣiyya*)," which, long ago, had belonged to the Arabs and was returning to them now after many centuries of tyranny and repression. Zaydān theorizes the *Nahḍa* as an awakening sparked by contact with Europe and especially France.[73]

> [Personal freedom] led to the dissolution of traditional restraints in society and thought and, as a part of that, the restraints in poetic style and poetic imagery. Some of the poets began imitating the European styles of ekphrasis and the like, and their feelings became refined through modern education. They comprehended human feelings and strengths, and they discovered the secrets of the human heart that the ancients had not understood. . . . Ideas among the Arabs and other civilized nations rubbed together, and they were forced by the natural logic of civilizations to learn one another's languages, read their literatures, and emulate them. . . . In sum, the poets shunned the restraints that fettered their forebears.[74]

For Zaydān, embracing "the spirit of the age" in poetry and prose involved a liberatory embrace of European styles. Modern authors of poetry and prose could pay less attention to "formal expression (*lafẓ*)," freeing themselves to pay attention to the "essence" of poetry and prose, which was "meaning (*maʿnā*)."[75] The period prior to the *Nahḍa* was, for Zaydān, one of intellectual and literary stagnation, dominated by the "scholastic mode (*ṭarīqa madrasiyya*)," in which "the meaning went as a sacrifice" to stylistic embellishments and ornamentation.[76]

Zaydān's paired notions of global literary interaction and literary decline should not, I think, be dismissed as a species of false consciousness or as the direct importation and naturalization of European ideas. Nevertheless, his era's literary critics and novelists engaged in a dramatic refashioning of *adab* so that it became recognizable as "literary." *Adab* was becoming part of "world literature" through global interaction, literary comparison, and social change. Zaydān and many others came to see the *maqāma*'s "ornamental" language as a serious defect when held up to European literature. As Hannah Scott Deuchar has shown, Zaydān was also part of a debate about translation and the Arabic language that emerged in the nineteenth century and continued well into the twentieth. The rich vocabulary in genres like the *maqāma* was seen by reformers like Zaydān as a kind of wasteful surplus that needed to be reined in and subjected to market logics.[77] A text like the *Ḥarīriyya* had no value in the global marketplace of literature because it was so resistant to translation and to the exchange-value logic of colonial capitalism. As Nādir Kāẓim has also shown in his 2003 study of the *Hamadhāniyya*'s reception, the *maqāma* form came to be seen in the early twentieth century as lacking the aesthetic simplicity and emotional depth of French Romanticism, while simultaneously missing the detailed treatment of character that could be found in French drama.[78] Critics in the twentieth century like Shawqī Ḍayf, who tried to defend the *maqāma*, claimed that earlier critics had erred in finding it "lacking" when compared to European narrative genres because it had never really been a narrative genre after all. It was rather a pedagogical or didactic one (*taʿlīm*). *Maqāma*s were merely vehicles for providing students with a way to learn rare words and rhetorical flourishes. For Ḍayf, the *maqāma* might be part of the pedagogical aspects of *adab*, but it was not part of "literature."[79] In this sense, al-Ḥarīrī's reputation as a major figure in the tradition has remained intact for many in the Arab world in the past century, even if he has been marginalized in the new educational and literary dispensations of the literary.

The entire debate over the *maqāma*'s literariness was necessarily conducted on the basis of normative definitions of literature. Because the *maqāma* supposedly lacked narrative or because its narrative was deemed mere window dressing to a pedagogical text, it was either banished from the precincts of literature or relegated to its undesirable neighborhoods. Some scholars have suggested that the repressive environment of medieval Islamic societies was to blame. As late as 1998, Rina Drory's entry on the *maqāma* in the *Encyclopedia of Arabic Literature* maintained that, due to the "powerful religio-poetic norms" governing Islamic society, the overt fictionality of the *maqāma* had to be masked with didacticism and "ultimately failed to fulfill a creative role in the dynamics of Arabic literature."[80] The implication of Drory's claim is that the hundreds of authors who wrote *maqāma*s after al-Ḥarīrī and al-Hamadhānī failed to be creative because the religio-poetic norms doomed them to constrained imitation. In a word, they lacked freedom—a haunted echo of Zaydān. Medieval Islamic societies, in Drory's account, were allergic to fiction, creativity, and play. I will return in Chapter 5 to the question of fictionality that Drory invokes. For now, it is worth considering how the discursive production of "literature" as a secular space of creativity is achieved through the concomitant assertion that the medieval past (and especially the *Islamic* medieval past) was full of fanaticism and pedantry.

Securing the reentry of the *maqāma* into the realm of the literary was achieved through reinterpreting the text as a subversive act of playful creativity that was smuggled into the culture of a closed-minded, medieval Islamic past. Consider, for example, Daniel Beaumont's reading of the *Hamadhāniyya* in which he argues that the trickster's ironic and playfully deceptive use of language is "fundamentally opposed to the thoroughly idealistic conception of language that pervades medieval Islam."[81] Beaumont is presumably referring to the Ashʿarī view that God's will is essentially legible through the sources of revelation. As Bernard Weiss puts it, medieval Muslims for the most part saw language "as a perfect instrument of communication when used by those who had truly mastered it."[82] It would be an oversimplification, however, to suggest that this theological commitment to language's legibility does not allow for allusion, deception, ambiguity, and difficulty. It erases the sophisticated tradition of language theory that developed in Islamic law, poetics, and exegesis. The poetics of the Ashʿarī scholar ʿAbd al-Qāhir al-Jurjānī, for instance, esteemed those kinds of language that could only be understood by the most adept of readers or listeners. The pleasure and wonder of discovering a text's hidden meaning found expression in a celebration of difficult, allusive, and potentially misleading language.[83] More troubling is the implication in modern scholarship that medieval Muslims were rigidly opposed to the kind of allusive and playful language found in the *maqāma* genre, which functions as a way of quarantining the *maqāma* from its Islamic context. The *maqāma* is transformed by this interpretive move into an island of secular, literary values in a fanatical medieval world. Building on this tradition of scholarship, Angelika Neuwirth states that the *Ḥarīriyya* "does not affirm the official law and order discourse of Islamic *ʿilm* [knowledge], but dissects its underlying psychological layers, shifting the focus from religious norms to their conceptual opposite, the *anti-norm*, represented by play and fiction, *adab*."[84] Neuwirth ominously codes Islamic knowledge as a discourse of "law and order," in a haunted continuation of Orientalist and secular postcolonial scholarly practices.[85]

In fact, the idea that the *Ḥarīriyya* and the *maqāma genre* in general were antinormative is an even older one. Thomas Chenery, the nineteenth-century translator whom we met earlier in this chapter, presumed the *Ḥarīriyya*'s overall "spirit" would offend pious Muslim audiences. He avers that "undoubtedly the spirit of the whole composition might well have offended the more scrupulous."[86] Chenery himself seems to find parts of the text distasteful, noting that "there is real moral excellence in much that [al-Ḥarīrī] writes," but these morally excellent discourses are "ill placed in the mouth of Abū Zayd."[87] Neuwirth's argument ironically coincides with Chenery's in that they both believe that the scrupulous Muslim would be irked by the *Ḥarīriyya*. The difference is that Neuwirth celebrates the supposed triumph of *adab* over dogmatic Islamic *ʿilm*, valorizing the perceived subversiveness of the *Ḥarīriyya*, whereas the censorious Victorians are left clutching their pearls. But both Neuwirth and Chenery maintain a vision of fragile pious Muslimness that cannot tolerate, much less celebrate, Abū Zayd al-Sarūjī. The result of both accounts is the erasure of the *Ḥarīriyya*'s central role in Islamic education, commentary culture, and aesthetics over the course of centuries. To take one example, when Tāj al-Dīn al-Subkī (d. 769/1368) compiled a biographical encyclopedia of Shāfiʿī legal scholars, he praised a prominent preacher in twelfth-century Rayy by saying that "he spoke as though with the words of the *Ḥarīriyya*."[88] The preacher's sermons in Rayy thus unproblematically resembled the trickster's sermons. Although some Muslims might have responded critically to the *Ḥarīriyya*, the idea that it was structurally and necessarily subversive is invented more or less out of whole cloth without reference to actual Muslim readers from the sixth–seventh/twelfth–thirteenth centuries.[89]

The Ghost of Bakhtin

Let us now return to Bakhtin's habitual haunting of literary readings of the *maqāma* and the role of his theoretical armature in the colonial economy of literature. Both Neuwirth and Chenery agree that Islamic piety is necessarily opposed to playful forms of *adab*, which implies a series of unstated assumptions about both *adab* and Islam. Neuwirth explicitly references Bakhtin to suggest that the *Ḥarīriyya*'s subversions are liberating. She portrays the antinorms of play and fiction as a kind of release valve for repressed energies. Bakhtin's notion of the carnivalesque, however, relies on the myths and teleologies of modernity. What Neuwirth and Bakhtin share is a kind of imagined "Middle Ages" that also stands in for everything dogmatic and monstrous about modernity.[90] Bakhtin claims that Rabelais's parodies were "opposed to the intolerant, dogmatic seriousness of the Middle Ages . . . [but] the history of culture and literature knew other forms of seriousness."[91] For Bakhtin, laughter "liberates from fanaticism," but that does not mean that all seriousness is necessarily fanatical. Indeed, he points out that "true, open seriousness fears neither parody, nor irony, nor any other form of reduced laughter, for it is aware of being part of an uncompleted whole."[92] Bakhtin associates this "open seriousness" with modernity, which, unlike the medieval world, was open-minded and multivocal. Bakhtin's valorization of the modern novel's multivocality is inextricably linked to his assumption that the medieval past was incapable of incorporating multiple voices.

When Bakhtin is made to travel to the medieval Islamic world, the landscape becomes haunted by Renan's account of Islam as essentially fanatical. The rigid dogmatism of Bakhtin's medieval world accords well with Renan's account of Islam, both of which together transform Muslim laughter into subversion. In fact, secularism and the institutions of literature continue to define themselves against the "medieval" sensibilities of fanatics in the present, especially against Muslims whose piety is made to seem anachronistic. As Michael Allan has shown with reference to the Rushdie Affair, the figure of the fanatical reader is still conjured up as the sinister Other to the cosmopolitan reader who thinks critically and who *recognizes* the secular values of literature.[93] The idea that medieval readers *failed* to recognize the *maqāma* for what it was (namely, literature) serves to indict them for their *lack* of literary sensibilities. When Chenery, Neuwirth, and Beaumont posit a pious, naively literalist, medieval Muslim reader who finds the *Ḥarīriyya* offensive, they make the text recognizable *as literature*. They insist that the space for "play and fiction" was, in that world, separate from and even opposed to religiosity. Thus, "literary" discourse was necessarily critical of religiosity's naivete. The *Ḥarīriyya*, once banished from the precincts of the literary, was permitted to return to the newly constructed realm of "world literature" under the auspices of the carnivalesque. It came to be celebrated by literary scholars for its antinomian antics, its critique of naive literalism, and its playful irreligiosity. When modern scholars project these values onto the *Ḥarīriyya*, they make it stand against the oppressive religiosity that Bakhtin helps us imagine was everywhere in the Middle Ages.[94]

My point here is that we do not need a better, more sophisticated reading of Bakhtin, stripped of its historical baggage and thus made more universalizable and more applicable to the Arabic case. Rather, we must historicize or, better yet, provincialize Bakhtin. As Dipesh Chakrabarty pointed out some decades ago, the European experience is deemed universalizable *as theory*, whereas other histories only flesh out and contribute to "the theoretical skeleton" that has already been established.[95] When our "most modern scholars" rely on the universalization of a particular definition of literature or analytical method for reading literature, they neglect to provincialize their own categories. What I am suggesting is that *any* definition of literature is always already normative because it relies on treating certain texts (usually novels) as central and prototypical while marginalizing texts that belong to different traditions of reading. As the foregoing chapter has demonstrated, when the concept of literature permeated the world in a colonial age, it inspired projects to reform the canon of *adab* along literary lines. When our own reading and interpretive practices unconsciously echo the logic of colonial critics and anticolonial reformers, we allow those ghosts to inhabit our minds. We are possessed.

This chapter's ghostly séance is not, however, an exorcism that frees us of our haunted entanglements with colonialism and our complicity in it. We cannot simply avoid the colonial economy of literature by ignoring it, and we cannot eliminate it by thinking otherwise. The colonial economy of literature is one symptom or manifestation of a material reality that is underpinned by the institution of world literature itself: its departments, associations, funding structures, linguistic policies, publishing houses, and so on. As Eve Tuck and K. Wayne Yang have argued, decolonization is not a metaphor but a material reality. To suggest that these new readings or the recovery of old readings would achieve decolonization can function as a "move to innocence" that would serve to deny that my own act of reading is also implicated in colonialism. As Tuck and Yang state, "When metaphor invades decolonization, it kills the very possibility of decolonization; it recenters whiteness, it resettles theory, it extends innocence to the settler, it entertains a settler future."[96] There can be no decolonizing reading of the *Ḥarīriyya* in a material sense because acts of reading cannot replace material decolonization. Nevertheless, world literature and national literatures are *imagined* geographies that do not map neatly onto territory and are contested in our metaphors and modes of thinking.[97] I therefore hold out the possibility of a noninnocent reading that brings into view both the forces that shape our geographies of the past and the practices that shaped knowledge production before world literature.

My proposal is both to make the erasures enacted by the colonial economy of literature apparent *as erasures* and to examine what has been erased. In making visible the epistemological shifts that caused these erasures, I am following in a tradition of critical scholarship on colonialism, world literature, and the *Nahḍa* that has been taken up by Haifa Saud Alfaisal, Michael Allan, Hannah Scott Deuchar, Peter Hill, Elizabeth Holt, Rebecca Johnson, Aamir Mufti, Samah Selim, Shaden Tageldin, and others.[98] What all these scholars and their studies share is a careful attention to the nineteenth century as a time of transformation, as well as a skepticism regarding the triumphal narratives of revival that continue to be regurgitated in scholarship.[99] As I have suggested above, these important accounts of nineteenth-century transformations tend to devote little attention to an account of *adab* as a social, material, and intellectual tradition prior to European colonial violence. A meaningful account of *adab* before world literature would engage with those interpretive practices that were unconcerned with colonial modernity and the new notion of "literature." Without taking these earlier archives and practices into account, we are left with an image of pre-nineteenth-century *adab* that is largely shaped *by* the nineteenth century. An example of this phenomenon is the constant buzz around *The Thousand and One Nights* and the scholarly delight in the renegade scholar Ibn Ḥazm (d. 456/1064).[100] It is not that these texts and authors are uninteresting, but they were, in their own ways, marginal in relation to their own precolonial contexts. Their omnipresence in modern scholarly discourse is a testament to the fact that *today's* readers find them interesting, useful, and, in one way or another, familiar.

The case of the *Nights* is instructive because it emerged from a decidedly marginal position in Arabic prose. Ibn al-Nadīm (d. 385/995) mentions the *Nights* in his catalog of Arabic books and describes it as "a wretched book of insipid stories."[101] As Kilito points out, the scholarly critics of earlier centuries did not appreciate the *Nights* because "it did not conform to the classical norm" in language and style. Although these stories must have appealed to some readers, the scholarly celebration of the text in the Arab world has emerged relatively recently in the course of the *Nahḍa*.[102] The text later became a global sensation and a true classic of "world literature" through the ministrations, appropriations, and augmentations of Antoine Galland and the Grub Street translators, among many others. Its ubiquity on world literature syllabi is mainly attributable to the fact that it has played a central role in the European literary imaginary. The *Nights* ironically became a synecdoche for classical Arabic literature as a whole. By contrast, Kilito contends that "the *maqāmāt* have become unreadable" as a result of the reordering of aesthetic values.[103] This shift in attitudes regarding both the *Nights* and the *Ḥarīriyya* came about because the social, material, and interpretive practices of reading had changed as a new literary culture swept the globe. Commentarial reading, which I discuss in depth in the following chapters, could not be assimilated into the literary and, as such, texts that foreground commentary or require commentary became "unreadable."

When Jurjī Zaydān looked back on the Ottoman era, he saw commentary culture as a symbol of a broader intellectual and social decline. In the commentarial age, commentary was a crucial component of a sophisticated scholarly culture for countless students of Arabic across the centuries from al-Andalus to Indonesia. Among those aspiring scholars was the young ʿAbd al-Laṭīf al-Baghdādī, whom we met in this book's introduction when his father Yūsuf brought him to listen to the *Ḥarīriyya* for the first time. As we will see in the next chapter, he would need much more than listening and memorization to unlock the secrets of the books that he studied and to understand the complex web of intertextuality in a commentarial culture of knowledge production. Commentary as a mode of reading was widely mocked in the nineteenth century for being meaningless exercises in superficial sophistication, as Ahmed El Shamsy has recently shown. However, these nineteenth-century attitudes do not help us understand the ways in which commentary culture operated. Commentary did not appear to ʿAbd al-Laṭīf as a "lifeless desert," and he did not worry that focusing on the canonical commented-on texts would rip his attention away from what neoclassical reformers would come to see as the real classics.[104] My contention, in short, is that the arrival of world literature rendered texts like the *Ḥarīriyya* fundamentally *unreadable* within the purview of literature because the narrative dynamics of the *Ḥarīriyya* were commentarial. That is, commentary was both a part of the narratives themselves and part of the socially and materially embedded reading practices that made the *Ḥarīriyya* a classic of commentarial culture.

Making the ghosts of literature's erasures and foreclosures familiar invites us to explore those alternative possibilities of reading and interpretation that could not be assimilated within the colonial economy of literature. When these ghosts become familiar to us, it becomes possible to parochialize our approach to reading literary texts and then to appreciate the interpretive possibilities of engaging with commentary culture. That discipline and practice of reading, with all of its social, material, and intellectual contours, are not merely of historical interest. This entire ethics of commentarial reading challenges the implicit hierarchies that are created when world literature demands transparency, translatability, and unfettered interpretive access. Texts like the *Ḥarīriyya* that resist these demands can be seen as an invitation to become more acutely aware of the heterogeneity of reading practices across time and space. To read before world literature is to provisionally inhabit interpretive approaches, the sophistication of which can only be appreciated when the implicitly normative claims of literature are recognized as particular, parochial, and historically conditioned.

Chapter 2

Reading in Commentary Culture

This chapter introduces the practices of reading and interpretation in the commentary culture that underpinned the reception and transmission of the *Ḥarīriyya*. I argue that commentary was neither a narrowly explanatory practice of elucidating texts nor an otiose crutch that was extraneous to the text. Rather, commentary was a multilayered and multifaceted discipline of reading, in which the goal was not simply to "understand" a text but to inhabit the entire discursive tradition to which that text belonged. When readers came to inhabit the tradition, their affective responses to sophisticated commentaries included wonder and joy, rather than simply "understanding." This affective component of commentary culture is often overlooked by modern readers who find commentary dull and potentially pedantic. To appreciate this social, material, and intellectual practice of reading, let us cast our imaginations back more than eight hundred years ago to Baghdad where a young ʿAbd al-Laṭīf al-Baghdādī would be introduced to the discipline of reading in commentary culture. That child's father, a man named Yūsuf, dreamed that his son would become a scholar one day. On May 8 of 1168 AD (28th of Rajab 563 AH), Yūsuf brought ʿAbd al-Laṭīf, only six years old at the time, to listen to the *Ḥarīriyya*, the collection of fifty stories about an eloquent trickster. When the young ʿAbd al-Laṭīf had listened to the whole book, he received a certificate attesting to this act of transmission that connected him back to the author through a single intermediary. ʿAbd al-Laṭīf would carry that material certificate with him for the rest of his life, but it was only the beginning of his multilayered interaction with the *Ḥarīriyya*.[1] Over the next few years, ʿAbd al-Laṭīf memorized a remarkable range of materials, including the *Ḥarīriyya*, the Quran, the poems of al-Mutanabbī, and primers on law and grammar. Finally, Yūsuf sent his son to study with Ibn al-Anbārī (d. 577/1181), a Baghdad luminary who composed a biographical dictionary of those devoted to *adab* and several treatises on Arabic philology.[2]

ʿAbd al-Laṭīf's first lesson was an unmitigated disaster. The lesson began with a reading from the preface of Thaʿlab's *Faṣīḥ*, one of the books that he had already memorized, which seemed fortuitous at first. But then Ibn al-Anbārī began speaking, offering his oral commentary on the text. ʿAbd al-Laṭīf could make neither heads nor tails of what the man was saying, and it seemed to him like a great deal of rapid-fire nonsense (*hadhar*).[3] This commentary was not simply an elucidation of the text. It was something much more sophisticated. When ʿAbd al-Laṭīf found himself utterly out of his depth, he also noticed that the other students were enjoying the teacher's commentary, visibly expressing "wonder." ʿAbd al-Laṭīf's confusion did not go unnoticed. "I eschew teaching children," Ibn al-Anbārī said. "Take him to study with my disciple al-Wajīh al-Wāsiṭī, and when he is more middling in his abilities, he may study with me."[4]

ʿAbd al-Laṭīf's new tutor would give the young student the knowledge and tools necessary to comprehend the commentarial culture that underpinned the practices of reading and scholarship. ʿAbd al-Laṭīf became his tutor's constant companion, helping al-Wajīh, who was blind, with his daily tasks. The student attended his teacher's study circle at the Ẓafariyya mosque in the morning, and then al-Wajīh would assign ʿAbd al-Laṭīf "all the commentaries (*jamīʿ al-shurūḥ*)" for the texts they had studied. Teacher and student would discuss the commentaries on a text until ʿAbd al-Laṭīf had mastered them. Finally, the tutor would have the text read aloud, and ʿAbd al-Laṭīf would produce his own commentary, presumably synthesizing what he had learned, to prove his mastery of the text and its commentarial tradition. After the morning study circle at the Ẓafariyya mosque, the tutor and the disciple would leave together for al-Wajīh's home. ʿAbd al-Laṭīf would then spend the evening assisting his tutor by reading aloud and memorizing the more advanced books that al-Wajīh was studying with Ibn al-Anbārī. He would also listen to al-Wajīh commenting on his assigned texts in the presence of his teacher. To understand the advanced oral commentary of Ibn al-Anbārī that seemed like nonsense, the young ʿAbd al-Laṭīf first needed to become an active participant in commentary culture, which involved reading existing commentaries, listening to a tutor's commentary, and finally executing one's own commentary for a teacher.[5]

This chapter argues that commentary culture was a multilayered discipline of reading, as illustrated by ʿAbd al-Laṭīf's movement through various stages: listening, memorization, immersion in commentaries, and finally producing commentaries himself. Furthermore, the culture of commentary involved social, material, and intellectual practices. The social relations between the tutor al-Wajīh and his pupil provided ʿAbd al-Laṭīf with an initiation into commentary culture. The material practice of producing certificates to attest to textual transmission allowed ʿAbd al-Laṭīf to certify his status as an authorized transmitter of the *Ḥarīriyya*, enabling him, in his old age, to bestow a chain of transmission back to al-Ḥarīrī on another generation of listeners.[6] The intellectual sophistication of commentarial reading was evident when ʿAbd al-Laṭīf could not comprehend his teacher's commentary on the *Faṣīḥ* of Thaʿlab. Commentaries were venues to perform knowledge and explore interpretive possibilities, and they also produced hierarchies among their readers and listeners. The students who understood their teacher's commentary marked themselves out through their affective responses to the commentary.

Whereas the previous chapter showed how the social and intellectual practices of commentary came to be seen as a mark of decadence and decline, this chapter draws attention to how ʿAbd al-Laṭīf and his contemporaries saw commentary as crucial to the social bonds of an intellectual community. Commentaries did not simply reside in texts. They resided in people who embodied those texts. As Rudolph Ware has argued regarding Islamic education in West Africa over the longue durée, those students and scholars "who underwent this process of embodied knowledge transmission became the books they studied."[7] The process of becoming a living embodiment of commentary was necessary in order to participate in the Islamic intellectual tradition in this era. Our dismissal or failure to understand the dynamic processes of commentarial culture means that we cannot read with ʿAbd al-Laṭīf al-Baghdādī but are forced to deracinate texts and read them "as literature." Without understanding the social, material, and intellectual contexts that underpin this act of becoming-embodied-knowledge, it is impossible to understand commentarial reading and the affective component of wonder, delight, and joy.

The present chapter begins by exploring how the *Ḥarīriyya*'s narratives about Abū Zayd and al-Ḥārith depict the relationship between commentary and affect. My argument is that these narratives reflect the commentary culture in which the *Ḥarīriyya* thrived. Next, this chapter analyzes the social practices of textual transmission and commentary that took place in reading sessions like the ones that were part of ʿAbd al-Laṭīf's education described above, in which scholars would read, transmit, and comment on texts. Finally, we turn to the value of commentarial genealogies, in which the ability of later generations to claim special interpretive authority was based on their ability to channel the commentarial legacy of earlier generations. This chapter as a whole is an introduction to commentarial reading, which is not a practice of merely elucidating texts but rather represents an entire ethics of reading, in its social, material, and intellectual dimensions.

Commentarial Reading and Affect in the *Ḥarīriyya*

To help us appreciate the stakes of commentarial reading, let us begin by taking a closer look at ʿAbd al-Laṭīf's first experience of Ibn al-Anbārī's commentary. The teacher's apparent babble and nonsense became eloquent to those who had mastered the massive archive of Arabic and Islamic knowledge. In other words, Ibn al-Anbārī's erudite oral commentary on the *Faṣīḥ* was incomprehensible to those who had yet to master the previously existing commentary tradition. This educational event alerts us to the multilayered nature of commentary. Some commentaries were more advanced than others, and each layer helped unlock more and more sophisticated layers that, at first, might seem excessive or incomprehensible. ʿAbd al-Laṭīf's first lesson also parallels many of the *maqāma*s in the *Ḥarīriyya* in which apparent nonsense is transformed into sense through the mediation of the trickster's commentaries. Consider, for example, *maqāma* #32 in which al-Ḥārith, who is encamped on the way to Medina after performing the pilgrimage to Mecca. He hears that the "jurist of the Arabs" is holding an assembly, so he goes with his companions to hear the learned man speak. When he arrives, he immediately recognizes that the jurist is none other than Abū Zayd, "the father of abominable lies."[8] Al-Ḥārith listens to one hundred *fatwā*s, all of which are incorrect or nonsensical. For instance, Abū Zayd is asked about the purification ritual for prayer: "Should someone performing ablutions rub his testicles?" He replies: "It is recommended to do so, but it is not obligatory."[9] The *fatwā* is obviously incorrect, and all the rest are likewise incorrect or nonsensical, but the crowd is full of admiration, and they lavish Abū Zayd with gifts.

Al-Ḥārith, meanwhile, does not reveal Abū Zayd for the rogue that he is. Instead, he follows him and berates him for pretending to be a jurist, at which Abū Zayd offers him a poem blaming fate for driving him to these deceptive performances. Abū Zayd then invites al-Ḥārith to join him on a pilgrimage. Al-Ḥārith replies, "Forget about me joining you, unless I learn the commentary (*tafsīr*)!"[10] In other words, al-Ḥārith has realized that these *fatwās* are not actually nonsense but are only nonsense in their apparent meaning. In fact, each *fatwā* contains a double entendre. In our example, the word "testicles (*unthayān*)" can also mean "ears," although this is a much less common meaning. It is a piece of lexical trivia. With that information in hand, the *fatwā* becomes perfectly correct because it is recommended (but not obligatory) to rub one's ears during ablutions. Once Abū Zayd explains what had bewildered and unsettled al-Ḥārith, the two set off to perform the pilgrimage together.

The trickster Abū Zayd provides al-Ḥārith with the commentarial key to unlock the meaning of these riddling *fatwās*. What had begun as nonsense turns to sense, but only for those like al-Ḥārith who seek out the commentary. The audience is left with their faulty understanding of God's law. The author of the *Ḥarīriyya* does not, however, leave his audience in the dark. The explanation of the double entendre can be found underneath each *fatwā*. For instance:

> *The questioner asked:* Is a non-Muslim living under Muslim rule permitted to kill an old woman *(qatl al-ʿajūz)*?
> *He responded:* Objecting to it is not permitted.
> The word for "old woman" also means "aged wine," and "to kill" means to mix the wine.[11]

Abū Zayd's audience, unaware of the commentary, is left to understand that a non-Muslim would be permitted to kill old women with impunity. By contrast, al-Ḥārith marks himself out as a worthy disciple of Abū Zayd by recognizing the absurdity of the *fatwās* and seeking out the commentary that transforms nonsense into sense. These authorial commentaries produce a powerful parallel between Abū Zayd and al-Ḥarīrī. Both the author and the rogue act as commentators. They give their audience, or at least some of it, access to a commentary. Both the fictional world and the social world beyond the text are governed by commentarial logics.

We know that these autocommentaries are, in fact, authorial because two manuscripts survive from the author's own lifetime, and both copies contain certificates in the author's own hand that authorize these copies. In fact, in all the early manuscripts of the *Ḥarīriyya*, there is a stable set of autocommentaries for the same nine *maqāmas*. In some cases, the commentary appears as interlinear commentary, as is the case with *maqāma* #32 with its riddling *fatwās*. In other cases, the autocommentary appears at the end of the *maqāma*, as is the case with #19.[12] Al-Ḥarīrī's autocommentaries often parallel the autocommentary that Abū Zayd provides his fictional audiences or, as in the *maqāma* with the riddling *fatwās*, only to al-Ḥārith who follows Abū Zayd and demands an explanation. When Abū Zayd does promise a commentary, he does not always deliver. In *maqāma* #44, he promises to explain his ambiguous speech to al-Ḥārith and his audience in return for payment, but he sneaks off before fulfilling his promise. Although the whole of the fictional audience is left frustrated, the author includes a commentary in two different forms for this episode.[13] *Maqāma* #44 has both an interlinear autocommentary and an autocommentary after the *maqāma*, a feature that al-Ḥarīrī explains in the introduction to the autocommentary that follows the *maqāma*: "I have [already] explained the secret of every riddle underneath it, not postponing its uncovering to those who read it. There remain some terms included in this *maqāma*, the interpretation of which might be obscure to some who encounter them. I wished to clarify them so that the reader might be saved from ambiguity's perplexity, the inconvenience of pondering, and the shame of searching and asking."[14] Whereas Abū Zayd the commentator postpones and then withholds the commentary, al-Ḥarīrī offers his readers immediate access. There is something paradoxical about this posture because the narratives stress the importance of seeking out explanations by interrogating the speaker himself, even if that means following him surreptitiously after he has departed. Al-Ḥarīrī's justification for interlinear commentary is that it saves the reader from experiencing that perplexity by providing the lexical explanations. The experience of perplexity and the experience of being given the keys to understanding coexist in the *Ḥarīriyya* and seem to heighten the hermeneutical drama because the reader cannot be sure whether the explanation will be provided immediately, postponed, or withdrawn completely. As we will see in Chapter 6, one *maqāma* portrays Abū Zayd offering a commentary that turns out to be just another ruse.

Abū Zayd's eloquent performances mesmerize audiences throughout the *Ḥarīriyya*, and they are the source of his subtle power. But the enigmatic quality of his speech is what prompts al-Ḥārith to treat Abū Zayd as a pedagogical authority. Consider, for example, *maqāma* #24, in which Abū Zayd crashes a boozy spring picnic.[15] The *maqāma* begins with al-Ḥārith and his companions enjoying wine and music when a man wearing an old, worn-out garment appears without invitation, irritating the gathered company. They are suddenly distracted from their uninvited guest by a line of verse that the musician has sung in which the word "union (*waṣl*)," referring to the union of beloveds, appears twice. The singer puts the first "union" in the accusative case and the second in the nominative case. When he is questioned, he swears that his reading is grammatically correct according to the early grammarian Sībawayh (d. ca. 180/796). The companions, however, break into two camps, one insisting that both ought to be nominative while the other insists the opposite.

The trickster Abū Zayd stays silent until this disunion over the word "union" subsides, but then he "smiles the smile of one who knows" and states that both instances of "union" admit either the nominative or accusative case.[16] The shabbily dressed man sees that the companions have girded themselves for war and are about to argue with him, so he goes on the attack with a rapid-fire series of allusively constructed grammatical riddles. For example, he asks, "Where do the men put on the veils of women and the ladies of curtained canopies appear wearing the turbans of men?" And: "What is the place where the ranks must be maintained between the striker and the one struck?"

Abū Zayd's audience is stunned by this display of grammatical knowledge and the allusiveness of the riddles themselves. Their sudden docility in the face of performative knowledge reflects the same pattern of affect and authority that we found in ʿAbd al-Laṭīf's first lesson with Ibn al-Anbārī. Al-Ḥārith tells us that when Abū Zayd's "terrifying riddles were poured out upon us, they brought confusion and barrenness to our minds," and the companions find themselves "incapable of swimming in his sea." As a result, al-Ḥārith's companions adjust their affective response to Abū Zayd and begin to treat him not as an onerous intrusion but as a source of authoritative knowledge. They exchanged "annoyance with him for a desire to learn from him," and they "traded weariness at seeing him for wanting a chain of transmission (*isnād*) from him."[17] Abū Zayd solves the riddles for his audience, and these solutions appear in the autocommentary that follows the *maqāma*, together with an explanation of grammatical case for the word "union," which had caused such discord.

The newfound harmony between Abū Zayd and his now-docile audience at the end of the *maqāma* is based on their recognition of the trickster as an authority from whom a chain of transmission or *isnād* might be desirable. *Isnād* is a technical term in the Islamic scholarly tradition that refers to the chain of scholars who transmitted a text from its origin. In the case of the hadith—the narratives that record the sayings and deeds of the Prophet Muḥammad—the *isnād* offers a mode of embodied authentication for the Prophet's legacy. After a canon of authentic hadith was established in books like the *Ṣaḥīḥ* of al-Bukhārī (d. 256/870), the embodied transmission of the Prophet's legacy did not go away but was transformed. The *isnād* became both a symbol and a ritual of one's connection with the Prophet. Having a short chain of transmitters between oneself and the Prophet became particularly desirable, and it became more common for very young children to hear hadith books with the oldest living person who possessed the shortest chain themselves.[18]

This ritual practice of hadith transmission goes some way to explaining why ʿAbd al-Laṭīf listened to hadith, the *Ḥarīriyya*, and numerous other texts in his childhood. As a child, one would collect certificates that testified to one's presence in the audience where a text had been read aloud. These audition certificates (*samāʿāt*, sing. *samāʿ*) might become relevant later in life and could take the form of individual certificates, copied into a personal manuscript of the text, for instance, or they could be lists of attendees inscribed in the manuscript from which the text was transmitted. Whatever a text's genre, whether it was hadith or a text like the *Ḥarīriyya*, having an audition certificate did not signify that a child or another auditor now understood the text but that the ritual of embodied transmission had taken place. In the case of hadith, for example, an illiterate layperson who had heard the text being read aloud could nevertheless become a vessel for the text and preside over its oral transmission to a new audience of listener-readers. That ritual of oral transmission and written certification was a highly prized social and material practice with important implications, although the precise form these practices took varied in different times and places across the Islamic world. In many cases, a scholar could not legitimately transmit that text to a new generation without having received that ritual transmission.[19]

Teaching a text, as opposed to transmitting it, was another matter entirely, and it required mastery. What exactly could determine a scholar's authority to explain a text was contested terrain and cannot be reduced to a matter of whether someone had an *ijāza* or "permission" to teach a text. Muslim scholars debated the meaning and necessity of *ijāza*s over the centuries, and modern scholarship often confuses *ijāza*s with audition certificates, as Garrett Davidson's study of postcanonization hadith transmission has shown.[20] What is clear from both the narratives of the *Ḥarīriyya* and the life story of ʿAbd al-Laṭīf al-Baghdādī is that mastery could be demonstrated through the performance of eloquent but difficult speech, the accompanying act of autocommentary, and the practice of commentary more generally. In fact, ʿAbd al-Laṭīf composed a series of aphorisms about the etiquette of refined, scholarly people in which he recommends that they elevate their speech above that of ordinary people by being "concise and eloquent . . . deploying some well-executed riddles (*alghāz*) and more or less ambiguous speech (*īhām kathīr aw qalīl*)."[21] An ideal scholar, according to ʿAbd al-Laṭīf, ought to act a bit like Abū Zayd. They should be cryptic and test the mettle of their interlocutors by forcing them to decode the elusive discourses that they encounter.

It is sometimes assumed that commentaries consist of mere glosses or explanations of the text. But this is hardly the case. As we saw with the lecture that confused ʿAbd al-Laṭīf on his first day of lessons, a commentarial lecture on a familiar text might baffle those who were uninitiated in the commentarial tradition. Recall that the commentary that flummoxed ʿAbd al-Laṭīf was on a text that he had already memorized. That commentary was designed to expound on the text in sophisticated ways for those who already understood the text's basic meaning and were familiar with the existing commentarial tradition.

Similarly, al-Ḥarīrī's autocommentaries are not limited to explaining words or riddles. The longest gloss in the autocommentary consists of a complete story that serves to reinforce the role of commentary as a phenomenon that discursively linked together the social, intellectual, and material realms. In *maqāma* #40, al-Ḥārith encounters Abū Zayd and his new wife quarreling, and he follows the pair when they bring their dispute before the judge of Tabrīz. The couple exchange a series of highly allusive insults that rely on comparisons with proverbially famous people and things, such as "She is more lying than Sajjāḥ!" or "He has more defects than the she-mule of Abū Dulāma!" The judge realizes that the two are not litigants but performers, and he joins in on the referential game, saying, "I see that the two of you are Shann and Ṭabaqa."[22] What does the judge mean?

The story of Shann and Ṭabaqa is the longest gloss in al-Ḥarīrī's entire autocommentarial corpus, and, in this case, he offers more than one competing explanation for the proverb. The first interpretation, which al-Ḥarīrī says is the one believed by most scholars, says that Shann and Ṭabaqa are the names of two tribes who met one another in battle. Rather than settling on this gloss and offering a fixed meaning for the proverb, he goes on to offer a second interpretation that he notes is less common. It is this rarer interpretation of the proverb, however, that is more compelling, fulfilling a pattern in which the more arcane interpretation of words and phrases is the more accurate (as we have already seen above in the riddling *fatwās*). According to this alternative story, Shann is a wily man from the Arab past who swears only to marry a woman who matches him (*tulāʾimuhu*), and he travels the land in search of her. Another man joins him on one of his journeys, and he hears Shann utter a series of strange questions. As the pair set out, Shann asks his companion, "Shall you carry me, or I you?" Later, as they pass a funeral, Shann asks, "Do you think the honoree is alive?" Shann's companion calls him the most ignorant man he has ever known, and when they arrive at his abode, he tries to amuse his daughter Ṭabaqa with Shann's nonsensical questions. "He only spoke accurately," she replies, and gives her father a commentary. She explains that by asking who should "carry" the other, he meant something like "carry the conversation" to pass the time on the road. When he asked if the dead man was alive, he was asking if he had left behind any progeny who would keep his memory alive.[23] The man gives his daughter in marriage to the enigmatic Shann.

The marriage of Shann and Ṭabaqa is also the marriage of the woman's brilliant interpretation (*taʾwīl*) and the man's riddling speech. Ṭabaqa's astute intelligence (*fiṭna*) marks her out as a fitting bride for the riddling Shann because she can transform his nonsense into sense. When the judge of Tabrīz calls Abū Zayd and his wife "Shann and Ṭabaqa," the explanation that these are tribes who went to war might seem most apt because the husband and wife are at war. However, the judge seems to be drawing on the second, less common interpretation to signal that he is aware that the two are only *apparently* at war but are actually witty compatriots. As with the riddling *fatwās* and the lessons of ʿAbd al-Laṭīf al-Baghdādī, layered commentary is a social and intellectual practice that turns nonsense into sense while building affective bonds of friendship, discipleship, and even marriage.

The *Ḥarīriyya* does not mark the beginning of *adab* commentary or of autocommentary more specifically. Anthologies of poetry like the *Mufaḍḍaliyyāt* of al-Mufaḍḍal (d. 164 or 170/780 or 786), for example, contain extensive commentary that glosses difficult words, provides alternative readings, and occasionally situates the poem in a particular narrative context. As for autocommentary, it is noteworthy that it can be found in a number of earlier texts depicting tricksters, vagabonds, and the criminal underworld. For example, in the *Kitāb al-Bukhalāʾ* of al-Jāḥiẓ, a chapter devoted to a certain Khālid b. Yazīd who specializes in begging (*kudya*) is followed by a commentary that seems to be composed by al-Jāḥiẓ himself. The stories and tropes around begging, tricksters, and vagabondage coalesced under the rubric of the "Tribe of Sāsān," a motley gang of vagabonds and charlatans of which al-Jāḥiẓ's Khālid b. Yazīd is the forebear.

Another autocommentary can be found in the richly inventive account of the Tribe of Sāsān composed by Abū Dulaf (d. fl. fourth/tenth century), who boasts in the opening lines of his poem about the tribe's freedom from worldly constraints. The ode consists of almost two hundred verses, providing a detailed taxonomy of tricksters and vagabonds. The poet's autocommentary on several verses is devoted to explaining the occasional rare word that belonged to the jargon of the tribe or to explicate the precise nature of a stratagem that is referenced in the verse.[24] The fictivity and acerbic commentary of Abū Dulaf's "Tribe of Sāsān" is made abundantly clear when the poet states that this tribe of vagabonds includes in their number the Abbasid caliph who must beg his Buyid "protector" Muʿizz al-Dawla (d. 356/967) for his bread. The caliph was a puppet of his Buyid overlords, but he was neither a beggar nor a member of this vagabond tribe. Abū Dulaf also lists various sorts of scholars among the Tribe of Sāsān, which implies that this poem is not to be taken as a sociological study of the medieval Islamic underworld but as a humorous and deflating analysis of the tricksterism and beggary common to all classes.[25] The link between the *Ḥarīriyya* and Abū Dulaf's ode to the Tribe of Sāsān exists both at the structural level, in that the author himself is providing autocommentarial glosses, and at the thematic level, in the sense that al-Ḥarīrī's trickster Abū Zayd is sometimes identified as a member of the Banū Sāsān. For example, the narrator claims in *maqāma* #49 that the Banū Sāsān considered Abū Zayd's advice to his son about how to live a life of vagabondage superior to the pious advice that is offered by Luqmān to his son in Quran 31:12–19 and was memorized among them like the supplications in the Fātiḥa of the Quran.[26]

The autocommentaries of al-Jāḥiẓ and Abū Dulaf are occasional affairs. By contrast, the irascible al-Maʿarrī (d. 449/1058) was a prolific autocommentator on both his poetry and his prose, which makes a good deal of sense because he was infamous for using rare and difficult words. Al-Maʿarrī hailed from a family of prominent Muslim judges and legal scholars, but he is best remembered for his pessimistic poetry and provocative proclamations about revealed religion. Centuries after his death, some Muslim scholars continued to attack him as an arch-heretic for supposedly claiming that his *al-Fuṣūl wa-l-ghāyāt* was a competitive emulation (*muʿāraḍa*) of the Quran.[27] The miraculous inimitability of the Quran was part of the theological claims to the text's divine origin. As the Quran itself states, "Were men and jinn to gather together to bring forth the like of this Quran, they would not bring forth its like, even if they were to help one another" (Q 17.88).[28] The polymath and biographer Yāqūt al-Rūmī (d. 626/1229) tells us that al-Maʿarrī downgraded the aesthetic achievement of the Quran. The story goes that when al-Maʿarrī was asked whether his *Fuṣūl* could compare with the Quran, he said: "The prayer niches have not yet polished [my *Fuṣūl*] for four hundred years."[29] This potentially apocryphal quip suggests that the Quran's perceived excellence is the result of its canonicity, rather than the inimitability of the revelation itself. Whether or not al-Maʿarrī ever said these words, the anecdotes reflect a concern among later readers about al-Maʿarrī's edginess, and I argue in Chapter 4 that these sorts of biographical writing were often polemical and interpretive.[30] In other words, a reader of al-Maʿarrī *might imagine* him to say such a thing based on a reading of his works. Yāqūt also tells us that al-Maʿarrī composed two autocommentaries on the *Fuṣūl*, both of which addressed its unusual vocabulary (*gharīb*) and its riddling passages (*lughz*), which already suggests a parallel with al-Ḥarīrī's autocommentarial activity.

Al-Maʿarrī also used autocommentarial writing to defend himself against his detractors who had, in his view, misinterpreted his words. His edginess and playful pessimism are particularly on display in his *Luzūm mā lā Yalzam* ("Necessitating the Unnecessary"), a collection of his later poems with supererogatory rhymes often referred to simply as the *Luzūmiyyāt*. In one of these, poems, studied in depth by Suzanne Stetkevych, he imagines a time in the far future when:

> People will ask, "What is Qurasyh? What is Mecca?"
> Just as people once asked, "What is Jadīs? What is Ṭasm?"[31]

Here, al-Maʿarrī imagines a future in which Islam has disappeared, but the final judgment has not arrived. It participates, as Susan Stetkevych points out, in a notion of time that is cyclical rather than teleological. The fickleness of fate (*dahr*) that erased the memory of previous societies will, in the end, come for us all. This apparent denial of the resurrection and its teleology of the final judgment are themes to which al-Maʿarrī returns again and again. In one verse, al-Maʿarrī describes death as "a long sleep without end (*mā lahu amad*)," which, in its most obvious sense, implies a denial of the resurrection when the dead ought to rise from their slumber. Al-Maʿarrī claims that "only an ignorant man objects to this verse" because what the line of verse *actually* means is that the sleep of death "has no *known* duration (*mā lahu amad maʿrūf*)."[32] The most obvious meaning and its heretical implications are thus discarded by the autocommentary.

Al-Maʿarrī's autocommentary exploits the ambiguity of the term *amad*, which can either mean end point or duration. Does death have no end (*amad*), or does it have no duration (*amad*) that can be known by mere humans? The former is heresy, while the latter interpretation, which is helped along by the autocommentary's interpolation of the word "known," is merely conventional. As al-Maʿarrī explains, no religious community claims to know the precise timing of the resurrection and the final judgment, which is known only to God.[33] Al-Maʿarrī's use of autocommentary to rebut a real or imagined critic does not survive as an independent text but was discovered in the margins of an undated manuscript at the British Museum (now the British Library). The discovery was made in 1954 by a Syrian researcher named Amjad al-Ṭarābulsī who was visiting London during his trip to the Twenty-Third Congress of Orientalists in Cambridge. He found the task of dating the manuscript to be no easy matter because the first and last folios are missing, but al-Ṭarābulsī noticed that the marginal scribbler seems to be a disciple of al-Maʿarrī himself who was recording the master's own defense of his writings.[34]

At the end of the day, it is likely impossible to know who exactly copied down these rebuttals. Al-Maʿarrī had many disciples, but none was more prominent than the son of a preacher from Tabriz who is usually known simply as al-Tibrīzī (d. 502/1109). It is said that in his youth, he made the journey from Tabrīz to Maʿarrat al-Nuʿmān, al-Maʿarrī's hometown, on foot, carrying a book of philology about which he had questions in his satchel. This copy of the book was so damaged by the monthlong journey that it seemed to have been immersed in water.[35] His studies with al-Maʿarrī proved crucial because, after his peregrinations, al-Tibrīzī eventually settled in Baghdad where he took up the professorship of *adab* and Arabic philology at the aforementioned Niẓāmiyya madrasa. There he taught some of al-Maʿarrī's works and counted among his students some of the most important scholars of hadith and the Arabic language.

Through al-Tibrīzī's role at the Niẓāmiyya and his status as the foremost philologist in Baghdad, al-Maʿarrī's oeuvre became assiduously transmitted and studied with the help of both the author's autocommentaries and the disciple's commentaries. For example, al-Maʿarrī's earlier poetry was collected into a book called *Saqṭ al-Zand* ("The Flint's Spark"). Al-Maʿarrī wrote an autocommentary on the work called *Ḍawʾ al-saqṭ* ("The Light of the Spark"), and he also wrote a prose introduction which was so challenging that he appended "an account of unusual vocabulary (*gharīb*) found in the introduction."[36] When al-Tibrīzī came to write his own commentary on al-Maʿarrī's *Saqṭ al-Zand*, he explicitly tells his reader that he has incorporated the more laconic glosses of his predecessor while attempting to offer the reader more clear guidance on the difficulties of reading these verses.[37]

In sum, al-Maʿarrī's oeuvre was shot through with commentary and commentarial reading practices. He used autocommentary to explain difficult words and to reinterpret problematic passages, but he also produced disciples who could authoritatively transmit and explicate his works within a scholarly milieu. With al-Tibrīzī in an influential post at the Baghdad Niẓāmiyya, this commentarial mode of writing, transmitting, and interpreting playful and difficult texts would have been familiar to the educated elites of Baghdad who had studied with al-Tibrīzī. That is to say, the *Ḥarīriyya*'s earliest audience would have likely been deeply familiar with texts that cried out for philological commentary, whether it was poetry like al-Maʿarrī's or scholarly texts on language and exegesis like the ones ʿAbd al-Laṭīf studied. What al-Ḥarīrī offered was a narrativization of the commentarial dramas that al-Maʿarrī performed.

Modern scholarship has overlooked the connections between al-Maʿarrī and al-Ḥarīrī because literary studies have tended to trace the origins and development of the *maqāma* genre on the basis of formal similarities or explicit references to influence.[38] The connection between al-Maʿarrī and al-Ḥarīrī, however, is to be found in the social, material, and institutional contexts. Commentaries and commentarial reading practices are not particularly "literary," and the drive to interpret *adab* as literature has therefore set aside these practices of glossing, riddle-solving, and rebuttal. Similarly, little attention has been given to the social and material contexts of *adab*'s reception and circulation. For the period before al-Ḥarīrī, little documentary evidence survives, but that is simply not the case for the life of al-Ḥarīrī. In fact, we have two manuscripts that survive from the author's own lifetime.

The Social Practice of Commentary

The story of the first of the two manuscripts that survive from the author's lifetime begins in the winter of 504/1111, when a handful of al-Tibrīzī's students and a few dozen others gathered around al-Ḥarīrī to hear his collection of *maqāmas* and the author's autocommentaries be read aloud. The process took over a month and was completed on February 18 (7th of Shaʿbān).[39] We have detailed knowledge of who attended these reading sessions because of a manuscript preserved in the Egyptian National Library, which is found under the shelfmark *Cairo Adab m105*.[40] The copyist was a prominent philologist and student of al-Tibrīzī named Abū al-Muʿammar al-Anṣārī (d. 549/1154) who had made his own manuscript copy of the *Ḥarīriyya* on the basis of the author's fair copy. Over the course of the month, Abū al-Muʿammar recorded the names of each attendee at the reading sessions.[41] On the final day, he inscribed a detailed audition certificate in his manuscript consisting of thirty-nine names, including the author.

Perhaps the most prominent name on this list is al-Jawālīqī (d. 539/1144), who was al-Tibrīzī's star pupil and had inherited his teacher's position as professor of *adab* and Arabic philology at the Niẓāmiyya. Al-Jawālīqī's august presence at the reading session must have lent the proceedings an air of special importance. (The very fact that al-Jawālīqī had been there would be fodder for biographers, to which we will return.) A number of other participants in the first reading of the *Ḥarīriyya* were either from important scholarly families in Baghdad or bore the title of judge (*qāḍī*).[42] Another name in particular stands out for us: Ibn al-Naqūr. He would later provide the young ʿAbd al-Laṭīf with his *isnād* back to the author. All in all, al-Ḥarīrī's audience consisted of a who's who of Baghdad's Muslim scholarly elite.

We should not imagine that al-Ḥarīrī himself read the text aloud. That task fell to Ibn Nāṣir al-Salāmī (d. 550/1155), a prominent philologist and hadith transmitter who was a member of the Ḥanbalī school of Islamic legal thought and had, like many others, studied under al-Tibrīzī. With the author and the reader sitting side by side, the session probably looked a bit like the illustration from a manuscript of the *Ḥarīriyya* that was completed by the copyist-illustrator Yaḥyā b. Maḥmūd al-Wāsiṭī in 634/1237. The many illustrations of the *Ḥarīriyya* have attracted no small amount of attention from art historians, and they have even been suggestively described as commentaries by Oleg Grabar. I would like to propose that one illustration can be understood as a visual double entendre that depicts both the scene of *maqāma* #2 and the social context of the *Ḥarīriyya*'s transmission (Figure 1).[43] In al-Wāsiṭī's illustration, the man sitting at the far right is clearly the authoritative figure in the room. All eyes are on him, and the necks of the listeners on the left are craning to see him with some hands held open as if they are posing questions. Second from the right sits a man who reads from an open book. We can imagine Ibn Nāṣir sitting next to al-Ḥarīrī with his copy of the *Ḥarīriyya* propped open while al-Ḥarīrī, sitting in front of the gathered crowd, answers questions about the text. We should, however, place more books in the hands of the audience members because we know that some of them like Abū al-Mūʿammar, the copyist of *Cairo Adab m105*, had their own copies.

In point of fact, this illustration does not depict a reading session at all but rather a scene in *maqāma* #2 in which Abū Zayd appears in Basra's library (*dār kutubihā*). One can see cubbies holding stacks of books in the background, above the heads of the audience. The man on the right is none other than Abū Zayd who, as we read in *maqāma* #2, seats himself at the periphery of those present (*jalasa fī ukhrayāt al-nās*). He then asks the man next to him about the book he is reading and finds out that it is a book of poetry. Abū Zayd decides to flex his versifying muscles by outdoing the reader's favorite verse in that book with verses of his own. This stranger's eloquence draws the attention of other onlookers who doubt that Abū Zayd is the author of these verses, and they test him to prove his eloquence by outdoing another beautiful line of poetry.

We see the crowd on the left posing their challenges with their gazes fixed on Abū Zayd on the right. But al-Wāsiṭī, the clever illustrator of this manuscript image, has created a visual double entendre that evokes both the scene of *maqāma* #2 and the reading sessions where the *Ḥarīriyya* was usually transmitted. The image does not depict Abū Zayd at the periphery of the library but in a position of honor and attention, seated next to a man with a book. Is it the book of poetry in *maqāma* #2 or a manuscript copy of the *Ḥarīriyya*? With this visual sleight of hand, the illustrator emphasizes the parallel between Abū Zayd and al-Ḥarīrī the author-commentator. Whereas the rogue Abū Zayd is extemporizing poetry that is superior to what his neighbor finds in his book, the author al-Ḥarīrī is himself the ultimate authority for the book that sits before him. At the same time, both Abū Zayd and al-Ḥarīrī possess remarkable language skills that allow them to embellish and outdo what came before. The visual double entendre also draws attention

Figure 1. An illustration depicting a scene in *maqāma* #2 from a seventh-/thirteenth-century manuscript that was illustrated by al-Wāṣiṭī. BnF, Arabe 5847, 5v.

to the shared role of autocommentator, which is played by both Abū Zayd and al-Ḥarīrī.

Turning back now to the earliest extant copy, the manuscript now known as *Cairo Adab m105*, contains a full set of the autocommentaries that were discussed above. They can be found in the main text block in almost all early copies of the *Ḥarīriyya*. What this means is that these autocommentaries were an integral part of al-Ḥarīrī's authorial manuscripts and the copies produced from those manuscripts. However, it is difficult to know how they were incorporated into the live reading sessions. Were they read aloud after the *maqāmas*? Were the riddles and glosses on parables offered to the audience in the midst of reading the text? This sort of stop-and-start reading might seem odd, but it would have been perfectly familiar to readers who, like ʿAbd al-Laṭīf al-Baghdādī, grew up listening to line-by-line commentaries on poetry, legal texts, and the Quran itself.

There is some evidence that al-Ḥarīrī also offered glosses orally to his audience in addition to the textual autocommentaries. For example, there is a report about oral commentary at the first reading session narrated by a disciple of al-Jawālīqī. The story goes that al-Jawālīqī raised a quibble regarding *maqāma* #21 in which the following line appears:

> Surely he will be gathered [on the Day of Judgment] as one more vile than the fungus of the field
> And he will be called to account for shortcoming and *al-shaghā*.[44]

This last word caused al-Jawālīqī some consternation, so he asked what it meant in this sentence. Al-Ḥarīrī said: "Excess (*al-ziyāda*)." Unsatisfied, al-Jawālīqī replied that "*Al-Shaghā* only refers to the uneven alignment of teeth, and it has no sense here."[45] This lexical quibble might seem trivial, but it gets to the heart of what we might call the *Ḥarīriyya*'s philological program. Al-Ḥarīrī pushed language to its limits and here al-Jawālīqī asserts that he has gone beyond the bounds. If *shaghā* refers to the uneven alignment of teeth, leading some teeth to exceed others in length and angle, it is relatively straightforward to see how the word might be used to refer to excess in general. But al-Jawālīqī is asserting that words ought to be used in ways that are lexically attested.

The correct use of language was also a concern of al-Ḥarīrī's. He wrote an entire treatise on the ways that elites misuse language entitled *Durrat al-Ghawwāṣ fī Awhām al-Khawāṣṣ* (The Diver's Pearl regarding the Errors of the Elites). There, he accuses elites of mispronouncing and misusing common words.[46] In other words, al-Ḥarīrī was not interested in breaking the rules, but he seems to have disagreed with al-Jawālīqī about what the rules required, pushing the limits of what a word could mean. An author's oral commentary, like the one al-Ḥarīrī offered al-Jawālīqī, could give the listener special access to how one ought to understand the rare or even unattested meaning of a word. It was up to the critics to argue about whether that usage was acceptable or not. The story of al-Jawālīqī's critique recalls a long-standing trope of the lexicographical provocateur, which can be found expressed in both al-Maʿarrī's ostensibly heretical poetry and a verse from the most famous ode by al-Mutanabbī (d. 354/965):

Even the blind can see my *adab*.
My words make the deaf hear.
I sleep easy upon the peculiarities [of my words],
while everyone stays awake on their account, disputing over them.

The poet brags that his erudite philological peculiarities and apparently anomalous words—his *shawārid*—keep his critics up at night, but he sleeps easy (literally, with heavy eyelids). He is never in doubt about his mastery of the language. It is perhaps unsurprising that al-Maʿarrī, the avid autocommentator and lover of obscure words, admired al-Mutanabbī of all the poets. He even wrote a commentary on al-Mutanabbī's poetry, which was transmitted by al-Tibrīzī.[47] By the time al-Ḥarīrī launched his text into the world, the social practice of commentary was part of the fabric of *adab*, its production, and its transmission. An author's lexical choices might challenge readers, spark debate, and bring delight, all of which was on display in the commentarial culture of reading.

Becoming Commentary and Transmitting Commentary

Becoming an embodied vessel of commentary was what allowed ʿAbd al-Laṭīf al-Baghdādī to ascend in the ranks of students to become a scholar. When it came to newly authored works like those of al-Maʿarrī and al-Ḥarīrī, there was the potential to learn the text with the author himself and to receive his explanations. Al-Tibrīzī studied with al-Maʿarrī, learned his texts and commentaries, and was rewarded when he came to Baghdad with a post at the Niẓāmiyya and a reverent coterie of students. Likewise, close disciples of al-Ḥarīrī became authorities on the text who could transmit it to the next generation. When ʿAbd al-Laṭīf *heard* the *Ḥarīriyya* as a child, he heard it from Ibn al-Naqūr, who was a disciple and bearer of authoritative commentaries. But he did not master the text or become able to comment on it himself until several years later when he began studying "all the commentaries" with his tutor.

Learning to embody the commentary tradition was a lifelong endeavor, and encounters with scholars who were close disciples of the author were not to be passed up. A case in point is the author's own son Abū al-ʿAbbās Muḥammad, known as Ibn al-Ḥarīrī. He was apparently not part of that first reading session (perhaps he remained in al-Mashān, the site of al-Ḥarīrī's family estates outside Basra), but he was considered an authority on his father's texts. When his father died, the son inherited a portion of his wealth and continued in his father's role as the head of the postal service, which also functioned as an intelligence apparatus. In the year 556/1161, a bureaucrat named ʿImād al-Dīn al-Iṣfahānī had been deputized by the caliph's vizier to collect taxes that were not forthcoming from Ibn al-Ḥarīrī.[48] ʿImād al-Dīn tells us that he graciously forgave the land tax that was owed (*aʿfaytuhu min al-kharāj*) and, seemingly to return the favor, Ibn al-Ḥarīrī welcomed him as a guest for some days. It was during that stay that ʿImād al-Dīn heard the *Ḥarīriyya* from the author's son, and he describes him as "a master of the text who has a clarificatory commentary on it."[49]

The exchange of these gifts, tax relief for companionship and commentary, was perhaps not uncommon in the world these two men inhabited. Patrons had lavished gifts on poets since the pre-Islamic period to prove their generosity and bring prestige to their courts. In the later Abbasid period, courts continued to be important, but both poets and prose authors sought payment and positions by means of their skill in producing beautiful language. ʿImād al-Dīn himself had secured a position at the Abbasid caliph's court by sending him a monumental panegyric ode in 552/1157–58 (he did not meet the caliph in person until two years later).[50] The gifting of beautiful language could secure patronage, companionship, and monetary reward. It was the warp and weft of the social fabric in a transregional, Islamic network. Giving and receiving particularly authoritative oral commentaries were likewise highly valued.

Fungible speech is also a theme in the *Ḥarīriyya*. Abū Zayd's eloquent performances (and commentaries on those performances) earn him companionship and coin, which directly parallels the ways in which professional scribes and bureaucrats exchanged poems and epistles for financial support. Devin Stewart has insightfully shown that the trickster of al-Hamadhānī's *maqāma*s participates in a kind of "begging" that is remarkably similar to the "exchange of words for wealth" that is found in al-Hamadhānī's professional epistles.[51] Words and wealth were not all that was exchanged in these encounters. After ʿImād al-Dīn had heard only forty of the fifty *maqāmas*, he fell gravely ill and was forced to return to Baghdad to recover. Al-Ḥarīrī's son was not so lucky. The contagion was transmitted to him as he transmitted the commentaries, and Ibn al-Ḥarīrī fell ill some days later, never to recover.[52]

This episode illustrates the ways in which poetry and commentary were part of an economy of gift exchange, but in some cases the exchange was more explicitly payment for services rendered. A student named Ibn Sukayna (d. 607/1210) once asked the hadith scholar Ibn Nāṣir, who had read the *Ḥarīriyya* aloud at the first reading session, if he would transmit to him al-Mutanabbī's poetry and al-Tibrīzī's commentary. Ibn Nāṣir agreed, but he told the student, "You always read hadith with me free of charge, but this is poetry, so I require payment." Ibn Sukayna tells us that his father gave him five dinars to pay for the lessons.[53] Ibn Nāṣir's distinction between hadith and poetry is suggestive because, although the practices of transmitting poetry and commentary were in some ways indistinguishable from those of hadith transmission, there is an insistence on differentiation here. It should be noted that this kind of report is unusual. Perhaps it was unusual or even unsavory to charge for access to a poetic commentary and this is why Ibn Sukayna's report was considered noteworthy. On the other hand, the biographical sources in this period often seem too polite to mention the nitty gritty of how this or that scholar made a living.

We should be careful not to project the religious-secular distinction that this anecdote might imply onto the Islamic past, particularly because it functions as a founding myth of modernity. At the same time, it is clear that Ibn Nāṣir made some distinction between poetry and prophecy, considering his authoritative transmission of al-Tibrīzī's poetry commentary to be a saleable commodity, whereas Prophetic hadith were not.[54] Of course, becoming a serious scholar who transmitted hadith was never extricated from worldly concerns. It was an expensive enterprise that usually involved extensive travel, lodging, and books, not to mention the presumption of passive income. At the very least, it entailed being able to forego remunerative labor and spend one's time memorizing and studying texts.[55] Whereas wealthy landowners like al-Ḥarīrī and his son might have felt that they were above charging fees for teaching, they nevertheless gained cultural capital from the *Ḥarīriyya*'s fame, and those assets could be converted into real material benefits like tax relief. Other privileged authorities like Ibn Nāṣir seem to have been of more modest means. The biographers state that when he died, he left behind his books, some worn-out clothes, and three dinars. The comment about his poverty seems designed to reinforce his asceticism in the style of the Baghdad Ḥanbalīs, but the biographical comments about his teaching fee may have been intended to point out his constrained financial circumstances, rather than a strict division between poetry and hadith.

Whereas descendants and disciples were privileged authorities in Iraq and in nearby regions where intercourse in trade and scholarship were frequent, the readers of the *Ḥarīriyya* in faraway lands had to rely on intermediaries even though the author was still alive. For example, only two months had passed since the first public reading of the *Ḥarīriyya* in 504/1111 when an Andalusian hadith scholar began frequenting the author's sessions. Abū al-Ḥajājj al-Undī (d. 542/1147–48) states that he had read the text aloud in the author's presence and heard the text more than once at al-Ḥarīrī's home in Baghdad.[56] There was evidently a flurry of reading sessions immediately after the first public reading had ended. When al-Undī returned to al-Andalus, he settled in Almería on the Mediterranean coast and returned to his trade as a blacksmith and a locksmith. But his scholarly travels to the east meant that he was also a source of texts, which he transmitted to eager students. One student, Ibn Khayr al-Ishbīlī (d. 575/1179), left behind a detailed catalog (*Fahrasa*) of all the books he studied. For the *Ḥarīriyya*, Ibn Khayr says that he had read it aloud in the presence of al-Undī in his shop (*bi-dukkānihi*) in 534/1140, once again mixing spaces of commerce and commentary. Ibn Khayr then includes the information about how al-Undī had received the text from the author, possibly copied from al-Undī's own certificate. We will return in the next chapter to the material practices like the production of certificates and catalogs of certificates that underpinned the transmission of the *Ḥarīriyya* and its manuscripts. For now, it is simply worth emphasizing once again that the transmission of texts was an intellectual activity that was embedded in social, embodied, and material practices.

Commentary grew with the transmission of text. Authorities would authorize the transmission of the *Ḥarīriyya* (which included the author's autocommentaries) by having it read aloud in their presence, but they could also provide recipients with glosses that they had heard from their teachers or with new glosses based on their own knowledge. As a result, not everyone who commented on the *Ḥarīriyya* would have composed a standalone text with their commentarial material. ʿImād al-Dīn says in his entry on Ibn al-Ḥarīrī that he "has a clarificatory commentary" on the *Ḥarīriyya*, but that does not mean that there is a lost book that contained the glosses of al-Ḥarīrī's son.[57] It seems more likely that Ibn al-Ḥarīrī's commentary was based on his own marginal notations on the text or his recollections, and his students might transfer those glosses into the margins or interlinear spaces of their own text.

Thus, almost all surviving manuscripts of the *Ḥarīriyya* contain marginal or interlinear notation of some kind (Figure 2). In some cases, it is obvious that the note was produced by a student listening to an oral commentary. For example, there is a marginal note in a manuscript of the *Ḥarīriyya* originally produced in the eighth/fourteenth-century in which the glossator had clearly misheard his teacher, realized his mistake, and corrected it. The gloss is for the term *al-aḥshāʾ*, a word referring to what is inside the human ribcage and belly. It is not a particularly unusual word, so perhaps the student was not a native speaker of Arabic and needed glosses of more ordinary vocabulary. Or perhaps their teacher was simply being thorough. In either case, the marginal gloss explains the term thus: "*al-aḥshāʾ*: It is what is in the insides, ~~such as the dog (*kalb*)~~ such as the heart (*qalb*)."[58] There are two different k-sounds in Arabic, one of which is pronounced like the English "k," while the other is produced further back in the throat like a glottal stop. It is impossible to mistake one of these letters for the other on the page because they are so orthographically distinct in the initial position in a word (كـ versus قـ) but it is certainly plausible that one might mishear one for the other. The student, transcribing his teacher's glosses, must have heard *kalb* instead of *qalb* before crossing out his mistake, having realized that it is only on rare and troubling occasions that one finds dogs inside human beings.

Manuscripts of the *Ḥarīriyya* with busy margins can be found all over the world, from Timbuktu to Nigeria to India and beyond. This phenomenon attests to an active project of commentarial reading that took place in countless reading sessions in private homes, places of business, palaces, madrasas, and mosques.[59] ʿAbd al-Laṭīf himself transmitted the *Ḥarīriyya* in the grand mosque of Aleppo later in life, although a North African mufti named al-Wansharīsī (d. 914/1508) issued a legal opinion (*fatwā*) that this text should not be studied in the mosque due to the lying (*kadhib*) and immoderation (*faḥsh*) that it contains. The question of the Islamicness of the *Ḥarīriyya* will be discussed in Chapter 6, but it is notable that we have ample evidence of al-Ḥarīrī's work being studied in mosques. Al-Wansharīsī's legal opinion was, of course, just one opinion, which carried the weight of his reputation but did not necessarily prevent people from carrying on studying the text in the mosque and scribbling in the margins as they did. The

Figure 2. A page from a seventh-/thirteenth-century copy of the *Ḥarīriyya* with annotations in multiple hands filling the margins and much of the interlinear space. The upside-down annotation in the lower margin is a quote from Ibn al-Khashshāb's critiques of *maqāma* #5. Leiden University Libraries MS OR 56, 27r.

mufti also notes in the same opinion that the imam of the grand mosque in Tunis only transmits the *Ḥarīriyya* in the vestibule or annex (*duwayra*) of the mosque.[60] Sometimes readings of the *Ḥarīriyya* would only take up a single session, which must have left little time for commentary. In other cases, only one or two *maqāma*s were read in a single sitting.[61] Presumably the latter was accompanied with a more extensive commentary and discussion, pointing again to the multilayered nature of commentarial reading.

In addition to these oral commentaries, some scholars began producing authored commentaries that circulated separately from the *Ḥarīriyya*. In other words, they produced manuscripts that only contained their glosses and comments on particular words or phrases in the text. Most of these commentaries were designed to accompany a reader of the *Ḥarīriyya* through the text, like the commentary of ʿAbd al-Bāqī al-Anbārī (d. 590/1194), which provides glosses to words in the order that they appear in the *maqāmas*.[62] In some cases, commentators produced different sorts of commentaries for different purposes. In the year 613/1216, the biographer Yāqūt was in Aleppo where he met a philologist who, while standing at the door of his house, listed off the titles of the books he had written, many of which were commentaries. He described one commentary on the *Ḥarīriyya* as "organized according to the order of the *maqāmas*" and another as "organized alphabetically (*ʿalā tartīb al-muʿjam*)." The man mentioned a third commentary on the *Ḥarīriyya*, which he described, rather mysteriously, as "organized in another way."[63] His alphabetical commentary survives in an undated copy in Princeton University's Firestone Library, and the introduction clarifies that he wrote this glossary after he wrote his commentary that ran in the order of the *maqāmas*, but there no mention of the third commentary.[64] These commentaries may reflect different approaches to reading. Whereas some readers might be expected to reference the commentary quite frequently as they worked their way through the text, others might read the text more quickly and only occasionally flip through this reference glossary to find what they needed.

In some cases, authored commentaries made their way back into the margins of later copies of the *Ḥarīriyya*. The Mamluk poet, philologist, and biographer Khalīl b. Aybak al-Ṣafadī (d. 764/1363) was famous for his fine handwriting, so he was sought after as a copyist of luxury manuscripts. One of the sumptuous copies of the *Ḥarīriyya* that he produced includes marginalia that al-Ṣafadī carefully transcribed from three different authored commentaries.[65] In other words, marginalia were not always a result of oral commentary or reader notation but could be produced by the copyist. Furthermore, al-Ṣafadī's marginalia are identified as belonging to specific commentators, namely Ibn al-Khashshāb, Ibn Barrī, and al-Panjdīhī, so they are not anonymous glosses but rather represent the various sides of philological debates that will be discussed in Chapter 4. When al-Ṣafadī extracted bits from these commentaries and added them to the luxury manuscript he produced, he was, in a sense, composing a new commentary by selecting and arranging parts of earlier commentaries in a new way. Thus, the lines between oral commentary, marginal commentary, and authored commentary can be rather blurry.

The Multiple Layers of Commentary

If we think back to young ʿAbd al-Laṭīf studying "all the commentaries" on every text that he studied with his tutor al-Wajīh, we begin to see how this complex of textual transmission and commentarial activity on the *Ḥarīriyya* reflects ʿAbd al-Laṭīf's multilayered encounters with texts. First he heard the *Ḥarīriyya*, then he memorized it, then he studied commentaries, then he produced commentaries. It should be emphasized once again that not all commentary was designed to explicate the text, as we saw when ʿAbd al-Laṭīf was dazzled and bewildered by the teacher's commentary on his disastrous first day of lessons. Commentaries on the *Ḥarīriyya* might also involve dazzling and digressive discourse that might overwhelm a beginner. A good example of this is the digressive commentary of al-Panjdīhī, which begins with an elaborate introduction written in erudite and difficult rhyming prose. Al-Panjdīhī appended an autocommentary to his commentary's introduction, much like al-Ḥarīrī did to his own *maqāmas*. This *maqāma*-like introduction then gives way to a commentary that is full of lofty rhetoric and digressions on the Quran and its divergent readings, the hadith, and other stories from the Islamic past.[66] The biographer Ibn Khallikān describes al-Panjdīhī and his commentary this way: "He was an excellent man of *adab* who concerned himself with the *Ḥarīriyya*. He commented on it, and his commentary was lengthy. He was exhaustive in a way that no one else had been. I saw a copy of it in five large volumes, while no other commentator has written that much or even half that much. It is a famous book that is widely circulating (*kathīr al-wujūd bi-aydī al-nās*)."[67] In other words, it was a commentary that was beloved for its prolixity. Like the *Ḥarīriyya* itself, al-Panjdīhī's commentary spread like wildfire. By the end of the sixth/twelfth century, it had made its way to al-Andalus where the Andalusian ʿAbd al-Muʾmin al-Sharīshī (d. 619/1222) took inspiration from it to write his own digressive commentary.

Al-Sharīshī's commentarial career is perhaps the best and most concrete illustration of the multilayered commentarial field. He is said to have composed three commentaries—a short or abridged commentary, a middle or philological commentary, and a long "*adabī*" commentary. The long commentary has been available in print since the nineteenth century, and there is a shorter commentary that remains in manuscript in Leiden University, which may be either the short or the middle commentary. Al-Sharīshī had evidently become something of an authority when he dispatched this shorter commentary to Sijilmasa in what is now Morocco, on the northern edge of the Sahara Desert. In al-Sharīshī's introduction to the shorter commentary in the Leiden manuscripts, he claims that a student had requested from him a commentary that would be free of cross-references between *maqāmas* so that each *maqāma*'s commentary might stand alone and be of service if a teacher were not available.[68] The student whom al-Sharīshī addresses may or may not have existed, given that the anonymous request was a common conceit, but al-Sharīshī claims that the request was made out of a desire "to make the text easier and more familiar to the children of his town, so that the difficulty and strangeness of its language might be removed from them, since their tongues are barbarous and their language uncivilized (*alsinatuhum barbariyya wa-lughātuhum ḥūshiyya*)."[69] Al-Sharīshī's dismissive attitude toward the linguistic abilities of non-Arabs is telling, as is the fact that his commentary was explicitly designed to take the place of what he viewed as a competent teacher. This philological commentary was designed to discipline readers in the embodied practice of reading difficult texts, whether or not they had a tutor available to them like al-Wajīh, the man who had helped transform ʿAbd al-Laṭīf into a walking commentary.

When al-Sharīshī found al-Panjdīhī's commentary, his sense of commentarial possibility shifted. Al-Sharīshī states in the introduction to his long commentary that he had already been engaged in studying the *Ḥarīriyya* for some time when he "came across the commentary of al-Panjdīhī," in which he "saw the desired aim" that had, until then, "been rolled up and eclipsed from my view." Al-Sharīshī then "began taking a second look" at the *Ḥarīriyya* in which he found "beneficial reports that I could not find in any other book."[70] He copied down these reports and reshaped them to build his own commentary, taking out the extensive chains of transmission that he found in al-Panjdīhī's commentary "to lighten the load for those who crave and desire the substance of the report."[71]

Al-Sharīshī did not throw out the material from his earlier commentary but rather added to it by cannibalizing portions of al-Panjdīhī's commentary. For example, in al-Sharīshī's middle commentary, one of his longer glosses is on Badīʿ al-Zamān al-Hamadhānī, the inventor of the *maqāma* genre and al-Ḥarīrī's predecessor. Al-Sharīshī gives his full name, quotes a report that he had composed four hundred *maqāma*s, and explains that al-Hamadhānī's inspiration for writing the *maqāma*s was the forty stories of Ibn Durayd. He also compares the *maqāma*s of al-Ḥarīrī and al-Hamadhānī, stating that he himself prefers al-Ḥarīrī's because it is "more copious and of greater benefit."[72] In the long commentary, al-Sharīshī maintains the material from his shorter commentary, but it is preceded by a lengthy quotation on al-Hamadhānī drawn explicitly from an *adab* anthology by al-Thaʿālibī (d. 429/1023). The quotation, which also appears in al-Panjdīhī's commentary, runs a page and a half in print.[73] Over the course of al-Sharīshī's long commentary, he draws on al-Panjdīhī frequently, but he was also apparently inspired by al-Panjdīhī's digressiveness to cite other poems and reports. Al-Sharīshī's anthologizing commentarial program expands on even the most expansive of commentaries to produce an erudite performance that was valued not for its *explanation* of the *Ḥarīriyya* but as an expansion on al-Ḥarīrī's work. The ways in which al-Sharīshī drew on and reformulated al-Panjdīhī's commentary are explored in detail in Chapters 6 and 7.

My point is that al-Sharīshī's commentary was clearly seen not as a series of desultory glosses on the text but as a work of scholarship in its own right. We can see this in the entry on al-Sharīshī penned by the Andalusian biographer Ibn al-Abbār (d. 658/1260). He tells us that he was at his teacher's house when he met al-Sharīshī in 616/1219–1220 for the first time. He listened to a portion of the commentary and was given license to transmit the rest of it on the author's authority. Like the *Ḥarīriyya*, al-Sharīshī's commentary required audition (*samāʿ*) and an authorization to transmit it (*ijāza*). It also tells us that students did not always listen to the entirety of a text before receiving the author's authorization to transmit it. A license might be issued to someone to whom the author wanted to transmit his text, regardless of whether they had mastered or even heard or fully read the text itself.[74]

Commentary, then, was not a narrow phenomenon devoted to explicating individual words in a text. That much was clear to ʿAbd al-Laṭīf when he saw his fellow students react with awe and appreciation at their teacher's baffling commentary on a work that the young man had already memorized and, one imagines, had thought he understood. When it comes to the *Ḥarīriyya*, commentary was a multilayered phenomenon that could take many forms. It could be oral or written. It could be found in the margins of a text or as a standalone work. It could consist of an alphabetical reference glossary, or a series of short glosses, or a lengthy and digressive anthology of poems and reports. It could also be part of the *maqāma*'s narrative itself, and it could transform nonsense into sense. Reading the *Ḥarīriyya* with ʿAbd al-Laṭīf, the project of understanding *adab* before world literature that I proposed in Chapter 1, requires us to see that commentary is not a crutch that is extraneous to the text. The multifaceted commentarial culture in which ʿAbd al-Laṭīf lived was something that informed almost every act of reading. The discipline of reading properly was not simply a matter of "understanding" the text with the aid of commentary. The goal was to inhabit the commentary tradition in such a way that one could express wonder and delight. To ignore commentary or to consider it unliterary and thus unworthy of attention is to erase the vibrant and sophisticated tradition that made the *Ḥarīriyya* one of the most celebrated texts in Arabic for almost eight centuries.

Chapter 3

The Social Lives of Manuscripts

When ʿAbd al-Laṭīf al-Baghdādī was in his late fifties, he found himself in Aleppo. There, he met Ibn al-ʿAdīm (d. 660/1262), the famous Aleppan historian and legal scholar who hailed from a prominent family of Ḥanafī scholars and judges. In those days, Ibn al-ʿAdīm had in his possession a valuable manuscript of the *Ḥarīriyya*, the same one that we encountered in the previous chapter—namely, the version we now know as *Cairo Adab m105*. That manuscript was part of the activities involved in the first public reading of the *Ḥarīriyya* in Baghdad back in 504/1111, which occurred over the span of several reading sessions. After some time, the manuscript made its way to Aleppo. ʿAbd al-Laṭīf and the manuscript thus found themselves in the same city in 614/1217–18, as attested by an audition certificate (*samāʿ*) made in the manuscript for that date that attested to a reading session near the central mosque of Aleppo. In the audience were children as young as two.[1] This manuscript can be thought of as containing part of a "living archive" that underpinned commentary culture. That is, in addition to the text of the *Ḥarīriyya*, the manuscript contains a curated collection of documentary evidence attesting to the way certain people interacted with the *Ḥarīriyya*.

Perhaps unsurprisingly, the reading practices of world literature and the discipline of Arabic literature that insist on reading *adab* "as literature" have little use for these documentary sources and archival logics. Even outside of the realm of literature, scholars have often assumed or asserted that Middle Eastern society and Islamic law were structured in a way that precluded the use of documentary sources prior to the Ottoman period. The idea that Islamic polities and societies lacked archives has now been thoroughly overturned, leading to a "documentary turn" in the study of premodern Islamic history.[2] But even as we learn more about the "archival practices" of law, governance, and the transmission of hadith, much less attention has been paid to the archival and documentary practices associated with the texts of the *adab* tradition. This chapter brings the *Ḥarīriyya* back into the conversation by examining the early manuscript tradition to see how readers engaged in archival practices to produce records of their reading and of their philological engagements with the text. Material artifacts like the manuscript *Cairo Adab m105* became authorities that paralleled the human textual authorities that we saw in the previous chapter. To produce these venerable textual authorities, readers engaged in intensive and multilayered processes of collation and certification.[3] In other words, they engaged in materially and socially embedded philological projects. As we will see throughout this chapter, medieval scholars took these practices and the documentary evidence they produced very seriously and often let them outweigh contradictory evidence for which only secondhand reports existed. Paying attention to the archival practices and material philology that produced manuscripts of the *Ḥarīriyya* contributes to the broader aims of this book—namely, to put us in conversation with the reading practices of medieval readers like ʿAbd al-Laṭīf al-Baghdādī. At the same time, this chapter directs our attention to the diversity of manuscript culture. Some manuscripts were not sites of archival practice but were nevertheless considered valuable and important for other reasons, for instance as personal copies of the *Ḥarīriyya* or as collector's items.

This chapter, then, is about the social lives of manuscripts. It demonstrates how manuscripts paralleled the embodied practices discussed in the previous chapter while at the same time reaching beyond the limitations of a human life span. This parallel of people and manuscripts can be seen in the case of ʿAbd al-Laṭīf and his encounter with *Cairo Adab m105*. Both the manuscript and the man began in Baghdad and ended up in Aleppo a century after the first reading of the *Ḥarīriyya*. How and why did both make this journey? We know that ʿAbd al-Laṭīf's route to Aleppo was circuitous. Even when he was a child, Baghdad was no longer the center of wealth, power, and scholarship that it had once been. Although it was still the seat of the almost-powerless Abbasid caliph, the Andalusian traveler Ibn Jubayr (d. 614/1217), who visited the city in 580/1184, found that nothing remained of its former splendor but its illustrious name.[4]

To make a name for himself, ʿAbd al-Laṭīf would need to leave home. He traveled to Damascus, Acre, Jerusalem, and then Cairo. In his travels, he met the luminaries of his age: the Jewish physician, philosopher, and

Torah scholar Moses Maimonides (d. 601/1204), the famed counter-Crusader Saladin (d. 589/1193), his sons, and his secretary al-Qāḍī al-Fāḍil (d. 596/1200), one of the most eloquent men of his age. In Cairo, ʿAbd al-Laṭīf was an active teacher of both the Quran and medicine. There, he experienced the trauma of the pandemic and famine that rocked Cairo in 597–598/1200–1202, and he wrote a searing account of cannibalism and desperation among that city's poor. Finally, he ended up in Damascus and then Aleppo, by which point he was a well-known scholar of philosophy and medicine, having abandoned his interest in alchemy years before that. He was not a specialist in the *Ḥarīriyya*, but he was a man of many talents who had received the text from a student of al-Ḥarīrī who had been present at the text's first reading. In stark contrast with our detailed knowledge of ʿAbd al-Latīf's peregrinations, however, we know almost nothing about how the manuscript made its way from Baghdad to Aleppo. We simply know that it was in the possession of the famous historian Ibn al-ʿAdīm by Rajab 600/March 1204.[5] That is when Ibn al-ʿAdīm began holding reading sessions on the basis of *Cairo Adab m105* and recording audition certificates with the names of audience members in the manuscript.

Archival Practices in the Reading of the *Ḥarīriyya*

The manuscript *Cairo Adab m105* was not simply a repository for the "text" of the *Ḥarīriyya* but also a repository of what can be called "archival practices." These practices were part of a sophisticated material culture of textual transmission. Readers like ʿAbd al-Laṭīf understood the unique authority of a manuscript like *Cairo Adab m105*. For one thing, manuscripts of the *Ḥarīriyya* took on particular significance due to their closeness to the author. In the same way that young scholars sought chains of *embodied* transmission back to al-Ḥarīrī, they also sought out chains of *material* transmission through manuscripts that had been read in the presence of the author or that had been collated against such a copy. The intensive and extensive collation work and archival practices produced manuscripts that were each imbued with unique authority.

In the previous chapter, we saw how commentary was a multilayered phenomenon that was both oral and written, but we also caught a glimpse of the way that the social practices of textual transmission were inscribed on manuscripts like *Cairo Adab m105*. That manuscript, as I have noted already, does not simply contain a list of attendees at the very first reading of the *Ḥarīriyya* but contains the records of many more reading sessions, thirty in all. In 1971 Pierre MacKay published a short monograph study of this manuscript in which he reveals this manuscript to be a rich source of information for the early reception of the *Ḥarīriyya*. MacKay provides reproductions of microfilms for the certificates in *Cairo Adab m105*, together with a detailed description of each certificate in this and a few other manuscripts. Rather than edit and translate these certificates, MacKay extracts the data and presents it systematically. This data includes the date(s) of the reading session, where it was held, the authorized transmitter, the reader, the audience members, and the recorder of the certificate. Some certificates are not decipherable or omit certain pieces of information, such as location, and although the certificates follow particular formulas, the "poetics" of these certificates is lost in MacKay's presentation, even as he helpfully includes images of the manuscript folios.

MacKay's study of *Cairo Adab m105* has, unfortunately, been almost entirely overlooked and rarely discussed in studies of the *maqāma* genre and of *adab* more broadly.[6] In part, this neglect can be chalked up to the broader neglect of the *Ḥarīriyya* in twentieth- and twenty-first-century scholarship, which we discussed in Chapter 1. There is, I think, more to it. MacKay's data does not offer much when it comes to reading the text "as literature." Whereas audition certificates have been fruitfully studied by scholars of history and Islamic studies, they have rarely been drawn on to interpret or contextualize Arabic "literary" texts. Literary approaches often (though not always) take for granted that the object of inquiry is the "text," abstracted from its material instantiation in the world. Most obviously, those literary interpretations that posit the *maqāma* as a subversive parody of Islamic knowledge production fail to take account of the fact that *Cairo Adab m105* bears witness to an enthusiastic reception of the text among Muslim scholars. Of course, a text's meaning far exceeds the interpretation of its earliest audience, but one wonders whether the neglect for MacKay's study and its conclusion that the early transmission of the *Ḥarīriyya* in Baghdad was mostly a Ḥanbalī affair has more to do with the secularizing drive of literary reading. Still, the urge to "liberate" the *Ḥarīriyya* from its Islamic reading practices is also an act of erasure—an erasure that is subtended by print culture, which often ends up preserving an abstracted and edited "text" or "work" while usually, but not always, excising or ignoring the various kinds of notes left behind by readers, owners, collators, and copyists.[7] These manuscript notes attest to the attempts of readers to preserve and understand the authorial version of the text, while paradoxically drawing attention to the existing variants in the manuscript tradition. These busy manuscripts are also pieces of *documentary* evidence that attest to acts of reading, collation, and teaching. Manuscripts like *Cairo Adab m105* became sites for archival practices that enhanced the value of the manuscript. The social life and history of a manuscript were part of what was interesting to its later readers. As one early twentieth-century Turkish scholar and librarian put it, "If a book is printed, there remains no flavor in it anymore."[8]

But manuscript culture should not be seen as a monolith or as the inverted opposite of print culture. Scholars and students today still scribble in the margins of their books (whether they own them or not).[9] Likewise, not all manuscripts were made to have their margins filled. The way that a reader interacted with a particular manuscript depended on a great many factors, which we will explore over the course of this chapter. How a reader treated a manuscript might depend on what sort of text or texts that manuscript contained, but those divisions of "genre" were not always the most important. If you step back and look at pages from two manuscripts containing interlinear glosses and margins full of detailed notes, you very well might be looking at a heavily annotated legal text or hadith collection on the one hand and a copy of the *Ḥarīriyya* on the other. At the same time, not all manuscripts of exactly the same text were treated in the same way. Some copies of the *Ḥarīriyya* are full of marginal notations or audition certificates or both. Others are pristine copies written in beautiful, fully voweled script. Still others are illustrated with scenes from the *Ḥarīriyya*.

Some manuscripts were considered particularly valuable because they served as authoritative witnesses to the text. Just as human transmitters of the text were valued for their proximity to the author, so too with manuscripts. *Cairo Adab m105* was a valuable manuscript precisely because it was associated with the first public reading and because it contained an attendance list of that first audience filled with impressive people. It also had a frontispiece or cover page on which we find the handwriting of al-Ḥarīrī himself (Figure 3). The main text on the page is written in large script in two different hands, first the hand of the copyist and then the hand of the author. It reads as follows, with the bold text in my translation signifying the portion that is in the author's hand:

> The *Maqāmāt* of Abū Zayd al-Sarūjī
>
> A composition of the most illustrious shaykh, the scholar and imam Abū Muḥammad al-Qāsim b. ʿAlī b. Muḥammad al-Ḥarīrī.
> The audition certificate of al-Mubārak b. Aḥmad b. ʿAbd al-ʿAzīz b. al-Muʿammar al-Anṣārī
> **The shaykh Abū al-Muʿammar al-Mubārak b. Aḥmad b. ʿAbd al-ʿAzīz al-Anṣārī, may God grant him success, heard on my authority the fifty *maqāma*s that I composed.**
> **Written by al-Qāsim b. ʿAlī b. Muḥammad in the City of Peace in Shaʿbān of the year 504.**
> **I have granted him a license to transmit everything of mine, both heard and written (*masmūʿ wa-taṣnīf*), after he has guarded against misreading (*taṣḥīf*) and textual corruption (*taḥrīf*).**[10]

This page endows with special authority both the copy and its owner Abū al-Muʿammar. Al-Ḥarīrī composed an audition certificate (*samāʿ*) that explicitly marks itself as a license to transmit the text (*ijāza*), and he has clearly marked that these documents are written in his own hand.[11] First, he uses the first person ("I composed," "on my authority"), and second, he identifies himself by name as the scribe of this certificate.

According to an anecdote in the medieval Islamic biographical tradition, this manuscript was far from the only copy that al-Ḥarīrī signed in this manner. The story goes that a student reading the *Ḥarīriyya* in the author's presence 514/1120–21 made an error that al-Ḥarīrī found to be more elegant than his original. He exclaimed, "By God, you've done well in your error. . . . Were it not that I have to this day written in my own hand upon seven hundred copies that were read in my presence, I would have changed it."[12] The figure of seven hundred is probably just a proverbial expression to indicate that he had signed a great many copies and is something like our numerical expression "I have a million things to do." However, it is significant that the story, taking place only two years before the author's death, portrays him as unwilling to change his text.[13]

The author's insistence on textual fixity might seem quixotic in a manuscript culture where each copy might acquire the imprint of a scribe's errors and enthusiasms. But it seems to have been precisely the author's awareness that textual variation might take place that led him to embed his

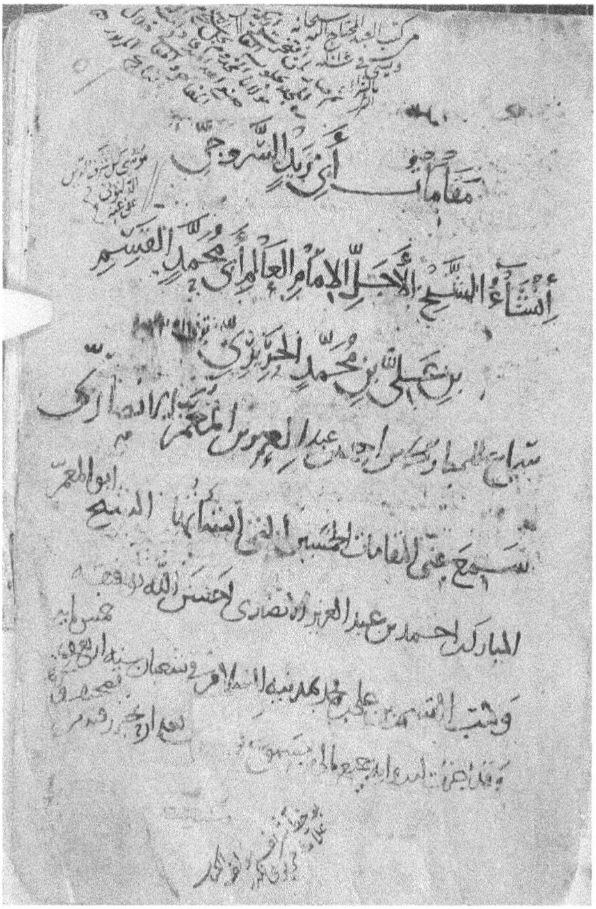

Figure 3. The original title piece of the *Ḥarīriyya* manuscript involved in the first public reading of the text. The top half in a thicker hand was written by the copyist and the bottom half by al-Ḥarīrī. Cairo Adab m105, 5v.

text in a scholarly world that had developed strategies for maintaining a text's integrity. In the final line of the certificate, al-Ḥarīrī states in his characteristic rhyming prose (deploying *taṣnīf, taṣḥīf,* and *taḥrīf*) that this license has been granted only after guarding against textual corruption. What might that mean? The process consisted of at least three steps. First, Abū al-Muʿammar must have copied *Cairo Adab m105* before the first public reading, presumably on the basis of the author's fair copy. He did so by making quires (*kurrāsas*)—that is, little booklets made up of four or five long pieces of paper called folios that were folded in half. A stack of five folios folded in half made quires of twenty pages each, and Abū al-Muʿammar filled these pages with what he found in the author's copy. Second, he collated his copy against the author's exemplar (*aṣl*). He apparently did this one quire at a time. We thus find notes at the bottom of the first page of most quires stating that "the exemplar has been collated with it (*ʿūriḍa bihā al-aṣl*)."[14] Finally, he participated in the first public reading in which his colleague Ibn Nāṣir al-Salāmī read aloud, possibly from the author's fair copy. After each reading session, Abū al-Muʿammar added a segment-certificate to mark the end of that session in the manuscript. For example, after *maqāma* #15, he writes that "listening to the text (*samāʿ*), read by Ibn Nāṣir in the presence of the author, reached this point on Saturday, the ninth of Rajab, in the year 504 for those mentioned in the certificate." That is, on January 21, 1111, the group had reached the end of *maqāma* #15. Although this is the first segment-certificate, there are some readers listed in the final audition certificate who only heard the first five *maqāma*s but not all of *maqāma*s #6 through #15. It seems possible that Abū al-Muʿammar added this segment-certificate because he anticipated a longer interval before they resumed reading. Indeed, as MacKay points out, the makeup of the audience changes after *maqāma* #15 to include more readers, such as the sons of a wealthy and distinguished Ḥanbalī scholar.[15] Perhaps they joined because they had heard about the exciting new work that would soon become all the rage.

The copyist Abū al-Muʿammar checked his text carefully, either during the initial collation or during the reading sessions. We can see evidence of this fact because, in *maqāma* #44, he noticed an error in his copy and corrected it. In that *maqāma*, Abū Zayd performs a string of verses that are nonsensical until the commentary unlocks the double entendre, much like the riddling *fatwā*s in *maqāma* #32. These riddling verses are modular units, the order of which is apparently arbitrary. When Abū al-Muʿammar made his copy, he misplaced one of the verses and left another out entirely. When he realized the discrepancy, he crossed out the misplaced verse and added both the missing verse and the misplaced verse in the margin, marking where the reader should insert them in the main text (Figure 4).[16] Corrections of this sort can be found throughout the manuscript.

Abū al-Muʿammar's meticulous acts of collation show that even a manuscript that was as close to the author as *Cairo Adab m105* required careful

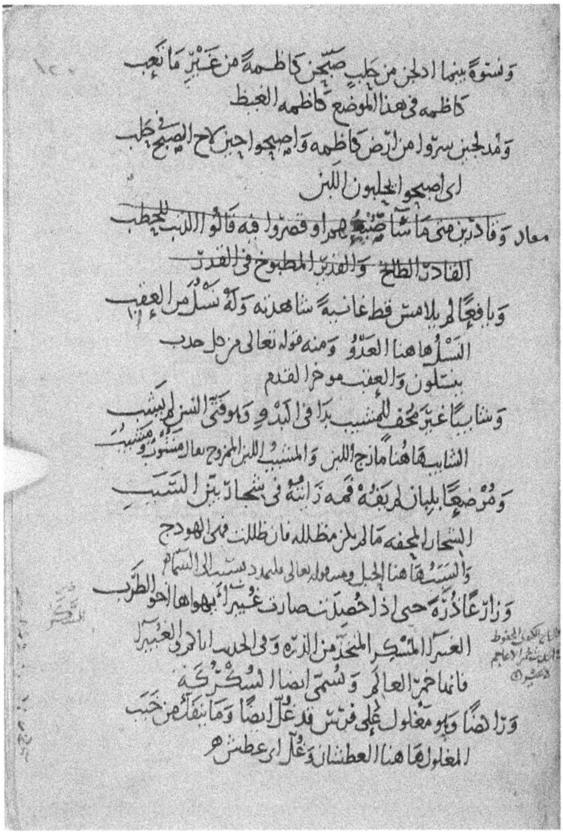

Figure 4. A page from *maqāma* #44 in which the copyist Abū al-Muʿammar has crossed out a line of verse that he had misplaced. In the lower right, there is one of "al-Tāj" Abū al-Yumn al-Kindī's philological critiques. Cairo Adab m105, 120v.

attention to make sure that it closely reflected the author's precise wording. There was, in other words, a drive to produce the most accurate, authoritative text possible. At the same time, the author's certificate on the frontispiece of this manuscript gave Abū al-Muʿammar a license to transmit both what the author had written and what he had heard (*masmūʿ*), perhaps referring to the author's oral commentary, which he offered in the course of reading. If that is the case, however, Abū al-Muʿammar apparently relied on his memory alone for al-Ḥarīrī's oral commentary because we find very few marginal annotations in *Cairo Adab m105*.

Later manuscript copies of the *Ḥarīriyya* were also collated against earlier copies that were considered particularly authoritative due to their proximity to the author. That is hardly surprising, given how much trouble the author and his closest disciples took to make the texts that he signed reflect a single, authorial original. After al-Ḥarīrī's death, Abū al-Muʿammar began transmitting the *Ḥarīriyya* in Baghdad on the basis of the manuscript he had copied, the one we know as *Cairo Adab m105*. Although his audiences were much smaller than the first public reading, some of his readers were given the honor of recording their audition certificates in his prized manuscript.[17] A few readers also sought and gained the privilege of collating their own manuscripts of the *Ḥarīriyya* against *Cairo Adab m105* to check the accuracy of their text.[18]

Collating the Text: Material and Embodied Transmission

Readers were keen to hear and study the *Ḥarīriyya* from authorities like Abū al-Muʿammar whenever the author was not available. Likewise, when copies of the *Ḥarīriyya* that had been endorsed by the author were not to be found, copyists and collators sought out second-generation copies that had been carefully collated against manuscripts that had been in al-Ḥarīrī's hands. A particularly stunning example of this material chain of transmission is a manuscript copied in Damascus on the fourteenth of Shawwāl 614/January 14, 1218, now held at the Bibliothèque Nationale de France under the shelf mark *BNF Arabe 7290*. It is a beautiful and carefully copied text, but its authority was augmented some two decades after it was originally made. In the holy month of Ramadan 632/1235, a man named ʿAlī b. Muḥammad decided to undertake a collation of this copy of the *Ḥarīriyya* in the presence of his father, which is attested in a colophon at the end of the manuscript (Figure 5).

Our collator ʿAlī had access to two manuscripts "upon which is the handwriting of al-Kindī." That is, they had been authorized by Abū al-Yumn al-Kindī (d. 613/1216), one of the most famous philologists of the age who was a star pupil of al-Jawālīqī and was known for his excellent oral commentary on numerous texts.[19] One of al-Kindī's manuscripts possessed particular authority because it had been collated against six other manuscripts, including

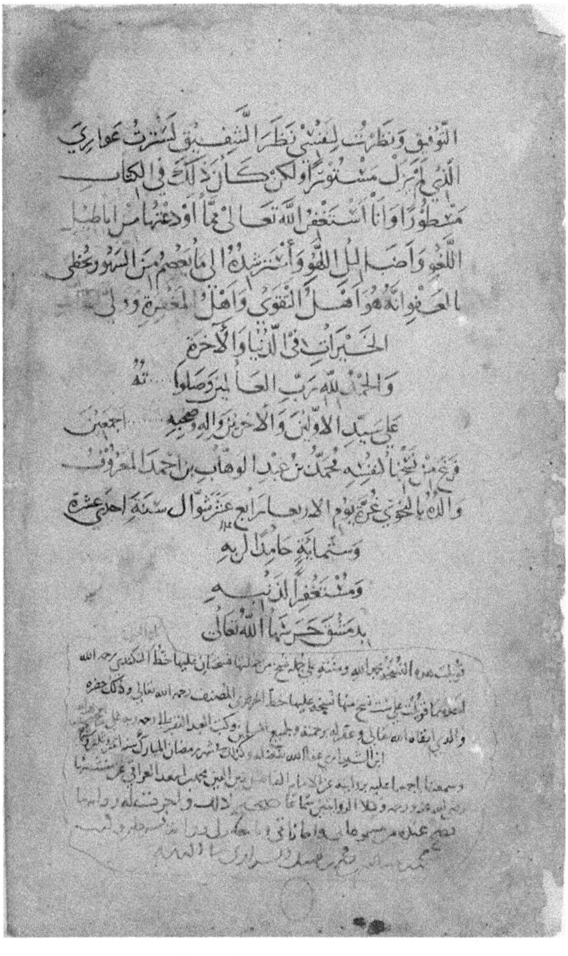

Figure 5. A page from a manuscript showing the collation note at the bottom of the page, bounded by an irregular line. BnF, Arabe 7290, 167v.

one "upon which is the handwriting of al-Ḥarīrī the author."[20] Finding a manuscript that had been authorized by al-Ḥarīrī himself was not always possible, but detailed collation notes like this one established a chain of textual transmission and collation. The discrepancies that ʿAlī found between these authoritative copies and his own manuscript could be registered in the margins of the text, and the collation note at the end of the manuscript established the authority of those corrections.

Textual transmission and embodied transmission of the sort we saw in the previous chapter took place side by side, as this certificate demonstrates. The first part of the collation certificate attests to the act of collation, whereas the second describes the embodied transmission of the *Ḥarīriyya*. In this second part, ʿAlī states that he heard the text and received a license to transmit the text on the authority of his father. The certificate then attests that his father, in turn, had heard the text from Ibn Ḥakīm (d. 567/1173),[21] a Baghdadi of the Ḥanafī school who had settled in Damascus and is credited with a commentary on the *Ḥarīriyya*. Ibn Ḥakīm thus serves as a first-generation authority on the *Ḥarīriyya* for ʿAlī's father, who belonged to the second generation. ʿAlī was therefore a third-generation reader who authorized his access to the text both by means of the chain of transmitters and by means of the extensive acts of collation he undertook against earlier manuscripts that had themselves been extensively collated.

Many scholars collected multiple chains of transmission for a single work, not necessarily because they wanted to shore up the reliability of those texts but because certain chains of transmission were valuable cultural capital. Having received a text from a venerable authority like al-Kindī or Ibn al-Naqūr was better than receiving a text from a lesser-known figure. Chains of transmission marked the possessor's position within a network of knowledge production and reproduction as well as their particular relationship to originator of a text, whether that was the Prophet in the case of hadith or al-Ḥarīrī in the case of the *Ḥarīriyya*. Documenting these chains of transmission was therefore of the utmost importance, which goes some way toward explaining the archival practices associated with manuscripts like *Cairo Adab m105* and ʿAlī's manuscript, known as *BNF Arabe 7290*.

The social logic behind producing these certificates was, however, complex and could go well beyond the accumulation of cultural capital. Documentary evidence of one's scholarly activities could act as a counterweight to other forms of evidence. For example, the key link in ʿAlī b. Muḥammad's embodied chain of transmission is Ibn Ḥakīm, a figure whose reputation was particularly poor among the philologically minded hadith transmitters of Baghdad who populated the first reading session and who were often either members of the Ḥanbalī legal school or closely associated with it.[22] We know of his spotty reputation because biographers recorded what his critics had to say. Ibn Nāṣir, the Ḥanbalī philologist and hadith transmitter who had read aloud the text of the *Ḥarīriyya* to its first audience, is recorded in the biographical sources saying that Ibn Ḥakīm was an "inveterate liar who never received audition for anything in Baghdad and whom I never saw among the hadith folk."[23] The same biography, however, quotes another source from the same Baghdad milieu responding directly to Ibn Nāṣir's accusation, saying that he had seen an audition certificate for a reading session that included Ibn Ḥakīm in the audience. What is more, it was written "in the hand of someone I trust."[24] In other words, Ibn Ḥakīm must have attended at least one scholarly reading session! The interest in documentary evidence in this biographical debate as a counterweight to the reported reputation of Ibn Ḥakīm illustrates that when scholars encountered manuscripts, some of them paid special attention to the certificates they possessed. The evidence of a trustworthy certificate could outweigh, or at least complicate, the opinion of a hostile contemporary.

Turning back now to *Cairo Adab m105*, the social logics of this ongoing archival practice associated with this manuscript are now more legible. It would have bestowed immense cultural capital to have one's name recorded in an important manuscript like *Cairo Adab m105*. It offered readers the chance to inscribe their names into a network of scholarly authority in a way that would reach beyond their own lifetimes, given that later readers paid attention not only to the text but to the names inscribed within the manuscript. As we have seen, these documentary witnesses to transmission were seen as reliable and potentially even more reliable than human memory—particularly if the recorder of the certificate was deemed trustworthy. Who owned a manuscript like *Cairo Adab m105* shaped who could participate in these archival practices, which presumably made this particular manuscript a valuable object for certain kinds of scholarly readers. However, this archival practice was not undertaken with the same enthusiasm across time but rather in fits and starts, suggesting that the manuscript was either used sparingly and on special occasions or that only certain users were permitted to participate in the archival practice of inscribing one's name. Whatever the case, the travels of this manuscript and its status as a valuable object can be partially traced through the audition certificates.

It seems that when *Cairo Adab m105* was still in Baghdad, it passed from the hands of its copyist and original owner Abū al-Muʿammar to Ibn al-Naqūr. Thus, sixteen certificates in the pages of the manuscript attest to reading sessions under these two authorized transmitters. After the death of Ibn al-Naqūr in 565/1170, the manuscript goes silent until the Rajab 600 (March 1204). At that point the Aleppan scholar Ibn al-ʿAdīm, whom we met at the beginning of this chapter, added new folios so that he could

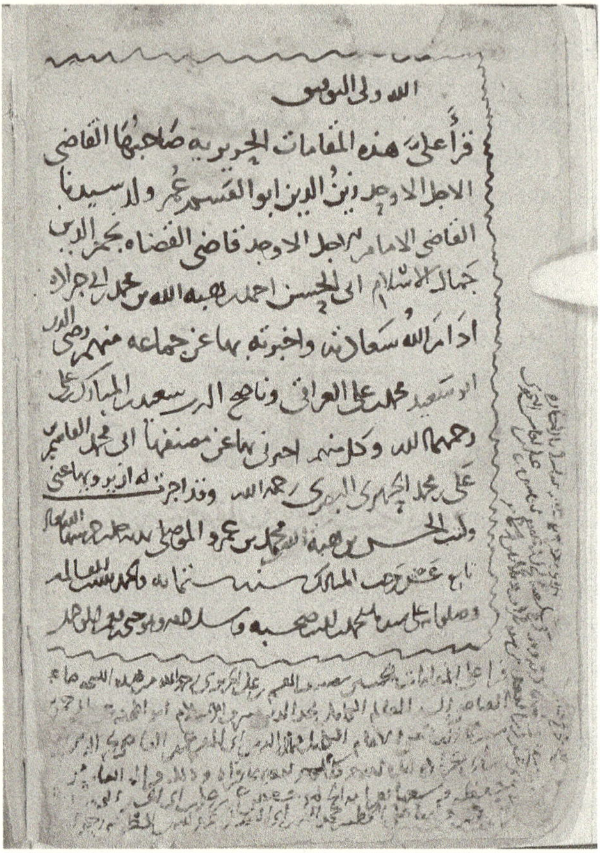

Figure 6. A page from Cairo Adab m105 with Ibn al-ʿAdīm's audition certificate at the top. At the end of the first full line, he is identified as the owner. Cairo Adab m105, 4r.

continue adding to the archive. He then held a reading with a man who had multiple single-link chains of transmission back to the author, and that authorized transmitter produced an audition certificate that seems to have functioned as a new frontispiece or "cover page" for the manuscript.[25] That first Aleppan certificate was designed to be noticed (Figure 6). The size of the script is significantly larger and more legible than most other notes, and the first line of the certificate identifies Ibn al-ʿAdīm as the owner of the manuscript (*ṣāḥibuhā*).[26]

Ibn al-ʿAdīm went on to hold several more readings using *Cairo Adab m105*, adding to the archive of certificates in the manuscript. In fact, he held a session with Abū al-Yumn al-Kindī, the philologist who had authorized the two manuscripts against which *BNF Arabe 7290* was collated. With the production of each certificate, the manuscript's archive of readers grew, but Ibn al-ʿAdīm was apparently reluctant to add marginal glosses in this copy. He did find room in the margins of his manuscript for the corrections and critiques of al-Kindī. Ibn al-ʿAdīm also mentions al-Kindī's corrections to the *Ḥarīriyya* in his major historical work, the *Bughyat al-Ṭalab* when he enters into a discussion of the island of Malta by reporting that, when he read the *Ḥarīriyya* with al-Kindī, he read the name of the island as "*Malaṭiyya*," as he found it in his own particularly authoritative manuscript (that is in *Cairo Adab m105*). Al-Kindī corrected him, saying that the name could only be read *Malaṭya*. This encounter left its mark in *Cairo Adab m105* where al-Kindī's alternative spelling is registered in the marginalia.[27] It seems that, in this case, al-Kindī was not trying to correct the text to recover the author's original spelling but was amending the text to conform to what he believed to be the correct spelling of Malta, and it may be that this drive for philological accuracy was occasionally at odds with the drive to reproduce the authorial original. Elsewhere, al-Kindī found fault with al-Ḥarīrī's word choice or citation of hadith, which he found imprecise or inappropriate (see, for example, the marginalia on the lower right of Figure 4).[28] Philological criticisms of this sort will be discussed in more detail in the next chapter. What we are interested in here is the archival practice that made *Cairo Adab m105* such a treasure trove of documentary evidence. A manuscript like this was clearly valued by its owner not simply because it allowed him to read the *Ḥarīriyya* but because of this book's storied history. It had passed through the hands of important scholars. Just as one sought out people with valued chains of transmission for hadith and for texts like the *Ḥarīriyya*, one sought out objects like *Cairo Adab m105*, which carried its history in its pages and gave the reader an opportunity to inscribe himself into that history.

We should not assume that this manuscript was the only place where a record of these reading sessions existed. Individual readers who owned manuscripts of the *Ḥarīriyya* produced audition certificates in their own manuscript and had them signed by their authoritative transmitters, just as Abū al-Muʿammar had done with the author in the pages of *Cairo Adab m105*. At the same time, it would not be practical for the mobile, scholarly class to travel with their entire libraries. Consider, for example, our friend ʿAbd al-Laṭīf al-Baghdādī. He certainly had a prodigious memory, having memorized many of the books that he had studied and commented on over the course of his education. He was not simply a "walking Quran," in Rudolph Ware's phrase, but also a walking *library* of textual material.[29] Rather than bring his whole library with him as he traveled, he carried a book that he called a *thabat*, which others called a *fihrist*. This book was a catalog or personal archive that contained ʿAbd al-Laṭīf's audition certificates.

ʿAbd al-Laṭīf's personal archive is not known to have survived, but evidence of its existence remains in *Cairo Adab m105*. As we saw at the beginning of this chapter, there are audition certificates in that manuscript for ʿAbd al-Laṭīf's reading sessions in Aleppo. Although ʿAbd al-Laṭīf's chain of transmission went through Ibn al-Naqūr, the reading session at which the young ʿAbd al-Laṭīf heard the text was not recorded in the manuscript. ʿAbd al-Laṭīf therefore decided to remedy the situation. He showed Ibn al-ʿAdīm his personal archive, which contained the certificate written by ʿAbd al-Laṭīf's father and signed by Ibn al-Naqūr. Ibn al-ʿAdīm then agreed to copy that certificate into his precious manuscript, which he duly notarized as being a copy of the audition certificate from the *thabat* of ʿAbd al-Laṭīf written in the hand of his father.[30] Without Ibn al-ʿAdīm's specificity about where he saw the original certificate, we would not know about ʿAbd al-Laṭīf's personal archive of certificates. The result of all these archival practices is that *Cairo Adab m105* contains a fully documented chain of transmission from al-Ḥarīrī at the first public reading to Ibn al-Naqūr, then from Ibn al-Naqūr to ʿAbd al-Laṭīf in the copied certificate, and finally from ʿAbd al-Laṭīf to Ibn al-ʿAdīm, his colleagues, and other young readers who attended sessions with ʿAbd al-Laṭīf.

The phenomenon of copied certificates turns out to be relatively common. As Said Aljoumani has shown, certificates might be copied from the manuscript's exemplar (*aṣl*) together with the text itself or from a different exemplar that contained a certificate for the transmitter or commentator, in order to reinforce their authority to teach and transmit the text.[31] In the case of ʿAbd al-Laṭīf, his original certificate was not recorded within an exemplar of the *Ḥarīriyya* but in a personal archive of certificates, perhaps in anticipation of the fact that he might copy them into manuscripts at a later date. Although Aljoumani's examples come mainly from hadith texts, the practice of making and copying certificates was clearly not uncommon for poetry and, of course, the *Ḥarīriyya*.

It is important to emphasize that the *Ḥarīriyya*'s readers were following a well-established practice of material philology when they produced certificates and copied certificates. The production and reproduction of certificates mirrored the embodied transmission of texts and commentaries from teachers to students. Take, for example, a manuscript containing the two commentaries by the Niẓāmiyya professor al-Tibrīzī, whom we met in the previous chapter and who taught al-Jawālīqī as well as many of the most enthusiastic readers and transmitters. The manuscript *Ayasofya 4095*, held at the Süleymaniye library in Istanbul, contains his commentary on the great pre-Islamic odes known as the *Muʿallaqāt*, as well as his commentary on the didactic poems of Ibn Durayd (d. 321/933).[32] Al-Tibrīzī's students transmitted his commentaries, including a certain Ibn al-Samīn (d. 549/1154), who transmitted those commentaries to his students. Those students, in turn, produced *Ayasofya 4095*, in which they both produced new documentary evidence of the text's authorized transmission and reproduced the documentary evidence of their teacher's connection to al-Tibrīzī. On the frontispiece, Ibn al-Samīn wrote an audition certificate for his student, dated Shaʿbān 545/1150.[33] At the end of Ibn Durayd's poem, there is a second, more detailed audition certificate written neither by the copyist nor by the teacher but by another attendee at these sessions who attests to the fact that the final session was on the thirteenth of Shaʿbān 545 (December 5, 1150). Just above the certificate attesting to the audition of the copyist of the manuscript, there is a "copy" or "image" (*ṣūra*) of Ibn al-Samīn's own certificate of audition from al-Tibrīzī.[34] As a result, the material practices of producing certificates within *Ayasofya 4095* tells the complete story of how al-Tibrīzī's commentary was passed down from a commentator, through two generations of students.

The handwriting of the copied certificate "image" belongs to a certain ʿAlī b. Yaʿīsh, an obscure figure whose distinctive handwriting is quite different from the handwriting of his colleague who copied al-Tibrīzī's commentary. Why did Ibn al-Samīn have a third party copy the certificate, rather than simply copy it himself? For one thing, having a third party involved may have added a layer of oversight to the process, assuring that the certificate was not simply a convenient invention of the person claiming its authorizing power. ʿAbd al-Laṭīf likewise did not copy his own certificate of audition for the *Ḥarīriyya* into *Cairo Adab m105*. Instead, Ibn al-ʿAdīm, the doyen of Aleppan scholarship and owner of the manuscript, made the copy for him. Perhaps Ibn al-ʿAdīm's handwriting was particularly recognizable and trustworthy, or perhaps it was the fact that manuscript culture was profoundly *social.* The production and reproduction of manuscripts and their certificates was not a solitary affair but one that involved the cooperative production of knowledge and its material artifacts.

A Forgery or the Author's Hand?

In addition to *Cairo Adab m105,* there is a second manuscript that survives from the lifetime of the author, but it has received even less attention. In fact, the status of the manuscript remains something of a mystery because one scholar in the 1950s declared it to contain a certificate in the hand of the author, whereas Pierre MacKay has categorically dismissed it as a forgery. So is it a forgery or not? That is the mystery we will try to untangle in the rest of this chapter. The manuscript is now held in Turkey and is known as *Istanbul University A4566.* It contains a certificate that purports to be in the hand of al-Ḥarīrī on the frontispiece (Figure 7), similar to the one found in *Cairo Adab m105 (see Figure 3).* The inscription on the frontispiece of the Istanbul manuscript reads as follows:

> The *Maqāmāt* of Abū Zayd al-Sarūjī
> Composed by al-Qāsim b. ʿAlī b. Muḥammad al-Ḥarīrī
> This copy of the *Maqāmāt* that I composed was read in my presence by the illustrious eminence Najīb al-Dawla Abū Zayd al-Muṭahhar b. Sallār b. Abī Zayd, may God grant him everlasting grace. He read it with both a verified recitation and a verified understanding (*riwāya muḥaqqaqa wa-dirāya muḥaqqaqa*).
> Written by al-Qāsim b. ʿAlī at the end of the month of Muḥarram in the year 514.

The main difference between *Cairo Adab m105* and the Istanbul manuscript is that the latter attests to a man named al-Muṭahhar b. Sallār reading the text aloud in the author's presence, whereas the Cairo manuscript attests to Abū al-Muʿammar hearing the text while another read it. In both cases, we find al-Ḥarīrī identifying himself by name as the one who composed the certificates on the frontispieces.

Figure 7. Title piece of a *Ḥarīriyya* manuscript that appears to have been copied by the author himself. Compare with Figure 3. Istanbul University Library A4566, 1r.

The intrigue of the Istanbul manuscript deepens when we notice that the title of the text on the frontispiece is written in the same handwriting or "hand" as the certificate below it. By contrast, the only portion of *Cairo Adab m105* in the author's hand is the certificate, whereas the top half where we find the title is in the hand of the scribe Abū al-Muʿammar. When we turn to subsequent pages of the Istanbul manuscript, we find the same, distinctive handwriting throughout. In other words, this is not simply a manuscript that al-Ḥarīrī authorized with a signed certificate. This appears to be a manuscript that al-Ḥarīrī copied entirely himself, sometimes called a "holograph." That is, unless it is a forgery.

The German Orientalist Helmut Ritter (d. 1391/1971) considered the certificate in the Istanbul manuscript authentic. In his 1953 article on the autograph manuscripts in Turkish libraries, he transcribes the certificate and reproduces an image of it, but he does not comment on the handwriting in the rest of the manuscript.[35] Ritter was intimately familiar with the Istanbul University library collection and with the persistence of manuscript culture in early Republican Turkey. He taught at Istanbul University during his long exile—which began after his 1925 conviction in Germany for "Päderastie"—his imprisonment, and subsequent release in 1926.[36] For him, the question of forgery does not arise.

For Pierre MacKay, on the other hand, the handwriting on the two certificates is so divergent that they could not possibly be written by the same hand. I am convinced otherwise, and it seems to me that the handwriting on the two manuscripts is remarkably similar. MacKay claims that al-Ḥarīrī's hand in *Cairo Adab m105* is "swift . . . with sometimes a slight tendency to horizontal crowding," in contrast to the less-crowded certificate in the Istanbul manuscript. He also expresses his surprise that we find no formal audition certificates in the pages of the Istanbul manuscript, which he suggests should be present on such an important manuscript.[37] These details do not, in my view, decisively expose *Istanbul University A4566* as a forgery. First, there is evidence of crowding in the Istanbul manuscript. The word "five hundred" in the date is stacked above the "fourteen." Second, the more monumental and careful handwriting of the Istanbul manuscript is hardly surprising because the Istanbul manuscript is a luxury copy rather than a scholarly one. The fact that the handwriting is clearer and more evenly spaced in the Istanbul manuscript is natural if we understand this manuscript to be a sumptuous gift to a valued disciple. It seems possible that al-Ḥarīrī produced several audition certificates back in 504/1111 after the first public reading of the text, which may have led to a more rushed scribal act. Furthermore, manuscript culture is not a monolith, so it is not necessarily surprising that the Istanbul manuscript lacks further audition certificates. A reader who encountered *Cairo Adab m105* might seek to be included in that manuscript's archive of audition certificates, but if that same reader encountered *Istanbul University A4566*, they might interact with it differently.[38]

The Istanbul manuscript, with its lack of audition certificates, is perhaps more comparable to another famous manuscript of the *Ḥarīriyya* that has garnered much attention among art historians: the illustrated manuscript *BNF Arabe 5847*, copied and illustrated in Ramadan 634/1237.[39] The script and illustrations are exquisite, and it was obviously quite a treasure. But there are no audition certificates whatsoever. It was, in all likelihood, a display copy, which shows no sign of ever being collated or of being part of active, scholarly study. Even the marginalia are decorative, zigzagging down the margin at regular angles. Although the Istanbul manuscript is not illustrated, it was undoubtedly recognized as a luxury item. Sometime after it was copied, decorative medallions were added to the frontispiece and the margins of the first twenty-one folios were embellished with gilt decorations. It is clear that these are later additions because the maker of these decorations studiously avoided covering over some marginal notation and even accentuated those notes associated with the author, although it seems possible that the gilding was intended to cover up other marginalia that was deemed undesirable.[40]

The question remains whether al-Ḥarīrī ever produced manuscripts of the *Ḥarīriyya* entirely himself. It seems plausible that he did. A report from the biographer Ibn Khallikān (d. 681/1282) tells us that other "holographs" of the *Ḥarīriyya* existed. In his biography of al-Ḥarīrī, he reports that sometime in the year 656/1258 he saw a copy of the *Ḥarīriyya* in Cairo that was written entirely in the hand of the author ("*jamīʿahā bi-khaṭṭ muṣannifihā al-Ḥarīrī*") with a dedication in the author's hand to the vizier Jalāl al-Dīn al-Ḥasan b. ʿAlī b. Ṣadaqa (d. 522/1128–29).[41]

It therefore seems that al-Ḥarīrī was in the habit of dedicating individual copies of the *Ḥarīriyya* in his own hand as gifts for important people. This pattern fits nicely with the story that was discussed in the previous chapter of ʿImād al-Dīn receiving commentary from al-Ḥarīrī's son in exchange for tax relief. The situation with the manuscript that Ibn Khallikān saw is a bit more complicated. According to Ibn Khallikān, al-Ḥarīrī's certificate on the frontispiece signified that he had dedicated the *Ḥarīriyya* itself to the vizier, not that he had dedicated a particular manuscript of that work to him. I believe Ibn Khallikān was mistaken. It does seem quite possible and even likely that al-Ḥarīrī dedicated the *Ḥarīriyya* to someone or other. He alludes to a patron in the *Ḥarīriyya*'s introduction, and Arabic poets and later prose authors had long dedicated their creations to wealthy patrons hoping for rewards. Indeed, the entire edifice of elite *adab* was bound up with a complex economy of gift exchange.[42] However, Ibn Khallikān was aware of a widespread story that al-Ḥarīrī had, in fact, dedicated the *Ḥarīriyya* to a different vizier—namely, Anūshirwān b. Khālid (d. 533/1138–39) who served the Seljuk sultan Muḥammad b. Malikshāh (r. 498–511/1105–18). As we have seen before in this chapter, scholars of the period tended to find documentary evidence more precise and reliable than narrative reports, so Ibn Khallikān decides that the manuscript evidence is "more sound."

I would like to offer a different solution to Ibn Khallikān's conundrum. It seems likely to me that al-Ḥarīrī made multiple holograph copies as sumptuous gifts to various patrons. Whereas many authors dedicated their *work* to a patron, al-Ḥarīrī produced *copies* of his famous work to offer as gifts to his patrons. In the case of Ibn Khallikān's holograph manuscript, it was a gift for the vizier Jalāl al-Dīn. The manuscript that Ibn Khallikān saw in Cairo does not survive, so my solution is far from certain, but we know from the historical record that Jalāl al-Dīn only rose to the vizierate in the year 513/1119–20, several years after al-Ḥarīrī first wrote and circulated the *Ḥarīriyya*. Al-Ḥarīrī could not have dedicated the work to the *vizier* Jalāl al-Dīn back in 504/1111, and it seems unlikely that he would have dedicated such a monumental *work* to Jalāl al-Dīn when he was merely the promising son-in-law of a vizier.[43] It is certainly plausible that al-Ḥarīrī rededicated the work to a new patron later in life, but it seems more likely that he was in the habit of producing luxury copies of his masterpiece for the wealthy and well connected. These manuscripts were then held in such high regard that their later owners might show them off to visiting bibliophiles like Ibn Khallikān.

Even if we accept that holographs of the *Ḥarīriyya* existed, we have not yet addressed MacKay's most pressing objection to the authenticity of *Istanbul University A4566*, which boils down to this: It is too good to be true. It turns out that the dedicatee of this manuscript is also identified in the biographical tradition as the author's inspiration for the rogue of the *Ḥarīriyya*, namely Abū Zayd al-Sarūjī. MacKay surmises that an "enterprising forger" familiar with the lore surrounding the *Ḥarīriyya* might be tempted to produce a manuscript with a certificate like this one to entice his customers.[44] The existence of such a forger is plausible, although we know very little about the premodern practice of forging Arabic manuscripts, as François Déroche has pointed out. We do know that calligraphers in the Ottoman period and perhaps much earlier trained by precisely imitating the style of earlier master calligraphers.[45] Perhaps this forgery was created in a later period by a master scribe imitating al-Ḥarīrī's hand. I know of no ironclad method to disprove this sort of supposition, but there are several problems with MacKay's theory.

For one thing, the idea that al-Muṭahhar b. Sallār was the inspiration for the character of Abū Zayd developed slowly and unevenly in the textual record, which potentially attenuates the value of this kind of forgery. There is no reference to al-Muṭahhar in the biographical work of ʿAbd al-Laṭīf's teacher Ibn al-Anbārī, who presumably would have had good information about the matter by virtue of being a student of al-Jawālīqī, a scholar who was present at the first reading of the *Ḥarīriyya*.[46] The first record of al-Muṭahhar that I can find is in the massive *adab* anthology from the late sixth/twelfth century by ʿImād al-Dīn al-Iṣfahānī, but he is not considered there to be a model for the fictional character. (The biographical entry is in a volume of the anthology that was printed in 1973, two years after MacKay's article was published, so he would not have had access to it.) There, we find a short entry on "al-Ṣadr Abū Zayd al-Muṭahhar b. Sallār Fakhr al-Dīn." It states that he was a disciple of al-Ḥarīrī, a tax official, and a resident of al-Mashān, the same town outside of Basra where al-Ḥarīrī's estates could be found. ʿImād al-Dīn then goes on to say: "I heard that al-Ḥarīrī composed (*ṣannafa*) the *Ḥarīriyya* for him and bestowed on them the name Abū Zayd upon his suggestion (*iqtirāḥihi*)."[47] It is perfectly believable that this version of al-Muṭahhar, a man who might have interacted with the author in his official capacities, would have received a luxury copy of the *Ḥarīriyya*. He was, after all, a disciple from the author's hometown who was part of the governing apparatus when al-Ḥarīrī was said to be serving as the caliph's spymaster in Basra, and according to ʿImād al-Dīn, he merely suggested the name Abū Zayd as an apt name for his eloquent rogue.[48]

As time went by, the versions of al-Muṭahhar's life story took on more and more characteristics associated with al-Ḥarīrī's trickster Abū Zayd. ʿImād al-Dīn's younger contemporary al-Qifṭī penned a short biography of al-Muṭahhar in which he claims that al-Ḥarīrī "composed the *maqāmāt* upon his tongue."[49] Al-Muṭahhar is no longer lending his name to the trickster; he is becoming the *Ḥarīriyya*'s trickster! So much so that al-Qifṭī adds that al-Muṭahhar was "known as al-Sarūjī." This is pure invention. The real al-Muṭahhar was not a man of Sarūj, a town just north of the present-day border between Syria and Turkey, over a thousand kilometers away from Basra. Instead, later biographers added this toponymic name to him as they increasingly blurred the distinction between the man and the character. If the supposed forger of *Istanbul University A4566* was attempting to parlay this lore about al-Muṭahhar, why would they not include the moniker al-Sarūjī in the manuscript's frontispiece? If the value of this manuscript lies in its interaction with this biographical lore, it seems odd that the strongest case for blurring the line between al-Muṭahhar and al-Sarūjī was not made in the certificate. In other words, the ostensible forger would have needed to be working after the blurring of al-Muṭahhar and al-Sarūjī took place in the biographical tradition but made the decision to leave out any explicit trace of that blurring other than the coincidental (and rather common) name Abū Zayd.

One further problem with the forgery thesis is that the story of al-Muṭahhar being the inspiration for Abū Zayd al-Sarūjī is a rather minor piece of *Ḥarīriyya* lore that only appears sparsely in the biographical tradition and never appears to my knowledge in the commentaries on the *Ḥarīriyya*. As MacKay himself points out, there exists an alternative story about al-Ḥarīrī's inspiration that is much more well attested in both the commentarial tradition and the biographical tradition. It also appears there replete with a chain of transmission through a well-known source: Ibn al-Naqūr. The main features of this more prominent origins story are as follows: Al-Ḥarīrī encountered an eloquent man named Abū Zayd al-Sarūjī begging in a Basran mosque, claiming that he had been imprisoned by Christians, a plausible story for someone from Sarūj. That night, when al-Ḥarīrī dined with his companions, he told them what he had seen, a story that roughly follows the plot of *maqāma* #48. Each member of the group then claimed to have witnessed the very same beggar in his own local mosque in a different guise. The shape-shifting trickster of the *Ḥarīriyya* was born.[50] We will have more to say about this story when we discuss the questions of fiction and named characters in Chapter 5, but what is important here is that we find two different stories about what inspired al-Ḥarīrī. One involves al-Ḥarīrī's erudite disciple and well-connected neighbor al-Muṭahhar and the other involves a stranger named Abū Zayd al-Sarūjī who begs eloquently in a Basran mosque. Some biographers like Yāqūt discuss both stories without registering the apparent contradiction. By the eighth/fourteenth century, al-Muṭahhar the scholar and tax official had, for some, entirely disappeared. Tāj al-Dīn al-Subkī (d. 771/1370) merges the two stories and claims that al-Muṭahhar was the name of that eloquent beggar whom al-Ḥarīrī met in a mosque.[51]

Having undertaken all this detective work in the lore of the *Ḥarīriyya*, let us return to the original question. Is the Istanbul manuscript of the *Ḥarīriyya* a clever forgery or not? The presence of the name Abū Zayd al-Muṭahhar b. Sallār on the frontispiece does not, I think, definitively prove the manuscript to be a forgery. The morphing of al-Muṭahhar's biographies is such a muddled and thinly attested affair that I find it difficult to believe a forger would undertake this kind of project. It would be particularly outlandish for a forger to produce this manuscript in the early sixth/twelfth century before the lore of al-Muṭahhar-as-Abū-Zayd emerged. Michael Cooperson, the editor of the new edition of the *Ḥarīriyya* published in 2020, has concurred with my assessment that *Istanbul University A4566* should, at the very least, be dated either to the lifetime of the author or to the period soon after his death.[52] The lore about al-Muṭahhar emerged much later. If this is a forgery, it was designed to closely imitate those holograph copies of the *Ḥarīriyya* that were known to exist.

The assessment by Cooperson and me that the manuscript must be from the early sixth/twelfth century is based in part on the very small number of differences between the Istanbul and Cairo manuscripts. The few places where the two manuscripts diverge can be particularly telling. In *maqāma* #4, for example, the narrator al-Ḥārith has listened to two unseen companions debating the nature of neighborliness. When morning comes, al-Ḥārith realizes that Abū Zayd al-Sarūjī and his son are "the companions of my night and the sources of my narration (*wa-musnadā riwāyatī*)."[53] This is the reading that we find in the Istanbul manuscript. In the Cairo manuscript, we find that the two are the "authors of my narration (*wa-ṣāḥibā riwāyatī*)," but there is a collation note in the margin that reads "*wa-musnadā*" and adds that this correction is based on a manuscript "in his hand"—that is, the author's hand. In other words, the apparent divergence of the Istanbul manuscript actually aligns with the authorial version that we find in the marginalia of the Cairo manuscript. The correction in the Cairo manuscript's margin appears to be in the hand of the copyist Abū al-Muʿammar and likely is the result of that multilayered collation of the text that took place both before the first reading session and during those sessions.

There are a handful of other cases where the Cairo and Istanbul manuscripts disagree in individual words or in the voweling of words, but the two texts are remarkably consistent.[54] When one word replaces another, it is a synonym. It is possible that these are errors, either in the Cairo or the Istanbul manuscript, but it is also possible that al-Ḥarīrī changed his text ever so slightly over the course of his life. Earlier in this chapter, we encountered a story preserved in the biographical tradition that attests to the author's unwillingness to change his text, even when he found an improvement. That story, together with the intensive practices of collation that venerated manuscript associated with the author, might suggest that the *Ḥarīriyya* existed in a textual culture that insisted on textual stability and the primacy of autograph manuscripts. Even so, that story about al-Ḥarīrī's refusal to change the wording of his masterpiece is not the final word on his views about textual stability. In light of these minor discrepancies, it seems more than likely that the Istanbul manuscript is an authentic holograph.

As for the impression of textual culture that we get from the manuscripts of the *Ḥarīriyya, it is* only part of the story when it comes to the material practices of producing and reproducing Arabic texts. It must be reiterated once again that manuscript culture is not a monolith. Consider, for example, the case of *Kalīla wa-Dimna*, a collection of stories about talking animals and fictional humans that was translated from Middle Persian in the second/eighth century by a bureaucrat and scholar named Ibn al-Muqaffaʿ. Like the *Ḥarīriyya*, *Kalīla wa-Dimna* was copied extensively in both illustrated and unillustrated manuscripts, and it was considered a paradigmatic work of *adab*. However, its manuscripts are marked by a high degree of textual variation to such an extent that Beatrice Gruendler has described its copyists (or some of them at any rate) as "coauthors" who creatively reworked the text even as they maintained the overall narrative structure.[55]

Here we have two works of *adab*—*Kalīla wa-Dimna* and the *Ḥarīriyya*—with two very different modes of transmission, one that is highly variable and another that is tightly controlled through collation. This is a significant difference that once again highlights why reducing all these texts to their formal features as they appear in printed versions or assessing them only in accordance with their "literariness" risks flattening out the diverse forms of reading and textuality that existed in the world of the *Ḥarīriyya*. The *Ḥarīriyya* was part of a deep and sophisticated philological practice, one that was shaped not only by the Quran and the Arabic grammatical and exegetical traditions but also by al-Ḥarīrī's predecessors like al-Tibrīzī who taught the poetry of the pre-Islamic bards and al-Maʿarrī. It is to that philological world that we turn in the next chapter by examining the generative critiques of Ibn al-Khashshāb, the disgruntled philologist who found flaws with al-Ḥarīrī's language.

What I ask that you take with you from this chapter is the following: Reading the *Ḥarīriyya* was, for many readers, far from a passive process. The material practices of textual reproduction were not always aimed at producing archives like *Cairo Adab m105*, but those scholarly practices were nevertheless designed to provide authorized textual authorities for present and future generations. The multilayered commentarial culture was designed to produce embodied textual authority in the form of expert commentators, and the material practices discussed in this chapter were designed to support and, in some cases, to supersede that authority. Material evidence could sometimes be trusted above human sources, provided that the proper archival practices had taken place, inscribing into the material record that specific forms of scholarly labor had occurred. Al-Ḥarīrī seems to have invested considerable effort in embedding his text in this scholarly world of textual reproduction. We might surmise that he did this because he knew that his colleagues would criticize him for any missteps, as al-Jawālīqī had reportedly done at the first public reading. As we saw in the previous chapter, he had accused al-Ḥarīrī of using the word *shaghā* to mean excess (*ziyāda*) when its proper lexical meaning referred to uneven teeth. As we will see in the next chapter, Ibn al-Khashshāb would take up al-Jawālīqī's mantle and try to pick apart the *Ḥarīriyya* with a mercilessness that would forever impact the reputation of both Ibn al-Khashshāb and al-Ḥarīrī.

Chapter 4

The *Maqāmāt* and Its Discontents

When ʿAbd al-Laṭīf al-Baghdādī arrived in Damascus at the age of twenty-eight, he met Abū al-Yumn al-Kindī, the illustrious philologist whom we met in the previous chapter. The two engaged in a series of debates about Arabic philology, in which ʿAbd al-Laṭīf triumphed, or so he tells us in his autobiography.[1] As far as I am aware, no record of their debates remains, but this philological debate obviously excited the two men's passions and animosities. For these two scholars, philology was a high-stakes affair. This chapter is about the intense philological debates that arose around the *Ḥarīriyya*, which were a crucial part of the text's reception among the scholarly elites. These philological modes of commentary do not conform to the interpretive practices of world literature, but this chapter contends that they reflect the sophisticated approaches to language and meaning that underpinned the *Ḥarīriyya*'s enthusiastic reception.

The *Ḥarīriyya* was a hot topic of philological debate, and one wonders whether ʿAbd al-Laṭīf and Abū al-Yumn al-Kindī discussed their differences about the *Ḥarīriyya* when they met in Damascus. After all, al-Kindī had been taught by Ibn al-Khashshāb, a virulent critic of al-Ḥarīrī, and al-Kindī left behind some of his philological quibbles in the margins of *Cairo Adab m105*, one of the manuscripts we discussed in the previous chapter. ʿAbd al-Laṭīf himself had also taken an interest in Ibn al-Khashshāb's discontented critiques, as well as the rebuttals of Ibn Barrī (d. 582/1187), a Cairene philologist of the same period who wrote a point-by-point defense of al-Ḥarīrī. ʿAbd al-Laṭīf was so fascinated by this debate that he wrote a commentary evaluating the two sides. ʿAbd al-Laṭīf's biographer provides a list of his works, an astonishing one hundred and sixty-nine titles on a wide variety of subjects. Among these, we find the following, rather lengthy title: "The

Book of the Fair Judgment between Ibn Barrī and Ibn al-Khashshāb regarding Ibn al-Khashshāb's Rebuttal of al-Ḥarīrī's *Maqāmāt* and Ibn Barrī's Defense of al-Ḥarīrī."[2]

As titles go, it is quite a mouthful, but it is at least helpfully descriptive. Unfortunately, ʿAbd al-Laṭīf's *Inṣāf* (*Fair Judgment*) does not survive, but several copies of the debate have come down to us that include Ibn Barrī's introduction. Ibn al-Khashshāb's rebuttals, or *Istidrākāt* (*Corrections*), as they are usually known in the manuscript record, are never transmitted on their own but always with responses of one sort or another. Philological debate was part of the landscape in which the *Ḥarīriyya* emerged and became a part of the Arabic canon, and ʿAbd al-Laṭīf's teacher had himself composed a treatise on the "fair judgment" between the two competing grammatical schools of Kufa and Basra.[3] As Jonathan A. C. Brown has stated with reference to the canonization of hadith collections, interpretive charity reflects and reinforces a text's canonical status. When readers see a text as canonical, whether it is scriptural, legal, or otherwise, they commit to interpreting it in the most flattering light, whether that means eliminating apparent contradictions or bringing it into line with interpretive expectations.[4] In the case of the *Ḥarīriyya*, early critics of the text were met with rebuttals from scholars who sought to make sense of the difficult and sometimes-experimental language of the text.

This chapter is about the *Ḥarīriyya*'s discontented critics, who sought to undermine a text that had become almost immediately canonical from al-Andalus to Central Asia during the author's own lifetime. This chapter is also about the *Ḥarīriyya*'s defenders who took on the critics and vanquished them, at least to their own satisfaction and the satisfaction of many others. When the dust settled on these debates, most readers found that Ibn al-Khashshāb's critiques had mostly missed the mark. The Mamluk man of letters Khalīl b. Aybak al-Ṣafadī concluded that "Ibn al-Khashshāb was only correct regarding a small portion of what little he said, and he was annoyingly disputatious in a large portion of what he said."[5] In addition to the rebuttals of Ibn Barrī, the sixth/twelfth century produced another defender of the *Ḥarīriyya* to pick apart Ibn al-Khashshāb's critiques—namely, the commentator al-Panjdīhī (d. 584/1188). He composed a lengthy, digressive commentary that inveighed vigorously against Ibn al-Khashshāb, drawing on philology, Islamic ethics, and ad hominem attacks on the critic himself to defend al-Ḥarīrī. As is clear from this debate over the *Ḥarīriyya* and from ʿAbd al-Laṭīf's contentious encounters with a fellow philologist, the field of philology was a fiery one that raised the passions of its participants. Indeed, most of Ibn al-Khashshāb's critiques and the rebuttals of al-Ḥarīrī's defenders are philological in nature.

These sixth/twelfth-century debates about language are hardly the stuff of literary analysis, and it is for this reason that they have been largely overlooked in a field that reads *adab* "as literature." Scholars in the past few decades have expressed their disappointment in premodern commentaries on Arabic poetry and prose for what they perceive as its atomistic, philological approach that supposedly has a deadening effect on the text.[6] These medieval philologists are ostensibly missing the "literary" point. But what I would like to suggest is that if we dismiss these apparently molecular, philological debates, then we are the ones missing the point. Or perhaps better, we are overlooking and even erasing the particular modes of reading and interpretation that underpinned the *Ḥarīriyya*'s success. As is clear from ʿAbd al-Laṭīf's autobiographical account of his encounter with the philologist al-Kindī, philological disagreement could inspire vigorous and high-stakes debates between rival scholars. As part of this book's broader project to read *with* ʿAbd al-Laṭīf and his contemporaries, we need to understand what made these debates so significant and compelling to the *Ḥarīriyya*'s readers.

The Stakes of Philological Critique

I argue here that the philological debates about the *Ḥarīriyya* were contestations over the nature of Arabic and the proper way of engaging with the language of God's message to humankind. Far from being pedantic, atomistic quibbles about the text, the positions taken in these debates express broad theoretical commitments about the nature of language itself. My intervention here engages with the new revisionist approaches to the study of commentary and especially *adab* commentaries. Pushing back against the assumption that commentary is derivative and lifeless, Everett K. Rowson published an important article in 2003 on two digressive *adab* commentaries in the eighth/fourteenth century. He shows how these commentaries function as erudite performances that delight their audiences while giving the reader "a panorama of world literary learning, and a potted lesson in the basics of their heritage."[7] As Rowson avers, these commentaries are not simply about explaining the text but delight in intertextuality. The reception of this revisionist account has proceeded in fits and starts since Rowson's article, and it is clear that the study of *adab* commentaries remains a marginal field of study, so to speak. In 2019 Adam Talib offered a word of caution to this emerging revisionist account by pointing out that scholars have tended to focus on the more obviously digressive, "creative" commentaries, particularly those of the Mamluk scholar and *adīb* Khalīl b. Aybak al-Ṣafadī (d. 764/1363). Talib claims that a distorted image of the Arabic commentarial landscape emerges from this selection bias in favor of those commentaries that conform more closely to our literary norms. What is left out are those commentaries that seek to police what Talib calls "orthodox diction."[8] Talib takes up a critique of a text by al-Ṣafadī that is quite similar to Ibn al-Khashshāb's critique of the *Ḥarīriyya*. Both the critics of al-Ṣafadī and al-Ḥarīrī take these authors to task for transgressing the boundaries of Arabic.

Talib cautions us not to approach the Arabic commentary tradition from what he calls the "virginity model of artistic creativity," in which analysis implicitly or explicitly valorizes what is new, original, and sui generis. As Rowson also pointed out, the point of commentary is to delight in influence (rather than to have anxiety over it because it takes away from one's claim to "originality"). As an alternative to the "virginity model," Talib proposes that we appreciate the Arabo-Islamic philological tradition as a form of "temporal drag," a term that he draws from Elizabeth Freeman's *Time Binds: Queer Temporalities, Queer Histories*.[9] Temporal drag is a performance of anachronism that is time-bending, just as drag is gender-bending. Gender, as Judith Butler and others have taught us, is a stylized repetition of acts. Talib asserts that the Arabic philological habitus is likewise a stylized repetition of authorial acts that is "predicated on historical fluidity, on the constant intervention of the past in the present."[10] Talib's productive and provocative invocation of queer theory nevertheless sits uncomfortably with his general account of premodern philology and aesthetics. As I understand Freeman's account of temporal drag, it is a queer performance that draws on the anachronistic pastness of the past precisely to *disrupt* the present and the present's too-comfortable relationship with time. Her examples of temporal drag offer "points of resistance" to the status quo's temporal order and to "chrononormativity."[11] This is surely not the case with the Arabo-Islamic philological tradition, by which I mean the broad array of language disciplines from lexicography to grammar poetics. The philological tradition was not seeking to disrupt the status quo but to describe and analyze the correct ways of doing Arabic. It was, in a word, normative.[12] Like temporal drag, it draws on the past, but unlike temporal drag it does not valorize what Freeman calls a "break with tradition as the hallmark of progress or artistic emancipation."[13] For the Arabo-Islamic philological tradition, time was not out of joint, and the pastness of the past does not appear as a disruptive anachronism but as a welcome tradition. The traffic between the past and the present was not marked by subversive interruption but by a normative and norm-producing relationship.

The fact that the Arabo-Islamic philological tradition is normative does not mean, however, that it is uniform. As the philological debates over the *Ḥarīriyya* discussed in this chapter reveal, commentators drew on the Arabic past both to attack and to defend al-Ḥarīrī. In doing so, these commentators made broader claims about the Arabic language. To understand how these debates functioned, let us begin with an apparently minor quibble that reflects much broader questions about the flexibility of language. The quibble concerns whether "poetic license (*ḍarūrat al-shiʿr*)" also applies to rhymed prose (*sajʿ*). Although rhymed prose does not follow the traditional meters of Arabic poetry, it nevertheless is metered in some way, often repeating the same morphological pattern at the end of a line or even throughout. The *Ḥarīriyya*'s rhymed prose is especially metrical. Consider the following line in *maqāma* #2, which I have underlined to highlight the rhyme and meter of the last two lines:

> I found Abū Zayd al-Sarūjī
> varying the patterns of his ancestry
> and casting about in his manners of making money.
> *Alfaytu Abā Zayd al-Sarūjī*
> *yataqallab <u>fī qawālīb al-intisāb</u>*
> *wa-yakhbiṭ <u>fī asālīb al-iktisāb.</u>*

Ibn al-Khashshāb takes issue with this line because the word "patterns (*qawālīb*)" is spelled with a long "ī" to match "manners (*asālīb*)." The problem is that the plural of "pattern (*qālib*)" ought to be written with a short "i": *qawālib*. The matter may seem obscure to one who does not know Arabic, so it helps to know that most nonhuman plurals in Arabic are extremely complicated. Although these plurals follow set patterns, the possibilities are so numerous that students of Arabic must simply memorize the plural form of any given word. Over time, however, they begin to discern patterns that determine how particular singular nouns take particular plural forms.

As Ibn al-Khashshāb points out, the plural form *qawālīb* would derive from the singular *qālāb* or *qālūb*, but these singular forms simply do not exist. What al-Ḥarīrī has done is to alter the standard morphology of one plural in order to fit the meter of another plural that has been properly formed—inventing *qawālīb* to match the well-attested word *asālīb*. Ibn al-Khashshāb cries foul. The Arabs, he claims, would only use altered plural forms like this in poetry because they were forced to work within the meter, and even then this kind of "poetic license" could only be used sparingly. It is unacceptable in prose where there is "choice and ample room"—that is, where there is no meter.[14] Ibn al-Khashshāb cites various authorities and verses of poetry to illustrate his point.

Before turning to the rebuttals to Ibn al-Khashshāb, it is worth noting that he cites the speech of "the Arabs," by which he means the Bedouin Arabs of the pre-Islamic and early Islamic period in whose language the Quran was revealed. Medieval scholars of Arabic were aware of the fact that their own language differed from that of the Arabian past. Earlier Abbasid scholars were said to have conducted philological research by spending time with Bedouin Arabs whose speech was presumed not to have altered because they, unlike their cosmopolitan counterparts, had not mixed their language with that of non-Arabs.[15] An entire genre of philological writing concerned with the misuse of Arabic emerged in the Abbasid period. These works were given the label "solecisms of the commoners (*laḥn al-ʿāmma*)," and they were ostensibly aimed at disciplining the linguistic errors of non-elites. Al-Ḥarīrī himself contributed to this genre, but he directed his attention to the errors of those very same elites with his *Durrat al-Ghawwāṣ fī Awhām al-Khawāṣṣ* (*The Diver's Pearl Regarding the Errors of the Elites*). As Colinda Lindermann has stated, this genre is not just about identifying errors but about "inscribing oneself in a tradition of engagement with linguistic purity and attaching oneself to the group of scholars who care about this purity."[16] In other words, it is a sociolinguistic project that is concerned with policing the boundaries of what constitutes proper Arabic. However, the boundaries of proper Arabic were contested.

When Ibn Barrī encountered Ibn al-Khashshāb's claim that the word *qawālīb* fell outside the bounds of proper Arabic, he responded by asserting that there is something called "prose license (*ḍarūra fī al-nathr*)" which resembles poetic license.[17] He identifies examples of unimpeachable Arabic prose in which words are altered to fit the meter of rhymed prose. One example he uses is a hadith in which the Prophet Muḥammad is said to have discouraged women from taking part in a funeral procession by saying: "Go back bearing sin and without reward (*irjiʿna maʾzūrāt ghayr maʾjūrāt*)."[18] Strictly speaking, the word for "bearing sin" should be *mawzūrāt*, not *maʾzūrāt*. The Prophet changed the *w* in the diphthong "*aw*" to a glottal stop (ʾ) to match the word *maʾjūrāt*, just as al-Ḥarīrī altered the plural of *qālib*.

Is there such a thing as prose license, as Ibn Barrī claims? The question is not an idle one. It goes to the heart of Ibn Barrī's engagement with what Arabic is, which he undertakes as he defends al-Ḥarīrī. Ibn Barrī is certainly not suggesting that we should discard the rules and regulations of the Arabic language, and he is not seeking to supplant the canonical sources for shaping and policing proper usage. However, unlike Ibn al-Khashshāb who generally tries to reinforce the standard rules of the game, Ibn Barrī tends to look for the exceptions to those rules. Ibn Barrī shows that al-Ḥarīrī is still playing by the rules, but he is taking full advantage of the exceptions to those rules that can be found if one mines the archive of early Arabic for all its oddities. To do so, he takes examples from the speech of the Prophet and from other early Arab sources to prove that alterations were acceptable in both prose and poetry.

The question remains, however, whether other critics accepted the existence of "prose license" or if Ibn Barrī conjured up the notion out of thin air. Although critics did discuss alterations in morphology and grammar to achieve harmony in rhyming prose, it seems that Ibn Barrī was the first to claim that there was something called "prose license." As Devin Stewart has shown, one of the earliest discussions of altering words in prose was that of Abū Hilāl al-ʿAskarī (d. ca. 400/1010), who wrote a treatise on "the two crafts"—namely, the crafts of prose and poetry. In a chapter discussing rhymed prose, al-ʿAskarī cites precisely the same hadith that we find in Ibn Barrī's defense of the *Ḥarīriyya*. Al-ʿAskarī does not call it an example of "prose license," but he does say that the Prophet altered the word to achieve a pleasing balance or harmony (*izdiwāj*), a term strongly associated with rhymed prose.[19] Thus, Ibn Barrī is taking an implicit discussion of a topic, perhaps even drawn directly from al-ʿAskarī, and making it explicit by giving it this label: prose license.

The term "prose license" appears very infrequently in the Arabic philological tradition. I have found only one example of the term being used outside of Ibn Barrī, and that is in the seventh/thirteenth century in al-Andalus. A grammarian named Ibn ʿUṣfūr (d. 669/1270) composed an entire treatise on both poetic and prose license in which he explains that rhymed prose permits changes like those found in poetry "due to the license in prose." He cites the same hadith that we find in Ibn Barrī and al-ʿAskarī, but he goes on to say that similar morphological alterations can even be found in the Quran.[20] He then adds that "due to the fact that rhymed prose is like poetry, it is permitted for al-Ḥarīrī to say . . . *qawālīb* in accordance with *asālīb*."[21] What Ibn ʿUṣfūr's discussion demonstrates is that the idea of "prose license" has an afterlife. The debate over the word *qawālīb* in the *Ḥarīriyya* is neither atomistic nor merely a matter of figuring out whether al-Ḥarīrī's usage follows the rules or not. In fact, there are no firmly established "rules." The rules are subject to debate and rearticulation, even as the terms of that debate remain firmly rooted in marshaling the canonical sources of the Arabic philological tradition. When Ibn Barrī and later Ibn ʿUṣfūr expanded what is possible in Arabic by granting license to prose, they were rejecting Ibn al-Khashshāb's concept of proper Arabic philological practice while at the same time agreeing with Ibn al-Khashshāb that proper Arabic practice was a matter of deriving rules from the same canonical Arabic sources.

Al-Panjdīhī takes Ibn Barrī's argument one step further. He points to the word *ḥājib*. It is morphologically similar to *qālib* with a long "ā" vowel and a short "i" on either side of the middle consonant. It turns out the *ḥājib* has a plural with a long "ī" (*ḥawājīb*), but it is not found in the lexicon or in the canonical Arabic sources from the pre-Islamic and early Islamic period. Instead, *ḥawājīb* occurs in a poem by the Abbasid poet al-Mutanabbī (d. 354/965). The commentator al-Panjdīhī reasons that if "*ḥawājīb*" is attested in Abbasid poetry, then "*qawālīb*" must also be permissible by analogy. This additional example from al-Mutanabbī may seem to us like minutiae, but al-Panjdīhī's contention is rather striking when we examine it more closely. Al-Mutanabbī is a canonical poet in the tradition, but he is rather late and far too urban to be considered a philological authority on the speech of the Bedouin Arabs. Additionally, his use of the word *ḥawājīb* is in poetry, which means that this word may only exist as an example of poetic license. All of this raises the question: Is the canon of authoritative sources for Arabic open or closed? Can a late-breaking word like *ḥawājīb* be used as the basis for analogy to derive *qawālīb*? Al-Panjdīhī claims that it can, but he notes that there is some debate about the legitimacy of this form of analogy. He states that some specialists in the principles (*uṣūl*) of language deem it permissible, whereas some consider it only permissible in poetry, and still others "say that prose license is like poetic license."[22] As al-Panjdīhī points out, this is a disagreement about the principles of language and whether the lexicon is capable of expansion and growth through analogy. A similar dispute about analogy played out in Islamic law. Scholars debated the extent to which analogy could be used to extend the reach of prohibitions on one intoxicating beverage to all others, including coffee when it appeared, or to apply the punishments associated with fornication to cases of sodomy.[23] Just as some Muslim legal scholars resisted the use of analogy to extend the reach of the law, some scholars like Ibn al-Khashshāb resisted the use of analogy to accept new spellings of old words.

The question of whether al-Ḥarīrī could adjust the morphology of a word to fit the rhyme thus becomes a much broader question about how flexible Arabic can be. Is "license" in poetry or prose a series of exceptions to the unchanging rules, or do these newly developed words like *ḥawājīb* become the basis for further lexical and morphological innovation? Of course, as Adam Talib has emphasized, the commentators themselves would not have identified concepts like "prose license" as innovations but as principles that had always existed in Arabic, as exemplified by the usage of the Prophet and his forebears. Whatever the case, the debate over prose license illustrates the broader theoretical commitments of the major participants in this debate. Ibn al-Khashshāb argues for a more restrictive view of language, while Ibn Barrī and al-Panjdīhī seek out flexibility to defend al-Ḥarīrī. In general, Ibn al-Khashshāb imagines Arabic as consisting of a fixed set of already-abstracted rules and a well-established lexicon. By contrast, Ibn Barrī and al-Panjdīhī do not accept that Arabic is limited by a discreet set of universally applicable rules. Instead, their rebuttals conceive of Arabic as an assemblage of resources and precedents on which authors and critics may draw. Although the term "prose license" did not exist before Ibn Barrī, he would likely not see himself as "innovating" but as discovering, identifying, and then giving a name to a feature of language that could already be found in Arabic's vast assemblage of resources.

Prescriptive and Flexible Theories of Language

We might call Ibn al-Khashshāb's position "prescriptive," while the position of Ibn Barrī and al-Panjdīhī we might call "flexible"—that is, capable of accommodating growth.[24] We saw an example of these two positions in Chapter 2 when the philologist al-Jawālīqī confronted al-Ḥarīrī about the word "*al-shaghā*" in *maqāma* #21. Al-Ḥarīrī glossed the word as "excess (*al-ziyāda*)," and al-Jawālīqī retorted that the word "only refers to the uneven alignment of teeth, and it has no sense here."[25] As we saw in Chapter 3, al-Ḥarīrī was reputed to have been averse to changing a single word in his *maqāmas*, preferring to transmit precisely the same text to each reader. It is said that he even refused to change the text when confronted with potential improvements. We might assume, then, that al-Ḥarīrī had heard the criticism of his colleagues but did not agree that the word *al-shaghā* could only ever refer to uneven teeth but that it could be properly used to signify excess in general.

It is only when we read several of Ibn al-Khashshāb's quibbles and the responses of al-Ḥarīrī's defenders that we can see that each side of these individual debates is expressing a broader theory of language that we can call "prescriptive" and "flexible." For example, Ibn al-Khashshāb takes up a line of critique in his response to *maqāma* #1 which is similar to the appraisal of the *Ḥarīriyya* that is attributed to his teacher al-Jawālīqī. The trickster Abū Zayd has performed an eloquent sermon and is trying to avoid being followed, "so that his dwelling (*marbaʿuhu*) might be unknown."[26] Ibn al-Khashshāb claims that the term *marbaʿ* specifically denotes a dwelling that one uses in the spring (*al-rabīʿ*), just as there are specific words for a summer dwelling and a winter dwelling appropriate to a nomadic lifestyle. He states that the author should have used the term *rabʿ* or even *manzil*, both of which refer to dwellings in general, a point that is "obvious to anyone who thinks on it."[27] Ibn Barrī responds to this point by citing poetry that uses *marbaʿ* in the general sense of a dwelling to prove that the meaning is not so restrictive. For example, he cites a pre-Islamic who composed an attack poem satirizing the Asad tribe for its weakness. One line of poetry reads: "You have gone and made your whips weak, even though spears assail you in every dwelling (*kull marbaʿ*)." Ibn Barrī quotes this line and explains that the word *marbaʿ* here refers to every place where the Asad tribe dwells, regardless of the season. He adds that the lexicographers have specified that the term *marbaʿ* refers to the spring dwelling because it is "the original meaning, which then became extended so that it was used for every place a man resides."[28]

In this example about the dwelling (or the spring dwelling), we can see once again that Ibn al-Khashshāb insists on the precise, lexical meaning of the term, while Ibn Barrī points to the potential for words to become "extended" beyond their original signification. His example is a pre-Islamic poet who either drew on this already-extended meaning or extended the meaning himself. In either case, the Bedouin Arabs, the keepers of the true Arabic, were themselves engaged in lexical expansion.

Al-Panjdīhī in his rebuttal is more willing to accept that the word *marbaʿ* refers specifically to spring dwellings, but, as he points out, there is nothing in the *maqāma* that points to the events taking place in the summer, winter, or fall. Therefore, al-Panjdīhī reasons, we can presume that the *maqāma* takes place in the spring.[29] His argument is composed in rhyming prose and thus carries a certain kind of emphasis and flourish that Ibn Barrī's analytical prose does not. However, al-Panjdīhī includes Ibn Barrī's rebuttal after his own, just for good measure.

Ibn al-Khashshāb's prescriptive critiques go beyond individual words. He also disdains al-Ḥarīrī's playful reworking of lexically attested proverbial expressions (*amthāl*). For example, al-Ḥarīrī begins *maqāma* #21 with the narrator al-Ḥārith describing his process of ethical self-cultivation, which eventually becomes so habitual that "undertaking it was a passion that I obeyed." Finally, the narrator settles in Rayy, by which point he says, "I had loosened the knots of error and knew truth from falsehood (*ʿaraftu al-ḥayy min al-layy*)."[30] This precise expression cannot be found in the Arabic philological tradition prior to al-Ḥarīrī, but we do find its inverse. For example, a contemporary of al-Ḥarīrī, a scholar known as al-Maydānī (d. 518/1124), compiled a reference work containing Arabic proverbial expressions, which was widely copied and is still used today. There, we find the expression "He does *not* know truth from falsehood" and a number of other phrases to express the ignorance of people who cannot distinguish one thing from another.[31]

Ibn al-Khashshāb initially bypasses all these lexical ambiguities and claims that al-Ḥarīrī erred because these sorts of expressions can only ever be used in the negative, not in the affirmative. He gives the following example: "So-and-so does not know a cat from a rat."[32] It would be utterly meaningless, he claims, to say that someone knows a cat from a rat, presumably because distinguishing hawks from handsaws is no great accomplishment. Ibn al-Khashshāb considers this principle well established in the books of the lexicographers, and he adds that the terms *al-ḥayy* and *al-layy* refer to "truth" and "falsehood." Ibn Barrī pounces on this last remark to say that al-Ḥarīrī intended the reader to know the proper gloss (*tafsīr*) for these two words. According to Ibn Barrī, the two words do not refer to truth and falsehood but to clear speech and obscure speech. In other words, al-Ḥārith arrives in Rayy having learned to distinguish what is manifest and what is hidden in language, a rather apt interpretation of the passage in the world of the *Ḥarīriyya* and one that may have been drawn from al-Ḥarīrī's glosses or those of his students.[33]

Ibn Barrī does not limit himself to correcting Ibn al-Khashshāb's glosses of *al-ḥayy* and *al-layy* but goes on to refute the critic's more general point. Ibn Barrī insists that proverbial phrases can be inverted and made affirmative, as we might expect, given his more flexible position on language. As Ibn Barrī points out, if someone were to claim that "so-and-so does not know a cat from a rat," then refuting that claim might lead one to say that so-and-so does indeed know a cat from a rat. Ibn al-Khashshāb is thus predictably more prescriptive when he insists that proverbial expressions remain as they are found in the textual sources. Ibn Barrī argues for more flexibility in linguistic expression based on the way people debate and disagree in everyday life—they regularly affirm what their opponents deny. Al-Panjdīhī, whose responses to Ibn al-Khashshāb are so often filled with rhymed prose and high rhetoric, simply glosses the proverbial expression. He does not even bother quoting Ibn al-Khashshāb or Ibn Barrī and it may be the case that he senses that he has already demonstrated Ibn al-Khashshāb's tendentiousness. It is certainly the case that al-Panjdīhī's digressions tend to grow shorter and less frequent as his commentary progresses.

In sum, when we read these apparently minute and atomistic critiques and rebuttals, it becomes apparent that these commentators on the *Ḥarīriyya* were not simply arguing over minor points of grammar and philology. Rather, they were expressing broader theoretical commitments about the nature of Arabic and its proper usage *by means of* these individual cases. All the commentators, whether more prescriptive or more flexible, were committed to enforcing correct Arabic as they perceived it, but their notions of correct diction were different. None of them were suggesting that we can simply remake the rules, much less break them when we wish, but they disagreed on what those rules were. They were not seeking to *disrupt* Arabic through their citational performances of the Arabic past, as the invocation of "temporal drag" might suggest. Nevertheless, some critics like Ibn Barrī *were* committed to a version of Arabic that was not bound by the lexicon or by a word's original spelling or signification.

The philological practices that underpinned the *Ḥarīriyya*'s reception were therefore decidedly heterogeneous, and competing scholars outlined different rules and different degrees of flexibility. It should be clear from what has been said so far that the aims of this heterogeneous philology were clearly not "literary" or "liberatory" in the usual sense. These scholars were instead part of a *discipline*. In some sense, they were part of what Talal Asad calls a "discursive tradition." The commentators were drawing on the authoritative resources of the past to make normative claims in the present that might shape the future of Arabic language and poetics.[34] The various shades of the more prescriptive and more flexible approaches to philology were thus not a battle between the normative and the antinormative. Rather, these were debates over the proper way to construct normativity within a discursive tradition.

Biographical-Interpretive Criticism and the Reception of Ibn al-Khashshāb

Ibn al-Khashshāb's critiques of the *Ḥarīriyya* did not serve his reputation well. For starters, his critiques do not seem to survive on their own in the manuscript record, which means that, as far as we know, copyists did not generally allow his views to stand uncontested. Rather, wherever they are found in the surviving record, his critiques are accompanied by the rebuttals of Ibn Barrī or al-Panjdīhī. Furthermore, Ibn al-Khashshāb's reputation in the biographical tradition seems to have suffered dramatically because of his critiques. I argue here, building on the work of Fedwa Malti-Douglas and other studies of the Arabic biographical tradition, that these biographies were not simply repositories of information about a person's life and intellectual career but were complex interpretive engagements with the person's deeds, works, and impact on posterity.[35] It is well known, of course, that many biographies were concerned with the reliability of hadith transmitters, which meant that questions of memory and morality were often foregrounded. However, I contend that biographical anecdotes were themselves acts of interpretation and what Mana Kia calls "commemoration," in which texts produce the social imaginary as they articulate it, shedding light on scholarly legacies and collective memory-building.[36] The interpretive act of biography represents a version of what Alexander Beecroft has called "implied poetics." Studying the classical Greek and Chinese traditions, Beecroft has suggested that biographies of past authors—particularly scenes of authorship—offer multiple and competing theories about literature "that may not be explicitly articulated but whose existence beneath the surface of the text can be inferred."[37] Whereas Beecroft's implied poetics refers to "unthought assumptions about literature that inform a biographer's conjectures," our biographers were operating relatively soon after the death of al-Ḥarīrī, which might lead us to assume that these stories are not purely conjectural. However, I argue below that biographers were not necessarily expressing unthought assumptions but were rather playing a knowing game of biographical-interpretive criticism. This mode of interpretation in the Arabic tradition is distinct from the "biographical fallacy" in which critics interpret a work through the prism of the author's life.[38] Instead, my evidence suggests that biography was a discursive game that was not concerned with the life of the actual author but was instead interested in investigating the value and significance of that author's texts through storytelling. As was the case with the apparently atomistic, philological debates mentioned above, biography was a way of engaging with much broader claims about Arabic, *adab*, and the place of texts like the *Ḥarīriyya* in society.

Our first example concerns the biographies of Ibn al-Khashshāb, which often emphasize his miserliness and moral laxity, and they seem to connect those aspects of his personality to his critiques of the *Ḥarīriyya*. Al-Dhahabī's (d. 748/1348) biographical entry on Ibn al-Khashshāb draws in part on the authority of Ibn al-Najjār (d. 643/1245) to say that Ibn al-Khashshāb was "miserly and careless about his reputation, playing chess in the streets, stopping to watch conjurers [or jugglers], and joking around." Immediately following this comment, Ibn al-Najjār mentions that Ibn al-Khashshāb wrote a critique of the *Ḥarīriyya*, and the biography then quotes a report from al-Qifṭī (d. 646/1248) stating that he was stingy. The biographer then tells us on the authority of Ibn al-Najjār that when Ibn al-Khashshāb wanted to buy a book, he would damage one of the folios while perusing it and then point out the defect to get a cheaper price. None of these stories reflect well on Ibn al-Khashshāb, although the biographer admits that "perhaps he repented."[39] But why embed the information about Ibn al-Khashshāb's critique of the *Ḥarīriyya* between two similar reports on Ibn al-Najjār's authority in this way? I would suggest that this eighth/fourteenth-century biography is carefully constructed to suggest that Ibn al-Khashshāb's corrections to the *Ḥarīriyya* are part and parcel of his miserliness and ethical failings. It is no accident that he is portrayed as being stingy *with books*. The biography thus functions as a different kind of rebuttal to Ibn al-Khashshāb's attack on the *Ḥarīriyya*.

The exception proves the rule. The only unequivocally positive biography of Ibn al-Khashshāb that I have seen in the near-contemporaneous biographical tradition is found in ʿImād al-Dīn al-Iṣfahānī's massive anthology of poetry and *adab* prose entitled *Kharīdat al-Qaṣr.* The biographer identifies Ibn al-Khashshāb as one of his teachers, so it is hardly surprising that his biography is laudatory. What is important is that ʿImād al-Dīn's biography makes no mention whatsoever of Ibn al-Khashshāb's critiques of al-Ḥarīrī.[40] Among Ibn al-Khashshāb's disciples and sympathizers, the critiques of the *Ḥarīriyya* were apparently not something to be memorialized.

Miserliness is thus a failing in *adab*, both in its ethical sense and in the philological, textual sense. It is not simply a matter of money; stinginess becomes an intellectual, interpretive vice. I would even suggest that some readers likely interpreted the biographical emphasis on Ibn al-Khashshāb's miserliness as a critique of his philological work, rather than a claim about his frugality. This might seem like an odd suggestion, but, as Marlé Hammond has shown in the context of poetesses, scholars seem to have extrapolated anecdotal details and scenarios in a poet's life on the basis of their poems.[41] To illustrate this point, let us turn now to an example of Ibn al-Khashshāb's miserly reading in which he extrapolates biographical details about al-Ḥarīrī on the basis of the existence of manuscript variation.

When Ibn al-Khashshāb was reading the *Ḥarīriyya*, he noticed a glaring instance of manuscript variation in the exordium of the *Ḥarīriyya*, which he claims is evidence of al-Ḥarīrī's ignorance. In a passage of al-Ḥarīrī's introduction beseeching the Prophet's aid and intercession, Ibn al-Khashshāb had found al-Ḥarīrī quoting what he claims is a Quranic description of Muḥammad, God's Messenger (*rasūl*). Ibn al-Khashshāb tells us that most of the manuscripts he encountered included the following verses: "It is the speech of a noble Messenger (*rasūl*) who is powerful, well-established with the Lord of the Throne—one who is obeyed and who is steadfast" (Q 81:19–21). However, some manuscripts contained a different passage from the Quran in its place—namely, "We have not sent you except as a mercy to the worlds" (Q 21:107).[42]

To interpret this discrepancy in the manuscripts, Ibn al-Khashshāb does not blame errant copyists but rather associates both variants with the author himself. It turns out that the word Messenger in Q 81:19 is traditionally understood to refer not to the Prophet but to Gabriel who conveyed God's message to Muḥammad. According to Ibn al-Khashshāb, al-Ḥarīrī was unaware of this fact when he used the verse to refer to the Prophet, and it took some time for him to realize his mistake. By that time, the *Ḥarīriyya* "had spread to the East and West, to Syria and Iraq." Thus, when he fixed his mistake by replacing Q 81:19–21 with a new verse that is traditionally understood to refer to the Prophet, al-Ḥarīrī began tracking down copies that had already begun to circulate in order to change them, a project that was ultimately unsuccessful.

Having established this unflattering biographical sketch of al-Ḥarīrī, Ibn al-Khashshāb pounces. He states that al-Ḥarīrī had erred both in his original Quranic quotation and in choosing to correct it. As Ibn al-Khashshāb points out, there is a minority opinion among the exegetes that thinks the word "Messenger" in al-Ḥarīrī's original version refers to Muḥammad and not Gabriel. The existence of this minority opinion justifies al-Ḥarīrī's original choice of Q 81:19–21 with its ambiguous word "Messenger." According to Ibn al-Khashshāb, al-Ḥarīrī erred when he replaced that verse with another because he did so unaware of the exegetical tradition that justified his earlier text.

Ibn al-Khashshāb's critique is an example of what readers came to see as a kind of "miserly reading," which I believe prompted biographers to portray Ibn al-Khashshāb as both stingy and lax in his morals. A more generous reader of the *Ḥarīriyya* might charitably assume that al-Ḥarīrī was aware of the minority exegetical opinion regarding the word "Messenger" in Q 81:19–21. Ibn al-Khashshāb's critique here is not "molecular" but biographical, conjuring up an evocative portrait of the author as a bumbling exegete. The portrait is in keeping with Ibn al-Khashshāb's argument that al-Ḥarīrī lacked mastery of the Arabic lexicon. In this case, the presence of actual, verifiable manuscript variation invited Ibn al-Khashshāb to construct a biographical anecdote that affirmed his uncharitable views about the value of the *Ḥarīriyya*. Just as later biographers portrayed Ibn al-Khashshāb as a miser on account of his miserly readings, Ibn al-Khashshāb portrayed al-Ḥarīrī as a bumbling exegete on account of the fact that some manuscripts contained Q 81:19–21 while others contained Q 21:107. I am not suggesting that the entire biographical tradition is a fabrication but rather that some—perhaps many—stories are extrapolated from close readings of an author's texts. Furthermore, I would submit that this case is not best understood as "fabrication" but as interpretation and textual criticism taking place in the form of biographical anecdotes.

As I have shown elsewhere, the manuscript variation that Ibn al-Khashshāb encountered can still be found in the manuscripts of the *Ḥarīriyya*, but it seems highly unlikely based on the manuscript evidence that this variation can be attributed to al-Ḥarīrī. It seems more likely the work of well-meaning copyists attempting to correct what they perceived to be an error.[43] One early commentator, a certain Abū al-Khayr al-Anbārī (d. 590/1194), was either unaware of the variation or was only concerned with the version he deemed to be authorial—namely, the version containing Q 81:19–21. In his commentary, he notes that exegetes differ as to whether the word "Messenger" refers to Gabriel or Muḥammad, thus giving his reader the key piece of information necessary to understand al-Ḥarīrī's interpretive game.[44] We have already seen in Chapter 2 that the *Ḥarīriyya* is full of apparent errors or even nonsense that can only be transformed into proper sense when the reader becomes aware of the rare meaning of a word. The same interpretive game is being played here. The reader who is familiar with the ordinary interpretation of the Quran would know that the word "Messenger" in Q 81:19 refers to the Prophet and thus identify its usage in the *Ḥarīriyya* as an error. Only a reader who is familiar with the recherché corners of the exegetical tradition would be able to recognize that it is not an error at all but part of the text's interpretive playfulness.

Ibn al-Khashshāb's refusal to play the text's interpretive game marks him out to enthusiasts of the *Ḥarīriyya* as a miserly reader. Al-Ḥarīrī's commentarial defenders reject this uncharitable attitude, but they counterintuitively accept the fact that it was the author and not later copyists who altered the text. Ibn Barrī insists that the author may well have been aware of the minority interpretation of Q 81:19–21 that claims the word "Messenger" refers to Muḥammad. In this version of events, it was not out of ignorance that he substituted Q 21:107 but rather out of a desire to abandon a verse about which exegetes differ so that he might "repair to that which no one disagrees about."[45] Whereas Ibn Barrī seems to admit his preference for the unambiguous Q 21:107, al-Panjdīhī is more resolute in his defense of the author whom he claims "did not err in the first instance when he chose to follow a unique opinion . . . and was correct in the second instance when he abandoned the weak and obscure opinion in favor of the well-known and obvious one."[46] As al-Panjdīhī explains, al-Ḥarīrī was "more secure in his religion" than to follow his whims or to cite the Quran according to supposition (*ẓann*) in a haphazard or random fashion.

Al-Panjdīhī's rebuttal is filled with the vocabulary of Islamic jurisprudence, accusing Ibn al-Khashshāb of fabrication (*iftirāʾ*) and saying that such slanderous speech is "proscribed and forbidden according to the law (*fī al-sharʿ*)." Furthermore, al-Ḥarīrī offered no confession (*iqrār*) that he interpreted the Quran on the basis of unsupported supposition, so it is prohibited to believe Ibn al-Khashshāb's slander. What is more, al-Panjdīhī argues that al-Ḥarīrī's choices of Quranic quotation are like the rulings made by the highest ranks of Muslim jurists (*mujtahids*). Those jurists are capable of performing independent interpretive work (*ijtihād*) to derive their legal opinions, rather than relying on adherence to an established school (*taqlīd*). Because a *mujtahid* is so well-versed in the Islamic scholarly tradition, he is not required to follow the majority opinion but is permitted to choose the less attested, less well-known interpretations.[47]

To sum up, we have on the one hand a critic claiming that al-Ḥarīrī was a bumbling scholar with a poor grasp of the exegetical tradition and on the other a sympathetic commentator maintaining that al-Ḥarīrī was comparable to the most expert Muslim jurists. Here again, in this example it becomes clear that these debates over single lines in the *Ḥarīriyya* are not atomistic. Rather, they reflect much broader questions about the text and the making of meaning. In this case, the question is about whether the *Ḥarīriyya* is properly "Islamic." Are its quotations of the Quran and hadith performed in ways that are firmly rooted in the Islamic scholarly tradition, or are they done haphazardly in ways that reflect poorly on the author and undermine any claim that the text should be treated as authoritative? We will return to these questions in Chapters 5 and 6 where we will see that some commentaries, like those of al-Panjdīhī and al-Muṭarrizī, treat the *Ḥarīriyya* as an Islamic text par excellence.

There were other debates about the *Ḥarīriyya*'s place in society and scholarship that critics carried out through biography. For example, some biographies seem concerned with the relationship between the *Ḥarīriyya* and the bureaucratic work of producing epistles in the chancery. This debate was litigated through two competing biographical anecdotes that emerged in the second half of the sixth/twelfth century to depict al-Ḥarīrī's adventures and misadventures in the chancery (the *dīwān al-inshā'*). The chancery scribe's role was to produce epistles on behalf of the ruler and other high officials. Through intricate rhyming prose, these epistles navigated the complex networks of power while communicating the breathtaking sophistication of the court and its elites.[48] The anecdotes depicting al-Ḥarīrī's spectacular success or, alternatively, his spectacular failure at the chancery in Baghdad were not, in my view, designed to convey events that took place in the author's life. Instead, these stories are better understood as examples of biographical criticism that sought to contest the place of the *Ḥarīriyya* in the world and specifically its usefulness for training chancery scribes.

Let us begin with the biographical anecdote that portrays al-Ḥarīrī as a man incapable of composing epistles in the chancery style, which appears in the magnum opus of Ḍiyāʾ al-Dīn Ibn al-Athīr (d. 637/1239) entitled *al-Mathal al-Sāʾir fī Adab al-Kātib wa-l-Shāʿir*. The work is not a collection of biographies but rather an influential work on Arabic style that presents itself in the title as a book that can offer both the chancery scribe (*kātib*) and the poet (*shāʿir*) a guide to proper behavior and composition (*adab*). The biographical anecdote about al-Ḥarīrī thus comes as something of a surprise in the introduction of this book unless we recognize that the function of biography here, as was the case in Ibn al-Khashshāb's critiques, is to make claims not about people but about texts.

Ibn al-Athīr mentions al-Ḥarīrī in the midst of vaunting chancery scribes who must be knowledgeable about every branch of knowledge, unlike the grammarian or theologian or legal scholar who specializes in only one. According to Ibn al-Athīr, even the best poets and prose authors are usually only skilled in a single genre, such as panegyric or satire or elegy. Al-Ḥarīrī revealed himself to be just such an author, unsuited to chancery writing, when he arrived in Baghdad from his estates in al-Mashān outside of Basra. In this telling, al-Ḥarīrī was already known for his *maqāma*s and therefore it was suggested that he would be suitable for the caliph's chancery. He was summoned to the chancery to write an epistle, a task that left him "speechless, his tongue incapable of both prolixity and terseness." He could not compose a single epistle. Ibn al-Athīr quotes two lines of an anonymous, satirical poem that was ostensibly written about this event:[49]

A shaykh of ours from Rabīʿat al-Faras
  Plucks out his beard in confusion.
God gave him speech in al-Mashān
  And has bridled him in Baghdad with dumbness

The anecdote serves to illustrate Ibn al-Athīr's point about the superiority of chancery scribes, but it also allows him to distinguish the narrative craft from the epistolary arts. Ibn al-Athīr explains that some people are amazed by this story, but they should not be because "the *Maqāmāt* all revolve around stories that move toward a resolution," whereas chancery writing "is a sea without a shore because the themes become new in chancery writing with the appearance of new circumstances."[50] The difficulty of chancery writing involves constraints and constant creativity that require the author to produce volumes and volumes of material, whereas al-Ḥarīrī was only able to compose a measly fifty *maqāmas*. Ibn al-Athīr cites the authority of none other than Ibn al-Khashshāb who is quoted saying that al-Ḥarīrī "is a man of the *Maqāmāt*," which he explains means that his only finely crafted prose is the *Ḥarīriyya*, while the rest of his writing is quite worthless.[51]

A starkly different biographical anecdote in another source quotes the same lines of poetry found in Ibn al-Athīr's version and provides an account of al-Ḥarīrī at the chancery, which implies that this is a competing interpretation of the *Ḥarīriyya*'s relationship to chancery prose. The anecdote is found in a more conventional source—namely, the massive biographical encyclopedia of Yāqūt (d. 626/1129), who was a contemporary of Ibn al-Athīr. According to Yāqūt, the chronology of events is completely reversed. Al-Ḥarīrī had not yet written the *Ḥarīriyya* when he came to the chancery. In his version, which he attributes to "someone whom I trust," al-Ḥarīrī had only written his first *maqāma* during a period when he was already engaged in the work of chancery writing, which he then mastered. It happened that he was in Baghdad and went to the chancery of the sultan (rather than that of the caliph as was the case in Ibn al-Athīr's story), which was full of talented and eloquent people. They had heard of his arrival but did not know of his skill, so one of the scribes asked him, "With what aspect of chancery writing are you engaged, such that we may discuss it with you?" Al-Ḥarīrī picked up a pen and said, "Everything which is related to this," pointing to the pen and inviting them to test his weighty claim. The scribes "each asked about the types of chancery writing of which he believed himself to be the master, and al-Ḥarīrī replied to all of them with the best possible answers, and he addressed them with the most perfect discourse such that he amazed them."[52]

The events at the chancery in these competing anecdotes could not be more different. In the first story, al-Ḥarīrī is stumped by a simple compositional exercise while in the second, he dazzles the experts with his ability to improvise eloquently about all chancery matters. One way of reading these biographies is to suggest that the tellers and re-tellers of these stories are debating whether the *Ḥarīriyya* is a useful text for training oneself to be a chancery scribe. Just as the debate about al-Ḥarīrī's Islamic credentials may be understood as an argument about the *Ḥarīriyya*'s place in the Islamic textual canon, these biographies seem concerned with the question of what a good chancery scribe needs to know and whether the *Ḥarīriyya* was a necessary part of that knowledge. It is noteworthy that both stories are making claims about the *breadth* of al-Ḥarīrī's knowledge. Is he simply a "man of the *Maqāmāt*," or is he a master of all disciplines related to writing, as a chancery scribe ought to be?

Yāqūt's story continues on to include more details that seem to reinterpret the other points of concern raised by Ibn al-Athīr's story, such as the verses about al-Ḥarīrī's writer's block and the stylistic divergence between al-Ḥarīrī's *maqāmas* and his other works. According to Yāqūt, al-Ḥarīrī's smashing success at the chancery brought him to the attention of Anūshirwān b. Khālid (d. 532–33/1137–39), who read the first and only *maqāma* that al-Ḥarīrī had written, which is reported to have been *maqāma* #48. Anūshirwān liked it so much that he encouraged him to write more. With that model *maqāma* in hand, al-Ḥarīrī returned to his hometown of Basra where he could gather his thoughts. He came back to Baghdad with forty *maqāmas*, and only then, according to Yāqūt, did he begin to have a reputation based on his *maqāmas*. However, he was accused by envious critics of falsely claiming to be the author of these stories. Some said he had taken possession of his *maqāmas* from a guest who died while staying with al-Ḥarīrī. Others said he purchased these stories from a Bedouin raider who pilfered them from a traveler from the Maghreb. The evidence for these accusations was that the *maqāmas* "do not match [the style] of his epistles, and they do not resemble his mode of expression."[53]

To prove that he had not stolen these *maqāmas*, al-Ḥarīrī's critics demanded that he compose another *maqāma*. Yāqūt tells us that al-Ḥarīrī sat in his abode in Baghdad for forty days filling pages and pages with ink, but he could not compose a *maqāma*, so he returned to Basra in defeat. But not for long. While back in Basra, he composed another ten *maqāmas* to add to the forty he had written before and brought them to Baghdad, at which point his greatness was clear to all. According to Yāqūt, it was this bout of writer's block that inspired the verses quoted above regarding al-Ḥarīrī being bridled in Baghdad but able to speak at his Basran estate. Yāqūt also explains the first line about al-Ḥarīrī picking his beard, saying he was afflicted with this compulsive behavior.

Yaqūt's longer and more detailed version is not necessarily the earlier or the more accurate account. In fact, there are reasons to suspect that Yāqūt's story was designed to make interpretive claims rather than convey details about the author's life. The accusations of plagiarism and their refutation in Yāqūt's story are clearly modeled on the Quran's "challenge" to those humans and jinn who doubt its divine origin. The Quran invites those who believe it to be human speech rather than divine revelation to "bring ten fabricated chapters like it and call upon anyone you can [for aid] besides God if you are truthful" (Q 11:13). Elsewhere, critics are challenged to bring a single chapter like the *sūra*s of the Quran (Q 10:38). This verse and others assert the Quran's miraculous inimitability. If humans cannot produce verses like those in the Quran, then the author must be God himself. Similarly, al-Ḥarīrī is said to have proved that he is the author of his first forty *maqāma*s by producing ten more like them.

There are two significant unstated assumptions underpinning Yāqūt's story. These assumptions are, I suggest, the interpretive work of biographical criticism. First, it is assumed that these *maqāma*s are inimitable because the authorial act is only reproducible by the author himself. Any person falsely claiming to be the author would be incapable of producing ten *maqāma*s like the first forty, just as humans are incapable of producing anything like the Quranic revelation. As we will see in Chapter 6, this idea that the *Ḥarīriyya* is Quran-like in its inimitability was a common theme in the early commentaries on the *Ḥarīriyya*. Second, Yāqūt's story implies that these *maqāma*s are produced through a difficult and intensive process of drafting, rather than through spontaneous eloquence. His attempts to write in Baghdad turn out to be unfruitful, but he fills pages with draft attempts. It is only back at home that he can complete the task. Whether al-Ḥarīrī wrote the text in Baghdad or Basra, the point of the story seems to be to differentiate these *maqāma*s from the spontaneous acts of expert epistolary writing that were required of al-Ḥarīrī in Ibn al-Athīr's story.

Writing biographical anecdotes was thus, I argue, a mode of textual interpretation. Telling dueling stories of al-Ḥarīrī in the chancery was not primarily undertaken to understand the life of the author but to make interpretive interventions about his text. It is possible that Ibn al-Athīr's story was a rewriting of Yāqūt's story or the other way around. Alternatively, both stories may have arisen out of a broader discourse about the relationship between the *Ḥarīriyya* and chancery writing. Ibn al-Athīr portrays storywriting as the easier task because the author is unconstrained by the exigencies of politics. He can shape the plot to fit whatever he wishes to say. Such writers, Ibn al-Athīr suggests, cannot write spontaneously and on demand. Yāqūt's story implies that one and the same author may be capable of eloquent discourse in the chancery but incapable of writing ten new *maqāma*s on the spot because the latter is actually more difficult. Between the lines, these stories may also reflect Ibn al-Athīr's anxieties about chancery education. According to him, al-Ḥarīrī arrived in the chancery having already become famous for his *maqāmas*. His ability to write stories had led some to believe that he would be suited to chancery work, and one wonders if Ibn al-Athīr's story functions as a warning to students that they need much more than an education in the *Ḥarīriyya*.

* * *

It is now clear that more was at stake than initially meets the eye in both the apparently pedantic debates between Ibn al-Khashshāb and his interlocutors and the biographical anecdotes that grew up around al-Ḥarīrī. Defending the *Ḥarīriyya*'s Arabic in the first instance and al-Ḥarīrī's mastery of the chancery arts in the second both sought to situate the text in the world. For the text's defenders, it was not a work full of solecisms and blunders but a model of proper, virtuosic Arabic. For the text's detractors, the text and its author belonged outside of the Arabic that really mattered. To understand and appreciate the minutely philological and biographical modes of interpretation requires us to set aside our expectations about what "literary reading" ought to look like. The philological, exegetical, and biographical critiques discussed in this chapter do not take on the formal features of "literary" criticism as it is practiced in the era of world literature. The goal of this chapter is not to express the critical insights of these early readers of the *Ḥarīriyya* in ways that make them comparable to modern criticism. Rather, I have suggested that we find important discussions about language, authorship, virtuosity, and aesthetic excellence expressed through the accumulation of evidence and example, as well as through imaginative biography. To be sure, none of our sources present a grand theory of how to read the *Ḥarīriyya*, but they do offer broader insights into how they believed language ought to work. Dismissing these insights as molecular and merely philological is to risk missing out on the sophisticated critical practice that underpinned the *Ḥarīriyya*'s reception and widespread celebration.

Chapter 5

Theorizing Fiction

Over the course of his life, ʿAbd al-Laṭīf al-Baghdādī had memorized, studied, and taught the *Maqāmāt* of al-Ḥarīrī. But how did ʿAbd al-Laṭīf understand the character of Abū Zayd al-Sarūjī? Did he believe that Abū Zayd was a real human being who walked the earth? Or did he think that al-Ḥarīrī had invented him out of thin air? In other words, did ʿAbd al-Laṭīf and other readers understand the *Ḥarīriyya* to be a work of fiction? In the decades after the *Ḥarīriyya* began circulating, some commentaries claimed that al-Ḥarīrī had, in fact, encountered an eloquent beggar named Abū Zayd al-Sarūjī in a Basran mosque. For some Orientalists, this story became a symptom of Islam's hostility toward fiction or, alternatively, the fact that no concept of fiction existed in the medieval Islamic world. As G. E. von Grunebaum puts it, "Arabic literary theory does not provide for fiction."[1] According to some formulations of this hypothesis, Muslim readers rejected inventive stories because they were considered tantamount to lies, and they had a pious desire for truth-telling. Whereas the modern critic who is familiar with literariness and the regime of world literature is imagined to be capable of recognizing the fictionality of a text like the *Ḥarīriyya*, the (medieval) Muslim reader supposedly *failed* to recognize it. As a result, Muslim authors who wished to color outside the lines were forced to justify or obfuscate the fictionality of their work in the face of this ostensible hostility.[2]

This mode of analysis, which I refer to as the "repressive hypothesis," has a lineage that goes back over a century and is deeply embedded in the processes that led to the emergence of world literature, which define fictionality in a narrow way so that it becomes the sole possession of literary modernity. Moreover, the repressive hypothesis possesses what Edward Said might call a remarkable "discursive consistency," which traffics in familiar stereotypes of a brittle, fanatical, and dogmatic Islam.[3] Consider Thomas Chenery, the Victorian translator of the *Ḥarīriyya* and editor of the *Times* of London. He declared in 1867 in the introduction to his translation that "the strict Moslems had always held works of fiction to be, if not blamable, at least unworthy to be written or perused by serious believers."[4] Over a century later, the erudite German philologist Wolfhart Heinrichs asserted that "we can conclude nothing more and nothing less than that Islam is averse to fiction."[5] In the 1998 *Encyclopedia of Arabic Literature*, Rina Drory stated that "official" Arabic literature, "governed by powerful religio-poetic norms, consistently claims the historicity of its texts" because fiction was unacceptable and condemned as lies.[6] There is a double-reification taking place in these statements. The first is of Islam and Arabic literature, which are reduced to a series of "orthodox" opinions. The second concerns "fiction," which becomes a kind of universal category that can be found (or not) in various times and places. According to the standard Orientalist view from Chenery to Drory, fiction was suppressed as a reaction to Islamic norms, which led to various "failures"—namely, the failure of readers to recognize fiction and the failure of truly fictional writing to emerge.

This chapter examines and picks apart the repressive hypothesis while taking a very different approach to the study of "fictionality" that seeks to avoid the reifications and false binaries of fiction/fact that continue to plague discussions of medieval Islamic textuality.[7] I propose to open up a space for what Julie Orlemanski has called a "comparative poetics of fiction," which pays attention to both the theoretical vocabularies of other contexts and what Nicolette Zeeman calls "literary theory expressed in 'literary' form."[8] In other words, we may find theorizations of fictionality that are expressed narratively rather than through explicit theoretical statements. Orlemanski's hermeneutic conception of fiction is rooted in the question of *how* people have linguistic capacities to depict the non-actual within particular discursive contexts, rather than the question of *who* has fiction "properly speaking." I argue that the specter of Muslim or Arabic hostility toward fiction in the premodern world derives from a particular mode of interpreting evidence that is underpinned both by the chronotopes and mythologies of a benighted, backward "Dark Ages" and the figure of the fanatical Muslim reader that was discussed in Chapter 1.[9] This chapter reinterprets that evidence to reveal sophisticated theorizations of fictionality, while offering new points of departure based on hitherto overlooked sources. By exorcizing the specter of a widespread hostility toward some universal category called "fiction," which was a foundational myth of world literature, it becomes possible to glimpse the various concepts and theorizations of fictionality that circulated among Muslim readers.

The overlooked sources for Arabo-Islamic theories of fictionality can be found, in part, within the vast commentarial tradition that grew up around the *Ḥarīriyya*. For example, an eighth/fourteenth-century commentator, whose work is only available in manuscript, states simply of the two protagonists in the *Ḥarīriyya* that the author "invented the two of them (*ikhtaraʿahumā*)."[10] He expresses no hostility or ambivalence about the status of this invention. Commentaries such as these have been neglected in the scholarship or, as we will see below, mobilized selectively to reinforce the repressive hypothesis. For example, we looked closely at Ibn al-Khashshāb's critique of al-Ḥarīrī in the previous chapter and his rather unfavorable reception in the broader commentary tradition. Nevertheless, his unique polemic against the *Ḥarīriyya*'s fictionality has been taken as a synecdoche for the attitudes of an entire "civilization," which supposedly possessed distinctive religio-poetic norms. I admit that Ibn al-Khashshāb's position is one of the available attitudes toward fictionality, but the idea that it is representative of an entire culture of reading is unsustainable.

Although none of the commentaries discussed here could be considered treatises on fictionality or the nature of narrative representation as such, we must read them as part of the networked intellectual tradition in which they were embedded. Because they were part of this tradition, individual words and phrases could call up entire archives of discourse. When these archives are pieced together, as I will do below, we can begin to see that these diverse theories of fictionality should not be viewed as incomplete or failed attempts to achieve the modern novel or to realize some universally applicable concept called "fiction." Rather, our notions of fictionality, as well as the medieval European accounts of fictionality discussed by Orlemanski, must be provincialized to avoid erasing the complex modes of understanding the relationship between textuality and reality that existed in the Arabo-Islamic tradition.

In what follows, I begin with an exploration of the *Ḥarīriyya*'s opening passage to elucidate my methodology of drawing on commentary to explore a networked intellectual tradition. I then turn to al-Ḥarīrī's so-called apology for fiction, which appears in al-Ḥarīrī's authorial preface or "exordium (*khuṭba*)." I situate this apology, which has been a key piece of evidence in the repressive hypothesis concerning fiction, within the commentarial literature and the broader archive of theorizing about the non-actual in Arabic. I show that it is, in fact, fruitful to read al-Ḥarīrī's so-called apology for fiction as an interpretive key to the text that allows the reader to theorize the text's fictionality. Finally, I return to the question posed at the beginning of the chapter regarding the characters Abū Zayd al-Sarūjī and al-Ḥārith b. Hammām; namely, what are we to make of the fact that biographies of these characters emerged in the first century after the *Ḥarīriyya* was written? Does it reflect a hostility toward fiction and an attempt to "adjust to the strict poetic norms of *adab*"?[11] I argue that this is an impoverishing and misleading interpretation of the evidence. A reassessment of this evidence suggests that there existed sophisticated understandings of the dynamic interaction between invented stories, stories about historical characters, and extratextual reality.[12]

Before analyzing the apology for fiction itself, it is useful to illustrate briefly my methodological approach of situating a passage of commentary within the broader textual tradition on which it draws to identify the networked nature of the tradition. By illustrating how commentarial reading operates, we can see that identifying intertextualities is not a way of providing alibis (for fictionality or other gambits) but rather a mode of making meaning. Let us begin with the opening passage of the *Ḥarīriyya*, in which the author invokes the aid of God and the Prophet Muhammad, and, in doing so, he introduces various thematic concerns in the book. It is a feature of many premodern Arabic books that the introductory invocations are to some degree "formulaic" but not at all meaningless. Instead, authors specifically tailored their praise and supplication to God to introduce the topics of their books. The *Ḥarīriyya* thus begins by saying: "We praise You for the clear eloquence (*bayān*) that You taught and the clarification (*tibyān*) that You inspired."[13] The reader thus immediately becomes aware, with or without a commentary, that this text takes up the question of language, eloquence, and communication. This may only be one thematic concern among several, but it is reinforced just one sentence later when al-Ḥarīrī says: "I seek refuge in You from the tongue's exuberance and loquacious babbling, just as I seek refuge in You from the shame of stumbling in speech and the disgrace of ineloquence."[14] What al-Ḥarīrī achieves here is twofold. First, he establishes a dichotomy between divine eloquence and erring human speech, and second, he alludes to a remarkably similar passage that is found at the beginning of a foundational work in Arabic poetics and aesthetics: *Kitāb al-Bayān wa-l-Tabyīn* (*The Book of Clarity and Clarification*) by al-Jāḥiẓ (d. 255/868–69).[15] By echoing the opening of that book, al-Ḥarīrī is suggesting that his book is somehow related to al-Jāḥiẓ's book and its theories of language and ethics.[16]

The digressive commentaries of al-Panjdīhī and al-Sharīshī both point out that this opening passage is an allusion to al-Jāḥiẓ's *Book of Clarity*.[17] However, the precise significance of al-Ḥarīrī's intertextual gesture to al-Jāḥiẓ and rhetorical technique is not spelled out in these commentaries. Rather, the commentaries situate al-Ḥarīrī's invocations within a discursive field involving eloquence (*bayān*) in general and with reference to al-Jāḥiẓ's *Kitāb al-Bayān* specifically. Commentary simply invites us to ponder the significance of the relationship. If we think back to ʿAbd al-Laṭīf's failed lesson, discussed in Chapter 2, in which the young student was incapable of understanding the commentary of a text that he had already memorized, we can see how commentary is not simply a mode of explanation but an intertextual exercise. The significance of intertextual references in a commentary might not be apparent to every student, just as they were not apparent to ʿAbd al-Laṭīf when he first encountered the advanced commentary of his teacher. To appreciate the sophistication of a commentary might require understanding all the previous commentarial interventions and their interrelations.

More importantly, the point of this digression is that an allusion to al-Jāḥiẓ here cannot reasonably be understood as a way of justifying the text by affiliating it with a venerable author. Instead, al-Ḥarīrī is *telling us something about the text at hand* by situating his book within an established discourse about eloquence. Evoking this passage in al-Jāḥiẓ emphasizes that the *Ḥarīriyya* is engaged in an established discourse on the relationship between speech and ethics, a point to which I will return later in the chapter.

Commentarial Reading and the "Apology" of Fiction

Turning now to al-Ḥarīrī's so-called apology for fiction, we should keep in mind this allusive practice and the role commentary plays in drawing attention to it. The passage in the *Ḥarīriyya* that has been interpreted as an "apology" for fiction appears near the end of the exordium. Al-Ḥarīrī expresses his concern that his "babbling" may backfire on him, even if his intentions are good. He quotes a passage from the Quran about that very sort of poor sinner who believes they are doing good but whose deeds lead them to perdition (Q 18.103). So far, the situation seems quite dire, but al-Ḥarīrī then extricates himself by anticipating those divergent responses to his text. In other words, he puts forward a typology of readers through which he expresses his robust understanding of textual multiplicity.

Al-Ḥarīrī's ideal reader, he says, is one who "scrutinizes things with the eye of his intellect (*naqada al-ashyā' bi-ʿayn al-maʿqūl*)." Such a person will "classify these *maqāmas* as things that impart knowledge (*ifādāt*) and will consider them like the invented stories (*mawḍūʿāt*) regarding beasts and inanimate objects (*al-ʿajmawāt wa-l-jamādāt*)."[18] What does al-Ḥarīrī mean by this rather cryptic allusion? Much of the rest of the chapter will be engaged in unpacking this passage, but first we should see who else is in the typology of readers. Al-Ḥarīrī admits there will be readers who defend him out of admiration or prudence, but he also knows that there will be those who attack him. He enumerates these sorts of critics. There is "an ignorant simpleton" who simply does not understand, as well as "a spiteful man who feigns ignorance and will disparage me for this composition, claiming that it is illicit in God's law." Al-Ḥarīrī goes on to ask whether one can find fault in someone composing stories "for instruction, not for falsification (*al-tanbīh lā li-l-tamwīh*)."[19] In short, al-Ḥarīrī claims that there is an edificatory role for the *Ḥarīriyya*, much like there is for animal stories, but some critics fail to recognize the text's salutary effects out of either spite or ignorance. The typology or hierarchy of readers now looks something like this:

1. The ignorant simpleton.
2. The spiteful reader who feigns ignorance, claiming it is illicit in God's law.
3. The prudent reader who pardons the author.
4. The admirer who defends the author.
5. The ideal reader who uses his intellect and reads them like stories of animals.

According to Jaakko Hämeen-Anttila and Rina Drory, this apology is simply a misdirection, which al-Ḥarīrī is forced to undertake due to the "venomous opposition" to fiction that he faced among his readers. As Hämeen-Anttila puts it, this passage "does not provide us with a key for reading his *maqāmas*" because it would have been impossible for al-Ḥarīrī to be honest and say: "I wrote them simply for entertainment and for making myself famous."[20] The fictional, entertaining element therefore supposedly needed to be smuggled in under the cover of didacticism, which is, after all, quite unliterary. According to Rina Drory, the hostility toward fiction was so great that the "the fictional world" and "self-proclaimed fictionality" in the *maqāma* genre was "gradually reduced to a mere skeleton." The supposed triumph of form over content, discussed already in Chapter 1, is framed in Drory's work as the result of Arabic's "normative poetics." Due to these normative pressures, the *maqāma* "failed to fulfil a creative role in the dynamics of Arabic literature." According to Drory, authors needed to be "very careful to relate their works to well-accepted literary traditions of the fables of *Kalīla wa-Dimna* . . . to prove the legitimacy of their writings."[21]

These claims strike me as strained interpretations of al-Ḥarīrī's typology of readers. If there truly was a widespread, pious suspicion or prohibition of fictional writing, and if those hostile readers needed to be placated, then why would al-Ḥarīrī describe those readers as spiteful and ignorant? These insults hardly seem like an attempt to placate critics. Would those readers whom he insulted truly be convinced by the subsequent invitation to read the *Ḥarīriyya* as animal stories? I would wager not. It would appear more plausible that al-Ḥarīrī's typology of readers includes a meaningful, intertextual gesture to stories about animals. As was the case with the allusion to al-Jāḥiẓ's *Book of Clarity* at the beginning of the exordium, al-Ḥarīrī's typology of readers is engaged in a citational game. In other words, I would suggest that the "apology" (really a typology) *does* offer us a particular kind of key that unlocks a particular mode of reading the text. But what kind of key is it? And what does it mean to interpret the *Ḥarīriyya* as one interprets animal stories? To answer that question, the commentators offer helpful points of departure.

Some medieval commentators, such as the Andalusian al-Sharīshī, suggest that this passage in the *Ḥarīriyya* about talking animals refers to *Kalīla wa-Dimna*, a collection of stories of Sanskrit origin about talking animals and fictional human beings. *Kalīla wa-Dimna* entered Arabic in the second/eighth century, and it was widely cited, discussed, and imitated, so it would be reasonable to assume that al-Ḥarīrī might have had *Kalīla wa-Dimna* in mind. According to the repressive hypothesis, al-Ḥarīrī only sought to associate his *maqāma*s with a venerable text like *Kalīla wa-Dimna* to defend his ostensibly offensive fictional endeavor. The repressive hypothesis has thus foreclosed any intertextual readings of the *Ḥarīriyya* and *Kalīla wa-Dimna*. If we examine these animal stories, however, it turns out that they have certain obvious features in common with the *Ḥarīriyya*. As we will see, the text takes up themes of eloquence, deception, and discovery in ways that suggest a particular interpretive key to reading the *Ḥarīriyya*. Modern scholars often refer to *Kalīla wa-Dimna* as an example of "mirror for princes" literature or, more broadly, advice literature.[22] Al-Sharīshī does seem to imply that there is a certain practical knowledge that can be gained from reading the *Ḥarīriyya*. In short, al-Sharīshī claims that what the *Ḥarīriyya* has in common with animal stories is that both offer the readers "experiences of the world (*tajārib al-dunyā*)" that might sharpen their intellects without subjecting them to actual risk.[23]

The Poetics of Virtual Experience

The poetics of virtual experience is the name I have given to the theorizations of fictionality that link the *Ḥarīriyya*, *Kalīla wa-Dimna*, and other texts that provide practical knowledge of the world without the risks of experiencing it firsthand. Authors prior to al-Ḥarīrī and commentators after him recognized that various texts, from stories about talking animals to fictional stories about imaginary humans to dubious anecdotes about historical figures could all provide the reader with a kind of practical wisdom. This poetics of virtual experience is not theorized in any one place, but if one draws together references from texts that appear to us to be part of quite distinct genres, it becomes possible to see how fictionality was not everywhere condemned as tantamount to lying but could be considered salutary and meaningful.

The poetics of virtual experience offers one possible way of reading the longest animal story in *Kalīla wa-Dimna*, which also gives the collection of tales its name. It tells the tale of two jackals named Kalīla and Dimna. The jackal named Dimna uses his cleverness and his eloquent wisdom to become a close adviser to the lion king. Although his brother Kalīla advises him against getting involved in politics, Dimna seeks out the lion to whom he offers his services. The lion, it turns out, has become afraid of a loud bellowing sound. The lion imagines that the loudness of the sound indicates the largeness of the creature's body. Dimna explains to the lion that not every sound ought to be feared, and, to drive his point home, he tells the story of the hungry fox who came upon a drum hanging from a tree. In this story, the fact that this drum was making such a loud sound made the fox believe that there would be plenty of meat inside, only to be sorely disappointed after all his efforts to crack it open to discover that it was hollow. This little story suggests that appearances and observable sounds can be deceiving. Having narrated this story about the fox to the lion, Dimna explains that he "coined this parable (*ḍarabtu laka hādhā al-mathal*)" in hopes that the lion would send him to investigate the sound, which he does.[24] Dimna discovers that the sound is coming from a harmless bull, which he reports to the lion, and the lion invites the bull to come to his realm. Eventually, the bull supplants Dimna as the lion's closest adviser and companion, frustrating Dimna, who uses his cunning to turn the bull and the lion against one another. Once again, he uses illustrative parables of varying lengths to make his point, this time to deceive the lion and the bull to the point that they fight, and the lion kills his friend the bull.[25]

Dimna and others in this story use short didactic stories or parables (*amthāl*, sing. *mathal*) to convince their audiences to follow particular courses of action. Stories have a rhetorical force. The problem is that even though these didactic stories appear wise, they are sometimes self-serving. Dimna uses stories about those who fail to act in a timely manner to urge the lion to preemptively strike the bull before it is too late, when in fact, Dimna is actually trying to deceive the lion to cover up his own deceptions and convince the lion to kill his friend hastily. He also urges the lion to heed his advisers—namely, himself. This piece of advice might be wise in one circumstance and foolish in another, depending on the worthiness of the adviser.[26] Dimna's deviousness inheres in his ability to mobilize wise words to achieve his own destructive ends. The lion trusts Dimna's advice even when he initially doubts it because Dimna's self-serving advice is framed as prudent wisdom. The lion's failure to see beyond the surface level and interrogate Dimna's interests is also a failure in *reading*. The lion is, in other words, an easy target because he cannot see that wise words can be put to devious ends. He is too easily swayed by stories. When Ibn al-Muqaffaʿ adapted *Kalīla wa-Dimna* from Middle Persian into Arabic, he added an epilogue in which Dimna is put on trial. However, Dimna's trial is not a moralizing tale about just desserts. Dimna immediately derails the trial with his rhetorical skills, and it is only through extralegal machinations, led by the lion's more politically adept mother, that Dimna receives his comeuppance.

The parallels between *Kalīla wa-Dimna* and the *Ḥarīriyya* are now relatively clear. The trickster Abū Zayd, like Dimna, manipulates his audiences through language, and the characters who fail to see through the rhetorical performances are doomed to fall into error. There are certainly differences between the two texts as well. Whereas Dimna deploys parables, Abū Zayd dazzles his audience with his eloquent performances in various Arabic poetic and prose genres. The courtroom scenes in the *Ḥarīriyya*, like Dimna's trial, show how Abū Zayd can bend the machinery of justice to his will. Al-Sharīshī, the Andalusian commentator, explains that al-Ḥarīrī invoked animal stories in his typology of readers because although they may not appear to accord with reality (i.e., animals do not speak), their hidden wisdom is beneficial:

> Al-Ḥarīrī was referring to books that are written in which the exterior sense has no reality whatsoever (*lā ḥaqīqata lahu fī al-ẓāhir*), but salutary wisdom has been included in its inner sense (*bāṭin*), like the book of *Kalīla wa-Dimna* and others that were composed on the tongues of what has neither intellect nor soul. Such is the case with the *Maqāmāt*. Even if its exterior sense is a lie (*kidhb*), its aim is to train, edify, and sharpen the intellect of the student. He might, therefore, acquire experiences of the world (*tajārib al-dunyā*) from the stories of al-Sarūjī, thus guarding against the calamities that might befall him and securing his intellect from negligence and trickery. In addition, it teaches the craft of writing prose and poetry, which is a most useful thing.[27]

Whereas the repressive hypothesis contends that medieval Muslim readers viewed fiction as tantamount to lying and therefore problematic, al-Sharīshī has no trouble stating that the *Ḥarīriyya* is meaningful while admitting that it may appear to be a lie on the surface. The text conveys apparent lies that contain true wisdom if one realizes that the text is not trying to convey information about something that actually happened.

Taken on its own, al-Sharīshī's reference to experiences (*tajārib*, sing. *tajriba*) might appear to be a kind of fuzzy appeal to the practical usefulness of stories. In fact, when al-Sharīshī's comments are placed within the broader tradition of sophisticated theorizing about storytelling, they appear considerably less fuzzy. For the poetics of virtual experience to come into view, we must piece together snippets from a vast assemblage of writings in the fields of philosophy, history, and *adab*. Our method here deliberately echoes the commentarial education of ʿAbd al-Laṭīf al-Baghdādī. Whereas commentary might appear to the uninitiated as opaque and nonsensical babble, it was a mode of bringing together intertextual references. To read with ʿAbd al-Laṭīf, we need the kind of commentarial reading that can piece together the significance of allusions to the broader tradition.

It is useful to begin with Ibn Sīnā or "Avicenna" (d. 427/1037), who was one of the most influential philosophers of all time. He also described the poetics of virtual experience, even as he dismissed it as inferior to poetry. In his massive philosophical summa, the *Kitāb al-Shifā'*, Ibn Sīnā addresses and reconfigures all the topics of philosophical inquiry from logic to metaphysics. In his book devoted to poetry and poetics, he draws on the centuries-long Arabic reception of Aristotle's *Poetics*. At the same time, he inflects the discussion with his innovative theory of modal existence in which he differentiated between those things that were impossible with regard to existence (like round squares), possible with regard to existence (like almost all of creation), and necessary with regard to existence (things that have already existed and the First Cause). For Ibn Sīnā, poetry is distinct from fabulated stories (*khurāfāt*), parables (*amthāl*), and stories (*qiṣaṣ*) because poetry induces the reader-listener's imagination about things that are possible (*mumkin*) or that have already happened and have thus become necessary (*ḍarūra*).

Ibn Sīnā states that activating the reader-listener's imagination (*takhyīl*) is the goal of poetry, which distinguishes it from books about nonexistent things like talking animals. He then clarifies this point by claiming that, even if *Kalīla wa-Dimna* were to be versified, it would not be considered poetry because its purpose is not to induce imagination but to "impart advice, which are the outcomes and experiences of certain scenarios that are ascribed to non-existent things." Imparting virtual experiences "has little need for meter," whereas poetry's ability to interact with the imagination seems to be augmented by its metrical quality.[28] For Ibn Sīnā, *Kalīla wa-Dimna* are fabulated stories because they traffic in "what exists only in speech (*wujūduhu fī al-qawl faqaṭ*)"—namely, talking animals. Nevertheless, Ibn Sīnā recognizes that fabulated stories serve a specific function—namely, to convey virtual experiences. At the same time, Ibn Sīnā insists that stories that convey virtual experience are most convincing when they are ascribed to figures who have actually existed. Stories are somewhat less convincing when told about invented human characters, whose existence is merely *possible*, and then even less so when placed in the mouths of talking animals, which are utterly invented.[29] In other words, it seems Ibn Sīnā is encouraging us to convey advice and virtual experience of the world through invented stories about people in the past or, barring that, about people with invented names (*qad ukhturiʿa lahu ism*).[30] Even as he denigrates books like *Kalīla wa-Dimna*, he offers a clear expression of the potential usefulness of fictional discourses.

Turning now to the century before al-Ḥarīrī, other authors of narrative prose likened their works to *Kalīla wa-Dimna*, presumably in response to the existence of sophisticated theories about virtual experience, ethics, and hermeneutics. Contrary to the repressive hypothesis, these authors do not condemn fictionality as a form of lying but rather celebrate the fact that their texts were fictional and could be seen as lying in a certain sense, presenting their texts as following the "*madhhab*" of *Kalīla wa-Dimna*. A *madhhab* refers to a "manner" or "way of going" and is also the word used to describe the different schools of thought in Islamic law. The first author to align his work explicitly with this *madhhab* was Ibn Buṭlān (d. 458/1066), who composed a text entitled *Daʿwat al-aṭibbāʾ* (*The Physicians' Dinner Party*), a prose narrative about an encounter between a miserly old doctor and a charlatan physician. Ibn Buṭlān, a Christian physician in Baghdad, describes his text as an "epistle . . . written according to the *madhhab* of *Kalīla wa-Dimna*, containing both jest that smiles to reveal earnestness and falsehood that expresses truth (*wa-bāṭil yanṭiq ʿan ḥaqq*)."[31] Drawing on the poetics of virtual experience, Ibn Buṭlān praises the outer falsehood of his fictional stories because they are employed to induce the reader to discover an inner truth (*ḥaqq*). Ibn Buṭlān adds a further paradoxical wrinkle to his intertextual gesture by making jest (*mazḥ*) reveal earnestness (*jidd*).

In other words, Ibn Buṭlān introduces his text as an ironized performance that implies the existence of a hierarchy of readers like the one laid out in the *Ḥarīriyya*'s introduction. As Linda Hutcheon has pointed out, irony produces hierarchies of knowledge in which those who "get" it possess a special kind of knowledge about what is *truly* going on: "Whether you see the power of irony working to exclude and to put down or, instead, to create 'amiable communities' between ironists and their intended audiences, the social nature of the participation in the transaction called 'irony' should not be ignored. From the point of view of the intending ironist, it is said that irony creates hierarchies: those who use it, then those who 'get' it and, at the bottom, those who do not."[32] The reader who "gets" *The Physicians' Dinner Party* will both laugh at the characters' naive seriousness and be privy to the text's underlying message. When Ibn Buṭlān's readers are asked to derive truth from falsehood, they are invited to engage in the work of interpretation and extracting truth. Once again, the *madhhab* of *Kalīla wa-Dimna* seems to be bound up with a kind of hermeneutical activity—seeing truth behind lies—that could train the reader to engage with the world in a more prudent manner.

The second author to refer to the *madhhab* of *Kalīla wa-Dimna* was Ibn Nāqiyā (d. 485/1092). He likewise refers to intellectual training as a feature of animal stories in the introduction to his *maqāma* collection, which appeared after al-Hamadhānī's but before al-Ḥarīrī's. Ibn Nāqiyā alludes to earlier authors who had taken a similar path (*madhhab*) by making their texts a form of training (*riyāḍa*) for the mind. According to Ibn Nāqiyā, this unnamed author, who may be al-Hamadhānī, is someone who produced a text that is "a challenge to the intellect that does not [require him] to shoot his arrow or send out his camels to scout for pasture."[33] In other words, it provides *virtual* experiences that do not require the reader to undertake risk in the real world. Ibn Nāqiyā goes on to say that the invented names in his *maqāma*s are equivalent to the "habit of poets when they write love poetry" and to the "sages when they place wisdom on the tongues of beasts."[34] He argues that this mode of storytelling is not proscribed (*maḥẓūr*), given that there are Arab proverbs, which are not referred to as lies, that are impossible to take seriously in their literal sense.[35] In this introductory passage, Ibn Nāqiyā distinguishes clearly between *lying* on the one hand and *invention* (including giving names to characters and making nonhumans speak) on the other. Thus, even before al-Ḥarīrī, we have a *maqāma* author thinking of his text in terms of *Kalīla wa-Dimna* and the poetics of virtual experience.

Prior to al-Ḥarīrī, the *maqāma* genre had already become firmly linked to animal stories, not to justify their existence to a hostile audience but to establish the hermeneutical approach that the *maqāma* demanded. This fact is given further credence in the organizational logic of an *adab* encyclopedia by al-Kalāʿī's (fl. sixth/twelfth century). Al-Kalāʿī was a near-contemporary of al-Ḥarīrī living in North Africa, but he was apparently unaware of the *Ḥarīriyya*. He was, however, aware of al-Hamadhānī's *maqāma*s, which he places in a chapter devoted to "*Maqāmāt* and Stories (*ḥikāyāt*)." These "stories" are, in fact, stories of talking animals, including some by al-Maʿarrī, who was discussed in Chapter 2. The fact that al-Kalāʿī places *maqāma*s in the same chapter with stories of talking animals suggests that there was a meaningful "*madhhab*" or "manner of writing" stories about both animals and humans that expected the reader to see beyond their artifice, irony, and fictionality of one kind or another.[36]

To review, we can see that both theorists like Ibn Sīnā and practitioners of *adab* like Ibn Nāqiyā and Ibn Buṭlān understood that a particular kind of writing that gave readers practical wisdom through virtual experiences of the world could be grouped together with *Kalīla wa-Dimna*. The markers of this grouping were not found in a work's formal features. Rather, all these texts were designed to provide the reader with virtual experiences of *reading* the world around them through the practice of reading and interpreting narratives. As it happens, *adab* authors were not the only ones to find the poetics of virtual experience useful.

Historiography and the Poetics of Virtual Experience

Historians in the century before al-Ḥarīrī also drew on the poetics of virtual experience to understand the usefulness of history and to differentiate their own stories about the past from the mere entertainments of other storytellers. Miskawayh (d. 421/1030) was a contemporary of Ibn Sīnā who studied both history and philosophy and composed works in both disciplines. In his history, *Tajārib al-Umam wa-Taʿāqub al-Himam* (*The Experiences of Communities and the Succession of Ambitions*), he discusses the notion of virtual experience with more specificity than we find in the works of his fellow philosopher Ibn Sīnā or the *adab* authors who speak more generally about the *madhhab* of *Kalīla wa-Dimna*. In particular, Miskawayh sheds light on the "virtual" aspect of the poetics of virtual experience. Although Miskawayh admits that some stories about the past are mere evening entertainments (*asmār*), he wishes to differentiate his own work from this form of amusement. Whereas other works might be unconcerned with separating the useful, exemplary stories from the entertaining ones, Miskawayh's account of the past was devoted to a kind of narrative usefulness.[37] Miskawayh says that reading about the events in the past can provide the reader with the experience of lifetimes not lived. These are not personal experiences but ones that are experienced "virtually" through narrative.

> I found that for this kind of event, if one knows an example similar to it that occurred in the past or an experience (*tajriba*) of a forebearer, then it can be taken as an example to be followed, which warns against what caused trouble to a people and encourages one to hold fast to what caused happiness to them. The matters of this world resemble one another (*innā umūr al-dunyā mutashābiha*), and its circumstances match each other. Everything of this type that a

person memorizes, it is as if it is his own experience (*ka'annahu tajārib lahu*) . . . as if he had lived the entirety of that era.[38]

Given that the events of this world recur in ways that resemble one another, being able to gain experience from the lives of others can make one worldly-wise beyond one's years.

Miskawayh also enumerates some examples of these events, such as "the subterfuges (*ḥiyal*) of war and the tricks (*makā'id*) of men," both those strategies that were successful and those that backfired on their perpetrators.[39] Here again, it becomes apparent that the discourse on virtual experiences is closely linked to the political problem of managing and deploying political maneuvers, some of which involve deception.[40] Again and again in *Kalīla wa-Dimna*, we see Dimna and other characters using their rhetorical skills to induce other characters to believe that their advice is wise, generous, and altruistic, even when that is not always the case. It is a crucial political skill to read and interpret the subterfuges of politics *and* to be capable of deploying successful subterfuges oneself.

The discussion of the poetics of virtual experience in both historical works and the *madhhab* of *Kalīla wa-Dimna* allows us to see how authors and readers understood these two kinds of texts to be closely related. In fact, in the decades after al-Ḥarīrī's death, historians writing in Persian would make this connection explicit. Ibn Funduq (d. 565/1169–70) wrote in his *Tārīkh-i Bayhaq* that readers of history are mistaken if they dismiss stories of the past because they are not completely "factual" but rather contain invented stories (*mawḍūʿāt va-muftarayāt*). They ought to know that "the stories that are in *Kalīla va-Dimna*, which are placed on the tongues of animals, are invented to provide benefits and experiences (*tajārib*), and are useful and acceptable."[41] As Julie Scott Meisami has demonstrated, Persian historiography presents itself here as a mode of edifying narrative that may also be entertaining. It is a guide to attaining "wisdom and virtue."[42] This framework for history is not uncommon in the Persian and Arabic historiographical tradition. The Timurid historian Mīrkhānd (d. 903/1498) contends that fabricated stories that are believed neither by their authors nor their listeners can nevertheless "provide incalculable profits and advantages."[43] Among the benefits of history that he lists is gaining experience (*tajruba*) through the experiences of others, which adds to one's own immediate experience.[44]

As Andrew McLaren has pointed out, it is almost certainly the case that Ibn Funduq was familiar with the *Ḥarīriyya* and its commentary tradition.

Ibn Funduq is reported to have written a commentary entitled *Sharḥ Mushkilāt al-Maqāmāt al-Ḥarīriyya* (*The Commentary on Difficult Words in the Ḥarīriyya*), which does not apparently survive.[45] Ibn Funduq could not have seen al-Sharīshī's commentary, which makes an explicit argument for reading the *Ḥarīriyya* within the poetics of virtual experience, because it had not yet begun circulating outside of the Islamic West. However, he may well have been familiar with the critiques of Ibn al-Khashshāb, who wrote the *Corrections* to the *Ḥarīriyya* that were discussed in detail in the previous chapter. Ibn Funduq's defense of history, which he admits contains a mixture of true information and invented stories, can be read as an oblique rebuttal to Ibn al-Khashshāb's critique of al-Ḥarīrī's so-called "apology for fiction," to which we now turn.

Ibn al-Khashshāb's Critiques

Given that there is such a widespread and sophisticated discourse on fictional stories that does not condemn them as lies but frames them as sources of practical wisdom, it no longer seems tenable to suggest that there was a widespread hostility toward all forms of fictional writing. There were, however, some scholars who were hostile toward fictional narratives about humans. An example of this view can be found in Ibn al-Khashshāb's vehement critiques of al-Ḥarīrī's typology of readers and his invitation to read the *Ḥarīriyya* like animal stories. Ibn al-Khashshāb's polemics seem to be outliers, but they have been taken in previous scholarship as representative of Islamic attitudes more broadly. As was demonstrated in the previous chapter, Ibn al-Khashshāb's critiques of the *Ḥarīriyya* on philological grounds were not well received and were deemed a kind of miserly interpretation of the text. It is crucial to understand Ibn al-Khashshāb's critiques and the rebuttals to them in order to appreciate some of the flaws in the repressive hypothesis.

Ibn al-Khashshāb argues that likening the *Ḥarīriyya* to the *madhhab* of animal stories is either "error or sophistry" because the stories of Abū Zayd are nothing like "the invented stories placed on the tongues of beasts."[46] According to Ibn al-Khashshāb, *Kalīla wa-Dimna* combines truth (*ṣidq*) and lying (*kidhb*), but it does so in a way that prevents lying from being confused with the truth. Everyone knows, he says, that a "a lion does not address a fox in a true sense (*ʿalā al-ḥaqīqa*)," and therefore the reader is immediately made aware of the fact that these stories are not intended to convey actual events. Rather, they are intended "only for experience (*bi-mujarrad al-tajriba*)," encouraging them to be prudent and to avoid errors in judgment.

The problem with the *Ḥarīriyya*, according to Ibn al-Khashshāb, is that the characters al-Ḥārith and Abū Zayd "could exist but did not, thus it is necessarily a lie that obscures the truth."[47] Abū Zayd is a realistic character and inhabits a world that is relatively recognizable. A reader could possibly misinterpret these stories as narratives of an actual eloquent man's exploits, instead of stories designed to impart experience. For Ibn al-Khashshāb, fictional stories must be patently unbelievable to be acceptable because the *Ḥarīriyya*'s mixture of the real and the fictional is misleading. When we take a broader view of the Arabic tradition, we find that Muslim historians who ostensibly were describing the past did not necessarily consider their work to be entirely "factual." As Ibn Funduq and Miskawayh point out, history itself is full of precisely the sort of mixture about which Ibn al-Khashshāb seems worried. Other historians like al-Ṭabarī (d. 310/923) took pains to point out that they were only transmitting what they had heard, not verifying the accuracy of the anecdotes they had collected.[48]

In a curious aside, Ibn al-Khashshāb adds that the invented rogue in the *Ḥarīriyya* is a lie "because the author does not assert his reality (*lā yaddaʿī ṣiḥḥatahu*)."[49] In other words, it would seem that the *Ḥarīriyya* is only a lie because al-Ḥarīrī fails to claim that his characters were real people. It is as if the bald assertion that Abū Zayd is a real, flesh-and-blood, historical figure would solve the whole problem. As it turns out, some readers did claim that Abū Zayd was real. Stories began circulating early in the sixth/twelfth century about al-Ḥarīrī's encounter with the "real" Abū Zayd, and these stories have been deployed by recent scholars as evidence of the repressive hypothesis. One of these stories states that al-Ḥarīrī encountered an eloquent beggar in the Banū Ḥarām quarter of Basra, after which al-Ḥarīrī met with his friends to recount the tale. In response, each of his companions claimed that he, too, had witnessed the very same beggar in his own local mosque in different guises. These stories of a "real" Abū Zayd, together with Ibn al-Khashshāb's critique, have played an outsize role in modern scholarship. They play a crucial role in Drory's claim that "official" Arabic literature, "governed by powerful religio-poetic norms, consistently claims the historicity of its texts" because fiction was unacceptable and condemned as lies.[50] (It has also been falsely asserted that Ibn Barrī used this story of the "real" Abū Zayd to rebut Ibn al-Khashshāb, but this is based on a faulty edition of the text that has only recently been superseded.)[51] Again, an interpretation of this anecdote as something that supports the repressive hypothesis seems strained. Even if we accept that al-Ḥarīrī actually met a beggar named Abū Zayd al-Sarūjī, the activity of round-robin storytelling suggests that his friends were playing an imaginative game. Furthermore, the story makes clear that al-Ḥarīrī only composed a single *maqāma* based on this supposed encounter, writing the rest of the *maqāmas* after the readers of his first *maqāma* demanded more. As we saw already in the previous chapter, Ibn al-Khashshāb hardly represented the mainstream philological position in the sixth/twelfth century. His philological *Corrections* was ferociously criticized by his contemporaries and successors in the commentary tradition. It should therefore come as no surprise that his critique of al-Ḥarīrī's invitation to read his *maqāmas* like animal stories was subjected to criticism, particularly in light of the well-established "poetics of virtual experience" described above.

Al-Panjdīhī offers a full-throated rebuttal to Ibn al-Khashshāb's critique that is worth quoting and commenting on in detail because it rejects certain key features of the poetics of virtual experience and roots fictionality in the Islamic tradition. He begins by stating that lying is not permitted, whether or not it provides the reader with experience. This stands in contrast to Ibn al-Khashshāb, Ibn Funduq, and al-Sharīshī, who all admit that certain stories that are not literally true are nevertheless justifiable under the poetics of virtual experience. Al-Panjdīhī rejects that stance:

> If lying which is not mixed with truth is permitted, then Ibn al-Khashshāb is victorious on this issue and is permitted to claim his reward. But lying is forbidden according to the *sharīʿa*. It is vile and ugly by nature. It is an offense against justice and is associated with wickedness and depravity, whether or not it is mixed with truth and whether or not one acquires experience (*tajriba*) and awareness (*tayaqquẓ*). The one who lies is customarily derided and scorned. He is disgraced and laughed at according to good taste (*ẓarf*). He is called a liar in this world and is punished in the hereafter.[52]

It should be emphasized that al-Panjdīhī is defending the *Ḥarīriyya* in this passage and throughout his commentary, so he is setting up what he sees as the properly Islamic terms of debate. Lying is unacceptable, but this text is not lying. He goes on to argue that lying in animal fables is even worse.

> The one who lies upon the tongues of beasts (*yakdhib ʿalā lisān al-ʿajmāwāt*) and falsifies in the guise of inanimate objects (*yaftarī ʿalā al-jamādāt*) has aggravated his loss and exacerbated his insolence because it is impossible for [animals] to speak. They lack speech and understanding. Mockery attaches to such a person and calamity follows him due to the shame of being called a liar and the violent punishment [of the hereafter].[53]

This attack on lying is rather different from the opinions of Ibn al-Khashshāb and al-Sharīshī (who himself drew heavily on al-Panjdīhī). Both Ibn al-Khashshāb and al-Sharīshī accept certain forms of exterior lying that is nevertheless truthful when one looks beyond the surface level. Al-Panjdīhī, as he often does, turns to the hadith of the Prophet. In this case, he seeks to identify the only situations in which lying is acceptable and show, as he often does, that Ibn al-Khashshāb's critiques are not only incorrect but also thoroughly misguided and un-Islamic.

> An authentic hadith from the Prophet says that he said: "Lying is only appropriate in three situations: A husband lying to his wife to please her, restoring relations between people, and lying in war." It is clear that Ibn al-Khashshāb slandered [al-Ḥarīrī] falsely, deceitfully, and misleadingly. He dug a pit for someone else, but he fell into it himself.[54]

Al-Panjdīhī is relentless in his criticism of Ibn al-Khashshāb, pouring out scorn and pulling out all the rhetorical stops to show how the critic was hoist by his own petard. When Ibn al-Khashshāb admits that lying is permissible, al-Panjdīhī seizes on the point, emphasizing that lying is un-Islamic. Al-Panjdīhī's rebuttal highlights for us the irony that Ibn al-Khashshāb's critique has been seen in modern scholarship as an expression of *the* Islamic view on fiction. Al-Panjdīhī also points out that there is no reason to assume that stories about talking animals are *necessarily* lies. The Prophet himself narrated stories that included talking animals, and these are sound reports that, according to al-Panjdīhī, "Muslims cannot deny."[55] Thus, al-Panjdīhī accuses Ibn al-Khashshāb of being un-Islamic because the latter proposes a hermeneutic in which any story about talking animals must be immediately dismissed as a lie.

Al-Panjdīhī's rejection of lying is not, however, a rejection of all forms of fictionality, as we can see from his response to al-Ḥarīrī's typology of readers. Al-Ḥarīrī invites his ideal reader to classify his *maqāmas* as both "invented stories (*mawḍūʿāt*)" and "things imparting knowledge (*ifādāt*)."[56] Glossing the first of these two terms, al-Panjdīhī does not shy away from the idea that the *Ḥarīriyya* consists of a certain kind of narrative invention. In fact, he explains that such stories are "fabricated (*ufturiya*)," a rather loaded term that is often used in the Quran to refer to the lies concocted about God by unbelievers (Q 3.94, 4.48, 6.21, etc.). Al-Panjdīhī adds that al-Ḥarīrī identifies his *maqāmas* as belonging to the category of fabricated stories like those of "beasts that have no speech, such as the stories of the lion, the jackal, the fox, and others in the book of *Kalīla wa-Dimna*."[57] Taken together with al-Panjdīhī's condemnation of lying, he seems to be implying that the *Ḥarīriyya* and *Kalīla wa-Dimna* consist of invented stories but not *lies*. To understand this distinction, we can turn to al-Panjdīhī's gloss of the term *ifādāt*, mentioned above. I have translated this term as "things imparting knowledge," which is to say that al-Ḥarīrī is claiming that his *maqāmas* are not mere entertainments but are beneficial to the reader. Al-Panjdīhī explains the term by recalling what immediately precedes this term in al-Ḥarīrī's exordium. There, he states that ideal readers must read with the "eye of the intellect." Those readers will "classify these *maqāmāt* among the things imparting knowledge." Al-Panjdīhī explains: "This means that someone who, with the eye of the intellect, examines these *maqāmāt* and contemplates these words ought to benefit from their secrets, seek illumination from their lights, follow the example of their forged foundations, slurp their refreshing meanings, be quenched with the sweetness of their expressions, writhe at the difficulty of their sermons, heed the hints of their sincere counsel, and be devoted to the treasures of their virtues."[58] As can be seen from this passage, al-Panjdīhī's "glosses" and "rebuttals" are far from dry and desultory. They are rhetorical performances in themselves, and here we see his insistence that the *Ḥarīriyya* requires a particular kind of reading that digs into its subtleties. Readers must use their intellects to uncover those benefits. One cannot simply take the stories at face value, but that does not mean that they are lies. Al-Panjdīhī does not specifically summon the poetics of virtual experience, but he does claim that there are benefits to reading certain kinds of invented stories, provided that they are read in the right way.

Given that al-Panjdīhī seems to accept that the *Ḥarīriyya* is a collection of invented stories but *not* lies, did he believe that Abū Zayd was a real human who walked the earth? The answer is complicated because al-Panjdīhī gives two distinct and seemingly mutually exclusive explanations for the reality (or not) of Abū Zayd, and this leads us to consider some theories of fictionality that lie outside of the poetics of virtual experience. Al-Panjdīhī says both that Abū Zayd was a real person and that al-Ḥārith b. Hammām is an everyman. Al-Panjdīhī's first explanation, replete with an *isnād* back to the author, relies on the biographical explanation that I have described above and that has been wrongly attributed to Ibn Barrī. According to this story, al-Ḥarīrī had met an eloquent beggar called Abū Zayd in Basra and shared the story with his friends, who then told their own stories of encountering this same eloquent beggar.[59] Al-Panjdīhī's source for the story is none other than Ibn al-Naqūr, an early authority on the *Ḥarīriyya*. In fact, Ibn al-Naqūr had been present at the first public reading of the *Ḥarīriyya* and had given the young ʿAbd al-Laṭīf his *isnād* back to the author. For that reason, his biographical anecdote carries special weight.

Al-Panjdīhī's second explanation is difficult to square with the first. It suggests an allegorical explanation for the name of the narrator al-Ḥārith b. Hammām. The word al-Ḥārith means literally "one who tills or sows," and al-Hammām can also mean one who is constantly concerned. In a passage not quoted by al-Sharīshī, al-Panjdīhī explains that al-Ḥarīrī "called himself al-Ḥārith, and he called his father Hammām because everyone without exception engages in cultivation, whether it be for the hereafter or the temporal world . . . and everyone is concerned with his religion or with this temporal world." What is remarkable is that al-Panjdīhī goes even further, making al-Ḥārith into a kind of everyman figure. He says that "every person is Ḥārith b. Hammām and Hammām b. Ḥārith in reality, though not in name."[60] Al-Panjdīhī also quotes hadith to the effect that Ḥārith and Hammām are "the most truthful names."

Taking all these bits of commentary together, it seems that al-Panjdīhī's point is that these stories are *true* without being *historically true*. Names do not need to refer to specific people but can refer instead to inner realities. This theory may seem similar to al-Sharīshī's suggestion that the exterior sense is a lie but that the inner sense is true, much like the stories of *Kalīla wa-Dimna*. However, there is a subtle but important distinction. Al-Panjdīhī's theory of fictionality does not admit that the outward form is a lie. Rather, we might surmise that he sees the outward form of these stories as the perceptible reality, which points to an inner reality. Al-Panjdīhī's solution to the identity of the named narrator is to argue that al-Ḥārith b. Hammām is the author's avatar but that this avatar also speaks to the universal human condition of self-cultivation. Al-Panjdīhī's claim that every person cultivates "either for the hereafter or for the temporal world" suggests that the *Ḥarīriyya* is, for al-Panjdīhī, a collection of allegorical tales about the universal human condition.

At the same time, we should be careful about trying to develop unified theories of fictionality on the basis of seemingly contradictory pieces of commentary. Al-Sharīshī, for example, puts forward multiple options when considering the relationship between narrative and reality, and he does so in different parts of his commentary. In his commentary on al-Ḥarīrī's introduction, al-Sharīshī presents the story of al-Ḥarīrī encountering Abū Zayd in the mosque, but then he offers a second option later on in his commentary on the first *maqāma*. Al-Sharīshī begins there by pointing to his earlier gloss, noting that "if it is believed that [Abū Zayd] was a specific person (*insān bi-ʿaynihi*), as has already been said in the introduction, then that is sufficient." However, al-Sharīshī then goes on to give an alternative explanation "if it is not believed." He then suggests that the name Abū Zayd may have some other meaning. The name Abū Zayd literally means "Father of Zayd," but it could be considered to be the byname for some nonhuman entity. For instance, al-Sharīshī suggests that some philologists understand Abū Zayd to be a name for old age, and al-Ḥarīrī "usually" describes Abū Zayd as being marked by old age and decrepitude. Alternatively, al-Sharīshī tells us that Abū Zayd may be a stand-in for fickle fate (*dahr*) because al-Ḥarīrī describes Abū Zayd "in ways that are only appropriate for fickle fate," pointing to a passage in *maqāma* #21.[61] If Abū Zayd is not a specific person who actually walked the earth but a kind of allegorical representation of fickle fate and old age, then how should we understand the narrator al-Ḥārith? Al-Sharīshī resorts to the everyman explanation that al-Ḥarīrī had called himself by the name al-Ḥārith b. Hammām "because he is among those who cultivate and have cares."[62]

In al-Sharīshī, the everyman al-Ḥārith that we found in al-Panjdīhī has been transformed into an avatar of the author who confronts fickle fate and old age in the person of Abū Zayd. Fate deceives and befriends al-Ḥārith throughout the course of the *Ḥarīriyya*. Although this allegorical reading is difficult to maintain throughout the text, that seems not to be the point for al-Sharīshī. He offers multiple, overlapping, and seemingly contradictory interpretations of the named characters, all of which coexist unproblematically with the poetics of virtual experience that he presented earlier, in which these stories are designed to function as animal fables that train the reader to avoid the pitfalls and deceitful dealings of this world.

None of these commentaries puts forward an interpretation of the text as a whole, but neither are these discussions atomistic. Al-Sharīshī links together the first and the twenty-first *maqāmas* to provide a citation supporting the interpretation of Abū Zayd as fate. Al-Sharīshī's glosses and interpretive digressions are provisional interpretive claims that offer different ways into the text for different sorts of readers. Al-Sharīshī admits that some readers will not believe the story of a real-world Abū Zayd and thus offers multiple alternatives for understanding Abū Zayd as an allegorical figure. The commentarial mode of reading exemplified here is not about providing a single, coherent literary reading of the text or a synthesizing interpretation. Rather, the commentators open up several avenues of interpretation. One can understand the *Ḥarīriyya* as a work about eloquence (*bayān*), as the allusion to al-Jāḥiẓ might suggest, but one can equally well consider how these fictional encounters with Abū Zayd provide opportunities to reflect on the vicissitudes of fate, just as one can use this text as a kind of virtual experience of life's pitfalls to protect oneself against those very same vicissitudes.

Semiotic Allegories: An Alternative Theory of Fictionality

Commentary offers a cacophony of interpretive possibilities, but it also points the way forward for future authors who picked up these theories of fictionality for their own projects. In closing this chapter, I would like to take a closer look at the allegorical theory of fictionality that explains the named characters as semiotic allegories for fickle fate, old age, the everyman, and so on. I propose that we understand these allegories as "semiotic" because they draw on the philological tradition. Al-Ḥārith is an everyman because the word "*ḥārith*" refers to one who cultivates, a condition that concerns all human beings in one way or another. Similarly, al-Sharīshī cites the philological tradition when saying that Abū Zayd is a proper name that is used as a byname for old age. Calling this commentarial analysis a semiotic allegory draws attention to the Arabic philological tradition of discourse around the relationship between the verbal form of a particular word (*lafẓ*) and the underlying meaning of that word (*maʿnā*).

The semiotic allegory became a theory of fictionality with a long afterlife that extended far beyond the *Ḥarīriyya* and its commentaries. The famous Ḥanbalī thinker Ibn al-Jawzī (d. 597/1200) composed a *maqāma* collection in the second half of the sixth/twelfth century, and he, like al-Panjdīhī, takes this semiotic approach to fictional discourse. Ibn al-Jawzī's *Maqāmāt* is not usually considered part of the *maqāma* tradition proper. Instead, Ibn al-Jawzī's and al-Zamakhsharī's (d. 538/1144) *maqāma* collections are considered, when they are considered at all, part of a "pious *maqāma*" tradition.[63] As we have seen, al-Panjdīhī understands the *Ḥarīriyya* to be a pious text par excellence when he situates it squarely within an Islamic textual universe. To a reader looking at the formal qualities of Ibn al-Jawzī's *Maqāmāt*, his *maqāma*s read much more like a collection of sermons than a series of picaresque narratives. However, Ibn al-Jawzī's introduction evinces an interest in theories of fictionality by discussing the extent to which animals can or cannot be personified. By claiming that talking animals represent an acceptable form of metaphorical speech, he is participating in the same semiotic account of fictional discourse that was compelling for Ḥarīrian commentators.

Ibn al-Jawzī argues in the exordium of his *Maqāmāt* that allusive and metaphorical language is superior to language that is self-evident.[64] He points to the exempla (*amthāl*) in the Quran as proof that this is the case. To make the case that allusive language is especially eloquent, he notes that the Quran personifies inanimate objects. For instance, the Quran refers to "a wall that desires to collapse" (Q 18:77) and to "the craftiness of the night and the day" (Q 34:33).[65] The Quran's status as the highest form of Arabic eloquence makes these desiring walls and crafty times of day a compelling justification for fictional personification. If walls can desire, could not animals speak? Could we not give human names to abstract ideas?

Moving from the Quran to the precedent set by wise people in general, Ibn al-Jawzī points out that the sages continuously told stories about animals and then launches into an extensive account of animal stories told by Arabs and pious forebears. Ibn al-Jawzī's citations and mode of argumentation here echo al-Panjdīhī and another late sixth/twelfth-century commentator on the *Ḥarīriyya*, Abū al-Khayr Salāma b. ʿAbd al-Bāqī al-Anbārī (d. 590/1193–94) who draws attention to *Kalīla wa-Dimna* but also discusses the pre-Islamic lore about animals and the personification of the moon and trees in some detail.[66]

Nowhere does Ibn al-Jawzī explicitly discuss *Kalīla wa-Dimna*, but his deliberate avoidance of the most obvious collection of animal stories in favor of "authentically Arabic" animal stories may be seen as an implicit reaction against the Persianate heritage that *Kalīla wa-Dimna* represented. Ibn al-Jawzī, like his near contemporary and commentator on the *Ḥarīriyya* al-ʿUkbarī (d. 616/1219),[67] does not mention these translated fables and instead focuses on the animal stories that are attributed to the Bedouin Arabs. Their venerable Arabic language possessed abounding metaphorical resources, and to deny that abundance is associated with miserliness. As Ibn al-Jawzī says: "There was a group of those who are lacking in their knowledge regarding the ampleness of language. When they heard someone say about a thing, 'That is nothing,' they would get angry and say, 'You have contradicted reality (*khālafta al-ḥaqīqa*).' This is ignorance on their part regarding the permissibility of metaphor."[68] The phrase "that is nothing" is, when taken literally, a lie when it refers to something that exists. For Ibn al-Jawzī, those who would denigrate this form of communicative speech—one that is easily understood by the listener as a meaningful, figurative expression—are simply lacking knowledge of Arabic's ample resources.

Ibn al-Jawzī's concern with the ampleness of language is part of his justification for inventing a fictional human character in his *Maqāmāt* who is none other than a personification of the author's intellect (*ʿaql*). He gives his intellect the name Abū Taqwīm, meaning "the one who sets things straight" or "the one who awakens." This personified intellect takes the place of the eloquent rogue in Ibn al-Jawzī's *Maqāmāt*. Instead of performing eloquent ruses, the intellect delivers eloquent sermons on pious themes. These scenes depicting Ibn al-Jawzī's conversations with Abū Taqwīm are justified, according to the author, because they are figurative representations of Ibn al-Jawzī's experience when he is "alone with the intellect in the house of thought."[69] What we would classify as fictional narrative is, for Ibn al-Jawzī, a metaphorical representation of a nonmaterial reality. Once again, nowhere is there any hint of hostility toward anything we would recognize as the modern category of "fiction." The semiotic account of fictional discourse situates the *Maqāmāt* within an Islamic ethical tradition and an Arabic linguistic tradition.

Far from being allergic to fiction, the Muslim authors and readers we have encountered in this chapter developed sophisticated theories for understanding the relationship between imaginative narrative and actual reality.

Fictional texts like the *Ḥarīriyya* were not condemned as lies on religious grounds by most readers and commentators. Rather, commentators like al-Panjdīhī condemned the critics of the *Ḥarīriyya* for being un-Islamic, just as Ibn al-Jawzī condemned critics of his mode of allegorical writing for misunderstanding the capaciousness of Arabic. In doing so, these commentators were following another intertextual allusion at the very end of al-Ḥarīrī's exordium, in which he claims that his work is intended as "instruction or a guidance to a straight path (*ṣirāṭ mustaqīm*)."[70] This is an allusion to the opening chapter of the Quran, which is central to Islamic prayer and in which the supplicant asks God to "guide us on the straight path" (Q 1:6). Al-Ḥarīrī seems to be suggesting that his *maqāmas* might offer the kind of Islamic guidance that one might expect to come from the Quran. In the next chapter, we will see how the embrace of the *Ḥarīriyya* as an Islamic text went even further, to the point that it was considered Quran-like in its inimitable eloquence.

Chapter 6

The Poetics of Islamic *Adab*

In October of 1229 AD (626 AH), ʿAbd al-Laṭīf al-Baghdādī sat in a mosque in Aleppo surrounded by students. He was now in his late sixties, an established scholar who had lived a rich life. He had survived the plague, experienced scholarly rivalries, and finally settled in Aleppo in his waning years. A colleague sat nearby, reading aloud the *Ḥarīriyya* in the presence of ʿAbd al-Laṭīf so that the gathered company could receive a chain of transmission through him back to Ibn al-Naqūr, who had heard the text in the presence of al-Ḥarīrī. Some of those in attendance at that Aleppan mosque had brought their sons, just as ʿAbd al-Laṭīf's father had brought his young son to hear the text when he was only six years old.[1] For those in attendance, there were several aspects of this event in October that were remarkable. They were in the presence of the manuscript that we know as *Cairo Adab m105*, a manuscript that had been present at the first public reading over a century earlier, and they were seated before a man who had a personal connection to that first reading. The thrill must have been immense.

What I wish to emphasize here is *where* this scene took place. It happened in a mosque. We know this because the attendance certificate produced for that session identifies a mosque in Aleppo as its location.[2] The sacred setting may come as a surprise to some, given that many modern scholars have assumed that medieval Muslim audiences (or at least piety-minded ones) would have found the *Ḥarīriyya* problematic and subversive to Islamic sensibilities. As Angelika Neuwirth puts it, the *Ḥarīriyya* "does not affirm the official law-and-order discourse of Islamic *ʿilm*, but dissects its underlying psychological layers, shifting the focus from religious norms to their conceptual opposite, the anti-norm, represented by play and fiction, *adab*."[3] This mode of reading insists on the secularity of *adab*. To read *adab* "as literature" in this manner is to conjure up a specter of fanatical piety as though it represents the medieval Islamic norm. Islam itself is posited as on the side of the reactionary catchphrase "law and order." As Michael Allan shows, this "specter of the fanatic" is one of the sinister Others against which secular literariness is defined.[4] Similarly, interpretations of the *Ḥarīriyya* that conjure up a hidebound, literalist Islamic piety enable modern critics to rescue the literary text from its unliterary readers and critics. Whereas world literature insists on reading texts like the *Ḥarīriyya* as a kind of secular literary endeavor, this chapter presents the Islamic readings of the text that appeared in the first century of the text's reception.

ʿAbd al-Laṭīf reading the *Ḥarīriyya* in the mosque invites us to reevaluate the relationship between Islam and *adab*. To quarantine playful and fictional texts and treat them as separate from Islam makes nonsense of the two earliest "programmatic" commentaries on the *Ḥarīriyya*, which both emphasize the text's Islamic credentials. Al-Muṭarrizī and al-Panjdīhī were introduced briefly in the "Dramatis Personae" at the beginning of this book. They both wrote their commentaries in the second half of the sixth/twelfth century and, I argue, considered the *Ḥarīriyya* to be a quintessentially Islamic book. In their view, it trains its readers to encounter God's word in the Quran, to understand its miraculousness, and to meditate on Islamic discourses like hadith.

In this chapter, I begin with an exploration of al-Muṭarrizī's thought, particularly the introduction to his commentary in which he sketches out a theory of poetics. Then the chapter turns to al-Panjdīhī, whose commentary is extremely digressive. Through these digressions, he situates the *Ḥarīriyya* within a realm of discourse and intertextuality that I call the "Islamic archive." The chapter then explores the *Ḥarīriyya*'s Islamic intertexts in Sufi poems and in the depictions of pious sermons in which pious ascetics confronted Muslim rulers with their injustices. In the conclusion of the chapter, we turn to the broader methodological question of what it means to be "Islamic" in the wake of Shahab Ahmed's magnum opus *What Is Islam?*, which has opened up a space for thinking about *adab* as Islamic, rather than as either un-Islamic or "Islamicate," a term introduced in the twentieth century by Marshall Hodgson to describe those more "secular" features of a culture that was imbued with Islamic language and ideas.

The Inimitable *Maqāmāt* of al-Ḥarīrī

Al-Muṭarrizī claims in the introduction to his commentary that the *Ḥarīriyya* is itself inimitable. He claims that it is possessed of *iʿjāz*, a word that usually refers to the Quran's miraculous inimitability and thus might come across as shocking to some readers. For readers unfamiliar with the Islamic tradition, the theological stakes of inimitability require some explanation. Beginning in the third/ninth century, the doctrine of *iʿjāz* emerged as a claim that the Quran could never be surpassed, although the precise reasons for this inimitability awaited further elaboration and debate in the centuries before al-Ḥarīrī. The doctrine has its basis in Quranic verses that challenge humans and jinn to invent something like the Quran. Their inability to do so is taken as evidence that the revelation is from God and not authored by a mere human.[5] In the course of Islamic history, several authors were accused of heresy because they were rumored to have either produced a competitive imitation of the Quran or to have dared to boast that they had surpassed it in eloquence.[6]

Al-Muṭarrizī does not claim that the *Ḥarīriyya* was an imitation of the Quran, but he does suggest that it is Quran-like in the way that he describes it. Al-Muṭarrizī says that the *Ḥarīriyya*'s "merits are without deficiency and its verses indicate its inimitability (*dallat ʿalā al-iʿjāz ayātuhu*)."[7] The word *āyāt* or "verses" is the word that one uses to describe the verses of the Quran, and it can also refer to marvels, miracles, and signs, and in al-Muṭarrizī's turn of phrase, it seems to encompass all of these at once. The words of al-Ḥarīrī's book are marvelous signs that prove that his book is inimitable.

If this does not seem radical and provocative enough, al-Muṭarrizī then goes further. He gives his readers an introduction to poetics that will allow them to realize the truth of his claims. What is striking is that al-Muṭarrizī's introduction to poetics is actually a series of quotations and paraphrases of two works by the foremost theoretician of Quranic inimitability of the fifth/eleventh century: ʿAbd al-Qāhir al-Jurjānī (d. 471 or 474/1078 or 1081). Al-Jurjānī, writing approximately half a century before al-Ḥarīrī composed his *Maqāmāt*, drew on his training as both a philologist and an Ashʿarī theologian to develop a poetics that would not only prove the Quran's innate aesthetic inimitability but also evaluate poetic excellence in human verse. Al-Jurjānī's two books on poetics are called *Dalā'il al-I'jāz* (*The Evidence of Inimitability*) and *Asrār al-Balāgha* (*The Secrets of Eloquence*).

Introducing his summary of Jurjānian poetics, al-Muṭarrizī addresses his readers to tell them that the purpose of this introduction to poetics is to "give you the touchstone of criticism and to throw you the reins of authority, so that you might distinguish between dross and gold."[8] Al-Muṭarrizī then seamlessly weaves together passages from al-Jurjānī's two books, a complex and sophisticated form of collation that I have discussed in some detail elsewhere.[9] For our purposes, it is simply important that his introduction presents Jurjānian poetics in a clear, concise, and systematic way.[10] Al-Muṭarrizī was obviously deeply familiar with al-Jurjānī's poetics. This might seem somewhat strange because al-Muṭarrizī himself was a member of the waning Muʿtazilī theological school, which had already lost considerable ground to al-Jurjānī's Ashʿarī school. Nevertheless, al-Muṭarrizī devoted much of his life and textual production in the realm of philology to transmitting and reformulating al-Jurjānī's ideas.[11]

It might be suggested that al-Muṭarrizī was using al-Jurjānī's theories to undermine their theological importance. After all, if al-Jurjānī's theories can prove that the *Ḥarīriyya* is inimitable just as much as it can prove the Quran inimitable, then perhaps Ashʿarī theology is not all it is cracked up to be. Indeed, early Muʿtazilīs had developed a different notion of Quranic inimitability, arguing that God had intervened and prevented anyone from imitating the Quran. However, by al-Muṭarrizī's time, this doctrine of divine diversion had been taken up by Shīʿī theologians, while prominent Muʿtazilīs like al-Qāḍī ʿAbd al-Jabbār (d. 415/1024) had already embraced the idea that the Quran's inimitability lay in its linguistic superiority and eloquence, which coincides with the Ashʿarī view.[12] In any case, al-Muṭarrizī evinces no hostility toward al-Jurjānī, so it seems more likely that he sees Jurjānian poetics as a perfect way to evaluate the *Ḥarīriyya*'s inimitable excellence.

At this point, it is worth giving a sketch of Jurjānian poetics to help us understand why al-Muṭarrizī might have seen the *Ḥarīriyya* as excellent and inimitable in Jurjānian terms. As Lara Harb has shown, al-Jurjānī emphasizes the importance of invoking wonder (*ʿajab*). But what kind of poetry can inspire wonder? For al-Jurjānī, it has to do with the pleasure of discovery. For example, a poet might say something like "I saw a lion" to express that they saw a brave person. It requires very little mental effort to understand this kind of metaphor because it involves a very straightforward substitution:

lion = brave person. This kind of metaphor is reducible to a simile (*tashbīh*) and expresses the idea that this person is *like* a lion in terms of their bravery. However, there are other forms of metaphorical language at a poet's disposal that are not so straightforward. For example, the poet Labīd (d. 40–42/660–63) describes his adventurous spirit in an evocative and complex way:

> I have ventured out on many a cold and windy morning,
> When the reins of the morning were in the hand of the north wind.[13]

This metaphor does not involve mere substitution. For al-Jurjānī, it is crucial that this kind of metaphor cannot be reduced to simile. Instead, it involves a kind of "borrowing," which is the root meaning for the Arabic term for metaphor—namely, *istiʿāra*. The wind borrows the notion of "hands" in order to take the "reins" of the morning. Neither the wind nor the morning properly possesses anything that could be represented by "hands" or "reins," which makes this metaphor irreducible to the simile's logic of substitution.

As al-Muṭarrizī puts it, paraphrasing al-Jurjānī: "Is it not clearly the case that Labīd has fashioned a hand for the north wind? It is known that there is no referent for which the hand acts as a substitute, as was the case in substituting the lion in place of the man."[14] In Jurjānian poetics, this nonreferential, nonsubstitutionary metaphor requires more effort on the part of the human intellect. It is therefore more pleasurable and more beautiful.[15] In al-Muṭarrizī's clarifying summary of a passage from al-Jurjānī, there are two types of comparative language: obvious (*ṣarīḥ*) and intellectual (*ʿaqlī*). If one simply compares things based on color, like a cheek to a rose, or on the basis of instinct, like comparing a lion to a man, there is no need for interpretation.[16]

For both al-Muṭarrizī and al-Jurjānī, it was important that the more sophisticated metaphors were only available to the more sophisticated sorts of people. Al-Muṭarrizī notes that "only someone who has a mind and whose insight rises above the class of the common folk (*al-ʿāmma*) can truly understand" the intellectual sorts of comparisons. By contrast, the comparisons like that of a cheek to a rose rely on mere sense perception, such that "every dolt and dummy shares in understanding them."[17] The experience of wonder (*ʿajab*) is not available equally to all comers in Jurjānian poetics. The more wonder-inducing poetry is only available to an elite. Moreover, those elites mark themselves out by way of their understanding. Recall that ʿAbd al-Laṭīf al-Baghdādī, back in Chapter 2, had a disastrous first lesson because he failed to express wonder at his teacher's commentary. The other students, more advanced than he was, registered their understanding of the teacher's complex, advanced commentary through an outward display of affect. In doing so, they marked themselves out as worthy students, whereas ʿAbd al-Laṭīf was exposed as an underprepared novice who needed training in the commentarial tradition in order to appreciate (in both senses of the term, to understand and enjoy) the erudite performance of his teacher.

As discussed above, poetics had theological consequences, and one's failure to understand the topic properly could lead to heresy. Because the Quran is understood to be an aesthetic and stylistic miracle, the process of rationally grounding one's assent to its guidance requires knowledge of poetics.[18] According to al-Muṭarrizī and al-Jurjānī, the failure to comprehend the different kinds of metaphors could also lead a reader into a theological error. Consider the Quranic passages that refer to the eyes and hand of God (e.g., Q 11.37 and Q 3.27). In the case of the Labīd verse about the north wind quoted above, there is no referent for the "hands" of the north wind. In passages closely paralleling al-Jurjānī, al-Muṭarrizī claims that people who do not understand this nonsubstitutionary metaphor will fall into "grave error (*al-ḍalāl al-baʿīd*)" because they will commit anthropomorphism. The unsophisticated assumption that all metaphors must be substitutionary has theological consequences because it threatens to diminish the oneness of God.[19] Al-Muṭarrizī is very selective in what he quotes and paraphrases in his remarkably condensed summary of Jurjānian poetics, so the fact that he mentions the theological implications of poetics suggests that it is an important issue for him. The question of hierarchy is likewise crucial because the unsophisticated reader is not simply one who does not experience wonder but also one who risks anthropomorphizing God.

In al-Jurjānī, al-Muṭarrizī, and al-Ḥarīrī, texts are tests. The ability to recognize a great work was the mark of a sophisticated and theologically adept reader. Al-Ḥarīrī's exordium likewise praises the reader who interprets his text with the "eye of the intellect."[20] In a different context, Pierre Bourdieu has argued that the appreciation of culture is productive of class. He states that "taste classifies, and it classifies the classifier."[21] In other words, showing an appreciation for the elevated, intellectual pleasures of reading complex poetry and prose is a way through which readers "distinguish themselves by the distinctions they make" (Bourdieu again).[22] Anyone who has hesitated to say that they enjoy reality television or low-budget romantic comedies because of what it might say about *them* is aware of the class dynamics at play here. In al-Ḥarīrī, this dynamic is dramatized when some fictional characters mark themselves out as excellent readers by seeing beyond Abū Zayd's verbal performances. For example, in *maqāma* #8, an old man and a boy appear before a judge in the town of Maʿarrat al-Nuʿmān. The two present their complaints to the judge. The old man claims to have lent a slave girl to the boy, but she was returned in bad health. The boy protests that the harm to the slave girl was accidental and that, as compensation, he had given him a slave boy who was equally beautiful and charming. Both complaints are exquisite rhetorical performances, which the judge recognizes because he is a perceptive reader. The judge, however, believes there is something hidden in their speeches and demands that the two "be clear or, if not, depart!"[23]

The two confess that no exchange of slaves had ever taken place. Instead, the terms "female slave (*mamlūka*)" and "male slave (*mamlūk*)" were intended to refer more generally to inanimate objects that are grammatically feminine (a needle) and masculine (a pencil). The terms *mamlūka* and *mamlūk* can simply mean "something owned." With this information, their initial complaints can now be reinterpreted, and it becomes clear that they were extended examples of double entendre (*tawriya*). The judge is impressed and gives them each some money for their troubles and for their eloquence, so the two depart. Soon after, the judge suspects that he has still not gotten to the bottom of things, and a particularly perceptive member of his entourage suggests that he order them to be returned to his court. When they return, he extracts a second confession. In fact, neither a needle nor a pencil had ever changed hands, and it was only their speeches that had called those objects into existence in the minds of their audience. The judge lets them off with a warning but what is important for our purposes is that he discovers, through persistent inquiry, that there is no referent for these words, just as there is no "hand" for the north wind. This scene is also noteworthy because each confession is also a kind of commentary, but the first commentary that Abū Zayd and his accomplice offer is not so much an explanation as a further deception.

In the previous chapter, we saw that al-Ḥarīrī's typology of readers identified the best sort to be one who "scrutinizes things with the eye of the intellect."[24] Al-Muṭarrizī's account of Jurjānian poetics likewise emphasizes the desirability of metaphors requiring intellection. He then uses al-Ḥarīrī's phrase in the conclusion to his commentary. Al-Muṭarrizī acknowledges God's blessings and then praises his own book for its usefulness and excellence. He claims that "whoever examines it with the eye of the intellect (*naẓara ilayhi bi-ʿayn al-maʿqūl*) will find wonderful goods and a desired harvest enfolded within it."[25] In other words, both reading the *Ḥarīriyya* and this commentary require one to read carefully, thoughtfully, and intellectually. Otherwise, one may lose out on its benefits and perhaps even be led astray.

It is quite telling that al-Muṭarrizī's commentary has played no role in the twentieth- and twenty-first-century interpretations of the *Ḥarīriyya* or the *maqāma* genre more broadly. To become part of world literature and the realm of the literary, these texts needed to be processed within the colonial economy of literature that I discussed in Chapter 1. They required the interpretive frameworks of Euro-American literary institutions and their authorizing forces. Al-Muṭarrizī's interpretive frameworks were, by contrast, rooted in Jurjānian poetics, which the commentator conceived of as the proper way to read the *Ḥarīriyya* with the "eye of the intellect," as al-Ḥarīrī encourages his readers to do in his preface.[26] For al-Muṭarrizī, at least, this is not a text that is about "excessive verbal performances," as Michael Cooperson has suggested.[27] In fact, al-Muṭarrizī insists that the use of rhetorical devices cannot be considered beautiful unless the verbal form (*lafẓ*) is well-matched to aid the text's meaning (*maʿnā*).[28] Al-Muṭarrizī summarizes al-Jurjānī's ideas about the relationship between form and content by stating that real eloquence resides in "the specific arrangement of meanings and the joining of words one after the other in a specific manner."[29] In Jurjānian poetics, whenever the precise expression of an idea is changed, it elicits a different cognitive experience in the reader, which cannot be reduced to a mere alternatively worded version of the same idea. Form and content are inextricably linked.[30] Given that al-Muṭarrizī presents his commentary and its introduction as a path to acquainting the reader "with the superiority of this book," it seems unlikely that he would understand the *Ḥarīriyya* as a triumph of form over content or as a book that is really about "excess" in its verbal performances. Rather, he saw it as Quran-like in its perfect and precise alignment of form and content. Indeed, Jurjānian poetics values the intellectual adventure that challenging language requires, but al-Jurjānī rejects ambiguity for ambiguity's sake or unnecessary complication in making a simple point. These kinds of overwrought phrases lead to weariness or require a great deal of effort for a paltry prize.[31]

Why do the performances of Abū Zayd in the *Ḥarīriyya* seem so excessive to modern readers? Recall that as far back as Thomas Chenery, the Victorian translator of the *Ḥarīriyya*, it was felt that al-Ḥarīrī "sacrificed" the story to the display of style. This view was part of a broader colonial critique of Islamic culture. As the anthropologist Charles Hirschkind has pointed out in his study of Egypt's soundscapes, "Europeans who came to the Middle East in the nineteenth century" perceived that "Muslims seemed too involved with surfaces and externalities," particularly in their interest in bodily movement, recitation, and the like.[32] These rituals and "externalities" were seen as superstitious distractions from the proper function of reason and rational religious devotion. According to Hirschkind, the notion of Muslim superficiality "was also elaborated in regard to genres of Muslim speech and writing, in what Europeans took to be a privileging of formal and aesthetic criteria over content and meaning."[33] Rhyming prose and the foregrounding of grammar and syntax were seen as signs of ostentation which reflected a broader cultural malaise that paid more attention to "external forms over inner meanings."[34] Although the derogatory edge of this outlook has largely fallen away, it has been my argument that literary interpretations of the *Ḥarīriyya* and the reading practices of world literature that underpin them are haunted by the ghosts of the nineteenth century. Supposing that the *Ḥarīriyya* is all form and little to no content ends up allowing these ghosts to shape our notions about what the text is "really" *about*. Or more precisely, it retrojects these later readings on the sixth/twelfth century.

The first century of readers (and listeners) who encountered the *Ḥarīriyya* most certainly did not see it as a text concerned with verbal pyrotechnics, any more than they thought the Quran was all about surface, not substance. Al-Muṭarrizī's claim that the *Ḥarīriyya* possessed inimitability like the Quran was also a claim about the appropriate way to appreciate and interpret the text. In both books, every word and phrase is precise and thus full of meaning, allowing for endless intellectual pleasure in the pursuit of meaning. For many readers, commentary was the appropriate response to such an inimitable text, as opposed to competitive emulation. A biographical anecdote illustrates this shift to commentary. The biographer and geographer Yāqūt (d. 626/1229) tells us that he met al-Shumaym al-Ḥillī (d. 601/1205), a scholar who rarely expressed admiration for any author. He was condemning various respected scholars for their foibles in a session that Yāqūt attended, and so the biographer finally asked if there was anyone whom he would be willing to praise. Al-Ḥillī replied that he knew of only three: al-Mutanabbī for his panegyric poetry, Ibn Nubāta (d. 374/984–85) for his sermons, and al-Ḥarīrī for his *maqāma*s. Yāqūt asked why al-Ḥillī had never tried to outdo al-Ḥarīrī with his own *maqāma*s. The cantankerous scholar finally admitted that he had tried three times to do so before giving up and turning to commentary, having realized that God had created him not to compete with al-Ḥarīrī but to "make apparent his excellence and to comment on his *maqāmas* with a commentary that is read and studied."[35] Although the language of inimitability is not specifically invoked here, Yāqūt states in a nearby passage that "were someone to claim that the *Ḥarīriyya* is inimitable, there would be no one to argue against him or refute his statement."[36]

By Yāqūt's day, of course, someone had claimed that the *Ḥarīriyya* was inimitable—namely, al-Muṭarrizī. As it happens, we know that Yāqūt had carefully read al-Muṭarrizī's commentary because of a passing comment Yāqūt makes in the preface to his geographical work, the *Muʿjam al-Buldān*. There, Yāqūt justifies the need for such a book by noting that scholars continue to make glaring geographical errors, one of which can be found in a certain commentary on the *Ḥarīriyya*. That commentary, he claims, identifies Tabriz as "one of the major cities of the Levant." This is an error that al-Muṭarrizī does, in fact, commit in his commentary (Tabriz is in northwestern Iran near Azerbaijan). Yāqūt nevertheless commends this commentary, without naming its author, for being dazzling to the intellect and for clarifying the "secrets of the *Ḥarīriyya*'s eloquence (*asrār balāghatihā*)."[37] In the precise wording of his praise, Yāqūt seems to be marking his awareness of al-Muṭarrizī's source for his commentary's introduction: al-Jurjānī's *Asrār al-Balāgha* (*The Secrets of Eloquence*).

Yāqūt also conveyed the idea that the *Ḥarīriyya* was Quran-like through his biography of al-Ḥarīrī. We have already encountered Yāqūt in the context of our discussion in Chapter 4, in which I claimed that biographical anecdotes can be understood as a mode of textual interpretation, rather than as way of conveying information about the lives of particular authors. Yāqūt's biographical entry on al-Ḥarīrī claims that the latter initially wrote forty *maqāmas* and then was accused of plagiarism. To prove he was the author, he produced ten more *maqāmas* like the first forty. This story echoes the Quranic challenge to those who claim it is human speech and not divine to "bring ten fabricated chapters like it" (Q 11:13). Al-Ḥarīrī's success in bringing ten *maqāmas* like his first forty both proves his authorship and plays on the notion of inimitability as a rubric for understanding the *Ḥarīriyya*'s uniqueness. Once again, we can see how discussing the *Ḥarīriyya*'s inimitability was not, in the long sixth/twelfth century, seen as a threat to the Quran's status as revelation. Instead, Quranic inimitability provided a framework for thinking about the relationship between texts, authors, and audiences.

But how can a text full of deceptions be considered similar to the Quran? Abū Zayd, whether we consider him a real human or not, shows us that language and discourses that assert their veracity are, as Philip Kennedy states, "incessantly discovered to be a pack of lies."[38] In this vein, Michael Cooperson has argued that Abū Zayd, in his "vaporous indeterminacy" should be understood as the Arabic language itself. He is "the language of God in the world of men," but, as a result of this paradox, language has become "unmoored from reality" and thus "unmoored from the sacred as well."[39] Drawing on the work of Kilito, Beaumont, and others, Cooperson suggests that the *Ḥarīriyya*'s saturation with Islamic discourses from the Quran to the Islamic sciences reflects a kind of melancholy. For these critics, there is in the *Ḥarīriyya* a kind of longing for a past in which language and reality were more closely aligned. As Cooperson puts it, "Language is left to fend for itself in a world that seems largely hostile to its purposes."[40] For Beaumont, the *Ḥarīriyya*'s unstable, deceptive language is "fundamentally opposed to the thoroughly idealistic conception of language that pervades medieval Islam."[41] He claims that "the Koran itself holds out the promise that the truth may be given direct representation in language," but his vision of the Quranic promise and the idealistic conception of language he takes to "pervade" medieval Islam does not hold up well to scrutiny. The ambiguity of language and the conventional, arbitrary nature of the linguistic sign were widely recognized among scholars of Islamic law and theorists of language.[42]

Even God's own speech could be marked by uncertainty when it circulates in the world of humans. The Quran itself points to its own ambiguities and to the challenge of its figurative language. The Quran distinguishes between "clear verses (*āyāt muḥkamāt*)" and "ambiguous ones (*mutashābihāt*)" (Q 3:7). Whereas the clear verses are called the "essence of the Book," the ambiguous verses are pursued by "those in whose heart there is swerving." This might seem to privilege the clear verses of the Quran, but the problem remains that the text does not identify which verses are clear and which are ambiguous. This sifting of wheat from chaff must be worked out by the believers. As the sixth/twelfth-century exegete and theologian Fakhr al-Dīn al-Rāzī points out in his multivolume commentary on the Quran, every sect in the world identifies as "clear" those verses that agree with their beliefs, while those that support their opponents' views are deemed "ambiguous."[43] What is more, the remainder of this same Quranic verse is itself ambiguous. The verse tells us *either* that no one knows the interpretation of the ambiguous verses except for God *or* that no one knows their interpretation except for God *and* those firmly rooted in knowledge. Al-Rāzī points out that exegetes are divided on which of these two readings is correct. Although some scholars claimed that humans should avoid interpreting these ambiguous verses, others like al-Sharīf al-Raḍī (d. 406/1016) and al-Qāḍī ʿAbd al-Jabbār (d. 415/1025) had devoted their exegetical projects to identifying and interpreting the ambiguous verses, presumably because they believed it was their duty to do so as scholars with firmly rooted knowledge.[44]

My point here is that Quranic exegetes both before and after the *Ḥarīriyya* took for granted the presence of ambiguity in the Quran. Their approaches to ambiguity might have differed, but their notions of language were not naively idealistic or marked by a longing for unambiguous legibility. Rather, there was a sophisticated understanding of the fact that human interpretive effort was required to understand the relationship between language and reality, particularly when that language was as rich and multilayered as God's own speech in the Quran. Perhaps the best expression of this idea in the Quran is the following: "God does not disdain to make a parable out of a gnat or something smaller. As for those who believe, they understand that it is the Truth from their Lord. As for those who disbelieve, they will say, "What did God mean by this parable?" Many are led astray by it, and many are guided rightly. Only the profligate are led astray" (Q 2.26). The Quran and its allusive language are a test. They can both serve as guidance and confuse people. Here again, as is the case in the *Ḥarīriyya*, readers mark themselves out as worthy by demonstrating their understanding of the text. The fact that surfaces can be deceiving is not a fault in the text but a feature of a particular kind of textuality that prizes the hermeneutical adventure. Indeed, the medieval exegetical tradition does not assume that Quranic language was or ought to be legible to all Muslims. If Abū Zayd is to be understood as the Arabic language itself, his elusiveness and invitation to hermeneutical adventures may be precisely what led scholars like Yāqūt and al-Muṭarrizī to describe the *Ḥarīriyya* in Quran-like terms.

Al-Panjdīhī's Digressions in the Islamic Archive

The *Ḥarīriyya* and the speeches of Abū Zayd are filled with Quranic allusion and, as we have seen, were understood by commentators as deeply intertwined with revelation. Abū Zayd's performances are filled with interpretive challenges like the one in *maqāma* #8 described above. The Quran is also full of interpretive challenges, and some verses might be misleading if a reader were to interpret them in the most obvious way. A deep knowledge of the Islamic sciences is usually considered necessary for interpreting the text because, for example, some Quranic verses are "abrogated" by verses that were revealed at a later time. Although such verses are no longer considered operative when deriving rulings in Islamic law and ritual practice, they continue to be recited.[45]

Might it even be the case that the *Ḥarīriyya* could help its readers encounter God's revelation? Al-Panjdīhī's commentary seems to explore this very possibility. It begins with an elaborate introduction in rhyming prose. Unlike al-Muṭarrizī, he makes no attempt to lay out a theory of poetics in this commentary's opening passages. Instead, al-Panjdīhī composes a kind of introductory *maqāma* of his own, complete with an autocommentary to explain the difficult words. Al-Panjdīhī praises the *Ḥarīriyya* in the highest possible terms and lauds al-Ḥarīrī's "inimitability in the concision of his expression (*iʿjāzuhu fī ījāzihi*)," which al-Panjdīhī considers to be the "alchemy of Arabic philology and a signpost for those who seek *adab*."[46] Al-Panjdīhī presents the *Ḥarīriyya* as the very best book of Arabic and *adab*, two pillars of knowledge that he considers to be the "interpreters of the Quran and the stewards of the Arabs—the foundations of the sciences and the connection with the traces of the past."[47]

For al-Panjdīhī, the *Ḥarīriyya* helps readers with the task of Quranic exegesis and connects them to the Islamic sciences. His digressive commentary then undertakes a kind of augmentation of the text's engagement with the Islamic sciences by linking line after line of the *Ḥarīriyya* to the Islamic discursive tradition or what I have called the "Islamic archive." The digressions include passages from the Quran, frequent quotations from the narrative and normative legacy of the Prophet Muḥammad (the hadith), stories of prominent Muslims, and even matters of Islamic law. Al-Panjdīhī also forcefully rejects the critiques of Ibn al-Khashshāb, as we saw in Chapter 4. His rebuttals are often elaborate rhetorical performances that insist on treating the text and its author with a deference and charity that reflects its canonicity.[48] Reading the *Ḥarīriyya* with al-Panjdīhī's commentary enacts a kind of meditation on this Islamic archive.

An example of al-Panjdīhī's digressiveness can be found in his commentary on *maqāma* #2, in which al-Ḥārith goes to the library in Basra longing for intellectual conversation. A man with a thick beard enters and greets the people seated there and proceeds to dazzle the assembled company with his poetic compositions, as discussed in Chapter 2. The word "beard (*liḥya*)" is not difficult or philologically interesting. Nevertheless, al-Panjdīhī takes the opportunity to explore what the Islamic archive has to say about beards. First, al-Panjdīhī begins with a general statement attributed to no one in particular: "It is said that the lightness of one's beard indicates happiness, cleverness, and a copious one indicates stupidity."[49] He then quotes hadith of the Prophet and other reports about prominent Muslims regarding beards. For instance, one hadith states that the Prophet made sure that his beard was no longer than it was wide. The lesson appears to be that one ought to keep one's beard trimmed to follow the normative example of the Prophet. The anecdotes verge on the humorous as well. One story tells of a man who saw the Prophet in a dream and expressed a desire to have a large beard. The prophet replied: "Your beard is fine. What you need is a sound mind."[50]

Al-Panjdīhī's commentary on beards does not stop here, and his discussion presents multiple opinions about beards. He goes on to quote reports of prominent early Muslims who themselves are discussing the Prophet's legacy. For example, the caliph and founder of the Umayyad dynasty Muʿāwiya (d. 60/680) sees a man with a long beard and discusses the matter with another companion of the Prophet named ʿAmr b. al-ʿĀṣ. According to ʿAmr, the Prophet took the measure of a man's intellect according to the length of his beard, his byname (*kunya*), and the imprint of his signet ring. Muʿāwiya then interviews the long-bearded man, asking him about his byname and his signet ring. He considers both of these to be impressive, leading Muʿāwiya to declare the man quite complete. In this story, long beards are not a sign of stupidity according to the Prophet but a sign of a man's intellect. However, Muʿāwiya's reputation was often considered highly questionable by later generations, given that he put up stiff resistance to the caliphate of ʿAlī after the latter's victory at the Battle of the Camel in the year 36/656. At the Battle of Ṣiffīn between the supporters of Muʿāwiya and those of ʿAlī, it was none other than ʿAmr b. al-ʿĀṣ (the companion with whom Muʿāwiya is speaking about beards) who commanded the cavalry for Muʿāwiya.[51] In later generations, the Umayyads in general were often, but not always, considered impious usurpers.

Was al-Panjdīhī inviting the reader of his commentary to view Muʿāwiya's endorsement of long beards with suspicion? Is ʿAmr b. al-ʿĀṣ's invocation of Prophetic precedent intended to cast aspersions on him as a reliable custodian of Prophetic precedent? The commentator al-Panjdīhī does not tell us one way or the other. Instead, he allows the ambiguity to stand before the reader. Al-Panjdīhī's digressive commentary is not pursuing the elimination of ambiguity, as one might expect from a less digressive philological commentary. The very digressiveness of the commentarial text allows for the presentation of multiple options, which might be settled by further oral commentary or left to the mind of the reader.

Given the inclusion of so much Islamic ethical material in al-Panjdīhī's digressions, one might naturally assume that his commentary condemns Abū Zayd for his deceptions. Indeed, it is sometimes suggested that the *maqāma*s of al-Hamadhānī and al-Ḥarīrī were not truly subversive but were intended to invite the reader to condemn the trickster's hypocrisies without explicitly telling the reader to do so.[52] Al-Panjdīhī is nothing if not a pious reader, after all, but he seems far more ambivalent about Abū Zayd than we might expect. On the one hand, he condemns Abū Zayd for his hypocrisy in *maqāma* #1. At the end of that *maqāma*, al-Ḥārith has followed Abū Zayd after the ascetic sermon in Sanaa, finding him indulging in meat and wine. Al-Ḥārith is horrified, pointing to the breakdown between word and deed, and al-Panjdīhī joins him in the commentary with an eloquent condemnation of scholarly hypocrisies. Al-Panjdīhī then cites the Quran, which states that "it is most hateful to God that you say what you do not do" (Q 61.2–3). Finally, the commentator quotes hadith condemning hypocritical preachers and scholars as some of the worst evils of this world.[53]

On the other hand, like al-Ḥārith, al-Panjdīhī is not always so disparaging of Abū Zayd. In fact, the commentator sometimes turns his ire against the narrator for being too harsh on the trickster. This is the case in *maqāma* #34, in which Abū Zayd sells a slave-boy to al-Ḥārith even though the boy is, in fact, Abū Zayd's own son. Al-Ḥārith, however, is distracted by the boy's beauty, which is compared to that of the ageless serving-boys of paradise.[54] The boy hints that he is in fact free by alluding to the Quranic story of Joseph in verse, "I am Joseph! I am Joseph! / I have taken away the veil, so if you are clever, you will understand, but I do not think you will understand."[55] After the sale, the youth drags al-Ḥārith to court to establish his freedom with the judge, which had been stipulated in the judge's presence by the youth's father on the previous day. The judge admonishes al-Ḥārith for missing the boy's warning and notes that "one who warns is like one who announces and makes something manifest. . . . He advised you, but you were heedless."[56] Al-Ḥārith is irate, but the judge argues that Abū Zayd and his son have actually done al-Ḥārith a favor because "he woke you up (*ayqaẓaka*)."[57] Al-Ḥārith disagrees and says that he will never speak to Abū Zayd ever again. It is at this point that the commentator intervenes to condemn the irate narrator, noting "That is not permissible (*dhālika lā yajūz*)." Al-Panjdīhī cites two hadith about the punishment of someone who shuns his brother. The first report warns that the punishment of Cain will attend anyone who shuns his brother for more than a year and that he will certainly suffer hellfire. The second report declares that it is not licit for a Muslim to shun his brother for more than three days, and that the first to make peace is the first to enter paradise.[58] Al-Panjdīhī, like the judge, refuses to scold Abū Zayd for his ruse and turns his attention instead to al-Ḥārith's shortcomings. The hypocritical preacher, who in *maqāma* #1 was identified by al-Panjdīhī as one of the great evils of this world, is now interpreted as a worthy friend of al-Ḥārith.

Al-Panjdīhī's ambivalence about Abū Zayd should encourage us to set aside our overriding concern about whether the reader is invited to celebrate Abū Zayd's subversions or condemn them. Perhaps determining our attitude toward the trickster is not really the point. Instead, it seems that the trickster invites a particular kind of reading, one that is wakeful and aware. The reader of *maqāma* #34 is asked to see beyond the surface level and to contemplate the Islamic archive in the broadest possible terms. Failing to see beyond the trickster's ruses is tantamount to a heedless and negligent form of reading that is as dangerous in life as it is when reading the scripture. Al-Ḥārith's declaration that he will abandon his ongoing companionship and closeness with Abū Zayd is a move that risks hellfire because it fails to be wakeful to the Prophetic example. At the same time, the Prophetic example and the Quran itself are ambiguous and require careful, wakeful reading, as the Quran itself warns and al-Panjdīhī's digression on beards reminds us.

In his preface, Al-Ḥarīrī emphasizes the importance of reading the *Ḥarīriyya* with the "eye of the intellect."[59] It is therefore unsurprising that we find several *maqāma*s in which a failure to read carefully is punished. In *maqāma* #34 discussed above, al-Ḥārith admits that the youth's beauty had distracted him and that "my mind was taken captive by his magic, and I was diverted from discovering the truth."[60] Similarly, in *maqāma* #10, Abū Zayd brings his son before a governor who is known for being attracted to boys rather than girls.[61] He pretends that his son is in fact a murderer who has killed his son, an accusation that the youth vehemently denies. During their performance before the governor, Abū Zayd slyly uses his eloquent accusations to highlight the youth's beauty. The governor is smitten and offers to pay the old man a sum of money to settle their dispute in the hopes of gaining the youth's favor. Abū Zayd agrees to the terms of the settlement, but the governor can only pay part of the sum up-front and promises the remainder on the following day. By then, the father and son have made off with the first installment.[62] In both *maqāmas*, a youth's physical beauty has led to reckless action and financial loss on the part of the character who fails to examine things with the "eye of the intellect." Both of these interpretive failures serve as contrasts to the judge in *maqāma* #8, discussed earlier, who perceives the performative nature of the rhetorical performances by Abū Zayd and his son.

The interpretive adventures of the *Ḥarīriyya* are, on the one hand, part of the poetics of virtual experience discussed in the previous chapter, teaching the reader how to avoid being duped by the ruses of this world. On the other hand, al-Panjdīhī and al-Muṭarrizī see the interpretive challenges as an effective laboratory for encountering the scripture and the broader Islamic tradition. I am not suggesting that the Islamic tradition is a trickster's tradition. It is likewise not the case that, as Chenery said introducing his translation of *maqāma* #11 with its sermon that "in the Moslem world, where religion is mixed up with the concerns of life, and pious discourse and phrases abound," it is no wonder that the author could "place in the mouth of a clever imposter the most serious warnings that can be addressed to mankind."[63] Rather, I am suggesting that the Islamic tradition has produced some of the most sophisticated theories of hermeneutics known to humanity and that in the *Ḥarīriyya* we find a narrative meditation on these hermeneutics that foregrounds the trickster Abū Zayd and his performances.

Al-Panjdīhī's digressions in the Islamic discursive tradition regularly draw attention to subtle ambiguities in the Quran that affect its exegesis. These exegetical ambiguities sometimes also draw attention to the ambiguity of Abū Zayd, who is both a marvel and a deceiver. In doing so, al-Panjdīhī draws a parallel between the interpretive problems of this world and of the sacred. For example, at the end of *maqāma* #34, in which al-Ḥārith had promised to shun Abū Zayd for the rest of his days, he ends up forgiving the rogue. In doing so, he alludes to the Quran, saying "I returned to him as a sincere friend and was welcoming to him, casting aside what he had done, even if it was an unheard-of thing (*shay'an fariyyan*)."[64] The allusion here is to the "Chapter of Mary" in the Quran. When Mary returns to her family after giving birth to Jesus, they are shocked and assume she has committed fornication. They exclaim, "O Mary, you have done an unheard-of thing (*shay'an fariyyan*)" (Q 19.27). As al-Ṭabarī (d. 310/923) notes in his monumental work of Quranic exegesis, this phrase is ambiguous because *farī* can mean "something amazing (*amr ʿajīb*)" or "a monstrosity (*fāḥisha*)."[65] Fakhr al-Dīn al-Rāzī, the sixth/twelfth-century exegete discussed earlier in this chapter, says that the text of the Quran "supports the interpretation that what is meant is an amazing thing that goes beyond the ordinary without [implying] revilement or censure, and it is possible that their intention is that it is a grave error (*ʿaẓīman munkaran*) and that it is an expression of censure."[66] In the following Quranic verse, Mary's family asks how such a thing could have happened, given that Mary's father was not a wicked man and her mother not a harlot, so it is noteworthy that al-Rāzī and others insist on this ambiguity. In part, it preserves the possibility that the unusual circumstances of Jesus's conception might *seem* like a monstrosity to his family who do not yet understand his miraculousness. When the infant Jesus speaks to them, the potential monstrosity of fornication is transformed into a wondrous and unheard-of thing: a child speaking eloquently from the cradle.

Al-Panjdīhī draws attention both to the fact that "an unheard-of thing" is a Quranic allusion and to the different connotations of the phrase, adding that "God knows best."[67] As is typical, he does not draw out the implications of this insight. When al-Ḥārith is made to use a Quranic allusion to Jesus to describe the actions of Abū Zayd, he is inviting us to see that something can be monstrous to some while being marvelous to others. Furthermore, the monstrousness of Abū Zayd's actions can be revealed as marvelous through deeper knowledge and appreciation, just as Jesus's speech from the cradle transforms the perception of a child belonging to an unwed mother.

A similar interest in Abū Zayd's ambiguity can be found in al-Panjdīhī's commentary on *maqāma* #32 in which Abū Zayd performs a series of legal opinions (*fatwās*) that contain double entendres, such that the most obvious interpretation is always false—a device known as *tawriya*.[68] There too, al-Panjdīhī examines a Quranic allusion that turns out to be ambiguous, but not because a word has different connotations, as was the case with *farī* (an unheard-of thing). Instead, al-Panjdīhī draws our attention to the variant canonical readings of the Quran: the *qirā'āt*. According to the Islamic tradition, there are a number of variant readings (*qirā'āt*) of the Quran that were all acknowledged and accepted by the Prophet.[69] These variations are generally very minor and usually involve changes in vowels or conjugation. To set the scene, *maqāma* #32 begins with al-Ḥārith witnessing the townspeople rushing to see this "jurist of the Arabs." He describes them "running as though they were hurrying to a sign that marks the way (*ka'annahum ilā naṣb yūfiḍūn*)."[70] This is an allusion to a Quranic passage that refers to the Day of Judgment when those who have mocked the Prophet will be humbled. The Quran describes them coming "out of their graves running as though they were hurrying to a way-marker (*naṣb*), their eyes submissive and covered in humbleness—that is the day they were promised" (Q 70.42–44).

This version of the Quranic verse with its reference to a "way-marker" is what appears in the earliest manuscripts of the *Ḥarīriyya*, but it is not the reading that one finds in most printed Qurans today. Among the several canonical recitations of the Quran that consist of mostly minor variations, one was adopted by the Ottoman Empire in the tenth/sixteenth century and then also used when the Egyptian government printed a highly influential Quran in 1342/1923.[71] In that now-standard reading, we find not *naṣb* but *nuṣub*. This tiny change in voweling alters the meaning of the term entirely: from "way-marker (*naṣb*)" to "idols (*nuṣub*)." In other words, the people in the town are rushing not toward a sign or guidepost but to the very same idols that they worshipped in their earthly lives and that marked them as polytheists. By pointing out the potential for variant readings in his commentary, al-Panjdīhī complexifies our interpretation of the townsfolk in *maqāma* #32 rushing toward Abū Zayd. Are they heading toward a way-marker that guides people or to a kind of idol who distracts the people from worshipping the one God? Once again, Abū Zayd is, in some sense, both. He is a guidepost along the way for those like al-Ḥārith who recognize that his *fatwā*s require interpretation and who receive deeper understanding of them through commentary, but he is a kind of idol for the townsfolk who accept his riddling *fatwā*s at face value. They will be led astray.

So far in this chapter, then, we have seen how the very thing that guides people rightly can also be the thing that leads them astray. Whether it is the Quran, the *Ḥarīriyya*, Abū Zayd himself, or the Prophetic legacy, readers seem to be constantly faced with a world of ambivalent signs and hermeneutical puzzles. As I have argued throughout, we should not see the *Ḥarīriyya* as subversive to or separate from Islam. Reading *adab* "as literature," as the modes of reading in the era of world literature have done, secularizes texts like the *Ḥarīriyya*, overlooking the Islamic contexts of their reception and interpretation.

Sufism, Politics, and the *Ḥarīriyya*

Conceptualizing the world as a hermeneutical puzzle in the way that al-Panjdīhī does has some obvious echoes in some strands of Sufi thought, in which the outer appearances of things and material reality itself are deceptive. To understand the truth of the world and the revelation, one must seek out its hidden secrets. It so happens that there is evidence of an explicitly Sufi interpretation of the *Ḥarīriyya* by the Sufi poet Ibn al-Fāriḍ in his *Naẓm al-sulūk*, an ode of over seven hundred lines often simply called his "poem rhyming in the letter *tāʾ*." These verses are significant for the reception of the *Ḥarīriyya* because the poem and its commentaries became part of the canon of the Akbarī school of Sufism, which developed in the wake of the influential figure of Ibn al-ʿArabī (d. 638/1240) and became one of the dominant strands of Islamic thought in the Eastern Islamic world down to the nineteenth century.[72] In the last quarter of the poem, Ibn al-Fāriḍ encourages the reader to contemplate the *Ḥarīriyya*:[73]

Contemplate the Sarūjian *Maqāmāt* and consider
his variegation—then you will happily accept my counsel.
You will understand the obscuring of the soul by senses (*iltibās al-nafs bi-l-ḥiss*)—
the inner meaning by its outer sense—in every shape and form.
Even if his words lie (*māna*), the Truth makes it
an allegory (*al-ḥaqq ḍārib bihi mathal*), but the soul is unserious.

For Ibn al-Fāriḍ, the disguises of Abū Zayd are a kind of metaphor for the disguises of the soul. The soul's outer shells of sense, shape, and form deceive and distract us from recognizing what lies within and beyond—namely, the soul. Therefore, although the words of al-Ḥarīrī and Abū Zayd may not be true in a literal sense, the reader can treat the text as an allegory for the deceptions of outer forms hiding inner truths. This reading is reinscribed in the commentaries, which latch on to the lexical significance of the term *iltibās*. The term *iltibās* can refer to that which obscures and causes ambiguity, but it is also related to a word for clothing (*libās*) and thus implies the more literal notion of disguise.[74]

Al-Farghānī, one of the commentators on this Sufi poem in the Akbarī tradition, takes note of the strangeness in the final line of the three verses quoted above, which refers to the soul as "unserious." It would be odd for this unserious soul to be the same "soul" that is disguised by sense perception. Furthermore, it is not al-Ḥarīrī who creates this allegory but the Truth, which is a name for God. Thus, Ibn al-Fāriḍ's poem seems to claim that it is God-the-Truth, not the author of the *Maqāmāt*, who has made an allegory of Abū Zayd al-Sarūjī's many disguises. For al-Farghānī, the unserious soul referred to in the poem is none other than al-Ḥarīrī, whom he describes as "lying, jesting, his soul unserious in understanding the soul and the Lord." Other commentators take this description of the unserious soul as a reference to the reader who might fail to see through the allegory of the soul, but al-Farghānī explains that God "the Truth, who acts through him [i.e. al-Ḥarīrī] and creates in him these words, brought forth this allegory . . . so that those with understanding could understand, contemplate, and consider the true nature of things (*ḥaqīqat al-amr*)."[75] As Samuela Pagani has pointed out, this notion of God creating new similitudes and allegories in the world "through human hands" (that is, through writers and artists) was held by scholars in the Akbarī Sufi tradition who drew on the legacy of Ibn al-ʿArabī. Among these theorists were al-Farghānī and ʿAbd al-Ghanī al-Nābulsī (d. 1143/1731).[76]

For Ibn al-Fāriḍ's commentator al-Farghānī, God could work through unwitting writers to produce meaningful metaphors that exceeded or even contradicted what the author had intended. This decoupling of the authorial intent from the Islamic meaning of an author's work stands in stark contrast to the approach of the commentators on the *Ḥarīriyya* discussed above. For al-Panjdīhī and al-Muṭarrizī, the text was a marvelous witness to the genius and Islamic erudition of the author. The author's intention was not, for them, to mislead and to jest. According to al-Farghānī, by contrast, the author can be seen as a jesting liar, but the text still cannot properly be interpreted as an affront to Islamic sensibilities, as some scholars in the modern period have suggested. Rather, the *Ḥarīriyya* is a message from God himself. It takes on the appearance of a meaningless jest to its uninformed readers and, ironically, to its very own author.

Before concluding this chapter, I want to turn our attention away from the *Ḥarīriyya*'s Islamic reception and toward its Islamic origins. Although much ink has been spilled on the question of the true origins of the *maqāma* genre, one rather clear textual precursor has been dismissed as unimportant, even though it bears a nearly identical name: the *maqām*. The terms *maqāma* and *maqām* are semantically identical and share the same plural (*maqāmāt*), but they refer to two distinct genres of Arabic prose. The *maqām* genre recounts tales of pious ascetics eloquently confronting Muslim rulers for their unjust rule and impious behavior. A chapter dedicated to the *maqāmāt* of the ascetics before caliphs and rulers can be found in the *adab* anthologies of Ibn Qutayba (d. 276/889) and Ibn ʿAbd Rabbih (d. 328/940).[77] The view that fictionality and frivolity are the defining features of the *maqāma* has led scholars to see this "literary" genre as fundamentally different from the Islamic *maqām*, with its piety and its references to specific historical figures.[78]

There are, nevertheless, overlooked parallels between the *maqām*s found in Ibn Qutayba and Ibn ʿAbd Rabbih on the one hand and the *maqāma*s of al-Hamadhānī and al-Ḥarīrī on the other. Let us begin with an example from Ibn Qutayba. The second of eight *maqām*s in his anthology portrays the Abbasid caliph al-Manṣūr (r. 136–58/754–75) overhearing a man in Mecca, who offers up the following prayer: "I complain to You [i.e., God] of injustice and corruption in the world and the greed that has intervened between the Truth and His people."[79] The caliph sends for the man and asks him to explain what he said, telling him that it has angered him. The man agrees to do so only if the caliph will grant him safety, which he does, so the ascetic tells him that the caliph himself is the greed that has intervened between God the Truth and His people. He accuses the caliph of greedily gathering the wealth of his subjects, all the while isolating himself from them, thus shirking his duties to God. The harangue goes on for two pages in the edition, culminating with al-Manṣūr breaking down in tears. The ascetic gives the caliph some advice on how to rectify matters and then disappears mysteriously.

There are evident parallels here between the *maqām* and the *maqāma*. The ascetic in this *maqām* is eloquent and mysterious, as the *maqāma*'s rogues often are. More importantly, the rogues regularly preach to their audience and decry the injustices of society. The distinction is that Abū al-Fatḥ and Abū Zayd are, it is assumed, insincere preachers. For example, in al-Hamadhānī's *maqāma khamriyya*, Abū al-Fatḥ plays a preacher who admonishes the narrator and his companions for being drunk at prayer after a night of carousing. The rogue then goes on to get drunk himself. This same theme is repeated in al-Ḥarīrī's *maqāma* #28. The insincerity of these rogue preachers is, however, attenuated in several cases. For example, al-Hamadhānī's *maqāma waʿẓiyya* begins abruptly with a brief introduction in which the narrator finds himself in Basra and encounters a preacher whose sermon takes up the rest of the *maqāma*. Within that sermon, the rogue quotes a different sermon given by ʿAlī b. al-Ḥusayn, known as Zayn al-ʿĀbidīn (d. ca. 85/713), the fourth imam of Twelver Shi'is and the grandson of ʿAlī b. Abī Ṭālib.[80] In other words, one of al-Hamadhānī's *maqāmas* is largely made up of a sermon attributed to a historical personage, just as many of Ibn Qutayba's *maqāms* were. Zayn al-ʿĀbidīn evokes the ruins of bygone communities discussed by the Quran and warns against the accumulation of possessions: "How much have you suffered from those with great power and armies and their helpers who have taken possession of this world (*dunyāhu*) and taken from it the objects of their desires—building fortresses and palaces, gathering together riches and troops?"[81] Zayn al-ʿĀbidīn's critique of power in the mouth of al-Hamadhānī's rogue and his warning against the accumulation of wealth echo some of the sermons in Ibn Qutayba's *maqāms*.[82] In his sermon-within-a-sermon, Abū al-Fatḥ does not convince his royal audience to repent but rather piques the interest of al-Hamadhānī's narrator, who asks the man who he is. Abū al-Fatḥ replies with a question, asking, "Were you unsatisfied with the outward appearance that I had altered such that you sought to know me and did not recognize me? I am Abū al-Fatḥ al-Iskandarī!"[83] The narrator is surprised by Abū al-Fatḥ's white hair, to which the rogue replies by extemporizing some poetry in which he calls his hair "a warner but a silent one" and "a portent of death."[84]

In this *maqāma*, al-Hamadhānī's rogue is offering a pious sermon that quotes a sermon by a historical figure, and he does not, in any obvious sense, participate in any jesting or hypocrisy. Abū al-Fatḥ is not found in a tavern drinking wine and reveling in his impiety. Rather, he admonishes the narrator (and the reader) for mistaking the transient appearances of this world for permanent truths. The distinction between the ascetic *maqāms* found in Ibn Qutayba and this Hamadhānian *maqāma* is less a matter of sincerity or historicity than it is a matter of the sermon's audience. The ascetics in Ibn Qutayba are speaking truth to powerful caliphs and kings, whereas Abū al-Fatḥ addresses an undifferentiated crowd in Basra.

In the *Ḥarīriyya*, Abū Zayd is a preacher in no fewer than seven *maqāmas*, and in one of these, he seems to channel the ascetics who speak truth to power. In *maqāma* #21, al-Ḥārith finds himself in Rayy where an eloquent man is preaching in an area "that brought together ruler and subject."[85] The sermon cautions against seductive deceptions, warning the crowd that the desire for fortune and wealth distracts human beings from what is truly important—namely, good works. The audience, moved by this sermon, is repentant and, once their wailing has died down, a voice cries out to the emir who is in attendance. The supplicant asks him to redress the wrongs of a certain treacherous functionary. But the ruler "inclined to his adversary and turned away from uncovering the injustice."[86] The supplicant then incites the preacher to give counsel to the ruler, and the preacher responds by standing and exhorting the ruler to address his shortcomings. First in verse and then in prose, Abū Zayd warns the emir of his duties as a Muslim ruler to his subjects and emphasizes the instabilities and uncertainties of power, telling him that "sovereignty is a changing wind and authority is lightning without rain."[87] Abū Zayd then raises the stakes of this ruler's precarity, using Quranic language to exhort the emir to avoid trading the hereafter for the here and now.

As with most of the pious *maqāms* in Ibn Qutayba's *ʿUyūn al-akhbār*, Abū Zayd's sermon in *maqāma* #21 of the *Ḥarīriyya* elicits the desired response of repentance from the ruler. The latter gives relief to the supplicant and rewards Abū Zayd the preacher with gifts. It is possible to interpret this scene as just another of Abū Zayd's ruses and to understand the complainant as one of Abū Zayd's confederates who prompt and facilitate his various ruses in several *maqāmas*. Indeed, in the final *maqāma* in which the rogue Abū Zayd repents, the reader is primed to suspect Abū Zayd's that this is yet another ruse.[88] There is, however, more than structural similarity that links this *maqāma* to Ibn Qutayba's *maqāms*. There is also an allusion to one of Ibn Qutayba's *maqāms* within al-Ḥarīrī's *maqāma* #21. After haranguing the ruler, al-Ḥārith follows Abū Zayd, as he often does, and the rogue recognizes him and extemporizes a poem, saying, "I am the one you know, O Ḥārith, the entertainer of kings, the wit . . . at times a brother to seriousness and at times frivolous."[89] Al-Ḥārith expresses his amazement that Abū Zayd "has acted piously even more than ʿAmr b. ʿUbayd!" This allusion to ʿAmr b. ʿUbayd (d. ca. 140s/750s), like hundreds of other allusions in the *Ḥarīriyya*, can pass by unnoticed if one is reading the text on its own, but when it is read commentarially, one realizes that this figure was famous for preaching against the injustices of the caliph al-Manṣūr. In fact, ʿAmr b. ʿUbayd is the ascetic preacher in the fourth of Ibn Qutayba's eight *maqāms*! In that version of the story, the caliph is speechless (*wajama*) when confronted by ʿAmr's eloquent sermon.[90] Likewise, the ruler in al-Ḥarīrī's *maqāma* #21 is described as speechless (*wajama*) in response to Abū Zayd's harangue.[91] In both stories, the sermon is aimed at exhorting the ruler to address injustices by responding directly to the petitions of his subjects.[92] In the story of

ʿAmr b. ʿUbayd, he advises the repentant caliph to prove his sincerity by responding to those "thousand injustices (*alf maẓlima*)" that are at his gates.[93]

The Andalusian commentator al-Sharīshī, whose digressive commentary is the subject of the next chapter, picks up on the references to ʿAmr b. ʿUbayd in *maqāma* #21 and offers the reader three stories about ʿAmr b. ʿUbayd, in which he harangues al-Manṣūr. Although he does not call these anecdotes *maqāms*, his digression is a way of indicating to the reader that Abū Zayd's sermon in *maqāma* #21 participates in a broad tradition of Islamic preaching against power. The *Ḥarīriyya* can be seen, then, as a text with a subversive message, but it is one that is directed not against Islam or Islamic discourses, as has sometimes been assumed. Rather, it participates in a subversive Islamic critique of the injustices of those in authority. The *Ḥarīriyya* joins a rich Islamic tradition of texts and authors that express a deep suspicion of political authority and reluctance to serve those in power.[94] One can find numerous anecdotes of Muslim scholars refusing to take up judicial posts, in addition to stories about those who set out to "command right and forbid wrong" by confronting rulers whom they considered unjust. An example cited by Michael Cook in his monograph on the topic involves a goldsmith from Marw who stood and harangued Abū Muslim (d. 137/755), the architect of the Abbasid revolution. The goldsmith was killed for his trouble. According to one version, he arrived shrouded for burial and preached harshly against Abū Muslim before a group of notables.[95]

With all these Islamic commentaries and intertexts, the claim that the *Ḥarīriyya* is subversive to the "law and order" discourses of Islamic *ʿilm* can now be recognized as misleading on two counts. First, the *Ḥarīriyya* was considered by its commentators and innumerable readers as a quintessentially Islamic text. Second, Islamic texts often express their suspicions about the forces of "law and order." As Abū Zayd puts it, quoting the Quran, those authorities "take power sow corruption in the land" (Q 2.205).[96] In other words, the *Ḥarīriyya* is not subversive because it is secular and "literary" but because it can be read as both Islamic and subversive to the coercive power of the state.

Making Islamic Meaning

The Islamic commentaries and intertexts explored in this chapter shed new light on the debate over how to conceptualize the Islamic tradition, a debate that has gained in intensity in recent years. It seems clear that many Muslim readers, but certainly not all, considered the *Ḥarīriyya* to be an Islamic text, although some readers of Ibn al-Fāriḍ would argue that it is Islamic despite the author's intention. In the nineteenth century, as the concepts and reading practices of world literature spread across the world, "literature" became associated with secular modes of reading. As we saw in Chapter 1, texts like the *Ḥarīriyya* came to be seen as un-Islamic or even anti-Islamic by many nineteenth-century Muslim reformers and Orientalists alike. The institutions and reading practices of world literature have transformed the *Ḥarīriyya* from a deeply Islamic text, one that was contested *on Islamic terms*, to a secular entertainment. In the twentieth and twenty-first centuries, the study of Islam in America drew on these same assumptions when conceptualizing Islam through law, theology, and the Quran, while overlooking or marginalizing those forms of Islamic *adab* that do not conform to the Sufi poetic mode.

Challenging what he calls the "legal-supremacist" view, Shahab Ahmed makes the case in his magnum opus *What Is Islam?* that we should conceive of precolonial Islam in the "Balkans-to-Bengal complex" as a multifarious practice of meaning-making. In other words, rather than think of Islam primarily in terms of norm-making, which privileges law and ethics, Ahmed offers a conceptualization of Islam as a "hermeneutical engagement" with the myriad manifestations of Revelation. For Ahmed, Revelation is not simply the sacred scripture but is rather to be understood expansively as including the prelinguistic truths that come before scripture, as well as the human "contexts" through which the Revelation and its Messenger flowed.[97] Ahmed's theorizations have their limitations, but his work offers the most powerful statement to date that the tradition of *adab* should not be understood as a "secular" or "literary" tradition but a tradition of Islamic meaning-making. As we have seen above, the premodern commentaries were not particularly concerned with urging the reader to condemn or celebrate the trickster. Rather, the aim of reading was to meditate on miraculous eloquence, the deeds of the Prophet, and the ambiguities of both the Quran and the world. There are certainly issues of linguistic and ethical normativity at play in the *Ḥarīriyya*, but to engage with the world and to engage with the text are, in this strand of the *Ḥarīriyya*'s reception, best seen as hermeneutical acts of high drama that were both enjoyable and meaningful to those who were trained to appreciate them.

Chapter 7

Gate-Crashing the Text

When ʿAbd al-Laṭīf al-Baghdādī was about thirty years old, he traveled to Jerusalem and participated in the *majlis* of Saladin, the famous ruler who reconquered Jerusalem from the Crusaders. A *majlis* (sometimes translated as "salon") was a key part of elite sociability in the medieval and early modern Islamic world in which the performance of erudition and eloquence took center stage. *Majālis* (the plural of *majlis*) were some of the key sites where *adab* took on its dual sense of learned discourse and proper comportment. To be a man of *adab* was to be able to participate in the *majlis*, both behaving elegantly and holding forth eloquently on a wide variety of topics. In ʿAbd al-Laṭīf's autobiography, he describes Saladin's *majlis* as "filled with scholars discussing various kinds of knowledge," while the "great king" listened and participated. If depictions of courtly *majālis* in our sources are any guide, the topic of conversation likely flowed from discussions of the Quran to recitations of poetry to the recounting of anecdotes and jokes to discussions of law and theology.[1] The *majlis* of Saladin was full of amicable, erudite discourse and, more than likely, combined conversations about scholarly topics with entertainments like poetry and music that made the assembled company feel at ease. ʿAbd al-Laṭīf describes the scene by quoting the Quran: "We stripped away the rancor from our breasts" (Q 7.43).[2] When ʿAbd al-Laṭīf attended this royal and courtly *majlis*, he was participating in a long tradition of knowledge production and performance that would have been familiar to learned men from Cordoba to the Caspian Sea and beyond. To be a learned and sophisticated man was to be capable of participating and appreciating this smorgasbord of discussion and performance that was the *majlis*.

The present chapter takes up the digressive commentary of al-Sharīshī, an Andalusian scholar hailing from the city of Jerez (*Sharīsh*). I argue that his commentary is structured as an entextualized *majlis*. That is, the commentary takes the elements and flow of a *majlis* conversation and puts them into a book devoted to the wide array of material found in the practice of *adab*. As a result, the commentary unfolds like a sparkling conversation, full of poetry and anecdotes, alongside the glossing of difficult words. Whereas a *majlis*'s sparkling conversation might meander from topic to topic based on the interests of its patron or the temperaments of its participants, al-Sharīshī's commentary is a *majlis* that usually lets the text of the *Ḥarīriyya* set the starting point of conversation if not, as we will see, determine its destination. The effect of al-Sharīshī's mode of digressive commentary is what we can call a "commentarial anthology" of *adab*.[3] As Everett Rowson has put it in a study of a later period, digressive commentaries "offered a unique way of presenting miscellaneous information" and allowed commentators and readers to delight in the intertextuality of the *adab* tradition.[4]

The digressions of al-Sharīshī's commentary, and of other digressive commentaries, offer an exploration of eclectic knowledge that mirrors the *majlis*. At the same time, the digressive commentary of al-Sharīshī seems to blur the boundary between text and commentary by "running alongside" the text and adding to it. Given that the scenes in the *Ḥarīriyya* often portray *majālis* in which al-Ḥārith and Abū Zayd participate, it may be best to think of al-Sharīshī's commentary as a kind of amplification of the text through which the commentator joins the author and his characters by juxtaposing his own commentarial *majlis* with the *majālis* depicted within the *Ḥarīriyya*. After all, Abū Zayd is often performing erudite discourse in *majlis*-like settings for judges, rulers, al-Ḥārith, and his companions.

The argument of this chapter unfolds in four parts. First, I introduce the *majlis* and the *adab* anthology. This section demonstrates how the two are intertwined conceptually and practically. The anthology, depending on its form, serves as a kind of textual aid to the *majlis*-goer (the *jalīs*) or as a textual representation of a *majlis* conversation, moving from topic to topic in more or less unexpected ways. Second, I show how al-Sharīshī's discussion of male-male love mimics the patterning of what one might find in the kind of anthology that mimics the *majlis*. Third, I suggest that al-Sharīshī's activity of running alongside the text of the *Ḥarīriyya* opens up a space to engage with material that goes well beyond what is actually introduced within the base text. I conceptualize this form of commentarial digression as "gate-crashing" the text. That is, al-Sharīshī acts as an uninvited guest, steering the conversation to serve his own ends. The *ṭufaylī* or "uninvited guest" is, in fact, a major theme of the *Ḥarīriyya* and *adab* more broadly.[5] Thus, al-Sharīshī's *ṭufaylī* commentary is paradoxically both an uninvited guest to al-Ḥarīrī's party and a text that responds to the *ṭufaylī* spirit of the *Ḥarīriyya*. Finally, I introduce the notion that some adaptations of the *Ḥarīriyya* can be understood as a form of commentary, taking up and reformulating the *Ḥarīriyya* in new ways. In one case, a sixth/twelfth-century Andalusian author wrote a *maqāma* featuring the same two characters as we find in the *Ḥarīriyya*: Abū Zayd al-Sarūjī and al-Ḥārith b. Hammām. As with commentarial gate-crashers, this *maqāma* author saw the *Ḥarīriyya* as what I will call an "open *majlis*," one that invited the ostensibly uninvited *ṭufaylī* to join, amplify, edify, and entertain.

Whereas the interpretive modes of world literature insist on paying attention to the literariness of a text, excising the *Ḥarīriyya* from the social and interpretive contexts that gave it life, this chapter roots the digressive commentary tradition in the social institution of the *majlis*. The outrageous citational games and baroque referentiality of the *Ḥarīriyya* find an enthusiastic interlocutor in al-Sharīshī's commentary, which expands on al-Ḥarīrī's text in both informative and unexpected ways. Whereas notions of the literary that flourished under the auspices of world literature have tended to view commentary as merely explanatory or supplementarily digressive, this chapter argues that the commentary participates in meaning-making. Moreover, this chapter theorizes commentary and adaptation from within the Arabic tradition in ways that are not rooted in the literary theory of world literature but are rather rooted in the concept of gate-crashing, which is central to both the *majlis*'s imaginary and the *Ḥarīriyya*'s narrative structure.

The *Majlis* as Live-Action Anthology

Let us begin with the relationship between the *majlis* and the *adab* anthology. For starters, it should be noted that there were many different kinds of *majālis*, some devoted to preaching, others devoted to transmitting texts, like the gatherings devoted to reading the *Ḥarīriyya* that we examined in Chapters 2 and 3.[6] Although some *majālis* might take place in courtly settings in which hierarchies would have been emphasized, others might take place among those of more or less equal station.[7] The kind of *majālis* with which we are concerned in this chapter are much more eclectic and harder to define because they were devoted to *adab*. These gatherings are sometimes referred to as the "intimate *majālis*" or *majālis al-uns*, but this friendly name should not obscure the fact that *majālis* were sites of intellectual competition and high-stakes performances. One needed to be erudite, elegant, and apropos to participate effectively. One needed, in other words, to have mastered a wide range of material from poetry to grammar to hadith to law.[8] As Wolfhart Heinrichs and others have pointed out, the term *adab* encompasses not simply a textual corpus or a genre but also a social practice of "having the apposite quotation at one's fingertips."[9] The *majlis* was therefore a paradigmatic place for people to participate in both the texts and practices of *adab*.

The *majlis* was also a model for *adab* texts more broadly. Authors could put before their readers an assortment of discourses by depicting either real or imagined *majālis*. There is perhaps no better example of this phenomenon of the *majlis* as an entextualized live-action anthology than the *Kitāb al-Imtāʿ wa-l-Muʾānasa* (*Book of Delight and Conviviality*) of al-Tawḥidī (d. 414/1023). This text purports to depict a series of *majālis* that took place over the course of many nights between the author, his patron, and a handful of other learned men. Al-Tawḥīdī depicts himself as a kind of live-action anthologizer, bringing together eloquent pieces of wisdom from different disciplines, from politics and philosophy to poetry and Quranic exegesis. In one evening's discussion, al-Tawḥīdī recounts the debate between a grammarian and a logician about which of the two disciplines was superior.[10] On another evening, al-Tawḥīdī puts before his patron a series of different opinions on the virtues and vices of Arabs and non-Arabs.[11] On still another evening, al-Tawḥīdī's patron asks him to discuss the value of poetry when compared to prose.[12] In each case, although in different ways, al-Tawḥīdī marshals the arguments for either side, quoting advocates with differing opinions or listing the merits and demerits of each, a point that will be important in what follows.

The result of al-Tawḥīdī's act of entextualizing these *majālis* is a text of digressive anthologizing that is often driven by the questions and demands of al-Tawḥīdī's patron, the vizier. As with a live *majlis*, however, any person participating in a *majlis* had the ability to shift the discussion in a new direction because conversation is unpredictable and proceeds, at times, through a kind of free association that delights in intertextuality. As the Arabic dictum has it, "Conversation is a many-branching thing (*al-ḥadīth dhū shujūn*)."[13] An example of this can be found in the twenty-fourth evening of the *Kitāb al-Imtā*ʿ, which begins in medias res. Al-Tawḥīdī states that those present at the *majlis* were discussing elephants, but their descriptions were of little interest or benefit.[14] Al-Tawḥīdī then decides to insert himself into the discussion and to change its direction somewhat, veering into more general questions about animal species, their habitats, and their natures, which then leads to a discussion of minerals and *their* natures. About a third of the way through the chapter, the vizier interrupts and asks a seemingly unrelated question concerning the difference between the Arabic words for spirit (*rūḥ*) and soul (*nafs*), and al-Tawḥīdī seizes on this invitation to discuss philosophies of the soul.[15] The vizier expresses his admiration for these insights, encouraging him as he often does to commit the conversation to writing.[16] It is at this point that, without further prompting, al-Tawḥīdī turns to an at-first seemingly unrelated topic. He tells the vizier that his teacher, the philosopher Abū Sulaymān (d. ca. 375/985), had recently asked after the vizier, seeking some intelligence about whether the vizier had received his letter and what the vizier's opinion was of his "service to his polity (*khidmatī li-dawlatihi*)."[17] Al-Tawḥīdī continues quoting Abū Sulaymān, who goes on at some length to discuss the burdens of the vizier's job and to put forward a kind of political theology on the relationship between religion and this-world (*al-dīn wa-l-dunyā*). Although not invited to the *majlis*, Abū Sulaymān's message to the vizier, or at least al-Tawḥīdī's version of it, can be brought into the conversation.

To summarize, the version of this evening's conversation presented in the *Kitāb al-Imtā*ʿ has gone from elephants to questions of the soul to the relationship between religion and politics. It would be impossible to assign this evening's conversation a topical label because, as presented in al-Tawḥīdī's text, it meanders from one topic to another in unexpected ways, sometimes due to prompting from the patron and sometimes due to al-Tawḥīdī's own sense of what is worthwhile and relevant. As we will see later on in this chapter, al-Sharīshī's digressive commentary sometimes unfolds in similarly unpredictable ways. For now, it is evident that the *Kitāb al-Imtā*ʿ is both an attenuated textual representation of a *majlis* and a kind of anthology that brings together diverse discursive materials. To become an expert *majlis* participant, one evidently needed to have a wide array of discourse at one's beck and call. To do that, one might study a different kind of anthology, one that organized its materials topically.

To become an effective *majlis* participant, one needed a great deal of variegated knowledge, and thus any man wishing to be good company must have been in want of a good *adab* anthology. Although one might pick up sundry anecdotes and poems here and there, a well-organized *adab* anthology could provide the reader with a range of material on the typical topics of *majlis* discourse. The *majlis* and the *adab* anthology were thus linked on a practical level. This point is emphasized by the Andalusian Mālikī legal scholar Ibn ʿAbd al-Barr (d. 463/1071), who lived more than a century before al-Sharīshī. Ibn ʿAbd al-Barr, despite being more famous for his role as a jurist, composed a massive *adab* anthology that emphasizes in both its title and its contents the intertwining of anthologies with *majlis* culture. He called his anthology *Bahjat al-majālis wa-uns al-mujālis*, which translates to "the delight of *majālis* and the pleasing companionship of the *majlis* participant." According to the anthologizer's introduction, "Perusing the arts of *ādāb* [the plural of *adab*]" is the most worthy pursuit after one understands the Quran and the Prophet Muḥammad's narrative and normative legacy (the *sunna*). Ibn ʿAbd al-Barr then states that the purpose of his anthology is to make those who memorize its contents "an adornment to his *majālis* and a pleasing companion to his fellow *majlis* participant (*zīnan fī majālisihi wa-unsan li-mujālisihi*)."[18] According to the anthologizer, his work is organized in this format to make it easier to memorize, and he also notes that most chapters begin with hadith of the Prophet, which he considers part of *adab*.

Ibn ʿAbd al-Barr claims that he has gathered together in each chapter different sides of a given issue so that one may either intelligently join with one's companion in his opinion or, if one wishes, "contradict him with the opposite opinion on that very same topic (*muʿāraḍatahu bi-ḍiddihi fī dhālika al-maʿnā*)."[19] As Luke Yarbrough points out in his study of a chapter within this anthology, each section presents "a selection of apposite prose and poetry that sometimes shows a decided moral drift, or drifts, but often merely furnishes the reader with eloquent sayings touching on a wide range of viewpoints and behaviors." More often than not, the anthologist does not intervene to point out which is the correct position, so it is not always clear what the "moral" of a particular chapter might be, or if one exists at all.[20] For example, the chapter on jesting includes sayings of the Prophet and other prominent figures endorsing the practice but also includes reports that condemn joking and excessive laughter.[21] The point of this anthology seems less about offering a particular "moral" lesson than arming *majlis* participants with what they need to join either side of a discussion.

Whereas the *Bahjat al-Majālis* is organized for ease of reference, other *adab* anthologists intentionally avoided thematic organization and structured their anthologies to move from one topic to another in unpredictable, yet structured, ways. These anthologies were, in other words, more *majlis*-like in their organization. An anthology of this type was authored by another Andalusian with whom al-Sharīshī was surely familiar—namely, Abū Isḥāq al-Ḥuṣrī (d. 413/1022). His *Zahr al-Ādāb* brings together a great deal of poetry and prose from the Islamic East, including twenty of al-Hamadhānī's *maqāmas*. Al-Ḥuṣrī states his goal in organizing his text as follows:

> It is a book in which the reader moves from prose to poetry, from natural to crafted, from disputation to adulation. . . . I have avoided organizing the verses that I have gathered into sections, while also avoiding putting one form far away from its like and isolating one thing from what is similar to it. I have made part of it interlinked (*musalsalan*) and left part of it unbound (*mursalan*), so that it might be elegantly chosen and its linkages well-formed. It includes both kinds of composition and contains both modes of compilation. . . . What remains I disperse in the rest of [the text] so that it is safe from boring long-windedness.[22]

Al-Ḥuṣrī's *Zahr al-Ādāb* moves from one topic to another in a kind of free association. Long sections of the text unfold with each new topic relating in some way to the previous one. The ideal of moving from one topic to another to avoid boring the reader is well-attested in earlier *adab* texts. It is found in the works of the third/ninth-century theologian and *adīb* al-Jāḥiẓ (d. 255/868–69), whose work, especially his lengthy *Kitāb al-Ḥayawān*, was seen by later digressive commentators like al-Ṣafadī as justification for their digressive style.[23] The jurist-*adīb* al-Muʿāfā b. Zakariyyā al-Jarīrī (d. 390/1000) explicitly compares the two ways of organizing material in the introduction to his anthology, listing some scholars who had made their work contain "separate chapters (*abwāban mubawwaba*)" addressing specific topics. The material in his book, by contrast, is "scattered, not organized into chapters," and it is for this reason that he calls his book *al-Jalīs al-Ṣāliḥ* (*The Suitable Majlis Participant*).[24] This ideal of mixing different kinds of discourses together was so readily accepted that we find the theologian and exegete Fakhr al-Dīn al-Rāzī (d. 606/1209) drawing on it in his exegesis of the throne verse in the Quran (Q 2.255). He notes that this verse combines theological, juridical, and narrative material and that moving from one to another "delights the heart, as though one is traveling from one country to another or moving from one garden to another or switching from eating one delicious food to eating another."[25]

Turning back to al-Ḥuṣrī's *Zahr al-Ādāb*, the anthologizer's digressive style is best illustrated through a brief account of the anthology's first digression, which is a disquisition on eloquence. Al-Ḥuṣrī's first anecdote concerns the Prophet Muḥammad and his encounter with two men, al-Zibriqān b. Badr and the poet ʿAmr b. al-Ahtam. The poet praises al-Zibriqān but then, when al-Zibriqān says the poet would say more were it not for his jealousy, the poet insults him. The Prophet is vexed by ʿAmr's contradictory statements, but the poet explains that he had first said the best of what he knew about the man but, when angered, said the worst of what he knew. ʿAmr insists that "I did not lie in the first instance and was truthful in the second."[26] This leads the Prophet to marvel that "some eloquence is magic, and some poetry is wisdom."[27]

After this anecdote, al-Ḥuṣrī's anthology offers biographies of both ʿAmr and al-Zibriqān before discussing a related phrase that praises eloquence as "licit magic (*al-siḥr al-ḥalāl*)." The anthology then includes a story in which the famously pious Caliph ʿUmar b. ʿAbd al-ʿAzīz (d. 101/720) uses the phrase "licit magic," then says that the poet Abū Tammām (d. 231/845 or 232/846) "took what ʿUmar said" and used it in his poetry to boast of his eloquence. More anecdotes and poems follow revolving around the use of this phrase until we find one poet using it to describe an eloquent woman whose speech was "licit magic" and who was a "snare for the minds" of men. The anthologist then briefly explores the motif of eloquent speech as an element of attraction, identifying other poets who used the same trope, including ʿUlayya (d. 210/825), the sister of Hārūn al-Rashīd. ʿUlayya's poem then leads to a discussion of her affection for an enslaved youth (*ghulām*) and her other poems. The anthologist then quotes some poets whose verses resemble those of ʿUlayya.

Al-Ḥuṣrī's anthology is digressively discursive and, in some sense, mimics the *majlis* itself. Unlike the *Bahjat al-Majālis*, which offers itself as a training tool and reference work for a *majlis* participant, al-Ḥuṣrī's *Zahr al-Ādāb* is an entextualized conversation. New topics are introduced not by chapter breaks but by picking up on some aspect of the previous poem or anecdote. In some sense, then, al-Ḥuṣrī's anthology operates as a digressive commentary on itself. Just as with al-Panjdīhī's commentary, where the mere mention of a beard can lead to various reports on beards, the mere mention of a person or a phrase in al-Ḥuṣrī's anthology can lead to one digression after another. As I noted in the Dramatis Personae with which this book began, al-Panjdīhī's commentary was al-Sharīshī's stated inspiration for composing his long commentary. According to al-Sharīshī's introduction, he had studied the *Ḥarīriyya* intensely, but when he came across al-Panjdīhī's commentary, he found it to be "the desired wish and the long-cherished goal that had, until that time, been veiled and concealed from me."[28] As we saw briefly in Chapter 6, al-Sharīshī's commentary cannibalizes al-Panjdīhī's material, while at the same time adding new material and removing some of the philological and scriptural references found in al-Panjdīhī.

What makes al-Sharīshī's commentary more closely resemble a *majlis* or an *adab* anthology is the new material that he adds. First, as al-Sharīshī explains in the introduction, he aims to draw attention to intertextualities, much like al-Ḥuṣrī does when showing how different poets drew on the poetry of others. According to al-Sharīshī, he seeks to "clarify the source of al-Ḥarīrī's speech (*tabyīn ma'khadh al-Ḥarīrī fī al-kalām*)." Second, al-Sharīshī tells us that his commentary will draw attention to the author's use of rhetorical figures (*ṣināʿat al-badīʿ*), such as paronomasia (*tajnīs*). Third, he says that the commentary will "spread wide the carpet of *adab*'s various kinds, bring forth great quantities of good poetry, both earnest and jesting, in the proper places for their appreciation, and match each section with that which increases its beauty and clarity."[29] The commentary thus enhances the beauty of the *Ḥarīriyya* by producing an anthology of poetry, prose, and erudition that follows the lead of al-Ḥarīrī's *maqāma*s and is as sparkling as a *majlis*'s conversation.

As al-Sharīshī puts it, the commentary "runs alongside Abū Muḥammad [al-Ḥarīrī] in accordance with the expansiveness of his gait and vastness of his territory." The result of this running alongside the author is an entextualized *majlis* that participates in and amplifies the text. Whereas al-Panjdīhī tends to restrict himself to a more narrowly construed Islamic archive, quoting poetry relatively rarely, al-Sharīshī shifts his attention to the broader remit of *adab*. For example, we saw in the previous chapter that, in *maqāma* #1, the narrator al-Ḥārith expresses his shock at Abū Zayd's hypocrisy. Al-Panjdīhī quotes the Quran and hadith about the evils of hypocrisy. Al-Sharīshī, by contrast, says that this story is reminiscent of stories about the Abbasid poet Abū Nuwās (d. ca. 198/813), who was famous for his love of wine, youths, and profligacy in general. Al-Sharīshī quotes two stories in which Abū Nuwās attends *majālis* that include pious sermons. In the first, he is found weeping, which is taken as a sign of his sincere repentance. It is discovered, however, that he is weeping over the beauty of a young man in attendance. In the second, he admits that he only attended "on account of this gazelle," by which he means a beautiful youth.[30] As with al-Ḥuṣrī's anthology, al-Sharīshī is juxtaposing thematically related material, but he is prompted not only by his own previous digressions but also by the text of the *Ḥarīriyya*.

Another striking example of how al-Sharīshī's digressions diverge from al-Panjdīhī's can be found in the opening passage of *maqāma* #10, in which the narrator sees "a youth (*ghulām*) who was forged in the mold of beauty."[31] As we might expect, al-Panjdīhī uses this opportunity to point out intertexts in the hadith of the Prophet involving beautiful youths. In al-Panjdīhī's commentary, we find two Prophetic reports about beauty. First, there is a story of the Prophet greeting an envoy from the ʿAbd al-Qays tribe, among whom is "a fair-faced youth."[32] The Prophet seats the youth behind him, explaining that "my brother David was ruined by a glance," alluding to the biblical story of his temptation by the beauty of Bathsheba, whom he sees bathing on the roof (2 Samuel 11). Versions of the David story that include his temptation are transmitted in the Islamic narrative tradition, such as in the *ʿArāʾis al-Majālis* of al-Thaʿlabī (d. 427/1035).[33] Al-Panjdīhī then follows this report with a second in which the Prophet is said to have stated that "God does not punish those with beautiful faces and deep black eyes (*sūd al-ḥadaq*)."[34]

By contrast, al-Sharīshī's response to the same passage about a beautiful youth in *maqāma* #10 is much more extensive and worth examining in some detail because it amounts to a short anthological essay on beauty, desire, love, and theology, which comes to seven pages in the modern printed edition.[35] It is not limited to Prophetic reports, although he includes the hadith reports that were quoted by al-Panjdīhī near the end of his digressive essay. Al-Sharīshī's goal in this portion of the commentary is, as he puts it, to mention "descriptions of comeliness and beauty, to the extent possible, to which I will add what is said about youths (*ghilmān*) in pleasing poetry that befits this place."[36] It is worth noting that al-Sharīshī emphasizes that what he mentions endeavors to be fitting for "this place"; that is, it conforms to the constraints of the context of a digressive commentary, just as a *majlis* participant might endeavor to make his statements appropriate for their context. He is also concerned with what it is "possible" to mention, alluding perhaps to his desire to avoid boring his reader with prolixity. In both of these matters, al-Sharīshī is echoing the norms of the kind of *majālis* described above, in which various kinds of poetry and knowledge were performed to delight the gathered company. The adept participant in a *majlis* was able to offer pleasing poems and other discourses without boring the listener.

As is often the case with anthologies, individual reports, poems, and interjections by the anthologizer are brought together. The discussion and the "argument," if there is one, emerges implicitly and through accumulation. Although difficult to summarize or separate into discrete sections, I have done both below to give the reader some sense of how al-Sharīshī's eclectic digressions unfold in volume one of the Beirut edition.

Al-Sharīshī on Beauty and Beautiful Youths:

I. Philology (page 376): A philological discussion of the colors associated with beauty (*ḥusn*), including a quotation from Ibn ʿAbd Rabbih's *adab* anthology *al-ʿIqd al-Farīd* and from al-Ḥarīrī's work on solecisms, the *Durrat al-Ghawwāṣ* about why it is said "beauty is redness." Several lines of poetry are cited to substantiate the philological discussion.

II. On Beauty (pages 376–78): A series of statements and stories appear that discuss the nature of beauty and the subtle differences between the words one uses to describe beauty. For example, it is said regarding a young woman (*jāriya*) that "she is pretty (*jamīla*) from afar and comely (*malīḥa*) from close up." It is explained that *jamīla* is said to refer to one who is beautiful when taken in all at once, whereas *malīḥa* refers to one who increases in beauty the more one looks. Several of these stories include verses, some of which call to mind other verses, which al-Sharīshī duly quotes.

III. The Appreciation of True Beauty (pages 378–79): There is a subtle shift in this section from discussing beauty itself to addressing the *appreciation* of beauty when al-Sharīshī quotes an unnamed source that "elegance is a matter of stature, excellence is in the neck, delicacy is in the limbs and waist, but the whole affair is a matter of speech (*al-sha'n kulluhu fī al-kalām*), and the axis is the intellect."[37] Another unnamed source suggests that beauty is made up of two aspects that can be described and a third that cannot be, though it is given many names, such as "the shape of the soul" and "the fire of passion." To the extent that this third property has taken hold in the heart, "the power of desire (*sulṭān al-hawā*) rules over the intellect." Al-Sharīshī identifies this report as the best that this section of commentary has to offer—its "cream (*zubda*)," which rises to the top. A poem by Imruʾ al-Qays is cited to praise natural beauty that requires no adornment, an apparently related point.

IV. Refined Male Love (pages 379–80): Al-Sharīshī then discusses two stories of famous scholars who loved other men. The first is about the famous grammarian Sībawayh, whose male student wore a veil to avoid distraction. The second is Abū Ḥātim al-Sijistānī, who, "in spite of his excellent character," loved his student al-Mubarrad, who had attended his study circles when he was a handsome youth. Al-Sharīshī quotes eight lines of al-Sijistānī's poetry on his beloved. The commentator then states that "being passionately fond of beauty is a trait that God has bestowed on his saints and great scholars, as well as those below them among the riffraff and the rabble." As he explains, the sweetness of the fruit depends on the goodness of the soil. Therefore, love for a noble soul can be good, whereas other sorts that are set in bad soil can be bad. He then quotes a certain *Kitāb al-Wishāḥ* to the effect that passion (*ʿishq*) clothed in chastity is noble, citing Quran 43.67: "Friends will be foes to one another on that day, except for the God-fearing."[38]

V. Theology and Love Theory (pages 380–81): Al-Sharīshī states that there is a group of Baghdadī theologians who believe that desire (*hawā*) is a test for humans that prepares them for love of the divine. Responding to the delight of the beloved's happiness and the difficulty of their anger helps them in understanding the appropriate relationship to God, who is, after all, more deserving of their love and devotion. A series of other statements apparently attributed to this group of theologians delve more into love theory. For example, they say that a lover (*ʿāshiq*) is so full of blessings that he can go without the basic necessities of life. As an example of this, they cite the story of the famous lovers Jamīl and Buthayna who spent two days together without food, surviving instead on one another's spittle. This is followed by a description of a kind of coquettishness as "one of the conditions of the beloved (*min sharṭ al-maʿshūq*)," a phrase with clear echoes in love theory.

VI. Prophetic Beauty (page 381): Al-Sharīshī states that all of God's prophets have been dazzlingly beautiful to their people, such that if one beholds a prophet for even a moment, one recognizes that he has the best form and the most perfect figure. This statement is preceded by a short discourse on the way that God only creates human forms free of blemish to honor them and that the outer form and the inner virtues are made to match one another.

VII. Reports of the Prophet (page 381): Here, al-Sharīshī quotes the same reports found in al-Panjdīhī, which state that those with beautiful faces will not be punished in hell and that the Prophet placed a beautiful youth behind him lest what befell the prophet David might happen to him.

VIII. Poems on Beauty (pages 381–83): Al-Sharīshī notes that poets have composed much poetry that describes beauty, and he introduces six excerpts by four different poets, which he considers "among the best." Regarding the first poem, he says that it is "as if it describes the youth whom al-Ḥarīrī mentions." The poets are Ibn Bassām al-Shantarīnī (d. 542/1147–48), Ibn Khafāja (d. 533/1138), Abū Nuwās, and Ibn Wakīʿ (d. 393/1003). Each is quoted here only once except for Ibn Khafāja, who is quoted three times. Both Ibn Bassām and Ibn Khafāja are Andalusīs who lived only decades before their fellow Andalusī al-Sharīshī, who was born in 557/1181.

The structure of al-Sharīshī's discussion of beauty moves from preliminary matters regarding how to define beauty to much more complex topics and finally to poetry. In fact, poetry makes up a little less than half of the entire digression because illustrative verses are quoted throughout. The digression covers a lot of ground. Taken together, it argues for an appreciation of beauty that transcends the carnal and an understanding of a pure form of love that is available only to elite intellectuals.[39]

The central sections (IV–VI) on the topics of refined male love, theology, love theory, and prophetic beauty demonstrate that this commentary should not be seen as "less Islamic" or "more secular or literary" than al-Panjdīhī's commentary. Al-Sharīshī not only includes the hadith reports that he finds in al-Panjdīhī but also expands the repertoire of material to include stories of scholars who were known for their chaste desire for male disciples. In doing so, al-Sharīshī amplifies the report about the Prophet in which he chastely placed the beautiful youth behind him to avoid temptation. Al-Sharīshī also puts forward the possibility that the experience of desire and passionate love provides a way to discipline the self to be more receptive to love of the divine. Although he stops short of endorsing this view of "a group of Baghdādī theologians," it fits nicely with the themes that emerge across al-Sharīshī's microanthology on love—namely, that beauty and desire have ethical and religious significance. Al-Sharīshī's discussion of beauty unfolds like the erudite conversation of an ideal *majlis* or like the *adab* anthology that mimics the *majlis*. In a sense, what al-Sharīshī produces is a *majlis* that "runs alongside" al-Ḥarīrī's *maqāmas*. Indeed, the literal meaning of the word *maqāma* ("an instance of standing") mirrors that of the term *majlis* ("an instance of sitting"), and al-Ḥarīrī's *maqāmas* are often narrative depictions of *majālis*, in which eloquent, erudite conversation flows.

Joining the *Majlis* Commentarially

The intertwining of *maqāma*, *majlis*, and *adab* anthology is particularly on display in the *maqāmas* depicting debates in which different characters (or sometimes Abū Zayd himself) take different sides on a particular topic. For example, in *maqāma* #3, Abū Zayd displays his eloquence by first praising a dinar coin in verse and then censuring it moments later.[40] As we saw earlier in this chapter, the anthology *Bahjat al-Majālis* explicitly frames its purpose as preparing a reader to discourse eloquently on both sides of an issue. Similarly, al-Ḥuṣrī's anthology *Zahr al-Ādāb* begins with a discussion of eloquence that is prompted by a poet who takes both sides of a question by first praising a man and then censuring him, which leads the Prophet to compare eloquence to magic because it can transform our perception. As for the medieval readers of the *Ḥarīriyya*, they were well aware that a mark of its author's eloquence was the fact that several *maqāmas* praised and censured one and the same thing. As the Mamluk man of *adab* al-Ṣafadī puts it: "The eloquence (*balāgha*) of the man [i.e., al-Ḥarīrī] is obvious from his discoursing on a thing in many of his *maqāmas* with both praise and censure. This is eloquence itself, to describe a thing with praise and then censure it, or with censure and then praise it, as he did in the *maqāma* of the dinar, and the one in which he debated the excellence of chancery writing versus accounting, and the one in which he discusses the virginal versus the deflowered woman, and marriage versus bachelorhood, etc."[41] What al-Sharīshī adds to these eloquent debates is twofold. First, he situates the phenomenon of praising and censuring one and the same thing within the *adab* tradition.

Second, al-Sharīshī amplifies Abū Zayd's speeches with anecdotes and poems from the *adab* tradition that support one side or the other.

Let us begin with what al-Sharīshī says about the Arab tradition of "praising a thing and censuring it (*faṣl fī madḥ al-shay' wa-dhammihi*)," the presence of which in his commentary is explained "on account of the fact that al-Ḥarīrī praised the dinar and censured it."[42] The commentator's strategy for discussing the topic is to reproduce selected passages from an earlier book on the subject by Ibn Rashīq al-Qayrawānī (d. 456 or 463/1063–64 or 1071), a North African poet and literary critic whose anthology of poetry, known as *al-ʿUmda*, has come down to us but whose monograph on praise and censure has not.[43] Al-Sharīshī has thus preserved for us excerpts from an otherwise lost work that, like an *adab* anthology, contains quotations from earlier poets and authors and, at the same time, includes the author's own analysis. Al-Sharīshī's excerpting of Ibn Rashīq begins with a quote from al-Jāḥiẓ defending the Arabs against their critics, real or imagined: "The people fault the Arabs and claim that they praise that which they also disparage (*yahjūn*), but this is false. Everything has two sides (*laysa shay' illā wa-lahu wajhān*), so when they praise a thing, they mention the comelier of its two sides. When they censure it, they mention the uglier of its two sides."[44] This statement attributed to al-Jāḥiẓ echoes the opening of both the anthologies by Ibn ʿAbd al-Barr and al-Ḥuṣrī. Recall that in al-Ḥuṣrī the Prophet was initially vexed that a poet had first praised and then censured a man because it gave the appearance of lying but that the poet explained how he had first mentioned the best aspects of the man and then the worst. Al-Sharīshī, quoting Ibn Rashīq, immediately points out, however, that whatever al-Jāḥiẓ might say, "most of these instances of praise and censure are forms of hypocrisy (*munāfaqa*), not fair-dealing (*munāṣafa*)."[45] Al-Sharīshī has now both praised and blamed the act of praising and blaming one and the same thing. He has given us both sides about giving both sides!

Let us now turn to the second way that al-Sharīshī responds to these debates by amplifying Abū Zayd's speeches with quotations from the *adab* tradition. The effect of al-Sharīshī's commentary is to insert Abū Zayd's extemporized eloquence (or rather, as al-Sharīshī says here, passages that are actually representative of al-Ḥarīrī's eloquence) into a broader discourse. His commentary is a *majlis* that is discussing a *majlis*—it joins the *maqāma*'s conversation, amplifying it and situating it within a field of quotable knowledge. In the case of *maqāma* #3 discussed above, al-Sharīshī draws explicitly on the monograph of Ibn Rashīq, which is itself an anthology of various stories and poems on the topic of praise and censure. In the commentary on the very next *maqāma*, however, we can see how al-Sharīshī picks up on a debate within the *maqāma*, while amplifying and situating it through his own anthologizing activity. *Maqāma* #4 begins with the narrator al-Ḥārith on his way to Damietta when he and his traveling companions stop for the night. He overhears a conversation between two nearby voices, one of whom asks the other, "What is your judgment on how you conduct yourself with your fellows and your neighbors?" The other voice replies with an eloquent speech on selfless hospitality, saying, "I care for the neighbor, even if he does me wrong; I strive to be friendly to one who attacks me; I bear with the companion, even if he causes me distress."[46] When he has finished, the first speaker chides him and calls him "my son," advising him to engage in a more transactional form of friendship, treating kindly and generously those who will do the same for him.[47] The narrator seeks out the source of these voices, and he recognizes Abū Zayd al-Sarūjī and his son wearing shabby clothes. Al-Ḥārith talks the two of them up to his traveling companions, and they collect gifts before sneaking off. Al-Sharīshī identifies the source of this debate in the Quran itself, which contains one verse that counsels patience in the face of wrongdoing (16.126), while the other insists that there is no blame on those who avenge being wronged (42.41).[48] Whereas Abū Zayd and his son performed their arguments eloquently, al-Sharīshī quotes the kinds of textual sources that we might find in an anthology. Al-Sharīshī's commentary on this episode "runs alongside" the debate between Abū Zayd and his son, participating in the debate over how human relationships ought to function and amplifying it with reference to the Quran, hadith, and poetry.

Al-Sharīshī's commentary is also marked by its Andalusian features and it is, in this way, like a *majlis*, responding and adapting to its audience. One of the best examples of this phenomenon is found in the commentary on *maqāma* #2, in which al-Sharīshī pays special attention to the differences between the Arabic vocabularies of the Islamic West and the Islamic East. Once again, a contrast between how al-Sharīshī sometimes follows al-Panjdīhī closely and sometimes diverges considerably is illustrative. This *maqāma*, which has been discussed in some detail in earlier chapters, has two parts. It is in the second part that Abū Zayd appears in a Basran library sporting a scruffy beard, the same beard that inspired the aforementioned commentarial digressions on beards. In the *maqāma*, Abū Zayd incites a conversation about poetry by asking what a fellow visitor is reading. The book turns out to be a collection of al-Buḥturī's poetry, and the reader quotes a line describing a woman's smile that he finds particularly compelling and original. Abū Zayd condemns the man's bad taste and insists that he compare it to a pair of verses on the same topic, which he then reveals to be his own composition. The commentaries of al-Panjdīhī and al-Sharīshī both discuss al-Buḥturī's life, his poetry, his participation in courtly *majālis*, and his interactions with fellow poets like Abū Tammām. In these digressions, the two commentaries are nearly identical.[49] Al-Sharīshī expands and prunes here and there, but he does not seem to think his audience is in need of any more explanation of these major poets of the Arabic tradition when compared to al-Panjdīhī's audience.

The situation changes considerably when the *maqāma* mentions the narcissus flower (*nirjis*).[50] The topic of flowers arises when the members of this scene's impromptu *majlis* express doubt about Abū Zayd's claim to be the author of his verses on al-Buḥturī's poetry, so they test him by demanding that he compose verses developing the theme of a new line of poetry that refers to a woman's tears as "pearls raining down from a narcissus."[51] As al-Sharīshī explains, many people dismiss this comparison of the eye and the narcissus because to them it is a yellow flower, and yellowness in the eyes is associated not with beauty or languid looks but with jaundice (*yaraqān*). To settle this matter, he asked one of his teachers (*baʿḍ ashyākhī*), who explained that the term *nirjis* among the people of the Islamic East refers not to the yellow narcissus, better known to us as the daffodil, but to a different flower that resembles the flower of the fava bean plant, which is white. Al-Sharīshī then goes on to give precise descriptions of this Eastern narcissus, citing poetry, and claiming that what the Easterners call *nirjis*, the Westerners call *bahār*. He notes the contrast of Western poetry, which compares the eye to the *bahār* flower, and he demonstrates that these verses closely resemble Eastern poetry about the *nirjis*.[52] This botanical-poetical investigation is not, however, a thorough study of poetic simile, and al-Sharīshī tells the reader to "examine the types of simile in [the commentary on *maqāma*] twenty-four, where you will find information on this type and others, God willing."[53] Al-Sharīshī is thus cognizant of his Andalusian audience and their potential prejudices about Eastern poetry with its metaphors that do not conform to the lived experience of Western readers. Similarly, in a passage of al-Sharīshī's commentary on *maqāma* #2 in which he evaluates Abū Zayd's poetry, he points out that Easterners wear black to mourn while Westerners wear white, once again citing poetry to prove this anthropological insight.[54]

Al-Sharīshī also attends to the desires of his audience even when they seem to run counter to his own. In his commentary on *maqāma* #8, al-Sharīshī recounts a charming story (*ḥikāya mustaẓrafa*) about the origins of a certain poem that he admits he wished to omit because he believed the anecdote to be both apocryphal and too famous to be worth mentioning. Nevertheless, he says, "one of the people of *adab* insisted that I mention it, so I have done so in an abridged form."[55] The story, it should be said, tells the tale of two destitute poets in rags who encounter one another on a stormy night. The first poet asks the other, "What are you?" The second replies that he is a poet and "the misfortune of *adab* has brought me to the state in which you see me." The two then jointly compose a poem and debate through the night about which of them is more destitute, agreeing in the morning to cast lots to decide who will remain and who will depart because, they reason, the presence of two ill-omened poets would be too much misfortune for a single town. The first poet, a certain al-Bakkī, loses and settles in Fez in present-day Morocco, where he becomes famous for afflicting its people with misfortune, a situation that al-Sharīshī considers too well-known to explain. This story of impoverished poets fits nicely with the *maqāma* genre's focus on eloquent rogues and beggars, and its popularity with the commentator's audience led to its inclusion in the text. The *majlis*, even when it is entextualized and curated as it is in al-Sharīshī's commentary, remains susceptible to the demands of its audience to redirect the conversation.

The inclusion of Western voices was not a given in *adab* anthologies from that region. One of the more famous anthologies is Ibn ʿAbd Rabbih's *Al-ʿIqd al-Farīd*.[56] It is said that the Buyid vizier al-Ṣāḥib ibn ʿAbbād heard about this book and sought to obtain it in hopes of learning something about the poetry of the Islamic West. When he was able to peruse the book, he remarked instead that it contained only sources from the East and reportedly exclaimed "These are our goods returned to us," a quote from the Quranic story of Joseph (12.65).[57] In yet another instance, al-Sharīshī is discussing al-Ḥarīrī's description of a sunset and juxtaposes two poems by the Baghdadi Ibn al-Rūmī (d. 283/896) with a poem by the Andalusian Ibn al-Zaqqāq al-Balansī (d. 528–30/1133–35). Al-Sharīshī also includes two lines of verse that an unnamed, young scribe (*warrāq*) had extemporized in the presence of al-Sharīshī's informant as he was leaving the city of Fez in the dusky evening.[58]

To sum up, al-Sharīshī's commentary "runs alongside" the *Ḥarīriyya* by anthologizing *adab* materials drawn from the early Arabic past and from his own Andalusī contemporaries. His commentarial *majlis* indicates what al-Sharīshī considers to be relevant intertextualities while seeking to offer the reader a kind of *adab* education structured around the *Ḥarīriyya*. At the same time, as I have hinted at in the introduction to this chapter, al-Sharīshī's commentary uses digressions to shift the conversation to topics that are unrelated to the words and motifs found in the *Ḥarīriyya*. In this sense, we can conceive of al-Sharīshī's commentary as a kind of "gate-crasher (*ṭufaylī*)." Al-Sharīshī's digressions are, in other words, not always prompted by the text of the *Ḥarīriyya* but seem to steal off in unexpected directions. Just as Abū Zayd joins *majālis* uninvited only to turn them to his own purposes, al-Sharīshī uses his digressions to introduce uninvited topics, bending the commentarial conversation to his will. At the same time, like Abū Zayd in *maqāma* #2, he introduces voices that seek to compete with and outdo al-Ḥarīrī's own words in a form of competitive emulation (*muʿāraḍa*). In other words, al-Sharīshī's form of gate-crashing is very much in keeping with both the spirit of the *Ḥarīriyya* and the spirit of the *majlis*, in which a gate-crasher becomes quite welcome by performing eloquently. To understand this phenomenon, let us turn to *maqāma* #16, in which both al-Ḥārith and Abū Zayd gate-crash a *majlis* and provide an opportunity for al-Sharīshī (and other Andalusians) to gate-crash the *Ḥarīriyya*.

Crashing the *Majlis*

Maqāma #16 finds the narrator al-Ḥārith in some unnamed locale in the Islamic West, the *maghrib*. He comes across a *majlis* and decides to insert himself into it as an uninvited guest—a *ṭufaylī*. A stranger also joins them, undoubtedly Abū Zayd, and the group decides to engage in a language game in which each member tries to invent a unique palindrome—that is, a phrase that is identical whether one reads it forward or backward. Al-Ḥārith cannot come up with one, so Abū Zayd takes his place, offering first a standard palindrome in prose and then, even more remarkably, extemporizing five lines of verses that are identical when read forward and backward. Although the members of the *majlis* beg him to stay and converse, Abū Zayd explains that he must return and bring his children a meal, so the members of the *majlis* supply him with food and send him with a messenger to ensure his return. Instead, Abū Zayd sends the messenger back with verses of admonition and advice to avoid overstaying one's welcome or visiting too often. One ought to seize one's opportunity (and any monetary gain) and then depart. It is, in a word, advice for a *ṭufaylī* on how to get while the getting is good and then get out before his hosts turn on him.

Al-Sharīshī takes the opportunity here to discuss the ethics of visiting (*ziyāra*), even though neither the term "visiting" nor "visitor (*zāʾir*)" appears in the text. He quotes stories and poems about visiting without a prior arrangement, but then he shifts abruptly to discuss a particular kind of visitor that is not mentioned in the *Ḥarīriyya*: the phantom or vision of the beloved (*ṭayf al-khayāl*), who visits the melancholy lover at night.[59] The *ṭayf al-khayāl* is certainly a visitor without an appointment, but al-Sharīshī has at this point strayed rather far from the text in which Abū Zayd is interested in how to be an effective *ṭufaylī*. Al-Sharīshī's decision to discuss the *ṭayf al-khayāl* is a kind of uninvited commentary, one that is not being shaped by the *Ḥarīriyya* per se. Just as al-Tawḥīdī steers the *majlis* in unexpected directions that are not directed by his patron's requests, al-Sharīshī steers his commentary as he pleases to cover topics that were not invited to the conversation by the text of the *Ḥarīriyya*. Al-Sharīshī's discussion of the *ṭayf al-khayāl* ends with a poem attributed to al-Sharīf al-Raḍī (d. 406/1015), which the poet says he composed in the year 387/997–98, leading his contemporaries to celebrate the originality of his variation on this theme, only to find a poem over thirty years later in the handwriting of his father with the same treatment of the trope. The poet then ponders whether his father had heard his poem and produced his own verses on the same theme or if he had forgotten hearing them and was unintentionally inspired to write this poem, a kind of poetic influence that he says is common among poets.[60] From visitors to visions to poetic influence, the digression diverges radically from the text on which it is ostensibly a commentary. Later Mamluk commentators would take this kind of digressive gate-crashing even further. Al-Ṣafadī's commentary on the *Lāmiyyat al-ʿajam*, a fifty-seven-line poem by al-Ṭughrāʾī (d. 514/1120), runs over eight hundred tightly packed pages in the nineteenth-century edition.[61] According to Kelly Tuttle, the commentary "branches off, often mid-explanation, into myriad digressions based on associations the author makes with words or ideas in the source-text." For Tuttle, this digression is intended to entertain and educate readers while also challenging and even frustrating them.[62] Even more than al-Sharīshī's subtle gate-crashing, al-Ṣafadī takes the reader well beyond the line of text in a kind of anthological romp. In another work, al-Ṣafadī even parodies the project of commentary itself by producing an erudite commentary on two lines of nonsensical poetry.[63]

What sets the *Ḥarīriyya* apart as a text to be commented on is that it seems to invite the ostensibly uninvited *ṭufaylī*. The text thematizes the eloquent *ṭufaylī* in *maqāmas* like #16, in which the *majlis* accommodates first al-Ḥārith and then Abū Zayd, suggesting that a *majlis* is made to be crashed, provided that the *ṭufaylī* can contribute in apt and elegant ways. Al-Sharīshī certainly leaped at this opportunity and, in doing so, joined other readers in the Islamic West who "gate-crashed" the text in other ways. For example, another Andalusian scholar named Aḥmad b. Muḥammad al-Kinānī added his own lines of verse to the text of a poem in *maqāma* #16. Al-Kinānī had traveled eastward in 579/1183–84, where he stayed long enough to complete the pilgrimage in 580/1184–85 and to hear the *Ḥarīriyya* from al-Khushūʿī, one of the last living transmitters of the text who had heard it from the author himself. According to al-Kinānī's biographer, the Andalusian scholar added two lines to the final poem in *maqāma* #16, in which both al-Ḥārith and Abū Zayd arrive as uninvited visitors to a *majlis*. The text of the poem reads as follows:

When you have picked the fruit of the date palm
  Do not save it for next year.
If you find yourself on the threshing floor,
  Fill your craw with the grain that's available!
Do not tarry when you have gathered goods
  and get stuck in the snare of the trapper.
And do not go too far when you swim,
  for safety is on the shore.
Address others saying "give now!"—Reply with "later!"
  Sell what you delay in exchange for what is present.
Do not visit a friend too frequently,
  for one is only bored by a constant visitor.[64]

Al-Kinānī, the Andalusī traveler, added the following two lines, matching the meter and rhyme of the earlier lines:

Do not grieve one who departs
  when you have glimpsed the brilliance of one arriving.
And do not stay silent too long in a gathering (*maʿshar*),
  even if you over-water the shrub (*wa-in zidta ʿabban ʿalā al-bāqil*).[65]

This Andalusian reader and transmitter of the *Ḥarīriyya* was joining in the "open *majlis*" of the text. The additional line of verse is, not coincidentally, an exhortation to welcome the newcomer. Al-Kinānī was adding his own voice to the text and, in some sense, was running alongside the *Ḥarīriyya* in a mode similar to al-Sharīshī. The *majlis* was a space for reciting the poetry of others and extemporizing poetry of one's own. Engaging with, responding to, and adding to the poetry of others was a quintessential *majlis* activity. The *majlis*, the *maqāma*, and the commentary were all arenas in which cocreating meaning could be achieved by running alongside the discourses of others. In the *Ḥarīriyya* itself, we have an example in *maqāma* #23 of a cowritten poem in which Abū Zayd and his son contribute alternating lines.[66]

Whereas al-Kinānī added lines, amplifying the text of the *Ḥarīriyya*, other Andalusian readers sought to compete with the text outright. In al-Sharīshī's commentary on *maqāma* #2, discussed above, he quotes some verses of Ibn Labbāl (d. 583/1188), another man from Sharīsh (Jerez), in which he performs a competitive emulation (*muʿāraḍa*) of Abū Zayd's poetry in the *maqāma*.[67] In a sense, Ibn Labbāl is participating in the *maqāma* itself, mimicking the activity of Abū Zayd, who takes a line of al-Buḥturī's poetry and seeks to outdo it with two lines of his own. Not to be left out, Ibn Labbāl also composes his own competitive emulation of al-Buḥturī's poem in the *maqāma*.

This kind of cocreation might seem odd in light of the claims by al-Panjdīhī and al-Muṭarrizī that the *Ḥarīriyya* is inimitable, although nothing invites attempts at imitation like an inimitable classic. Al-Sharīshī's digressive commentary, by contrast, is explicitly designed to augment the effect of the *Ḥarīriyya*, whether that is to increase the impact of a sermon on the soul or to more effectively relieve the reader's sorrows by adding to the text's amusing passages. In other words, this is a text that is open to improvement through amplification. There is also good reason to think that al-Sharīshī did not think that the *Ḥarīriyya* was beyond criticism. Indeed, he criticizes al-Ḥarīrī's long-windedness in *maqāma* #15, a story in which Abū Zayd solves an inheritance riddle after a long introduction revolving around hunger and food. The latter topic is taken up quite differently in al-Hamadhānī's *maqāma*, but al-Sharīshī takes the opportunity to critique both. "Abū Muḥammad [al-Ḥarīrī] was prolix in this *maqāma* to the point that it is a burden to the listener (*al-sāmiʿ*). Badīʿ al-Zamān al-Hamadhānī has a *maqāma* with a related theme that is clipped short (*batrāʾ*). If al-Hamadhānī's *maqāma* were lengthened and al-Ḥarīrī's were shortened, then the two would balance out."[68] Al-Sharīshī goes on to quote the entirety of al-Hamadhānī's too-short *maqāma*, which runs only about a page in the printed edition.

Reading al-Sharīshī's commentary is, in many ways, a well-rounded education in the world of *adab*. The *Ḥarīriyya* touches on many of the canonical topics and motifs of *adab*, and even when it does not in the case of the phantom of the beloved (*ṭayf al-khayāl*), al-Sharīshī draws the reader's attention to it through digression. The commentary's amplification of the *Ḥarīriyya* is a celebration of *adab*'s intertextuality. Gate-crashing the text, as al-Sharīshī's commentary does, is not a rebellion against *adab* but rather a way of participating in the self-conscious intertextuality of the *adab* tradition. The *Ḥarīriyya*'s open *majlis*, its layered referentiality, and the social context of its transmission invited readers across the Islamic world to participate in the text's amplification as they participated in its transmission.

Adapting the *Maqāma*

There was at least one other way to participate in the *Ḥarīriyya*'s open *majlis*: write a new *maqāma*. As I noted at the outset of this book, the *maqāma* was one of the most productive prose genres in the precolonial period, and many authors were drawing explicitly on and responding to earlier models. This was, after all, what al-Ḥarīrī had done. He explicitly refers to al-Hamadhānī's *maqāma*s as a model for his own in the preface of the *Ḥarīriyya*. Al-Sharīshī appreciatively notes the excellent decorum (*adab*) of al-Ḥarīrī in alluding to al-Hamadhānī's superiority, "even though he knew that his *maqāma*s were superior to al-Hamadhānī's."[69] Several of the themes and topics in the *Ḥarīriyya* are clearly drawn from a particular *maqāma* by al-Hamadhānī. For instance, al-Ḥarīrī's *maqāma* #18 is clearly a response to al-Hamadhānī's *maqāma maḍīriyya*, both of which begin with the eloquent rogue refusing food and then explaining to the gathered company why he has done so with an elaborate story. We thus find al-Ḥarīrī running alongside al-Hamadhānī, not through the citation of similar works of *adab* already in existence but through the production of new material. Al-Sharīshī even notes in his commentary the point at which al-Ḥarīrī's *maqāma* diverges from al-Hamadhānī's version, which coincides with the moment the two rogues launch into their stories to explain their rude refusal of a host's food. Al-Sharīshī also quotes the portion of al-Hamadhānī's *maqāma* that inspired that of al-Ḥarīrī.[70]

What would happen if we were to read al-Ḥarīrī's *maqāma* commentarially? That is, what if we understood the adaptation of al-Hamadhānī's *maqāma* as a series of interpretive choices, in a way that resonates with our treatment of Ḥarīrian commentary? In a sense, reading commentarially is no more than reading intertextually, but in the context of the *maqāma* tradition, these forms of intertextuality are often dismissed as mere imitation. The nineteenth-century translator Thomas Chenery dismisses al-Ḥarīrī's *maqāma* #18 by saying that "whatever merits it may possess are, however, diminished by the circumstance that it is a close imitation, and in parts almost a literal copy, of one by Al Hamadhâni," a view that continues to haunt scholarship on al-Ḥarīrī and the *maqāma*.[71]

My proposal is that al-Ḥarīrī's narrative choices in the adaptations of and variations on al-Hamadhānī's *maqāma*s are fruitful sites of interpretive engagement. In al-Hamadhānī's *maqāma maḍīriyya*, the rogue Abū al-Fatḥ refuses to eat the savory *maḍīra* stew because he had once been invited to a loquacious merchant's house to eat *maḍīra*. The arrival of the food is postponed over and over again as the merchant boastfully describes his wife, his possessions, and an enslaved male youth in excruciating detail. After a description of the merchant's toilet, the increasingly frustrated Abū al-Fatḥ finally gives up and departs, while the merchant chases after him yelling "Abū al-Fatḥ! The Maḍīra!" The youths think that *al-maḍīra* is Abū al-Fatḥ's nickname, and they start repeating the merchant's cry, prompting Abū al-Fatḥ to throw a stone in their direction. The stone pierces a man's skull, leading to a two-year imprisonment for Abū al-Fatḥ and his oath never again to eat *maḍīra*.[72] As Fedwa Malti-Douglas has shown, this *maqāma* draws on the narratives of misers (*bukhalāʾ*) and gate-crashers (*ṭufaylīs*).[73] The merchant manages to delay the fulfillment of a promise and to control the flow of discourse, both of which are normally the stratagems of Abū al-Fatḥ himself.[74] In the outer frame-story of the *maḍīriyya*, Abū al-Fatḥ is the one denying his companions the opportunity to eat *maḍīra*, substituting speech for food in a way that mirrors the activity of the merchant.

Al-Ḥarīrī's *maqāma* #18 parallels al-Hamadhānī while inverting and reshaping several features. It begins with Abū Zayd threatening to depart if a certain dish is served, but his quarrel is not with the food itself but with the glass vessel, which is transparent. When the diners ask after the reason for Abū Zayd's sudden outburst, he explains that a glass vessel is a spiller of secrets (*al-zujāj nammām*), and he has vowed for years never to share space with a spiller of secrets.[75] To explain his strange behavior, Abū Zayd relates a story about how he once possessed a beautiful and eloquent enslaved woman (*jāriya*) whom he guarded jealously. While hosting a neighbor (*jār*) for food and drink, he becomes intoxicated and makes the mistake of describing her beauty, her fine recitation of the Quran, and her sweet singing voice. Although he catches his mistake and swears his neighbor to secrecy, it is too late, and he blabs to the governor who is seeking a gift for his prince. Abū Zayd is forced to give up the woman, and this explains his aversion to that which betrays its secrets, whether they be friends or transparent vessels. Whereas al-Hamadhānī's *maqāma* ends rather abruptly at this point, al-Ḥarīrī's continues on with Abū Zayd reciting an invective poem against his neighbor. The host admires Abū Zayd's praise of the *jāriya* and his invective against the *jār*, so he showers him with gifts to the point that Abū Zayd cannot decide whether to complain about his neighbor or thank him for betraying his secret.[76]

Al-Ḥarīrī inverts al-Hamadhānī's *maqāma* in several respects. Whereas al-Hamadhānī's rogue Abū al-Fatḥ encounters a merchant who could not stop boasting of his possessions, al-Ḥarīrī makes it the rogue himself who boastfully describes his *jāriya*. Whereas al-Hamadhānī's merchant avariciously defers the fulfilment of a promise through language, Abū Zayd uses language negligently to disclose that which he had hoped to keep hidden. Al-Hamadhānī's *maqāma* depicts language as a kind of stand-in for absent material objects. Looking more broadly at al-Hamadhānī's oeuvre, it might be said that language is regularly "exchanged" for coin. As Devin Stewart has convincingly argued, the rogue's begging speeches find direct parallels in al-Hamadhānī's epistles in which he beseeches his patrons for material support. In this version of "literary mendicancy," the role of language is to transform immaterial language into the material rewards associated with commerce. Al-Ḥarīrī recasts language as the revealer of secrets. To speak is to put oneself at the mercy of rapacious tyrants, their agents, and their obsequious subjects like Abū Zayd's secret-spilling neighbor. Of course, Abū Zayd never really lets his language reveal more than he wishes, and one suspects that a more discerning audience might discover that neither the enslaved woman nor the neighbor in *maqāma* #18 ever existed but are brought into being by Abū Zayd's language. (The discerning reader of the *Ḥarīriyya* may likewise realize that Abū Zayd is summoned into being through language.) Whereas al-Hamadhānī's hero is sometimes exposed to actual violence, al-Ḥarīrī's Abū Zayd uses language to navigate nearby coercive authority, extracting their wealth while talking his way out of trouble. A similar obfuscation occurs in *maqāma* #8, discussed in Chapter 6, in which Abū Zayd and his son perform an eloquent dispute over damage done to one another's slaves. In that *maqāma* they eventually admit that their descriptions are elaborate double entendres, and the dispute is actually over mundane household objects. Under further scrutiny, they admit that the entire dispute was contrived; the items were conjured into mental existence through language. In *maqāma* #8, the purpose of eloquent language is not to reveal that which is hidden but to provide an eloquent and impenetrable shield of discourse. As Philip Kennedy has pointed out in his reading of the final *maqāma* in the *Ḥarīriyya*, in which the rogue repents his sins, the reader has been trained to understand that speech is an alibi for yet another ruse.[77] The eloquent rogue, after all, is just as capable of eloquently confessing as he is of eloquently transgressing, just as an elegant *majlis* participant can praise and censure one and the same thing.

If we read al-Ḥarīrī's *maqāma* #18 as a commentary on al-Hamadhānī's *maqāma maḍīriyya*, we can see that the slight refraction of al-Hamadhānī's meditation on hospitality, miserliness, and the ethics of boastful speech becomes al-Ḥarīrī's warning about the dangers of language when it is used as a means of communication rather than obfuscation. For al-Ḥarīrī, transparent language is folly because it renders one's property and one's intentions visible to capricious rulers and false friends. Better to be elusive by way of opaque language that can amaze, impress, and entertain without giving away what lies below the surface.

Just as al-Ḥarīrī modeled some of his *maqāma*s on al-Hamadhānī's, scores of authors would pen new *maqāma*s and *maqāma* collections over the following centuries. Many of those authors would draw on the themes and topics of the early *maqāma* collections in ways both obvious and subtle. A clear way in which some authors would announce that they sought to "run alongside" al-Ḥarīrī and al-Hamadhānī was that they would name their own characters in ways that echoed the names Abū Zayd al-Sarūjī and al-Ḥārith b. Hammām, just as al-Ḥarīrī echoed the character names of al-Hamadhānī. A handful of examples from both the Islamic East and West illustrate the point:

Maqāmāt of Badīʿ al-Zamān al-Hamadhānī
ʿĪsā b. Hishām / Abū al-Fatḥ al-Iskandarī
Maqāmāt of al-Ḥarīrī
al-Ḥārith b. Hammām / Abu Zayd al-Sarūjī

Maqāmāt of al-Saraqusṭī[78]
al-Sāʾib b. Tammām (via al-Mundhir b. Ḥumām) / Abū Ḥabīb al-Sadūsī
Maqāmāt of Abū Bakr al-Ḥanafī (fl. late sixth/twelfth century)[79]
al-Fāris b. Bassām / Abū ʿAmr al-Tanūkhī
al-Maqāmāt al-Qurashiyya of Ibn al-ʿAṭṭār (d. 691/1291)
ʿĀmir b. Tammām / Abū Burayd al-Tanūkhī
al-Maqāmāt al-Zayniyya of Ibn al-Ṣayqal al-Jazarī (d. 701/1301)[80]
al-Qāsim b. Jaryāl / Abū Naṣr al-Miṣrī
al-Maqāmāt al-Jalāliyya of al-Ḥasan b. Abī Muḥammad al-Ṣafadī (fl. early eighth/fourteenth century)[81]
Thāmir b. Zammām / Abū Fayd al-Lujūjī

Although not all iterations of the *maqāma* genre featured character names that closely follow those of the *Ḥarīriyya*, we find this kind of playful emulation echoing down into the four nineteenth-century *maqāma*s of al-Shidyāq spread across his four-volume magnum opus *Al-Sāq ʿalā al-Sāq*. He calls his narrator al-Hāris b. Hithām (that is, al-Ḥārith b. Hishām but pronounced with a lisp).[82] All of the *maqāma* authors mentioned here take up and adapt the themes and narrative strategies of the *Ḥarīriyya* in one way or another. For example, al-Ḥanafī takes up the theme of praising and censuring one and the same thing that we find in the *Ḥarīriyya*. Whereas al-Ḥarīrī usually allows Abū Zayd to both praise and censure the dinar, al-Ḥanafī distributes the roles between his eloquent rogue al-Tanūkhī and the narrator al-Fāris b. Bassām. Ibn Ṣayqal al-Jazarī amplifies the philological difficulty of the text. As Maurice Pomerantz has pointed out, the *maqāma* collection of Ibn al-ʿAṭṭār is closely modeled on the *Ḥarīriyya*.[83] In the margin of the manuscript beside each *maqāma* heading, save one, there is a marginal note identifying this *maqāma* as "corresponding (*muqābala*)" to a particular *maqāma* in the *Ḥarīriyya*.

This act of *muqābala* is also known as "competitive emulation (*muʿāraḍa*)." Competitive emulation could be either appreciative and celebratory, as in the case of Ibn al-ʿAṭṭār, or dismissive and derogatory.[84] As an example of the latter, the philologist Malik al-Nuḥāt (d. 568/1173), wrote a competitive emulation of the *Ḥarīriyya* in which he complained that al-Ḥarīrī's collection had become famous even though it contains "widespread solecisms throughout and weak language."[85] By contrast, Ibn al-ʿAṭṭār humbly describes his effort as "following in his footsteps . . . even though I know I am not suited for this aim."[86] For Ibn al-ʿAṭṭār, an appreciative form of running alongside the *Ḥarīriyya* could be achieved not only through commentary but through emulating individual *maqāma*s. The characters in his *maqāma*s are new, but they are reenacting themes and plot lines that have already been established by a prior text. These *maqāma*s are, in a sense, running alongside the *Ḥarīriyya*, not by collating a series of reports on the same topic as we might find in a commentary but by producing new narratives that mirror earlier *maqāma*s. For example, *maqāma* #4 in Ibn al-ʿAṭṭār's collection "corresponds" with *maqāma* #3 in the *Ḥarīriyya*, in which Abū Zayd both praises and censures a dinar and receives a dinar for each poem.[87] Ibn al-ʿAṭṭār's *maqāma* reproduces the same plot with new characters, new locations, and new language.

A different approach to competitive emulation came from an Andalusian who was among the first Andalusian readers of the *Ḥarīriyya*: Ibn Abī al-Khiṣāl. He wrote a *maqāma* that might best be referred to as the fifty-first adventure of Abū Zayd al-Sarūjī and al-Ḥārith b. Hammām because he uses the very same characters as al-Ḥarīrī does in his *maqāma*s. He has appropriated al-Ḥarīrī's characters and composed a *maqāma* that draws on the themes and tropes of the *Ḥarīriyya* while reformulating them in various ways. Ibn Abī al-Khiṣāl was a major Andalusian poet, bureaucrat, and epistolographer who was known in his day as "the one who holds the two vizirates (*dhū al-wizāratayn*)," but he was also an avid author of competitive emulations (*muʿāraḍa*s).[88] His *muʿāraḍa*s of al-Maʿarrī and al-Ḥarīrī seem to be appreciative appropriations; he wanted to participate in a kind of cocreation that would allow him to share in the narrative and philological traditions of the Islamic East, while producing his own material.

This fifty-first adventure of Abū Zayd and al-Ḥārith by an Andalusian author is, as Jaakko Hämeen-Anttila has pointed out, formally distinct from al-Ḥarīrī's *maqāma*s. It is considerably longer than any of al-Ḥarīrī's *maqāma*s, and its diction is different.[89] As with several of al-Ḥarīrī's *maqāma*s, Abū Zayd appears elderly and in shabby clothes, and he complains eloquently of his poverty and its effects on his wife and children.[90] The listeners are inspired to be generous with the elderly man, but al-Ḥārith is suspicious and does not join his fellows in their charity. It is here that Ibn Abī al-Khiṣāl's *maqāma* offers a fascinating reversal of the normal course of events in a Ḥarīrian *maqāma*. It is the rogue Abū Zayd who encounters a mysterious figure who turns out to be none other than al-Ḥārith. Conjuring the narrator to reveal himself, Abū Zayd says:

> "O strange form and doubting visage! Is there some matter that has made you sit and single yourself out? Will whatever brought you forth reveal you? Are you a vanguard for cut-throats, or is this the weakness of ascetics?"
> [Abū Zayd] paused forebodingly, then he took an arrow from his quiver and said, "State your lineage or receive your recompense (*intasib wa-illā fa-ḥtasib*)!"[91]

In the *Ḥarīriyya*, we find various characters demanding that Abū Zayd explain himself. Judges, governors, and al-Ḥārith (not to mention al-Hamadhānī's narrator ʿIsā b. Hishām) demand that the rogue identify his lineage, his purpose, or his hidden meaning.[92] In this fifty-first adventure of al-Ḥārith and Abū Zayd, the narrator takes this turning of the tables in stride, telling Abū Zayd to save his attacks for his enemies, "for you are the mighty Abū Zayd!"[93]

This happy meeting between the two does not last because, as we have seen, for example, in *maqāma* #2 of the *Ḥarīriyya*, Abū Zayd disappears, leaving behind a few verses. Ibn Abī al-Khiṣāl then amplifies Abū Zayd's departing verses commentarially, much like al-Sharīshī's own commentary, by quoting two poems with different rhyming endings that he introduces saying that these poems "are similar to that one (*wa-ilā dhālika*)."[94] Although the narrative thus far might stand as a *maqāma* on its own, Ibn Abī al-Khiṣāl engages in a variation on the two-act model of *maqāma* #2, in which al-Ḥārith reencounters Abū Zayd in a new locale by chance. In Ibn Abī al-Khiṣāl, however, al-Ḥārith tracks his friend down in a suburb of Baghdad where he is spending his newfound wealth on wine, eventually going into debt with the tavern owner (*khammār*). Al-Ḥārith has a long conversation with this tavern owner to secure Abū Zayd's release, a conversation that, as Hämeen-Anttila points out, allows the narrator to display his own rogue-like eloquence. And Hämeen-Anttila is surely correct that this *maqāma* allows for some balance, or perhaps even blurring, between the characters of al-Ḥārith and Abū Zayd. Whereas Hämeen-Anttila would, however, praise Ibn Abī al-Khiṣāl for his "novelistic" innovations and dismiss al-Ḥarīrī for "mere linguistic trickery," it seems more fruitful to read Ibn Abī al-Khiṣāl's adaptation *commentarially*. The author recombines various elements of earlier *maqāma*s while amplifying certain themes and trends. He recognizes that al-Ḥārith has some roguish eloquence in him that allows him to overcome the tavern owner and to become the mysterious figure in a gathering whose lineage must be demanded.

Riffing on the Tradition

The experience of reading al-Sharīshī's amplifying, commentarial participation with the *Ḥarīriyya* is the experience of watching a master of the craft of *adab* riffing on the tradition. To "run alongside" a text, as al-Sharīshī did, was an interpretive, commentarial act that blurred the boundary between commentary, emulation, and adaptation. To some extent, we can think of *adab* in general as a cross-temporal *majlis* that one can join, be invited to, and be expelled from. You can crash a *majlis* in an elegant way that makes your gate-crashing welcome, but to do so requires an immense body of knowledge and an ability to create something pleasing and apropos for an audience already intimately familiar with that immense body of knowledge. As I have argued, reading al-Sharīshī's commentary as a *majlis* invites us to read the post-Ḥarīrī *maqāma* tradition as a kind of commentary, drawing the attention of readers to particular unrealized possibilities within the *Ḥarīriyya*. If al-Sharīshī's commentary "runs alongside" with the *Ḥarīriyya* by drawing on the past, the *Ḥarīriyya*'s adaptations "run alongside" the classic *maqāma*s in a way that looks to the future. The *Ḥarīriyya* is thus a hinge text or nexus in the *adab* tradition, refracting its own cannibalization of the *adab* tradition in a way that would inflect the unfolding of Arabic prose for centuries to come.

Al-Sharīshī's commentary both resembled a *majlis* and circulated in *majlis*-like contexts. In the year 616/1219–20, the Andalusian biographer Ibn al-Abbār (d. 658/1260) found himself in the house of his teacher in Valencia, where he met al-Sharīshī and heard the commentator reading his commentary aloud to him and his teachers.[95] The biographer listened to a portion of the massive commentary and received a license to transmit its entirety. In other words, the entextualized *majlis* of al-Sharīshī's commentary was also an actual *majlis* that had been scripted ahead of time and in which the commentator would read the text aloud and lead his audience through a series of digressions. This live-action digressive anthology could exist both in a book and in a scripted *majlis* conversation.

In closing, let us think back to ʿAbd al-Laṭīf's early education, discussed in the opening of Chapter 2, in which the young student first encountered his teacher's baffling commentary and then became immersed in the tradition by studying "all the commentaries." To truly learn any text, ʿAbd al-Laṭīf had to become a commentator on that text himself, who could weave together the strands of the tradition in ways that both edified and delighted his audience. Reading with ʿAbd al-Laṭīf, as this book has invited us to do, involves diving into the rich intertextuality of *adab* and recognizing the ways in which commentators and readers participated in that tradition. The interpretive mode associated with world literature is, in the final analysis, one that seeks to excise the text from the interpretative traditions that gave it life. It certainly makes meaning of these texts, but it cannot appreciate the rich citational game of the commentarial tradition or the sophisticated intertextualities of gate-crashing writers who made the *maqāma* one of the most vibrant genres of Arabic writing before world literature.

Conclusion

> The notion of discontinuity is a paradoxical one: because it is both an instrument and an object of research; because it divides up the field of which it is the effect; because it enables the historian to individualize different domains but can be established only by comparing those domains.
>
> —Michel Foucault, *Archaeology of Knowledge*

> Yet any translation which intends to perform a transmitting function cannot transmit anything but information—hence, something inessential. This is the hallmark of bad translations.
>
> —Walter Benjamin, "Task of the Translator"

I have argued in this book that there is a considerable rupture between literary reading practices and those associated with commentary culture. Moreover, I have demonstrated that this rupture is not merely conceptual. The social, material, and intellectual practices—an entire ethics of reading that has been discussed and analyzed in this book—underpinned the production and interpretation of *adab* in an age of commentary. The curious thing about any claim about discontinuity, including the one that I have presented in this book, is that rupture functions as both a method and an object of research. Foucault describes this form of historical research as one that "transforms documents into monuments" and "deploys a mass of elements that have to be grouped, made relevant, placed in relation to one another to form totalities."[1] There is, therefore, a risk of a certain kind of circularity in the logic of an argument for discontinuity. One could, for example, dispute the thesis of this book by pointing out that there are certain continuities between commentarial reading and literary analysis. It is true, for example, that there are modes of literary analysis that are playful and that identify tantalizing intertextualities, just as al-Sharīshī or al-Panjdīhī have done in their digressive commentaries. Why not, then, seek out and emphasize these resonances?

One reason for telling a story of rupture is that it helps explain how radically the reception of the *Ḥarīriyya* was altered by the educational and ideological transformations of the nineteenth century. The overwhelming enthusiasm for the *Ḥarīriyya* in centuries past was not the result of poor literary tastes, as Charles Pellat had suggested, nor was it due to a preference for verbal pyrotechnics. One man's ostentatious fireworks might be another's resolutely practical internal combustion engine. This book has sought to make meaning out of the *Ḥarīriyya*'s richly allusive and elusive language in a manner that foregrounds the myriad ways in which participants in commentary culture made meaning of the text. Reading *adab* "as literature" is certainly a legitimate project, and I am not denying that the *Ḥarīriyya* can be interpreted and appreciated with the tools of literary analysis. What reading *adab* as literature cannot do is tell us how the *Ḥarīriyya* was understood by its earliest readers or by subsequent generations of readers who engaged with the text in Arabic and through the mediation of many other languages from across what might be called the Arabic Cosmopolis.[2]

When al-Ḥarīrī deliberately inserted his text into the infrastructure of Islamic knowledge production, he could not know for certain that it would spread like wildfire and become an Islamic classic for centuries. However, when al-Ḥarīrī filled the audience of the text's first reading with Baghdad's leading scholars and then made himself available to scholarly visitors from across the world for the remainder of his life, he was doing all he could to dispatch his book to a wide world of readers who would appreciate a richly allusive and elusive text that invited glossing and commentary. When those participants were reading, listening to, and experiencing the *Ḥarīriyya*, perhaps they saw themselves and their commentary culture reflected in the hermeneutical adventures of Abū Zayd and al-Ḥārith. When Abū Zayd is depicted as a man who produces riddling speech and intensely allusive rhetoric, only to follow it with an explanation, perhaps readers recognized the structures of their own commentarial world. When Abū Zayd demonstrates his eloquence by both praising and censuring a dinar in *maqāma* #3, perhaps they contemplated the power of language in their own societies. These hermeneutical dramas and rhetorical performances may feel like "mere" language games to many of us, but they were embedded within a cosmopolitan scholarly culture in which playing with language was often a high-stakes affair.

One way to think about the rupture between reading literarily and reading commentarially can be illustrated by comparing two translations of the *Ḥarīriyya*. The first is a recent "literary" translation by Michael Cooperson that seeks to achieve what Walter Benjamin calls "the unfathomable, the mysterious, the 'poetic,' something that a translator can reproduce only if he is also a poet."[3] The second translation is a series of Persian glosses, which we might call a commentarial translation. It conveys mere "information," which is the mark of all "bad translations," according to Benjamin. But I would hasten to add that these judgments about good and bad translations are rooted in the dispensation of world literature and its literary judgments. My contention is that translations make interpretive arguments and that different kinds of translation projects can reflect different social, material, and intellectual approaches to reading and interpretation. Cooperson's translation of the *Ḥarīriyya* sets out to restage the linguistic marvel of the *Ḥarīriyya* by performing a series of exquisite experiments in the English language. He re-creates each *maqāma* in English using a different dialect, jargon, or authorial style, from Singlish to legalese to Chaucer.[4] Just as al-Ḥarīrī plumbed the depths of the Arabic language, Cooperson presents his translation as an exploration of the possibilities of English.

Cooperson's exuberant literary translation stands in stark contrast to a Persian translation that was completed in 587/1191. Composed by Sirāj Kātib (fl. sixth/twelfth century), it is a word-by-word interlinear translation that does not stand on its own but rather perches between the lines of the Arabic text. When one sees it on the manuscript page, it is recognizable as an interlinear *commentary*, glossing each Arabic word in Persian, just as countless commentaries would provide Arabic glosses for difficult Arabic words. Whereas Cooperson calls this a "timid" translation, I would suggest that what we have here is an example of translation that participates in the reading practices of commentary culture.[5] This commentarial translation does not aim to reproduce the text's effects in a new language or to replace and displace the original. It does not even put the translated words in the order they would appear in a Persian sentence. The purpose, as Sirāj Kātib explains in his short introduction, is to allow readers to encounter and appreciate the Arabic of al-Ḥarīrī with the help of a series of glosses.[6]

There is trouble brewing in this neat binary that I have presented between a modern, literary translation and a premodern, commentarial one. Nothing is quite so simple. For one thing, the binary may be insufficiently differentiated, and we should keep open the possibility of other revolutions in reading practices and publics between the lifetime of our friend ʿAbd al-Laṭīf al-Baghdādī and the radical changes that took place in the colonial era, such as the ones proposed recently by Nir Shafir and Khaled El-Rouayheb.[7] For another, one of Cooperson's models for his bold, literary translation is the Hebrew translation of the *Ḥarīriyya* that was completed by Judah Alharizi (Yehūdah al-Ḥarīzī, d. 622/1225) in Aleppo around the time that ʿAbd al-Laṭīf wandered the streets of that same city.[8] This wildly inventive Hebrew translation emerged before world literature. So, is Alharizi's translation a "literary" one? The more immediate question may be whether it is a translation at all. As Abraham Lavi puts it, "one can hardly recognize the original Arabic" when one reads the Hebrew versions because so much has changed. The names of the protagonists are replaced with biblical names, such that Abū Zayd al-Sarūjī becomes Heber the Kenite of Zaanannim (Ḥeber ha-Qênî mi-Ṣaʿănannîm; Judges 4:11), while al-Ḥārith becomes Ithiel (ʾÎṯîʾēl; Proverbs 30:1). Al-Ḥarīrī's Quranic quotations and allusions are replaced with biblical ones or passed over in silence.[9] Should we consider this to be an adaptation rather than a translation? One problem with calling it an adaptation is that Alharizi also composed a book of original *maqāma*s in Hebrew, which continued to feature Heber the Kenite as the eloquent rogue![10] Just as Ibn Abī al-Khiṣāl wrote the fifty-first Arabic adventure of Abū Zayd al-Sarūjī, al-Ḥarīzī wrote fifty new adventures about Heber the Kenite (who is also Abū Zayd, traveling under a new name). The boundary between Alharizi's translation-cum-adaptation and his original *maqāma*s is blurrier than it might first appear.

My point is not to establish some clear distinction between translation and adaptation. Rather, what I aim to suggest is that the dispensation of world literature allows us to recognize Alharizi's transformation of the *Ḥarīriyya* as a "literary" project, whereas Sirāj Kātib's glosses are distinctly "unliterary." One is considered bold, while the other is timid. The argument of *Before World Literature* is that literariness has haunted our readings of texts from the past and that we should make these ghosts familiar to us and invite them to unsettle our interpretive instincts. It is not the case that we must do away with the category of "literature" or "the literary" altogether. Rather, we should use these concepts carefully and recognize the limitations, assumptions, and genealogies that come along with them.

Cooperson's analogy between his translation and the Hebrew translation of Alharizi is apt in many ways. It is not always possible to "recognize the original Arabic" from which Cooperson draws, and it is no accident that it is the only book-length work of the Library of Arabic Literature in which the translation never appeared together with a facing-page Arabic text. When we compare the stated aims of Cooperson's English version with the ideological underpinnings of Alharizi's broader project, however, there are considerable divergences between the two translation projects. In the introduction to Alharizi's collection of original *maqāma*s, he praises al-Ḥarīrī for surpassing all other authors but claims that the themes and metaphors of his marvelous book were, in fact, purloined from Hebrew. Alharizi imagines asking one of the eloquent pieces of rhetoric in al-Ḥarīrī's book where it came from, to which it would respond, "I was stolen from the land of the Hebrews."[11] Alharizi frames his competitive adaptation and, by implication, his earlier translation of al-Ḥarīrī as acts of restitution that could restore to the Hebrew language its pilfered glory. By contrast, Cooperson's translation of the Arabic is seeking out analogous resources in English to allow al-Ḥarīrī's text to resonate within the literary field of a global English. As Karla Mallette puts it, the translation is a "love letter addressed at once to al-Ḥarīrī's Arabic and to the English language."[12] Cooperson's translation is not concerned with proving the precedence and excellence of the English language or its literary tradition. Alharizi, by contrast, is anxious about the success of the *Ḥarīriyya*, and he engages with the claims of its unique inimitability through a paradigm of competitive emulation rather than one of "literary" translation. The stakes of translation and adaptation across languages and religious communities may come further into focus in future studies by recalling that the *Ḥarīriyya* had been described by Alharizi's contemporaries as "inimitable," just as the Quran was inimitable. Language and its relative merits might have theological implications.

My hope is that the discussion of commentary culture in the pages of *Before World Literature* will offer avenues for approaching the richly competitive terrain of aesthetics and knowledge production in the premodern Islamic world and beyond. The vibrant commentary culture that underpinned the reception of the *Ḥarīriyya* was unconcerned with the norms, values, and reading practices of world literature. Therefore, if we want to read with ʿAbd al-Laṭīf, or perhaps better, if we want ʿAbd al-Laṭīf's mode of reading to inform and unsettle our approach to textual analysis, then we must take into account the social, material, and intellectual practices of reading in commentary culture. To become initiated into this ethics of reading, ʿAbd al-Laṭīf had to become a walking commentary, which would allow him to participate in the elite circles of knowledge production as he traveled from Baghdad to Cairo to Aleppo. Although I do not aim to make the readers of this book into embodiments of commentary culture, the preceding chapters have offered avenues for thinking about the stakes of reading and interpreting texts in the life of ʿAbd al-Laṭīf's world that cannot be assimilated to the contours of the literary.

It is certainly true that most texts in the Arabic tradition are not like the *Ḥarīriyya* because they do not have extensive commentary traditions or manuscript records. In that sense, *Before World Literature* does not necessarily offer an exact model of how to study other texts. Instead, it presents a provocation and a mode of thinking about how to practice an unsettled philology of *adab*—what Aamir Mufti, drawing on Erich Auerbach and Edward Said, called "a homeless (and restless) philology" that denaturalizes the world.[13] This book explores a practice of reading that offers resistances to the results of our own "close reading" because, as I have argued above, the hermeneutical expectations in this era were shaped by the reading practices of commentarial culture. The *Maqāmāt* of al-Ḥarīrī was such a central feature of Islamic education and the broader Arabic Cosmopolis that the practices of reading and interpretation that underpinned its success can provide resistances to our interpretive instincts. If nothing else, the reading practices of commentary culture can provincialize literariness and allow us to think differently about reading texts before world literature.

Notes

The following abbreviations appear in the notes.

HMC	al-Ḥarīrī, *Maqāmāt Abī Zayd al-Sarūjī*. Edited by Michael Cooperson. New York: New York University Press, 2020.
BNF	Bibliothèque Nationale de France
GAL	Carl Brockelmann, *Geschichte der arabischen Litteratur: Zweite den supplementbänden angepasste Auflage*. Leiden: Brill, 1943–49.
GALS	Carl Brockelmann, *Geschichte der arabischen Litteratur: Supplementbänden*. Leiden: Brill, 1937–42.
EI2	*Encyclopaedia of Islam*, Second Edition Online. Edited by P. J. Bearman, Thierry Bianquis, Clifford Edmund Bosworth, E. J. van Donzel, and Wolfhart Heinrichs. Leiden: Brill, 2012.
EI3	*Encyclopaedia of Islam*, Three Online. Edited by Everett K. Rowson, Gudrun Krämer, John Abdallah Nawas, and Marc Gaborieau. Leiden: Brill, 2007–.
MSR	*Mamluk Studies Review*
ZMDG	*Zeitschrift für Geschichte der arabisch-islamischen Wissenschaften*

DRAMATIS PERSONAE

1. al-Ṣafadī, *Kitāb al-Wāfī*, 28:229; al-Dhahabī, *Siyar aʿlām*, 19:269–71.

2. Lindermann, "Shared Set of Solecisms."

3. ʿImād al-Dīn al-Iṣfahānī, *Kharīdat al-qaṣr (ʿIrāq)*, 4.1:676.

4. The critiques of the biographer Ibn al-Najjār (d. 643/1245) are preserved in al-Dhahabī, *Siyar aʿlām*, 20:527. The laudatory biography is found in ʿImād al-Dīn al-Iṣfahānī, *Kharīdat al-qaṣr (ʿIrāq)*, 3.1:7–18.

5. E.g., al-Panjdīhī, *Maghānī*, Suleymaniye MS Murad Molla 1549, 48v.

6. al-Ṣafadī, *Nuṣrat al-thāʾir*, 61.

7. *HMC*, 177.

INTRODUCTION

Epigraphs: Marx and Engels, *Communist Manifesto*, 223–24. Kilito, *Les séances*, 212.

1. Leezenberg, "Rare Pearl," 154; Casanova, *World*; Mufti, *Forget English!*, 130–45; Allan, *In the Shadow*; Beecroft, *Ecology*. Some of these accounts are rooted in Talal Asad's critique

of secular modernity. For Asad, the medieval Islamic tradition, like Michel Foucault's invocation of the classical tradition, is not designed "to make detailed statements about the past but to offer viable alternatives to liberal conceptual frameworks in the present." Katz, "Multiplicity," 680.

2. The most vocal advocate for reading *adab* as literature was Jaraslov Stetkevych, whose essay will be discussed in detail below.

3. The context for Macaulay's claim is part of an argument in favor of introducing English education in India. Macaulay, "Minute," 109; U. Bhattacharya, "Teaching of English."

4. Cooperson, "Note on the Translation," xxxviii, n. 4.

5. Enderwitz, "Adab," and the sources cited there. Heinrichs, review of *'Abbasid Belles-Lettres*.

6. Ibn Abī Uṣaybiʿa, *Literary History of Medicine*, §15.40.2.

7. ʿAbduh states that he spent a year and a half studying the commentary of al-Kafrāwī (d. 1202/1788) on the grammatical work *Kitāb al-Ājurrūmiyya*. He claims that the teachers would ambush their students with technical terms from grammar and law without explaining them. *Al-Aʿmāl al-Kāmila*, 2:320.

8. Ibid., 2:321–22.

9. Haj, *Reconfiguring Islamic Tradition*, 67–108. ʿAbduh was also deeply interested in the educational ideas of Herbert Spencer (d. 1321/1903), whose essay on education was familiar to ʿAbduh. The latter visited Spencer in England in the early 1900s. Elshakry, *Reading Darwin*, 161–218.

10. Hirschfeld, review of *The Maqamat*, 409–10.

11. Chenery, introduction, 20.

12. Margoliouth and Pellat, "al-Ḥarīrī." The entry in the second *Encyclopaedia of Islam* takes over much of the material from D. S. Margoliouth's entry in the first *Encyclopaedia of Islam*, but these comments about taste are Charles Pellat's contribution.

13. Salma Jayyusi, in her response to Thomas Bauer's critical review of the Cambridge History of Arabic Literature volume on the postclassical period, endorsed the view of *Nahḍa* critics, who "rejected the vacuity and serious aesthetic fatigue" of the poetry that preceded them, which was full of "banality, repetitiveness, and artificiality." Jayyusi, "Response," 194–95; Bauer, "In Search of 'Post-Classical Literature.'" Sinan Antoon and Abdelfettah Kilito have both lamented the marginalization of large portions of the Arabic poetic tradition that engage in jesting and obscenity. Antoon, *Poetics of the Obscene*, 22; Kilito, *Al-Maqāmāt*, 41–42. Useful overviews of the notions of decline are Gündüz, "Ottoman-Era Arabic Literature"; and von Hees (ed.), *Inḥiṭāṭ*.

14. Kāẓim, *Al-Maqāmāt wa-l-talaqqī*, 144–49. Some scholars saw the text as essentially pedagogical rather than literary or even narrative. Ḍayf, *Al-Maqāma*, 8–9.

15. Throughout the text, I refer to *maqāma*s by their number rather than their name because, although the numbers remain stable, a few of the names do not.

16. *HMC*, 7–10.

17. *HMC*, 9.

18. *HMC*, 10.

19. *HMC*, 11–14, 182.

20. This tendency is discussed fully in Chapter 1. Neuwirth, "*Ayyu ḥarajin*" and "al-Ḥarīrī's Travel"; Stewart, "*Maqāma*," "*Maqāmāt* of Aḥmad b. Abī Bakr," and "Of Rhetoric, Reason, and Revelation." The same view has been expressed regarding al-Hamadhānī's

maqāmas in Beaumont, "Trickster." The other approach has been to suggest that the reader is invited to condemn the trickster. Monroe, *Art of Badīʿ al-Zamān*, 44–45.

21. MacKay, "Certificates," 9–11. For general accounts of Islamic commentary culture and its transformations over time, see Blecher, *Said the Prophet*, 4–14; Davidson, *Carrying on the Tradition*, 5–45; A. Ahmed, *Palimpsests*, 4–7; and Sayeed, *Women and the Transmission.*

22. Katsumata, "Style of the *Maqāma*."

23. Claims of inimitability will be discussed in Chapter 6. According to a survey of book collections in Damascus around 1900, the *Ḥarīriyya* tied for first place with no less venerable a book than the Quran. Hudson, *Transforming Damascus*, 88.

24. Marx and Engels echo this rhetoric of possession in the epigraph to this introduction, which is also the epigraph to David Damrosch's work. Marx and Engels state that, as in the case of material goods, "intellectual creations of individual nations become common property." Cited in Damrosch, *What Is World Literature?*, xiii.

25. Alagunfon, *Classical Arabic "Maqāma."*

26. al-Ṣafadī, *Nuṣrat al-thāʾir*, 59.

27. Ibid.

28. Ibid., 61.

29. Cooperson, "Probability," 69.

30. Alan Jones states that Arabic commentaries are "mines of information, most of it recondite, but they are worse than useless when one wants to try to understand any literary feature in a poem." Jones, *Marāthī and Ṣuʿlūk Poems*, viii, 146. Margaret Larkin takes a less dismissive approach but ends up with the same conclusion. Larkin, "Abū l-ʿAlāʾ," 481–82.

31. Pollock, "Philology in Three Dimensions," 399.

32. Mufti, *Forget English!*, 207, 240.

33. Ibid., 241.

CHAPTER 1

1. For some examples of Bakhtin in readings of the *maqāma*, see Neuwirth, "*Ayyu ḥajarin*," 243, and "Woman's Wit"; Elinson, "Market Values"; and Rosen, "Beard as Spectacle." For a general critique of Bakhtin's portrayal of the medieval period, see Ganim, "Medieval Literature as Monster." Stereotypes of the medieval also haunt other uses of European theory to read Arabic literature. Daniel Beaumont draws on Lacan's seminar on *The Purloined Letter* to argue that the unstable, deceptive, ironic language in the *Hamadhāniyya* and the *Ḥarīriyya* is "fundamentally opposed to the thoroughly idealistic conception of language that pervades medieval Islam." He claims that "the Koran itself holds out the promise that the truth may be given direct representation in language." Beaumont, "Trickster and Rhetoric," 12. This account of medieval Islamic thought and the Quran do not hold up well to scrutiny. The ambiguity of language and the conventional, arbitrary nature of the linguistic sign were widely recognized among theorists and practitioners of Islamic law in the medieval period and among theorists of language. See Vishanoff, *Formation of Islamic Hermeneutics*; Bauer, *Die Kultur der Ambiguität*; and Adamson and Key, "Philosophy of Language." The idea that Arabic and Islam hold idealistic notions about language has become so taken for granted that it has made its way into such works as Benedict Anderson's *Imagined Communities*, where he claims that global communities of the past were imagined through "an idea largely foreign to the

contemporary Western mind: the non-arbitrariness of the sign. The ideograms of Chinese, Latin, or Arabic were emanations of reality, not randomly fabricated representations of it." *Imagined Communities*, 14.

2. Bakhtin, *Rabelais*, 121–22.

3. Mattar, *Specters of World Literature*, 10.

4. As Jennifer Wenzel points out in a different context, "Gestures toward universality or planetary community that do not grapple with this unevenness can effect a *gentrification* of the imagination, displacing communities and epistemologies in the name of breaking down barriers." *Disposition of Nature*, 9.

5. The title of Kilito's *Lan Tatakallam Lughatī* has been translated, a bit problematically, as "Thou Shalt Not Speak My Language." The title does not contain a negative imperative, as one finds in the Arabic version of the Ten Commandments, for example, but rather a negation of the future. Thus, I prefer "You Will Not Speak My Language."

6. Kilito, *Lan tatakallam lughatī*, 15.

7. Margoliouth and Pellat, "al-Ḥarīrī."

8. Kilito, *Lan tatakallam lughatī*, 18–20; Pellat, *Le milieu baṣrien*, 8–9.

9. Kilito, *Lan tatakallam lughatī*, 21.

10. J. Stetkevych, "Arabic Poetry," 108.

11. W. Jones, *Poems*, 85; Said, *Orientalism*, 115.

12. J. Stetkevych, "Arabic Poetry," 118.

13. Damrosch, *What Is World Literature?*, 281. As Damrosch notes, translatability is distinct from value because "a work can hold a prominent place within its own culture but be read poorly elsewhere, either because it doesn't translate well or because its cultural assumptions don't travel" (289). For Damrosch, juxtaposing a series of "foreign" works allow for them to interact in a field of possibilities with "intercourse in every direction" (Marx and Engels's "apt phrase"), whereas it seems to me that the directions of intercourse are much more delimited (300).

14. Chen Bar-Itzhak, for instance, seeks to "demonstrate the injustices inflicted upon literary works of world literature when read through the hegemonic, Anglo-American theoretical canon." Bar-Itzhak, "Intellectual Captivity," 81.

15. Kilito, *Les séances*, 212. Although Kilito recognizes the recent pedigree of the "literary," he nevertheless draws on the strategies of European literary criticism to interpret a unitary "message" in the *maqāma*. He concludes that the *Ḥarīriyya* "is a reflection upon *adab*, on its function and also on its purpose." The *Ḥarīriyya*, he suggests, should be seen as a grimly sardonic comment on the state of a fallen intellectual world where men are no longer generous and where *adab* is no longer valued. It is, in other words, social criticism. The further irony in this conclusion, Kilito notes, is that Abū Zayd earns a living with the money he earns from performing *adab* (233–40). See also Kilito, *Al-Ghā'ib*. Elsewhere, Kilito identifies his approach as "structuralist (*bunyawī*)." See, for example, the subtitle to his 1997 book, *Al-Adab wa-l-gharāba*, which refers to "structuralist studies in Arabic literature (*dirāsāt bunyawiyya fī al-adab al-ʿarabī*)." Wadād al-Qāḍī considers Iḥsān ʿAbbās's recognition of al-Hamadhānī's *maqāma* as social criticism (*al-naqd al-ijtimāʿī*) to be a turning point in *maqāma* criticism. Al-Qāḍī, *Maqāmāt Badīʿ al-Zamān*, 152, and "Badīʿ al-Zamān."

16. Mufti, *Forget English!*, 11.

17. Wenzel suggests that "the tragedy of Orientalism repeats as the farce of World Literature." *Disposition of Nature*, 7; Said, *Orientalism*, 127. Mufti posits that "Orientalism may be understood as a set of processes for the reorganization of language, literature, and culture

on a planetary scale, which effected the assimilation of heterogeneous and dispersed bodies of writing onto the plane of equivalence and evaluability that is literature." Mufti, "Orientalism and the Institution of World Literature," 488. In his monograph, a very similar passage appears in which world literature has been substituted for Orientalism. He states that "world literature . . . has functioned as a *plane of equivalence*, a set of categorical grids and networks that seek, first of all, to render legible *as literature* a vast and heterogeneous range of practices of writing from across the world and across millennia" for comparison and evaluation. Mufti, *Forget English!*, 11.

18. This "unequal distribution of epistemic capital" is discussed in Chen Bar-Itzhak, "Intellectual Captivity." Examples of this distribution of epistemic capital might be found in the cast of theorists (Arendt, Derrida, and Heidegger) found in Chea, *What Is a World?*.

19. Allan, *In the Shadow* and "How *Adab* Became Literary"; Apter, *Against World Literature*; B. Bhattacharya, *Colonialism, World Literature*; Mattar, *Specters of World Literature*; Mufti, *Forget English!*.

20. See von Hees, *Inḥiṭāṭ*; Bauer, "In Search of 'Post-Classical Literature'"; Gündüz, "Ottoman-Era Arabic Literature"; and El-Rouayheb, *Islamic Intellectual History*. For a comprehensive survey of the decline narrative and scholarly engagements with it, see Sajdi, "Decline."

21. Bauer, "Mamluk Literature," "In Search of 'Post-Classical Literature,'" and "'*Ayna hādhā min al-Mutanabbī!*'"; Hirschler, *Written Word*; al-Musawi, *Medieval Islamic Republic of Letters*; Muhanna, *World in a Book*.

22. El Shamsy, *Rediscovering*, 32, 36–37, 39–40, 60.

23. Margaret Larkin notes that "the commentaries on al-Mutanabbī's *Dīwān* are virtually devoid of anything we would today call aesthetic or subjective criticism." She admits that this is not taking commentary on its own terms and that "aesthetic critique" was "beyond the ability and/or interests of *aficionados* such as al-Maʿarrī." Larkin, "Abū l-ʿAlāʾ," 481–94. Some scholars have suggested that modern literary approaches could reconstruct what a hypothetical reader in the past would have understood. Julie Scott Meisami suggests that the "new and different" ways that modern scholars have approached Arabic poetry may be "new and different to us, that is, but perhaps closer to those of medieval poets and critics themselves." Meisami, *Structure and Meaning*, 15. For James T. Monroe, "literary criticism . . . aim[s] to interpret works of art for a hypothetical audience of more or less unskilled readers in need of help in understanding the subtleties in the text, and ultimately, its message." Monroe, *Art of Badīʿ al-Zamān*, 93. For the *Ḥarīriyya*, Katia Zakharia's work has engaged with the commentaries to some extent, but her approach tends to criticize these commentators for failing to ask certain questions and for treating the text in simplistic or unconvincing ways. Zakharia, *Abū Zayd*, 69–75.

24. As El Shamsy points out, later reformers and editors would emphasize the indigenous Arabic philological tradition. El Shamsy, *Rediscovering*, 200–206.

25. Geert Jan van Gelder has pointed out that complaints about cultural and intellectual decline are common across the history of *adab*. Even as authors complained about the "corruption of the age (*fasād al-zamān*)," they continued to celebrate the poetry and prose of their contemporaries. Van Gelder, "Good Times, Bad Times." In the *Ḥarīriyya*, Abū Zayd al-Sarūjī regularly complains of the corruption of the times, but his response is not society-wide cultural renovation.

26. Said, *Orientalism*, 127–30. Although properly his family name is made up of three words (Silvestre de Sacy), I follow Said's convention of referring to him as Sacy.

27. Sacy, *Chrestomathie*, vol. 1, avant-propos (no page number).

28. Orfali, "Sketch Map"; Savant and Mahdi, "History of Iranian Cities"; Hermansen and Lawrence, "Indo-Persian Tazkiras"; Kia, *Persianate Selves.*

29. A complete manuscript in the hand of the author was said to have cost two thousand dirhams (equivalent to five times the annual salary of a madrasa librarian). Muhanna, *World in a Book*, 107.

30. The one-page introduction to this recycled anthology from the early modern period contains a two-line epigram just above the formulaic invocation that states, "In the name of God, the Merciful and Compassionate." Hārūn al-Rashīd is presented with a slave girl for purchase, and he asks if she is a virgin. She replies: "God save me from a stale market!" He finds this witty and pleasing, so he purchases her. His son al-Maʾmūn is presented with another slave girl and asks in a dialectical Arabic: "Are you a virgin, or what (*am aysh*)?" She replies: "Or what!" He also finds this pleasing and purchases the slave girl. Anonymous, Staatsbiliothek Berlin, MS Sprenger 1243, iv. On this trope in *adab* of the witty slave girl's repartee with potential buyers, see Myrne, *Female Sexuality*, 110–12.

31. Ulrich Marzolph discusses examples of European anthologies from the seventeenth and eighteenth centuries. Marzolph, "Literary Genre."

32. Sacy, *Chrestomathie*, 1:3. The verse appears in the sixth story of the eighth chapter of Saʿdī's *Gulistān*. Saʿdī, *Gulistān*, 167. On the significance of the *Gulistān*, see S. Ahmed, *What Is Islam?*, 493; and Ingenito, *Beholding Beauty*, 101–2.

33. Tageldin, *Disarming Words*, 33–44.

34. al-Ṭahṭāwī, *Takhlīṣ al-ibrīz*, 94, and *Imam in Paris*, 191.

35. al-Yāzijī, *Epistola critica*, 2.

36. al-Shidyāq, *Leg over Leg*, 4:685. Al-Yāzijī, in fact, calls his epistle: "On correcting what he neglected in his transmission of the content of the Ḥarīriyya, and editing its commentary." The two key terms in this title are "transmission (*riwāya*)" and "correcting (*tadāruk*)," each of which refers to a specific activity of the Arabic scholarly tradition. Sacy's edition is, like the manuscript copies that preceded it, a "transmission" of a text, whether that text was poetry, prose, or even hadith of the Prophet. As for "correcting (*tadāruk*)," it associated al-Yāzijī's epistle with a long tradition of scholars writing line-by-line philological critiques and emendations (*istdirākāt*) of recently written scholarly works (see Chapter 2). An early twentieth-century Cairene edition also refers to Sacy as "the commentator." al-Ḥarīrī, *Kitāb al-Maqāmāt* (1912), 1.

37. Sacy, "Avertissement," v. Al-Ṭahṭāwī notes in his travelog that many of the aesthetically praiseworthy features of Arabic may be considered poor style among the French. For example, he notes that paronomasia (*jinās*) is meaningless for them and that a form of double entendre known as *tawriya*, in which only the less obvious meaning of the word is intended, would be considered appropriate only rarely and only in comedic literature. Al-Ṭahṭāwī, *Takhlīṣ al-ibrīz*, 91, and *Imam in Paris*, 185.

38. Preston, preface, xiv.

39. Said, *Orientalism*, 130.

40. The three labels (Oriental, Asian, and Arab) are seemingly interchangeable for Renan and allow him to direct his critiques at different levels of generality. He is aware of the fact that the text was enthusiastically read and taught across the Islamic world, "from the Volga to the Niger, from the Ganges to Gibraltar," as he puts it. He is nevertheless willing to compare al-Ḥarīrī's insight into the foibles of his society to Balzac's *La Comédie Humaine*, a collection of interlinked stories depicting French society in the first half of the nineteenth century. Renan, "Les séances," 297, 294.

41. Renan, "Les séances," 298.

42. Ganim, "Medieval Literature as Monster."

43. Renan, "Les séances," 300.

44. Renan, "Les séances," 295.

45. Renan, *L'Islamisme*, 2–3. Quoted in Norman, "Disputing the 'Iron Circle,'" 693. Renan explicitly states elsewhere that "l'avenir, Messieurs, est donc à l'Europe et à l'Europe seule. L'Europe conquerra le monde et y répandra sa religion, qui est le droit, la liberté, le respect des hommes, cette croyance qu'il y a quelque chose de divin au sein de l'humanité." Renan, *De la part*, 28; cited in Mallette "Orientalism," 242.

46. On ʿAbduh, his relationship with al-Afghānī and Freemasonry, see Kateman, *Muḥammad ʿAbduh*, 88–126; and Büssow, "Muḥammad ʿAbduh."

47. ʿAbduh, *al-Aʿmāl al-Kāmila*, 3:335–36.

48. ʿAbduh, *al-Aʿmāl al-Kāmila*, 3:336–37.

49. Renan, "Les séances," 295, 300. Mufti has pointed to Johann Gottfried Herder as one of the progenitors of "the romantic and organic national concept as such, whose notion of language and culture is so deterministic as to spill over into the territory theorized decades later . . . as biological race." *Forget English!*, 62.

50. The notion that the postclassical has unjustly displaced the classical is also found in a recent work by Ahmed El Shamsy, *Rediscovering*, 5, 149. The discourse of decadence has also recently been treated by David Fieni, in *Decadent Orientalisms*.

51. On the controversies of authorship regarding the *Nahj al-Balāgha*, see Qutbuddin, "*Nahj al-balāgha*."

52. ʿAbduh, "*Khuṭbat al-Mufassir*," 4.

53. Heinrichs, "*Muwallad* (2)."

54. Chenery, introduction, 20.

55. Hirschfeld, review, 410. Although he considers al-Ḥarīrī to be al-Hamadhānī's "more brilliant imitator," it is al-Hamadhānī "who, as to taste, is distinctly superior to Hariri."

56. Hala Auji has noted some significant continuities between early Arabic printing and manuscript formats. Auji, *Printing Arab Modernity*, 12 and 115–17; Schwartz, "Meaningful Mediums." As Salam Rassi has said, "The domains of scribal, commentary, and print culture in the nineteenth century were intimately connected." Rassi, "Scribal," 408.

57. El Shamsy, *Rediscovering*, 150. El Shamsy is unaware of the Istanbul edition's colophon that identifies al-Nabhānī as the editor, stating that this edition "had been edited and printed a few years earlier by al-Shidyāq, but it is not clear whether ʿAbduh knew this . . . [and] ʿAbduh's edition was arguably superior." In fact, ʿAbduh mentions the Istanbul edition in his editorial introduction, and it is difficult to see how ʿAbduh's bowdlerized edition based on unidentifiable manuscripts is superior. By contrast, al-Nabhānī identifies the manuscripts that he used in his edition in ways that make them identifiable to researchers today.

58. al-Hamadhānī, *Maqāmāt* (Istanbul), 100.

59. Ghazal, "'Illiberal' Thought," 215–16.

60. al-Hamadhānī, *Maqāmāt* (Istanbul), 100; Ghazal, "Yūsuf al-Nabhānī," 120; Dreher, "Collection"; Chiabotti, "Yūsuf b. Ismāʿīl al-Nabahānī."

61. El Shamsy, *Rediscovering*, 153. On education reforms and epistemic shifts in Islamic law from those based on language to those modeled on the natural sciences, see Nakissa, "Epistemic Shift."

62. Hourani, *Arabic Thought*, 114–15, 132.

63. Gesink, *Islamic Reform*, 155–56; ʿAbd al-Mutaʿāl, *Tārīkh al-iṣlāḥ*, 58–59; ʿAbduh, *Al-Aʿmāl al-Kāmila*, 3:199–200.

64. al-Hamadhānī, *Maqāmāt* (ʿAbduh), 7.

65. al-Hamadhānī, *Maqāmāt* (ʿAbduh), 96, and *Maqāmāt* (Istanbul), 33. Sarah R. Bin Tyeer discusses some of the other changes to the text in ʿAbduh's edition. Bin Tyeer, *Qur'an*, 220–21n3. On the textual history of the *Hamadhāniyya* generally, see Orfali and Pomerantz, *Maqāmāt*.

66. El Shamsy, *Rediscovering*, 171.

67. Al-Ṭahṭāwī says that this French distaste for homoeroticism is similar to the "innate disposition of the Arabs," a gesture that admits the widespread presence of homoerotic poetry while insisting that true Arabness is, in fact, in agreement with modern French attitudes. He implies that there ought to be a classicizing return to an "original" Arab norm. Al-Ṭahṭāwī, *Takhlīṣ ibrīz*, 87–88. Ironically, he nevertheless quotes homoerotic poetry, of both the more chaste and the more obscene varieties (46, 90). See also the translation: al-Ṭahṭāwī, *Imam in Paris*, 143, 181, 184. ʿAbduh would likely have also been familiar with bowdlerization in the English context, given that he was friends with the poet Wilfrid Scawen Blunt (d. 1341/1922). Kateman, "Tellings of an Encounter."

68. al-Ḥarīrī, *Assemblies* (Chenery), 1:220–21.

69. Roberts, "Translation."

70. ʿAbduh, *al-Aʿmāl al-Kāmila*, 3:55. Zaccone's novel, to which ʿAbduh refers, is also known as *La dame d'Auteuil*.

71. For an example of rulers attempting to censor material, see al-Ṭabarī, *Annales*, 3:2131. For scholars, see the *ḥisba* tradition, discussed in Klein, "Between Public and Private," and M. Cook, *Commanding Right*. See also Deuchar, review of *Popular Fiction*.

72. Antoon, *Poetics of the Obscene*, 21.

73. Zaydān, *Tārīkh Ādāb*, 1251. For a detailed treatment of Zaydān, his literary projects, and his interaction with the "Ottoman literary biome," see Arslan, "Entanglements." For transformation and uses of the term *nahḍa*, see Deuchar, "Nahḍa: Mapping a Keyword"; and Patel, *Arab Nahdah*, 11.

74. Zaydān, *Tārīkh Ādāb*, 1424.

75. Zaydān, *Tārīkh Ādāb*, 1425.

76. Zaydān, *Tārīkh Ādāb*, 1084.

77. Deuchar, "Loan-Words," 203.

78. Kāẓim, *al-Maqāmāt wa-l-talaqqī*, 144–49.

79. Ḍayf, *al-Maqāma*, 8–9.

80. Drory, "*maqama*," 507–8.

81. Beaumont, "Trickster and Rhetoric," 12.

82. Weiss, *Search for God's Law*, 116.

83. Keegan, "Throwing the Reins"; Harb, *Arabic Poetics*, 28–30, 262–63.

84. Neuwirth, "*Ayyu ḥajarin*," 243. See also Neuwirth, "Adab Standing Trial."

85. Allan, *In the Shadow*, 9–25; Majid, "Can the Postcolonial Critic Speak?" The notion that Islamic knowledge is necessarily invested in "law and order" ignores the role of antinomian piety in Sufism. Karamustafa, *God's Unruly Friends*. Furthermore, as Shahab Ahmed has argued, these attitudes should not be characterized as antinomian but "para-nomian" or "supra-nomian" in order to "emphasize that this stance does not necessarily place itself *against* the law as it does *beside*, *beyond*, and *above* the law." S. Ahmed, *What Is Islam*, 454.

86. Chenery, introduction, 34.

87. Chenery, introduction, 34–35. According to Chenery, other distasteful aspects of the *Ḥarīriyya* would not offend the less scrupulous Muslims: "To pass suddenly from the most solemn subjects of pleasantry, to place in the mouth of a clever imposter the most serious warnings that can be addressed to mankind may be morally objectionable; but in the Moslem world, where religion is mixed up with the concerns of life, and pious discourse and phrases abound, it excites little repugnance." Al-Ḥarīrī, *Assemblies* (Chenery), 1:163.

88. The preacher in question was Fakhr al-Dīn al-Rāzī's father Ḍiyā' al-Dīn (d. 559/1164). Al-Subkī, *Ṭabaqāt*, 7:242.

89. In some areas, such as Yorubaland in West Africa, the *Ḥarīriyya* continues to be a central feature of Islamic education to this day. As Sulaiman Adewala Alagunfon has shown, one of Abū Zayd's eloquent incantations found in *maqāma* #12 came to be treated by Muslim scholars in this region as "one of the best prayers against theft, natural disaster, and accidents of various kinds." Alagunfon, *Classical Arabic*, 108.

90. Ganim, "Medieval Literature as Monster."

91. Bakhtin, *Rabelais*, 121.

92. Bakhtin, *Rabelais*, 122–23.

93. Allan, *In the Shadow*, 9, 21–34.

94. Bakhtin, *Rabelais*, 121.

95. Chakrabarty, "Postcoloniality," 3.

96. Tuck and Yang, "Decolonization," 3.

97. Tapji Garba and Sara-Maria Sorentino say that because "metaphor makes geography," therefore "settler colonialism cannot be adequately theorized *without* metaphor." Veracini, "Colonialist and Decolonial"; Garba and Sorentino, "Slavery Is a Metaphor," 776.

98. Alfaisal, "Politics" and "Liberty and the Literary"; Allan, *In the Shadow*; Deuchar, "Loan-Words"; Hill, *Utopia*; Holt, *Fictitious Capital*; Johnson, *Stranger Fictions*; Mufti, *Forget English!*; Selim, *Novel*; Tageldin, *Disarming Words* and "Hugo, Translated." C. Ceyhun Arslan's recent book *Ottoman Canon*, though focused on the nineteenth century, addresses the presence of "classical" Arabic texts in late Ottoman scholarship, but Arslan's book was published too late to be fully addressed here.

99. Ahmed El Shamsy, in an echo of the triumphalist narrative, describes Arabic-Islamic scholarship on the eve of the print revolution as dominated by "scholasticism, which manifested itself in the literary form of basic teaching manuals overlaid by a superstructure of numerous layers of postclassical commentary" and by esotericism "that disparaged book learning." He claims that his account "should not be read as a rehash of the nineteenth-century narrative of decline, which dismissed postclassical Islamic thought as a mere lifeless shell waiting to be revived and filled by European Enlightenment." El Shamsy, *Rediscovering*, 61. It should be noted that proponents of the decline paradigm were not uniformly in favor of European Enlightenment ideals. Furthermore, the sources for El Shamsy's account of postclassical learning and commentary culture are rooted in the views of its Arab critics who tell a heroic story of their triumph over an obscurantist and irrational past.

100. The extent of European interest in Ibn Ḥazm can be gleaned from the size and scope of a recent edited volume: Adang, Fierro, and Schmidtke, *Ibn Ḥazm of Cordoba*.

101. Ibn al-Nadīm, *Kitāb al-Fihrist*, 3:322; van Gelder, review of *Sheherezade*.

102. Kilito, *Arabs and the Art of Storytelling*, 123–24.

103. Ibid.

104. El Shamsy, *Rediscovering*, 37, 41.

CHAPTER 2

1. ʿAbd al-Laṭīf's autobiography is preserved in Ibn Abī Uṣaybiʿa, *Literary History of Medicine*, §15.40.2–6. This material does not contain precise dates, but the details about ʿAbd al-Laṭīf listening to the *Ḥarīriyya* are found in the manuscript *Cairo Adab m105*, 3v; MacKay, "Certificates," 18. For studies of ʿAbd al-Laṭīf's autobiography, see Toorawa, "Autobiography" and "Portrait"; and Bonadeo, *ʿAbd al-Laṭīf*.

2. ʿAbd al-Laṭīf refers to his teacher as Kamāl al-Dīn, and he is also known as Abū al-Barakāt, but he is usually known as Ibn al-Anbārī, the author of *Nuzhat al-alibbāʾ*. Ibn Abī Uṣaybiʿa, *Literary History of Medicine*, §15.40.2; Hämeen-Anttila, "Marginalia Harīriana," 259; Brockelman, "al-Anbārī, Abū al-Barakāt."

3. The line in ʿAbd al-Laṭīf's autobiography reads: "*fa-qaraʾtu ʿalayhi khuṭbat al-Faṣīḥ fa-hadhara kalāman kathīran mutatābiʿan lam afham minhu shayʾan lākin al-talāmīdh ḥawlahu yuʿjabūn minhu thumma qāla anā ajfū ʿan taʿlīm al-ṣibyān iḥmilhu ilā tilmīdhī al-Wajīh al-Wāsiṭī.*" The available translations seem to imply that ʿAbd al-Laṭīf thought that his teacher was, objectively speaking, not making any sense, but we know that ʿAbd al-Laṭīf eventually understood his teacher's lessons after studying the commentary tradition. Ibn Abī Uṣaybiʿa, *Literary History of Medicine*, §15.40.2; Bonadeo, *ʿAbd al-Laṭīf*, 116. ʿAbd al-Laṭīf's effusive praise for his teacher Ibn al-Anbārī is preserved in the biographical tradition. Al-Dhahabī, *Siyar aʿlām*, 21:115.

4. Ibn Abī Uṣaybiʿa, *Literary History of Medicine*, §15.40.2.

5. The testing of a student's knowledge guarded against what is now called an "illusion of fluency." To illustrate the condition of a superficial reader, the Umayyad-Abbasid bureaucrat and litterateur Ibn al-Muqaffaʿ likens him to a man who wishes to learn eloquent speech and so is given a piece of parchment (*ṣaḥīfa ṣafrāʾ*) on which a friend has written down the forms (*taṣārīf*) and meanings (*wujūh*) of words. Having studied it intensely for a day, the man goes to a gathering of people known for their knowledge, cultivation, and cleverness. In his conversation with these wise and clever men, he inevitably commits a solecism and is told by the men there that he has misused a word. The man is shocked, wondering how he could have erred, thinking that this crib sheet should be sufficient for his linguistic education. Ibn al-Muqaffaʿ, *La version arabe*, 47.

6. Some of the listeners to whom ʿAbd al-Laṭīf transmitted would have been as young as four, emphasizing that listening to a text often occurred well before one could read or memorize. MacKay, "Certificates," 23–24.

7. Ware, *Walking Qurʾan*, 69.

8. *HMC*, 164.

9. *HMC*, 165.

10. *HMC*, 178.

11. *HMC*, 172.

12. Keegan "Commentators," 303n29.

13. *HMC*, 253–54. The host gives Abū Zayd an ʿĪd camel and a robe like Saʿīd's; the former gift is explained in two different ways by al-Ḥarīrī's autocommentary, a feature discussed further below. *HMC*, 254–58.

14. *HMC*, 254.

15. *HMC*, 115–19.

16. *HMC*, 116.

17. *HMC*, 117.

18. As Richard Bulliet points out, young listeners were already common in the fourth/tenth century. Bulliet, "Age Structure," 105–17; Sayeed, *Women and the Transmission*, 168–77. Garrett Davidson points out that al-Dhahabī (d. 748/1348) also identified the fourth/tenth century as the era in which students of hadith began bringing their young children to hear hadith. Davidson, *Carrying on the Tradition*, 69; al-Dhahabī, *Siyar aʿlām*, 18:369.

19. Davidson, *Carrying on the Tradition*, 51, 165–77.

20. There has been a great deal of confusion in secondary literature over the terminology of audition certificates (*samāʿāt*) and certificates granting permission to transmit or teach a text (*ijāzāt al-riwāya* and *ijāzāt al-tadrīs* or *ijāzāt al-dirāya*). The last of these terms is rather rare, and scholars like al-Suyūṭī continued to insist that only audition was required to transmit a text, whereas teaching was permitted for anyone who had mastery. Davidson, *Carrying on the Tradition*, 109–11.

21. Ibn Abī Uṣaybiʿa, *Literary History of Medicine*, §15.40.8.

22. *HMC*, 217–218.

23. *HMC*, 223–224.

24. Bosworth, *Mediaeval Islamic Underworld*, 1:xii.

25. The poem does also contain potential realia, such as mass-producing amulets, associated with itinerant urban groups, as well as linguistic data. Schaefer, "Material Nature," 182; Richardson, "Tracing." Bosworth's edition of the poem is in Bosworth, *Mediaeval Islamic Underworld*, 2:3–39, 191–213. For Muʿizz al-Dawla, see lines 110–11. For scholars, see lines 65, 124, and 125.

26. *HMC*, 289; also 11, 155.

27. Blankinship and Pizzone, "Self-Commentary as Defensive Strategy."

28. It is usually assumed that any claim that a human could compete with the Quran would have been deeply problematic for medieval Muslim sensibilities, although we will see in Chapters 5 and 6 that this situation was considerably more complicated than is often assumed.

29. Yāqūt, *Muʿjam al-udabāʾ*, 305; Stewart, "Rhythmical Anxiety."

30. The notion that biography is a way of interpreting a poet's work or of reshaping a scholar's legacy is not new. Malti-Douglas, "Controversy" and "Dreams"; Cooperson, "Ibn Ḥanbal"; Jaques, "Other Rabīʿ." Some of the relevant scholarship on this topic has been compiled and analyzed by Jonathan Lawrence, who argues that these stories are more than commentary and "point to a way of reading texts that assumes they have exegetical contexts in the extra-textual world to which they refer, with the awareness that life is contradictory, messy, and uneven." Lawrence, "It's All Just Poetry," 327.

31. Following Suzanne Stetkevych's translation in Stetkevych, "Irony," 514; Sperl, *Mannerism*, 97–154; Smoor, "Delirious Sword."

32. al-Maʿarrī, *Zajr al-nābiḥ*, 21.

33. Ibid. Al-Maʿarrī's autocommentary states that there are many Quranic verses famous for their omission (*ḥadhf*), implying that his poetry also requires the reader to supply omitted words.

34. al-Ṭarābulsī, "*al-Muqaddima*," 6–11.

35. Yāqūt, *Muʿjam al-udabāʾ*, 2824; Sellheim, "al-Tibrīzī"; al-Ṣafadī, *Kitāb al-Wāfī*, 28:228. Travel time based on *al-Ṯurayyā*, the online gazetteer. Seydi and Romanov, *al-Ṯurayyā Project*.

36. al-Maʿarrī, *Shurūḥ Saqṭ al-Zand*, 1:6.

37. Ibid., 1:4.

38. More recently, Kevin Blankinship has noted the similarity between al-Maʿarrī and al-Ḥarīrī. "Al-Maʿarrī's Anxious Managerie."

39. MacKay, "Certificates," 9.

40. Pierre MacKay referred to this manuscript as Cairo Adab 105, but the "m" is crucial because it signifies a different collection of manuscripts, the *makhṭūṭāt khāṣṣa* or "private manuscripts," which likely derive from private libraries. Lacking the "m" made it difficult to acquire enhanced images of this manuscript for some years, although Guy Burak was kindly able to provide me with reproductions of the microfilms. Karim Malak solved the mystery of the missing "m" for me, and I am extremely grateful to both Guy Burak and Karim Malak.

41. On the attendance lists that preceded audition certificates see Aljoumani and Reier, "Documentary Depth."

42. MacKay, "Certificates," 9–11.

43. Grabar, "Pictures or Commentaries," 94–99. For studies of the *Ḥarīriyya*'s illustrations, see O'Kane, "Text and Paintings"; George, "Illustrations" and "Orality"; and Roxburgh, "In Pursuit."

44. *HMC*, 101.

45. Ibn al-Anbārī, *Nuzhat al-alibbāʾ* (Baghdad), 264. The text of the *Maqāmāt* quoted in Ibn al-Anbārī is corrupt and has *al-ghalā* for *al-falā*, which would make the text speak of the "fungus of the cooking pot" rather than the "fungus of the field." The text also has *yuḥāsan* instead of *yuḥāsabanna*, making nonsense of the second hemistich. This edition of Ibn al-Anbārī and its reprints must be treated with some caution. A nineteenth-century lithograph edition has the correct reading. Ibn al-Anbārī, *Nuzhat al-alibbāʾ* (Cairo), 455.

46. Lindermann, "Shared Set of Solecisms," 81; al-Ḥarīrī, *Durrat al-ghawwāṣ*.

47. Larkin, "Abū l-ʿAlāʾ."

48. He says that he was acting as "the tax farming deputy of the vizier ʿAwn al-Dīn (*nāʾib al-wazīr ʿAwn al-Dīn fī al-ṣadriyyāt*)." ʿImād al-Dīn al-Iṣfahānī, *Kharīdat al-qaṣr* (*ʿIrāq*), 4:676. For *ṣadriyya* as a tax office, see Dozy, *Takmilat al-Maʿājim*, 6:428.

49. ʿImād al-Dīn al-Iṣfahānī, *Kharīdat al-qaṣr* (*ʿIrāq*), 4:676.

50. Ibid., 1:36; See Keegan, "Rethinking Poetry."

51. Stewart, "Professional Literary Mendicancy."

52. ʿImād al-Dīn al-Iṣfahānī, *Kharīdat al-qaṣr* (*ʿIrāq*), 4:676.

53. al-Dhahabī, *Siyar aʿlām*, 20:269. For Ibn Sukayna, see al-Dhahabī, *Siyar aʿlām*, 22:333.

54. There has been much debate about the extent to which the distinction between secular and religious domains is a purely modern (or modern Western) phenomenon. For Shahab Ahmed, the reification of the term "religion" presupposes that the religious is "self-evidently distinguishable from the 'non-religious.'" Ahmed, *What Is Islam?*, 178. Others have sought to show how premodern Muslims possessed a concept of "religion" that was analogous to the modern one. Abbasi, "Islam and the Invention of Religion" and "Did Premodern Muslims Distinguish," 188. Still others have sought to redefine "the Islamic secular" as a "psychodynamic disposition or orientation" that takes account of "the keen and conscious awareness of the ubiquitous gaze of the God of Islam," while existing alongside and complementary to Islamic law. Jackson, *Islamic Secular*, 50. In the case of Ibn Nāṣir, charging for the study of poetry may have been an effort to distinguish it as a worldly affair (*dunyawī*) that is "not a domain entirely outside of or separate from *dīn*; rather, it is a distinct constituent of a broader

'sacred canopy'" (50). The poetry of al-Maʿarrī and the prose of al-Ḥarīrī does not become less Islamic or secular by being identified by Ibn Nāṣir as distinct from the quasi-scriptural discursive corpus of the Prophetic hadith. The diverse moral rubrics that coexisted within Islamic discourses have been discussed incisively in Katz, *Wives and Work* and "Multiplicity." See also the debates on secularism that have emerged in and around the work of Talal Asad and Saba Mahmood. Mahmood, *Religious Difference*; Asad, *Formations*.

55. The ability of nonscholars to attend reading sessions was more limited, a pattern that can be seen in Hirschler, *Written Word*, 32–81.

56. Ibn Khayr, *Fahrasat Ibn Khayr*, 474; al-Dhahabī, *Siyar aʿlām*, 20:186–87.

57. ʿImād al-Dīn al-Iṣfahānī, *Kharīdat al-qaṣr (ʿIrāq)*, 4:676.

58. al-Ḥarīrī, *Maqāmāt*, Princeton MS Garrett 131Hq, 32v.

59. The locations of some reading sessions can be found in MacKay, "Certificates." One took place in a Fāṭimid palace (33, fig. 29), another in a mosque (27, fig. 31), and others in madrasas (25, 27, figs. 21, 32).

60. MacKay, "Certificates," 23–24; al-Wansharīsī, *al-Miʿyār*, 1:24.

61. MacKay, "Certificates," 21, 23, figs. 19, 23.

62. al-Anbārī, *Sharḥ*, Suleymaniye MS Laleli 1847.

63. Yāqūt, *Muʿjam al-udabāʾ*, 2218.

64. al-Wāsiṭī, *Sharḥ Maqāmāt al-Ḥarīrī*, Princeton MS Garrett 2908Y, 1v–2r.

65. al-Ḥarīrī, *Maqāmāt*, Danish Royal Library, MS Cod. Arab. Add. 83; Gacek, "Copenhagen Manuscript."

66. Keegan, "Digressions in the Islamic Archive."

67. Ibn Khallikān, *Wafāyāt al-aʿyān*, 4:390.

68. Leiden distinguishes between two remarkably similar commentaries by al-Sharīshī, calling one the short commentary and the other the middle commentary. Al-Sharīshī, *Sharḥ*, Leiden MS Ar. 5804 is identified as the short or abridged commentary (*mukhtaṣar*), and al-Sharīshī, *Sharḥ*, Leiden MS Or. 470 is identified as the middle commentary (*mutawaṣṣit*).

69. al-Sharīshī, *Sharḥ*, Leiden MSS Or. 470, 1v, and Ar. 5804, 7r.

70. al-Sharīshī, *Sharḥ* (Beirut), 1:7.

71. Ibid. The full passage reads as follows: "I saw in his commentary the desired aim, the coveted wish, and the persistent goal that had, until that time, been rolled up and eclipsed from my view. I began to take a second look, buckling down for serious work, being neither lazy nor tired. I saw with my own eyes the light of meaning in the blossoms of words (*nūr al-maʿnā fī nawr al-lafẓ*). Things became clear to me as I reaped the harvest. I studied it to its utmost, and I copied down its benefits, which I had yet to find in any book. I took from it hadiths with their *isnād*s that I might include and reports going back to the Prophet (*āthār marfūʿa*) that I might set down. . . . I removed the *isnād*s, though I might have included them, to lighten the load for those who crave and desire the substance of the report."

72. al-Sharīshī, *Sharḥ*, Leiden MSS Or. 470, 3r, and *Sharḥ*, Leiden MS Ar. 5804, 9v. In the long commentary, this passage is rephrased to be more impersonal, saying that the *Ḥarīriyya* surpassed the *Badīʿiyya*. Al-Sharīshī, *Sharḥ* (Beirut), 1:24.

73. al-Sharīshī, *Sharḥ* (Beirut), 1:22–23; al-Panjdīhī, *Maghānī*, Suleymaniye MS Murad Molla 1549, 17v–18r.

74. The text reads: "*samiʿtu ʿalayhi baʿḍahu wa-ajāza lī saʾirahu bi-riwāyatihi*." Ibn al-Abbār, *Kitāb al-takmila*, 136–37; Davidson, *Carrying on the Tradition*, 108–51.

CHAPTER 3

1. Pierre MacKay labels the certificates in which ʿAbd al-Laṭīf is the transmitter as "X" and "Y." MacKay, "Certificates," 18, 20–25.

2. An outline of this "documentary turn" can be found in Hirschler, *Monument*, 5–9; El-Leithy, "Living Documents, Dying Archives," 390; Livingston, "Paperwork"; Sijpesteijn, *Shaping a Muslim State*; Hirschler, "From Archive"; and Rustow, *Lost Archive*, 474n55. For an articulation of the view that documents were less important in Islamic societies, see Chamberlain, *Knowledge*, 13–16.

3. On collation, see Rosenthal, *Technique and Approach*, 26–27; and Gacek, *Arabic Manuscripts*, 271.

4. Cited in Tim Mackintosh-Smith, introduction, xviii, n20; and Cooperson, "Abbasid 'Golden Age.'"

5. MacKay, "Certificates," 20, fig. 4.

6. A few favorable reviews of MacKay's monograph emerged with minor corrections. Otherwise, it has only been cited a handful of times, usually by those interested in the history of education, rather than in the study of *adab*. R. B. Serjeant, review of "Certificates"; Beeston, review of "Certificates"; Wagner, review of "Certificates." MacKay is also cited in Stern, "Some Noteworthy Manuscripts"; Vajda, "Oral Transmission"; and Witkam, "Human Element."

7. From the perspective of an editor of a print edition, a manuscript is usually a "witness" to the text that can be compared to other "witnesses" to identify variants to the text, but even in editions that include extensive description of the manuscripts, one rarely finds the kind of detailed study of manuscript notes along the lines of Pierre MacKay's 1971 study. Among the exceptions is an edition of Ibn Aʿtham's *Kitāb al-Futūḥ* published in Hyderabad in which the marginalia are fully transcribed in the edition's footnotes. Ibn Aʿtham, *Kitāb al-Futūḥ*; McLaren, "Dating Ibn Aʿtham's History," 184n3. My thanks to Andrew McLaren for this information.

8. The Turkish scholar's name is Hoja Ismail Efendi, and he was Helmut Ritter's friend. Ritter, "Autographs," 64.

9. During an undergraduate year at Oxford University, I would read my course of study's "set texts" in the Bodleian Library, a nonlending library where one was regularly obliged to sit in the reading room to complete one's readings. Students from previous years had inevitably marked up the Bodleian copies of these set texts and, at times, had carried on arguments with one another over the interpretation of particular passages. Finding the annotations of friends and colleagues in borrowed books is often illuminating. I also recall flipping through my brother's copy of Freud's *Moses and Monotheism*. He had circled one of Freud's footnotes on the arbitrariness of biblical exegesis and scribbled Pink Floyd's turn of phrase in the margin: "Shine on, you crazy diamond."

10. al-Ḥarīrī, *Cairo MS Adab m105*, 5v. The text on the title piece translated here is also reproduced in a seventeenth-century encyclopedic supercommentary on the Mantle Ode. Al-Baghdādī, *Ḥāshiya*, 1:275.

11. Garrett Davidson has shown that there is a good deal of confusion in the secondary scholarship around the use of the term *ijāza*. As he points out, the "term *ijāza* literally means 'permission', and the permission to transmit hadith (*ijāzat al-riwāya*) has long been conflated in secondary literature with the permission granted to qualified individuals to teach (*ijāzat al-dirāya* or *ijāzat al-tadrīs*) or issue fatwās (*ijāzat al-iftāʾ*)." Whereas permission to transmit

a text could be granted to someone through correspondence or a short meeting, the idea that one had to possess an *ijāzat al-dirāya* to teach was contested. Davidson, *Carrying on the Tradition*, 109–10. The use of Arabic technical terms in Euro-American secondary scholarship sometimes conjures up ahistorical phantoms in our understanding of the sources. See, for example, the problems of putting analytical weight on the terms *tafsīr bi-l-raʾy* and *tafsīr bi-l-maʾthūr* in Saleh, "Preliminary Remarks," 36–37.

12. Yāqūt, *Muʿjam al-udabāʾ*, 2205.

13. The number seven and its multiples had long been used for this purpose in the Near East. Conrad, "Seven and the *Tasbīʿ*," 45.

14. E.g., al-Ḥarīrī, *Cairo MS Adab m105*, 36r, 45r, 66r. As MacKay points out, the collation notes cease after the sixth quire, which he lists as 64b. MacKay, "Certificates," 7; Gacek, *Arabic Manuscripts*, 210–13.

15. al-Ḥarīrī, *Cairo MS Adab m105*, 44r. Pierre MacKay suggests that this first segment was broken up into four sessions because one of the auditors, Abū al-Faḍl Ibrāhīm al-Mukarrimī is found near the end of the audition certificate where it is stated that he heard *maqāma*s #1–5, 7–12, and 16–50. Some other readers also heard only the first five *maqāmas*. Thus, MacKay proposes four sessions to cover *maqāmas* 1–5, 6, 7–12, and 13–15. The Ḥanbalī scholar whose sons attended *maqāma*s #16–41 is Abū Saʿd al-Mubārak b. ʿAlī al-Mukharrimī (d. 513/1119).

16. al-Ḥarīrī, *Cairo MS Adab m105*, 120v–121r.

17. It is unlikely that all instances of Abū al-Muʿammar overseeing readings of the *Ḥarīriyya* were recorded in this manuscript, given that there is generally a long lag between readings, sometimes lasting years. MacKay, "Certificates," 12–14.

18. E.g., certificate E in MacKay, "Certificates," 13.

19. MacKay, "Certificates," 21. Al-Kindī is reader #244 in MacKay's list. Yāqūt describes him as producing a kind of running commentary on every book that was read before him. He could answer almost any question on a text to the point that students asked why they needed the book when his pronouncements were so decisive and eloquent. Yāqūt, *Muʿjam al-udabāʾ*, 1332.

20. al-Ḥarīrī, *al-Maqāmāt*, *BNF Arabe 7290*, 167v.

21. The manuscript refers to Ibn Ḥakīm as Zayn al-Dīn Muḥammad b. Asʿad al-ʿIrāqī. ʿImād al-Dīn claims that the year was 566, not 567. ʿImād al-Dīn al-Iṣfahānī, *Kharīdat al-qaṣr (ʿIrāq)*, 3.1:267; al-Qurashī, *Al-Jawāhir*, 3:89–92.

22. MacKay has called the early transmission of the *Ḥarīriyya* "ostentatiously Ḥanbalite," although his method for identifying individual scholars as members of the Ḥanbalī school is problematic, relying as he does on a late biographical dictionary that includes scholars who were never identified as Ḥanbalīs in earlier biographical works. MacKay, "Certificates," 10; Keegan, "Commentarial Acts," 120–32.

23. al-Qurashī, *Al-Jawāhir*, 3:90.

24. Ibid.

25. Konrad Hirschler calls these "secondary title pages." Hirschler, *Monument*, 123.

26. al-Ḥarīrī, *Cairo MS Adab m105*, 3v; MacKay, "Certificates," 20, 53.

27. Ibn al-ʿAdīm, *Bughyat al-ṭalab*, 251. I am indebted to Benedikt Reier for this reference. Al-Ḥarīrī, *Cairo MS Adab m105*, 99v. It seems clear that *Malaṭiyya* was the preferred reading of al-Ḥarīrī. See al-Ḥarīrī, *Maqāmāt*, Istanbul University MS A4566, 122r. Ibn al-ʿAdīm reports that al-Kindī, on the authority of al-Jawālīqī, considers the other pronunciations

to be solecisms of the sub-elites ("*fīmā talḥan fīhi al-ʿāmma*"), emphasizing the polemical valence of the term *ʿāmma* and the fact that many scholars were accused of belonging to it. The copy that was collated with al-Kindī's manuscript, which reads *Malaṭiyya* in the body of the text and then *Malaṭya* in a collation note. Al-Ḥarīrī, *Maqāmāt, BNF MS Arabe 7290*, 159r; *HMC*, 193.

28. al-Ḥarīrī, *Cairo MS Adab m105*, 120r.

29. Ware, *Walking Qur'an*, 12.

30. al-Ḥarīrī, *Cairo MS Adab m105*, 3r; MacKay, "Certificates," 18, 52. For the *thabat* and similar genres, see Davidson, *Carrying on the Tradition*, 241-75.

31. Aljoumani, "Ṣuwar al-ijāzāt," 98. These copied *ijāza*s have caused some to identify a Yale University manuscript as al-Ghazālī's autograph. See Griffel, "Is There an Autograph."

32. *Ayasofya 4095* is a composite manuscript, that is, it contains more than one text by more than one copyist that were later bound together. Al-Tibrīzī, *Sharḥ al-qaṣāʾid, Ayasofya 4095*. For the phenomenon, see Hirschler, "Development."

33. al-Tibrīzī, *Sharḥ al-qaṣāʾid, Ayasofya 4095*, 1r. The teacher, Ibn al-Samīn is Abū al-Maʿālī Aḥmad b. ʿAlī b. ʿAbd Allāh al-Baghdādī al-Khabbāz; see al-Dhahabī, *Tārīkh al-Islām*, 11:958–59. Not to be confused with his grandson of the same teknonym, Abū al-Maʿālī. Al-Ṣafadī, *Kitāb al-Wāfī*, 7:85.

34. al-Tibrīzī, *Sharḥ al-qaṣāʾid, Ayasofya 4095*, 134v.

35. Ritter, "Autographs," 69.

36. van Ess, *Im Halbschatten*, 36.

37. MacKay, "Certificates," 28.

38. It should be noted that Istanbul University MS A4566 contains collation notes in which a collator has provided corrections drawn from a copy that he indicates is authoritative. See, for example, folios 38v and 114v. In other words, some collation did occur with this manuscript, and the "errors" in this authorial copy might suggest that this cannot be understood as an autograph. Errors as slight as these do not, in my view, rule out the possibility that al-Ḥarīrī himself committed them or made slight changes to his text over time. Furthermore, the manuscript against which the Istanbul manuscript was collated might itself contain faulty readings.

39. For some studies of *BNF Arabe 5847*, see O'Kane, "Text and Paintings"; and Roxburgh, "In Pursuit of Shadows."

40. al-Ḥarīrī, *Maqāmāt*, Istanbul University MS A4566, 2v.

41. The passage describing the holograph runs as follows: "*qad kataba ayḍan ʿalā ẓahrihā annahu ṣannafahā li-l-wazīr Jalāl al-Dīn ʿAmīd al-Dawla Abī ʿAlī al-Ḥasan b. Abī al-ʿIzz ʿAlī b. Ṣadaqa wazīr al-Mustarshid ayḍan wa-lā shakk anna hādhā aṣaḥḥ min al-riwāya al-ūlā li-kawnihi bi-khaṭṭ al-muṣannif.*" Ibn Khallikān clarifies that he is referring to the vizier who died in 522/1128–29. Ibn Khallikān, *Wafayāt al-aʿyān*, 4:64.

42. Sharlet, *Patronage and Poetry*, "Thought That Counts," and "Tokens of Resentment"; Gruendler, "Abbasid Praise Poetry" and *Medieval Arabic Praise Poetry.*

43. al-Dhahabī, *Tārīkh al-Islām*, 11:377.

44. MacKay, "Certificates," 29.

45. Déroche, "Fakes," 94, 96–97.

46. Ibn al-Anbārī, *Nuzhat al-alibbāʾ* (Baghdad), 262–65.

47. ʿImād al-Dīn al-Iṣfahānī, *Kharīdat (ʿIrāq)*, 4.1:679; Yāqūt, *Muʿjam al-buldān*, 5:131.

48. ʿImād al-Dīn al-Iṣfahānī, *Kharīdat (ʿIrāq)*, 4.1:601.

49. Al-Qifṭī also mentions that a judge from al-Wāsiṭ in Iraq studied one of al-Ḥarīrī's grammatical works with Abū Zayd al-Muṭahhar in 538/1143–44. For al-Qifṭī, al-Muṭahhar is

still a man of this world and a disciple of al-Ḥarīrī's scholarly work. Al-Qifṭī, *Inbāh*, 3:276. The phrase "known as al-Sarūjī" in al-Qifṭī's entry on al-Muṭahhar does not appear to be an interpolation. The editors drew from a manuscript copied before al-Qifṭī's death, and I have seen the same phrase in a manuscript copied in 646/1248, the same year as al-Qifṭī's death. Al-Qifṭī, *Inbāh*, Suleymaniye MS Feyzullah 1382, 95v.

50. Yāqūt, *Muʿjam al-udabāʾ*, 2203; al-Panjdīhī, *Maghānī*, Suleymaniye MS Murad Molla 1549, 23r–v, and *Maghānī*, Suleymaniye MS Hamidiye 1195, 9r–v; Ibn Khallikān, *Wafayāt al-aʿyān*, 4:63. The story is also quoted in the printed edition of Ibn al-Khashshāb's critique of the *Ḥarīriyya* with Ibn Barrī's rebuttal. Scholars have misidentified this story as part of Ibn Barrī's rebuttal, but it is an interpolation into the manuscript that the scribe identifies as such with a chain of transmitters that includes al-Panjdīhī. See Chapter 5 on fiction.

51. Yāqūt, *Muʿjam al-udabāʾ*, 2203, 2207; al-Subkī, *Ṭabaqāt*, 7:267–68.

52. Cooperson, "Note on the Translation," xxvii.

53. *HMC*, 21.

54. Examples of variation can be found in *maqāma* #9, in which the Cairo MS reads "*shiyamī*," whereas the Istanbul MS reads "*khuluqī*." In *maqāma* #12, the Cairo MS reads "*labūsuhu labūs al-ruhbān*"; the Istanbul MS reads "*shāratuhu shārat al-ruhbān*." In both cases, the meaning is more or less the same. *HMC*, 44, 55.

55. Gruendler, "Rat and Its Redactors"; Keegan, "Before and After *Kalīla wa-Dimna*" and "Elsewhere Lies Its Meaning."

CHAPTER 4

1. Ibn Abī Uṣaybiʿa, *Literary History of Medicine*, §15.40.3; Bonadeo, *Philosophical Journey*, 125n88.

2. Ibn Abī Uṣaybiʿa, *Literary History of Medicine*, §15.40.9.

3. Ibn al-Anbārī, *al-Inṣāf.* On these debates and Ibn al-Anbārī's work, see Olivieri, "*Kitāb al-ʾInṣāf*."

4. Brown, *Canonization*, 42–46.

5. al-Ṣafadī, *Nuṣrat al-thāʾir*, 58–59.

6. How to interpret the divergences between medieval commentators and modern literary critics has been a major question for scholars of the twentieth century. Margaret Larkin concludes her article analyzing al-Maʿarrī's commentary on al-Mutanabbī by asking why there is "virtually no discussion of essentially aesthetic criteria and poetic issues, such as poetic voice, lyricism, or for that matter, even the political and cultural realities that form the backdrop of the poem?" Larkin answers that this "simply is not what Arabic criticism, let alone commentaries, did." Whereas Wolfhart Heinrichs described the critics' "failure . . . to understand complex structures," Larkin insists that the absence of this properly literary discussion does not reflect an absence of understanding that readers must have had but left unwritten. Larkin, "Abū al-ʿAlāʾ," 492. Regarding the interpretation of poems, Williams Jones had described Arabic poems as "pearls at random strung," while A. J. Arberry rejected this view and claimed that Arabic poems possessed unity and coherence. Pritchett, "Orient Pearls Unstrung," 119–25, and the sources cited there. Heinrichs and van Gelder have argued that medieval Arabic criticism was interested only in the single line. Julie Meisami, Suzanne Stetkevych, Stefan Sperl, and others demonstrated that whole poems could be interpreted productively, rejecting the "pearls at random strung" thesis. By contrast, van Gelder states that

analyzing whole poems simply reveals "structures that were hitherto unsuspected; revelations that can serve to test methods, support theories, even add to our appreciation of the poems; or, if such an analysis does not serve anything, it may be its own reward as a neat exercise in inventivity and ingeniousness." Van Gelder, *Beyond the Line*, 200; Heinrichs, "Literary Theory: The Problem of Its Efficiency"; Talib, *How Do You Say*, 183–94. As Sperl points out, van Gelder's thesis "does not mean that whole poems must lack coherence or be devoid of a unified message . . . because medieval criticism has passed them over in silence." Sperl, *Mannerism*, 6–7. Meisami has suggested that structural interpretation does not merely provide insight into the poem's significance for us but rather what it must have meant to the poets and critics themselves. Thus, Meisami states that what she calls structuralist analysis has "challenged such fragmentary approaches and urged us to read these poetries in new and different ways (new and different to us, that is, but perhaps closer to those of medieval poets and critics themselves). They show us that structure and meaning are inextricably, vitally linked—as any good medieval poet, or critic, knew." Meisami, *Structure and Meaning*, 15. Here, Meisami makes the bold claim that critics can use the ahistorical interpretive techniques of structuralism to recover what the poem should have meant to its historical author and its best readers, an argument James T. Monroe also makes for the *maqāma*. Monroe, *Art of Badīʿ al-Zamān*, 93. Although structural interpretation may shed light on what a text *might* mean to us or to others, there appears to me to be no necessary or determinative relationship between a text's structural features and its meaning as that unfolds over time.

7. Rowson, "Alexandrian Age," 109–10.

8. Talib, "Al-Ṣafadī, His Critics," 110.

9. Ibid., 114–19.

10. Ibid., 114.

11. Freeman, *Time Binds*, 3.

12. Jonathan Owens describes early approaches to Arabic linguistics by figures like Sībawayh as "explicatory descriptivism." Even the descriptive element of Arabic linguistics is one that seeks to describe particular kinds of Arabic language users. Owens, "Grammatical Tradition," 105.

13. Talib, "Al-Ṣafadī, His Critics," 132.

14. Ibn al-Khashshāb, "Risāla," 4.

15. Sībawayh may have relied on encounters or second-hand reports in urban areas, rather than travels to the desert. Carter, *Sībawayhi*, 40–42; Gruendler, "Early Arabic Philologists," 93–94; Weipert, "al-Aṣmaʿī."

16. Lindermann, "Shared Set of Solecisms," 75. The earliest treatises on solecisms of the commoners is from the second half of the second/eighth century (57).

17. Ibn al-Khashshāb, *Istidrākāt*, Suleymaniye MS Fazil Ahmed Pasha 1203, 11r; *Naqd Ibn al-Khashshāb*, Yale MS Landberg 503, 8r–v. The passage is corrupt in the defective print edition but leaves us with the same result. See now Ibn al-Khashshāb, *Istidrākāt* (Maḥmūd) and *Istidrākāt* (Ḥasanʿalyān).

18. Ibn al-Khashshāb, *Istidrākāt* (Ḥasanʿalyān), 56. The context of this saying is found in Ibn Ḥajar's commentary on al-Bukhārī's *Ṣaḥīḥ* in *Bāb ḥaml al-rijāl al-janāza dūn al-nisāʾ*. Although this hadith is discussed in a commentary on al-Bukhārī, it does not appear in al-Bukhārī's *Ṣaḥīḥ* collection itself because it does not meet his stringent standards for inclusion. See Ibn Ḥajar al-ʿAsqalānī, *Fatḥ al-bārī*, 3:217.

19. al-ʿAskarī, *Kitāb al-Ṣināʿatayn*, 261.

20. Ibn ʿUṣfūr, *Ḍarāʾir*, 14.

21. Ibid., 15.

22. al-Panjdīhī, *Maghānī*, Suleymaniye MS Murad Molla 1549, 58v. The use of analogy was considered foundational to the Arabic grammatical tradition, with some declaring that "grammar as a whole is analogy." Suleiman, *Arabic Grammatical Tradition*, 25.

23. Haider, "Contesting Intoxication"; Adang, "Ibn Ḥazm on Homosexuality."

24. There are numerous forms of prescriptivism in linguistics. Hallberg, "Standard Language Ideology."

25. Ibn al-Anbārī, *Nuzhat al-alibbāʾ* (Baghdad), 264, and *Nuzhat al-alibbāʾ* (Cairo), 455.

26. *HMC*, 9.

27. Ibn al-Khashshāb, "Risāla," 9; Ibn al-Khashshāb, *Istidrākāt*, Suleymaniye MS Fazil Ahmed Pasha 1203, 7v.

28. Ibn al-Khashshāb, "Risāla," 9. The verse is quoted in al-Akhfash al-Aṣghar, *Kitāb al-Ikhtiyārayn*, 504. Ibn Barrī also quotes another line of verse that is found in al-Mufaḍḍal's *Mufaḍḍaliyyāt* together with a gloss by the anthologist. Al-Mufaḍḍal, *al-Mufaḍḍaliyyāt* (Lyall ed.), 49.

29. al-Panjdīhī, *Maghānī*, Suleymaniye MS Murad Molla 1549, 48v.

30. *HMC*, 99.

31. al-Maydānī, *Majmaʿ al-Amthāl*, 2:160. Although the general meaning of the expression is clear, al-Maydānī registers several other interpretations of the words *al-ḥayy* and *al-layy*. They might mean "truth" and "falsehood," but the words also might refer to "urging camels on" and "restraining them."

32. It should be noted that this expression also has divergent interpretations, one of which echoes the interpretation about camels but is rather about driving goats out to pasture or calling them back.

33. Al-Ḥarīrī's defenders did not invent the notion that *ḥayy* and *layy* refer to clear and obscure speech. It is not found in al-Maydānī, but it is found in other reference works on proverbial expressions, such as the works of Abū Hilāl al-ʿAskarī (d. ca. 400/1010) and Ibn Fāris (d. 395/1004). The latter happened to be an associate of al-Hamadhānī and, more importantly, wrote a collection of riddling *fatwā*s that inspired *maqāma* #32 in which Abū Zayd plays a riddling mufti. Ibn Fāris, *Mutakhayyar al-Alfāẓ*, 164; al-ʿAskarī, *Jamharat al-amthāl*, 2:419.

34. Asad, "Idea," 20.

35. As noted above, biography as debate over reputation and legacy in the Arabic and Islamic traditions has been the subject of a number of other studies. Malti-Douglas, "Controversy" and "Dreams"; Cooperson, "Ibn Ḥanbal"; Jaques, "Other Rabīʿ"; Lawrence, "It's All Just Poetry" 327; Haider, "Lunatics and Loving Sons"; Cooperson, *Classical Arabic*.

36. Kia, *Persianate Selves*, 172.

37. Beecroft, *Authorship*, 19.

38. On the biographical fallacy and the "reverse biographical fallacy," see ibid., 2. For a detailed study of Ḥarīrian biographies, see Zakharia, *Abū Zayd*, 23–33.

39. The biography concludes with a report of someone seeing Ibn al-Khashshāb in a dream after the latter's death saying that God had forgiven him after shunning him and other scholars of his sort. al-Dhahabī, *Siyar aʿlām*, 20:526–27.

40. ʿImād al-Dīn al-Iṣfahānī, *Kharīdat al-qaṣr* (*ʿIrāq*), 3.1:7–18.

41. Hammond stops short of claiming that these anecdotes are utter fabrications. Hammond, *Beyond Elegy*, 142–47.

42. Ibn al-Khashshāb, "Risāla," 3.

43. Keegan, "Commentators."

44. al-Anbārī, *Sharḥ*, Suleymaniye MS Laleli 1847, 8v.

45. Ibn al-Khashshāb, "Risāla," 4.

46. al-Panjdīhī, *Maghānī*, Suleymaniye MS Murad Molla 1549, 14r–v; al-Panjdīhī, *Maghānī*, Suleymaniye MS Hamidiye 1195, 5v.

47. al-Panjdīhī, *Maghānī*, Suleymaniye MS Murad Molla 1549, 14r–v; al-Panjdīhī, *Maghānī*, Suleymaniye MS Hamidiye 1195, 5v.

48. Gully, *Culture of Letter-Writing*, 84–93.

49. Ibn al-Athīr, *al-Mathal al-sā'ir*, 1:38–39.

50. Ibid., 1:39. The anecdote is likewise described as a defense of epistolary writing with which the *maqāma* shared some common ground in Gully, *Culture of Letter-Writing*, 4.

51. Ibn al-Athīr, *al-Mathal al-Sā'ir*, 1:40.

52. Yāqūt, *Mu'jam al-udabā'*, 2203–4.

53. Ibid., 2204.

CHAPTER 5

1. Von Grunebaum, *Medieval Islam*, 287; Leder, "Conventions of Fictional Narration," 34.

2. Seeger A. Bonebakker discusses a wide range of texts that, in his view, have some relation to fictionality, the fantastic, and storytelling. He does note that a variety of opinions might have circulated but treats the idea that Muslim scholars had reservations about fiction as his "working hypothesis." Bonebakker, "Nihil Obstat," 22, and "Some Medieval Views," 22–24.

3. Said, *Orientalism*, 273. The term "repressive hypothesis" recalls Foucault's *History of Sexuality*, which is sometimes understood as rejecting Freudianism, but I take his project to be one of reconceptualizing our understanding of sexuality away from a repression/freedom dualism to explore the discourses about sexuality and their relationships to different configurations of power. Although the discourses on fictionality do not map precisely onto those of sexuality, there are important resonances in the repression/freedom dichotomy. D. Cook, "Foucault," 157.

4. Chenery, introduction, 30.

5. "Aus dem Angeführten konnen wir zunächst nicht mehr und nicht weniger schließen, als daß der Islam der Fiktion abhold ist. Ob dieses Verhalten aus einer niedrigen Einschätzung der Phantasie und aus der religiosen Bedenklichkeit menschlichen Schöpfertums zu bergrunden ist, konnen wir mangels aus einschlägiger Texte nicht entscheiden." Heinrichs, *Arabische Dichtung*, 43. On the *Maqāmāt* more specifically, see Kilito, *Les séances*, 125–39; and Zakharia, "Norme et fiction." The most prominent proponent of the idea that narrative "fiction" can be separated out from factual content is Stefan Leder. See Leder, "Use of Composite Form." A critique of this view in the analysis of historical writing can be found in Meisami's, "Mas'ūdī," 149–52. For a summary of the debates on "fiction" in Islamic historiography, see Haider, *Rebel*, 10–15. The first moves to establish a more detailed history of the Arabic conceptualizations of fictional writing (a *Begriffsgeschichte*) can be found in Isabel Toral-Niehoff's "'Fact and Fiction.'"

6. Drory, "*maqāma*," 507.

7. For other critiques of the fact/fiction binary, see Stephan, "Modalities of Fictionality"; and Keegan, "Al-Tawḥīdī, Fictionality."

8. Orlemanski, "Who Has Fiction?," 155, 158; citing Nicolette Zeeman, "Imaginative Theory." Orlemanski's approach recognizes the problems of universalizing accounts of fiction that identify certain "signposts" of fictionality that tend to be drawn from the features found in the modern novel. At the same time, she also critiques the view that fiction was "invented" at some point in history, often the dawn of European colonial modernity. Orlemanski, "Who Has Fiction?," 148–50.

9. The idea that Muslim authors and readers working in Arabic were distinct can be seen in Drory's claim that the very same authorial technique of declaring that the work is invented "from the heart" is one that "clearly assumes two opposite functions when appearing in Hebrew or in Arabic contexts." Drory, *Models and Contacts*, 18n12. Orlemanski also discusses how the ideologies of secular modernity have inflected the study of fiction. Orlemanski, "Who Has Fiction?," 147.

10. al-Qazwīnī, *Kitāb al-Mughnī*, Suleymaniye MS Esad Efendi 2819, 10v.

11. Drory, *Models and Contacts*, 29.

12. It seems possible that the anxieties of fiction ascribed to the medieval Islamic world are, in fact, a figment of the scholarly imagination that grew out of debates around fictionality in Europe in the seventeenth through nineteenth centuries. As Nicholas D. Paige points out in *Before Fiction*, authors prior to the nineteenth century regularly asserted that their fictional characters were "real." Overthrowing this "ancien régime" of the novel may have helped produce the assumptions underpinning the Orientalist assumptions about Arabic fiction, but this is a topic too expansive and exploratory to be dealt with here. Paige, *Before Fiction*. See also Gallagher, "Rise of Fictionality."

13. *HMC*, 3.

14. *HMC*, 3.

15. al-Sharīshī, *Sharḥ* (Ibrāhīm), 1:14.

16. Montgomery, "al-Jāḥiẓ's *Kitāb*," 115–17.

17. Al-Panjdīhī points this out after a long philological discussion of the words al-Ḥarīrī uses, and he quotes the opening passage of al-Jāḥiẓ's *Kitāb al-Bayān*. Al-Sharīshī adds that this is an example of parallelism (*muqābala*), part of the rhetorical arts. Al-Panjdīhī, *Maghānī*, Suleymaniye MS Murad Molla 1549, 7v; al-Sharīshī, *Sharḥ* (Ibrāhīm), 1:14–15.

18. *HMC*, 5.

19. Ibid., 5–6.

20. Hämeen-Anttila, *Maqama*, 151–52.

21. Drory, "*maqāma*," 507–8. See also Drory, "Three Attempts" and *Models and Contacts*, 11–46. The constraints and pressures of a religious system do not, of course, necessarily impede creativity. The inventiveness of the hadith genre was well known to Muslim scholars. Ignaz Goldziher even identifies the Prophetic condemnation of forged hadith as a fabricated response to the rise of forged *ḥadith*. Goldziher, *Muslim Studies*, 2:127. Ibn al-Jawzī transmits a story in which Ibn Ḥanbal and Yaḥyā b. Maʿīn overhear a storyteller elaborating a fantastical story on their authority. When the two hadith men confront them, the storyteller has a ready answer; he has been speaking on the authority of other people with the same names. Ibn al-Jawzī, *Kitāb al-Quṣṣāṣ*, ¶24. Quoting unreliable hadith reports was, in fact, a widely accepted practice, suggesting that the cult of authenticity may be, in part, a modern one. Brown, "Even If It's Not True."

22. Keegan, "Elsewhere Lies Its Meaning."

23. Al-Sharīshī, *Sharḥ* (Ibrāhīm), 1:44.

24. Ibn al-Muqaffaʿ, *Version arabe*, 62.

25. Ibid., 92.

26. Ibid., 75–76.

27. al-Sharīshī, *Sharḥ* (Ibrāhīm), 1:44.

28. The passage preceding this quote is somewhat convoluted and possibly corrupted in the extant manuscript available to me. Nevertheless, it is clear that he does not consider a versified *Kalīla wa-Dimna* to be poetry. Ibn Sīnā, *al-Shifāʾ*, 7:54. Complicating matters further is the fact that this passage includes the term *muḥākāt*, which is the Arabic term for mimesis, but as Lara Harb has argued, the understanding of mimesis in Ibn Sīnā and other philosophers working on the Aristotelian tradition had little to do with "imitation" or "representation" of reality but were based on "comparison" through simile and metaphor. Harb, "Mimesis," 2.

29. "*fa-inna al-tajriba ayḍan idhā istanadat ilā mawjūd aqnaʿat akthar mimmā tuqniʿ idhā istanadat ilā mukhtaraʿ wa-baʿda dhālika in istanadat ilā mawjūd mā yaqdir kawnuhu*." Ibn Sīnā, *al-Shifāʾ*, 7:55.

30. Ibn Sīnā notes that there is a kind of speech for which names are invented (*ukhturiʿa lahu ism*) and do not really exist, as well as stories that deal with particular circumstances (*aḥwāl juzʾiyya*) that did actually exist. Even stories engaged in what existed and can exist are not necessarily poetry and thus do not induce imagination because they do not engage in the universal. He admits that poetry also traffic in particulars, but it is mixed with the universal (*al-kullī*). Ibid., 7:54.

31. Ibn Buṭlān, *Daʿwat al-Aṭibbāʾ*, 13, and *Doctors' Dinner Party*, ¶o.1.

32. Hutcheon, *Irony's Edge*, 17; citing Booth, *Rhetoric*, 28.

33. Ibn Nāqiyā, "Maqāmāt," 123.

34. Ibid.

35. In the examples he cites of Arab proverbs, he refers explicitly to the existence of talking animals in the narrative heritage of the Arabs (as opposed to the translated work of *Kalīla wa-Dimna*). These two distinct genealogies for talking animals would also divide the commentators on the *Ḥarīriyya*.

36. al-Kalāʿī, *Iḥkām ṣanʿat al-kalām*, 198–209.

37. McLaren, "Ibn Aʿtham's History," 283.

38. Miskawayh, *Tajārib al-Umam*, 1:59. The contents of Miskawayh's history occasionally take up precisely these sorts of example. Miskawayh discusses the *ḥiyal* of Alexander the Great and the *ḥiyal* and *makāʾid* of Muʿāwiya. Miskawayh, *Tajārib al-Umam*, 1:82-84, 1:370-71. Miskawayh's claim that "the matters of this world resemble one another" was not a new idea. A similar sentiment was expressed as early as ʿAbd al-Ḥamīd b. Yaḥyā al-Kātib (d. ca. 132/750) where he describes the role of the *kātib* as one who guides beasts (*sāʾis al-bahāʾim*) using subterfuges to do so (*ḥiyal*). ʿAbd al-Ḥamīd, *ʿAbd al-Ḥamīd*, 286.

39. Miskawayh, *Tajārib al-Umam*, 1:59.

40. McLaren, "Ibn Aʿtham's History," 277–86.

41. Ibn Funduq, *Tārīkh-i Bayhaqī*, 16; quoted in Meisami, *Persian Historiography*, 213.

42. Meisami, *Persian Historiography*, 213.

43. Mīrkhānd, *Tārīkh-i Rawḍat al-Ṣafāʾ*, 14–15.

44. Ibid., 11. Here, Mīrkhānd specifically references the "practical intellect (*ʿaql-i tajārubī*)."

45. McLaren, "Ibn Aʿtham's History," 287.

46. Ibn al-Khashshāb, "*Risāla*," 4–5. Ibn al-Khashshāb's phrase "*al-mawḍūʿāt ʿalā alsinat al-ʿajmawāt*" is remarkably similar to Ibn Funduq's phrase in Persian about placing stories on the tongues of animals: "*bar zabān-i ḥayavānāt nahādah-and*."

47. Ibid., 5.

48. See Keegan, "al-Tawḥīdī, Fictionality," 342; and McLaren, "Ibn Aʿtham's History," 130.

49. Ibn al-Khashshāb, "*Risāla*," 5.

50. Ibn Khallikān, *Wafayāt al-aʿyān*, 4:63; Yāqūt, *Muʿjam al-udabāʾ*, 2203; Drory, "*maqāma*," 507; Stewart, "ʿĪsā b. Hišām's Shiism," 15n5.

51. This rebuttal, on which the theorizing of Zakharia and Drory rests, is undoubtedly a later interpolation. It appears in at least one manuscript: Princeton University Library, Garrett 134H. This manuscript is wrongly attributed to ʿAbd al-Laṭīf al-Baghdādī. The interpolated rebuttal is simply the story of al-Ḥarīrī encountering the "real" Abū Zayd, but it is introduced with an *isnad* as though Ibn Barrī had received the story from a certain Ibn Ḥammuwayh, a scholar who would have been a child or even just a glimmer in his parents' eyes when Ibn Barrī composed his rebuttals. According to the *isnād*, Ibn Ḥammuwayh transmits the story on the authority of the commentator al-Panjdīhī, who wrote his commentary after Ibn Barrī had already completed his rebuttal, which makes the *isnād* impossible, barring time travel. In fact, al-Panjdīhī quotes Ibn Barrī, not the other way around. Al-Panjdīhī, *Maghānī*, Suleymaniye MS Murad Molla 1549, 54r. The story of the "real" Abū Zayd who encountered al-Ḥarīrī is found in al-Panjdīhī's commentary, but it is not part of his rebuttal to Ibn al-Kashshāb's critique. Al-Panjdīhī's use of the story will be analyzed in detail below. Katia Zakharia identifies the interpolation as Ibn Barrī's response to the attack on fiction and even provides the Arabic text of "Ibn Barrī's" response in an appendix, but she omits the *isnād* that cites al-Panjdīhī through al-Ḥammuwayh. Zakharia, "Norme et fiction," 219, 229; Kilito, *Les séances*, 257. This older printed version of Ibn al-Khashshāb is also missing all the material about *maqāma*s #8 and #13. The first of Ibn al-Khashshāb's critiques of *maqāma* #4 is also missing. Ibn al-Khashshāb, "*Risāla*." There are now a pair of new editions that are much more reliable, although they appeared late in the drafting of this book. One retains the erroneous Ibn Barrī rebuttal in the body of the text, while the other does not seem aware of the manuscripts that contain the interpolation. Ibn al-Khashshāb, *Istidrākāt* (Maḥmūd), 58, and *Istidrākāt* (Ḥasanʿalyān), 37–39.

52. al-Panjdīhī, *Maghānī*, Suleymaniye MS Murad Molla 1549, 32v, and *Maghānī*, Suleymaniye MS Hamidiye 1195, 11v.

53. al-Panjdīhī, *Maghānī*, Suleymaniye MS Murad Molla 1549, 32v, and *Maghānī*, Suleymaniye MS Hamidiye 1195, 11v.

54. al-Panjdīhī, *Maghānī*, Suleymaniye MS Murad Molla 1549, 32v, and *Maghānī*, Suleymaniye MS Hamidiye 1195, 11v.

55. al-Panjdīhī, *Maghānī*, Suleymaniye MS Murad Molla 1549, 28v, and *Maghānī*, Suleymaniye MS Hamidiye 1195, 11v.

56. *HMC*, 5.

57. al-Panjdīhī, *Maghānī*, Suleymaniye MS Murad Molla 1549, 28r.

58. *HMC*, 5. al-Panjdīhī, *Maghānī*, Suleymaniye MS Murad Molla 1549, 28r, and *Maghānī*, Beyazid MS V2611, 13v.

59. al-Panjdīhī, Suleymaniye MS Murad Molla 1549, 23r–v.

60. al-Panjdīhī, Suleymaniye MS Murad Molla 1549, 23v–24r, and al-Panjdīhī, Suleymaniye MS Hamidiye 1195, 9r.

61. al-Sharīshī, *Sharḥ* (Ibrāhīm), 1:48–49. The example al-Sharīshī cites for a description of Abū Zayd as fickle fate is the following poem at the end of *maqāma* #21:

My wolf wreaks havoc in every flock
to the point that I am like the heir of humankind—

I aʾm their Shem, their Ham, and Japheth.

Because Abū Zayd defeats all comers, he is like fortune or fickle fate, which eventually defeats all humankind and is thus their "heir" because it "inherits" what we leave behind. The reference to Noah's three sons is somewhat more obscure, and the commentaries offer little help beyond saying that these are the progenitors of various racialized groups. Presumably, these three brothers are the heirs of humankind because all of humankind perishes in the flood. Al-Sharīshī, *Sharḥ* (Ibrāhīm), 3:32–33; Al-Panjdīhī, *Maghānī*, Suleymaniye MS Hamidiye 1195, 111v; *HMC*, 103.

62. Al-Sharīshī, *Sharḥ* (Ibrāhīm), 3:32–33. The passage is mangled in the Beirut edition, which I have generally cited due to its availability. However, it is not a true edition but a resetting of the nineteenth-century Būlāq edition with the addition of some scholarly footnotes. A single line of the Būlāq edition is completely missing, suggesting that it was simply skipped in the process of resetting the text. For the correct reading, one must therefore reference the old Būlāq edition on which all later printings of al-Sharīshī seem to be based. Al-Sharīshī, *Sharḥ* (Būlāq), 1:20.

63. Hämeen-Anttila, *Maqama*, 179–83. Regarding al-Zamakhsharī and the pious *maqāma* more generally, he notes that "the closest model for these *maqāma*s is the earlier pious literature and pious *maqāmāt* which are somewhat outside the present subject."

64. See the discussions of ʿAbd al-Qāhir al-Jurjānī in Chapter 6.

65. Ibn al-Jawzī, *Maqāmāt*, Suleymaniye MS Nuruosmaniye 4271, 1v.

66. al-Anbārī, *Sharḥ*, Suleymaniye MS Laleli 1847, 20r. For al-Anbārī, see Yāqūt, *Muʿjam al-udabāʾ*, 1379–80; and Hämeen-Anttila, "Marginalia Ḥarīriana," 259. When the *Ḥarīriyya* is seen through its commentarial tradition, Ibn al-Jawzī's *Maqāmāt*—a reception of the *Ḥarīriyya* which is similar to al-Panjdīhī's commentary on the *Ḥarīriyya* in so many respects—no longer seems a marginal, pious contribution to the central, picaresque tradition of *maqāma*s. His *Maqāmāt* becomes instead a meaningful engagement with the interpretive questions raised by *maqāma* texts and their commentators.

67. al-ʿUkbarī, *Sharḥ al-alfāẓ*, 64–65.

68. Ibn al-Jawzī, *Maqāmāt*, Suleymaniye MS Nuruosmaniye 4271, 3v.

69. Ibid., 4r.

70. *HMC*, 6.

CHAPTER 6

1. MacKay, "Certificates," 24.

2. Later *maqāma* collections were also transmitted in mosques. For example, *al-Maqāmāt al-Jalāliyya* by the Mamluk historian al-Ḥasan b. Abī Muḥammad al-Ṣafadī (fl. early eighth/fourteenth century) contains notes attesting to the fact that it was read in a mosque in Tripoli. Pomerantz, "*Maqāma* Collection," 640.

3. Neuwirth, "*Ayyu ḥajarin*," 243. For a discussion of Bakhtin in medieval Arabic literature, see Bin Tyeer, *Qurʾan*, 269–75.

4. Allan, *In the Shadow*, 9.

5. The verses that challenge humans and jinn to bring chapters or books like the Quran are Q 2.23–24, Q 10.38, Q 11.13, Q 17.88, Q 28.49.

6. Abū al-ʿAtāhiya is said to have boasted that he wrote a poem better than chapter 78 of the Quran. Al-Iṣfahānī, *Kitāb al-Aghānī*, 4:29. More famously, Ibn al-Muqaffaʿ and al-

Maʿarrī were both accused of attempting imitations of the Quran. Grigoryan, *Neither Belief*, 50–53; von Grunebaum, *Tenth-Century Document*, xiv, n. 7.

7. al-Muṭarrizī, *Īḍāḥ* (Lahore), 32; Muṭarrizī, *Īḍāḥ*, Suleymaniye MS Nuruosmaniye 4061, 1v.

8. al-Muṭarrizī, *Īḍāḥ* (Lahore), 33.

9. These borrowings and paraphrases are not noted in the current editions of al-Muṭarrizī's commentary. Keegan, "Throwing the Reins," 113–20.

10. The order is more logical according to al-Jurjānī himself because it begins with more general topics before moving on to the more specific ones. Al-Jurjānī refers to various unspecified reasons for abandoning this more intuitive model of presentation. Margaret Larkin has argued that al-Jurjānī's polemical, dialectical context helps explain the unusual, discursive structure of the work. Keegan, "Throwing the Reins," 116; Larkin, *Theology of Meaning*, 14–15.

11. Keegan, "al-Muṭarrizī."

12. Zadeh, "'Fire Cannot Harm It,'" 58; citing ʿAbd al-Jabbār, *Tathbīt*, 86–91.

13. al-Jurjānī, *Asrār*, 43; al-Muṭarrizī, *Īḍāḥ* (Lahore), 36. See Heinrichs, *Hand of the North Wind*.

14. al-Muṭarrizī, *Īḍāḥ* (Lahore), 36.

15. Harb, *Arabic Poetics*, particularly 144–46; al-Jurjānī, *Asrār*, 126.

16. al-Muṭarrizī, *Īḍāḥ* (Lahore), 38. Drawing from al-Jurjānī, *Asrār*, 82–84.

17. al-Muṭarrizī, *Īḍāḥ* (Lahore), 38.

18. In the eighth/fourteenth century, another scholar carrying the name al-Jurjānī wrote a book about eloquence. This al-Jurjānī was Muḥammad b. ʿAlī, a Shi'ite and a student of al-ʿAllāma al-Ḥillī (d. 726/1325), who put the importance of poetics succinctly: The rulings of the *sharīʿa* depend on the truth of the Quran, which depends on it being revealed from God, which depends on it being beyond human capability. Thus, without first proving the divinity of the Quran, assenting rationally to the demands of the revelation becomes impossible. Muḥammad b. ʿAlī b. Muḥammad al-Jurjānī, *al-Ishārāt*, 1. For a disambiguation of the scholars who carry the name al-Jurjānī, see Harb, "al-Jurjānī, ʿAbd al-Qāhir."

19. al-Muṭarrizī, *Īḍāḥ* (Lahore), 36.

20. *HMC*, 5.

21. Bourdieu, *Distinction*, 6. The relationship between language and status in Islamic contexts has been elaborated by several scholars, especially Cheikh-Moussa, "Avarice ou sophistique?"; Marlow, *Hierarchy and Egalitarianism*; Heck, *Construction of Knowledge*, 26–93; and Messick, *Calligraphic State*, 1–74. Shahab Ahmed discusses the tension between egalitarianism and hierarchy in Islam in *What Is Islam?*, 374–77. As Konrad Hirschler has argued, the period when the *Ḥarīriyya* and al-Muṭarrizī's commentary circulated was also marked by increased literacy and scholarly engagement by non-elites. This point is not disputed here, and it seems rather likely that this broader literacy contributed to the need for scholars to use texts like the Ḥarīriyya to distinguish themselves from nonscholars and literate non-elites. As Hirschler points out, scholarly reading sessions that excluded the broader public tended to take place in private homes, reinforcing distinctions on a spatial level. Hirschler, *Written Word*, 32–70.

22. Bourdieu, *Distinction*, 6.

23. *HMC*, 38.

24. *HMC*, 5.

25. al-Muṭarrizī, *Īḍāḥ* (Lahore), 557–58. There is considerable variation in the manuscripts for this passage, and I have therefore generally followed two manuscripts of

al-Muṭarrizī: Suleymaniye MS Nuruosmaniye 4061, 236v; and Suleymaniye MS Haci Selim Aga 973, 227v.

26. *HMC*, 5.

27. Cooperson, "Note on the Translation," xxix.

28. al-Muṭarrizī, *Īḍāḥ* (Lahore), 70.

29. Ibid., 44.

30. Abu Deeb, *Al-Jurjānī's Theory*, 53; Harb, *Arabic Poetics*, 212–15, 248–49; al-Jurjānī, *Dalā'il*, 481–82, and *Asrār*, 101–16.

31. al-Jurjānī, *Asrār*, 129–30; Abu Deeb, *al-Jurjānī's Theory*, 280; Harb, *Arabic Poetics*, 144.

32. Hirschkind, *Ethical Soundscape*, 15.

33. Ibid.

34. Ibid.

35. Yāqūt, *Muʿjam al-udabāʾ*, 2205–6.

36. Ibid., 2205.

37. Yāqūt, *Muʿjam al-buldān*, 1:9–10. Al-Muṭarrizī's error can be found in his commentary on *maqāma* #40, which takes place in Tabriz. al-Muṭarrizī, *Īḍāḥ* (Lahore), 437.

38. Kennedy, *Recognition*, 306.

39. Cooperson, introduction, xxvi.

40. Ibid.

41. Beaumont, "Trickster and Rhetoric," 12.

42. See Vishanoff, *Formation of Islamic Hermeneutics*; Bauer, *Die Kultur der Ambiguität*; and Adamson and Key, "Philosophy of Language." These assumptions are deeply held, taking on the guise of common sense to the point that they have, as I pointed out in the first note in Chapter 1, made their way into such works as Benedict Anderson's *Imagined Communities*, where he claims that global communities of the past were imagined through "an idea largely foreign to the contemporary Western mind: the nonarbitrariness of the sign. The ideograms of Chinese, Latin, or Arabic were emanations of reality, not randomly fabricated representations of it." *Imagined Communities*, 14.

43. al-Rāzī, *Mafātīḥ al-Ghayb*, 7:188. The same Quranic verse goes on to say of the ambiguous verses that "no one knows their interpretation except for God and those who are firmly rooted in knowledge say we believe in it, all is from our Lord." As al-Rāzī points out, exegetes disagree as to whether or not "those who are firmly rooted in knowledge" are included among those who know the interpretation of these verses. Al-Rāzī makes detailed and cogent arguments for the translation I have given here, but he notes multiple respected exegetes who would read the verse slightly differently; namely, "No one knows their interpretation except for God and those who are firmly rooted in knowledge—they say we believe in it."

44. See Thaver, "Encountering Ambiguity."

45. Burton, "Naskh"; Madelung, review of *Abū ʿUbaid*.

46. The word "signpost" here is *sīmīyāʾ*, which can also refer to natural magic. However, al-Panjdīhī provides a commentary on his introduction in which he glosses this term as *ʿālāma*. Al-Panjdīhī, Maghānī, Suleymaniye MS Murad Molla 1549, 4r.

47. al-Panğdīhī, Maghānī, MS Beyazid V2611, 1v–2r.

48. On charitable interpretation as a sign of canonization, see Brown, *Canonization*, 30, 42–46.

49. al-Panjdīhī, Maghānī, MS Murad Molla 1549, 63v.

50. Ibid., 64v.

51. Wensinck, "ʿAmr b. al-ʿĀṣ."

52. Monroe, *Art of Badīʿ az-Zamān*, 19–38. See also Stewart, "Of Rhetoric, Reason, and Revelation," 207–17. As mentioned earlier, it is also sometimes assumed that pious Muslim audiences would have condemned the *Ḥarīriyya* as a whole or, failing that, the trickster. al-Ḥarīrī, *Assemblies* (Chenery), 1:34; Neuwirth, "*Ayyu ḥajarin*," 243; Beaumont, "Trickster and Rhetoric," 12; Hämeen-Anttila, *Maqama*, 151–52.

53. al-Panjdīhī, Maghānī, Suleymaniye MS Murad Molla 1549, 50r–v. For a transcription and translation of the entire passage, see Keegan, "Digressions," 93–94.

54. *HMC*, 184; El-Rouayheb, *Before Homosexuality*, 130–36.

55. Ibid.

56. *HMC*, 187.

57. *HMC*, 188.

58. al-Panjdīhī, Suleymaniye MS Hamidiye 1195, 165v.

59. *HMC*, 5.

60. *HMC*, 185.

61. *HMC*, 46.

62. *HMC*, 48.

63. al-Ḥarīrī, *Assemblies* (Chenery), 1:163.

64. *HMC*, 189.

65. al-Ṭabarī, *Tafsīr*, 15:521–22. The exegete al-Thaʿlabī (d. 427/1035) seems to prefer a straightforwardly negative connotation: "a grave error (*munkar ʿaẓīm*)." Al-Thaʿlabī, *al-Kashf*, 6:212.

66. al-Rāzī, *Mafātīḥ al-ghayb*, 21:208.

67. al-Panjdīhī, Suleymaniye MS Hamidiye 1195, 166v.

68. Two kinds of double entendre are considered distinct in the Arabic tradition. *Tawriya* refers to a situation in which the less likely meaning is intended, which is distinct from *istikhdām*, in which both meanings are understood to be intended by the author. Bonebakker, *Some Early Definitions*, 9–23, 84.

69. According to the Islamic tradition, the third caliph, ʿUthmān, produced a unified Quranic codex and undertook the burning of the now noncanonical copies held by various companions. Recently, very early copies of the Quran have been discovered in which the order of verses and chapters varies, but the canonical variant readings tend to be much more minor. For an overview of this phenomenon and its interpretation in the Muslim and non-Muslim scholarly traditions, see Nasser, *Transmission*, 5–34.

70. *HMC*, 164.

71. Leemhuis, "Readings of the Qurʾān."

72. Qureshi, "Ibn ʿArabī and the Akbarī Tradition," 98.

73. For the text of the poem, see al-Farghānī, *Muntahā al-madārik*, 2:224. These lines are also translated, with some differences, in Nicholson, *Studies in Islamic Mysticism*, 257–58.

74. al-Kashānī (or al-Qashānī) describes the parable as "a similarity that is found between the obscurity of the two—the obscuring of al-Sarūjī in each of his disguises, and the obscuring of the soul in the form of sense perception." Published as al-Qashānī, *Kashf al-wujūh*, 237–38. Two more commentaries can be found in the margins of an early twentieth-century Azharī edition of Ibn al-Fāriḍ. Ibn al-Fāriḍ, *Al-Juzʾ al-awwal*, 1:202–3.

75. al-Farghānī, *Muntahā al-madārik*, 2:224. Al-Kashānī, by contrast, glosses this unserious soul as the carnal soul that enjoins evil (*al-nafs al-ammāra*), a reference to Quran 12.53,

76. Pagani, "Reality and Image," 520. Ibn al-Fāriḍ was not directly influenced by Ibn al-ʿArabī, but he and his poetry were certainly claimed by the school. Post, "Taymiyyan," 309.

77. The names of these chapters are slightly different. Ibn Qutayba calls them *maqāmāt al-zuhhād bayna yaday al-khulafā' wa-l-mulūk*. In Ibn ʿAbd Rabbih, they are the *maqāmāt al-ʿubbād bayna yaday al-khulafā'*. Ibn Qutayba, *ʿUyūn al-Akhbār*, 2:333–43; Ibn ʿAbd Rabbih, *al-ʿIqd al-Farīd*, 3:93–100.

78. Hämeen-Anttila argues that "one should not overdo the connection between the two genres" and that outside of the terminological similarity, "there is little that makes the pious *maqāmāt* more cognate to Hamadhānian *maqāmas* than many other prose anecdotes." Hämeen-Anttila, *Maqama*, 74. ʿAbd al-Mālik Murtāḍ emphasizes that the *maqāms* are distinct because these are derived from "recitation and transmission (*muʿawwaluhum fīhā al-riwāya wa-l-naql*)." In other words, unlike the *maqāmas*, the *maqāms* are "historical stories about that which happened to historical personages (*ḥikāyāt tārīkhiyya waqaʿat li-ashkhāṣ tārīkhiyyīn*)." ʿAbd al-Mālik Murtāḍ, *Fann al-maqāmāt*, 213–14.

79. Ibn Qutayba, *ʿUyūn al-akhbār*, 2:333.

80. al-Hamadhānī, *Maqāmāt* (Beirut), 130.

81. al-Hamadhānī, *Maqāmāt* (Beirut), 132.

82. Ibn Qutayba, *ʿUyūn al-akhbār*, 2:334. There is also an example in the *maqāmāt al-zuhhād* of a sermon within a sermon (2:342).

83. Reading *ghayyartuhā* for ʿAbduh's *ghayyartahā*. Al-Hamadhānī (Beirut), 136; al-Hamadhānī, *Maqāmāt* (Istanbul), 48.

84. al-Hamadhānī, *Maqāmāt* (Beirut), 136.

85. *HMC*, 99.

86. *HMC*, 101.

87. *HMC*, 102. The term I have translated here as "sovereignty" is *dawla*, which itself is implicated in the lexical field of precarious uncertainty. It is a word that can also refer to changing forms. For example, *dālat lahu al-dawla* or *dālat ʿalayhi al-dawla* refers to fortune turning toward or away from someone.

88. The ambiguity of Abū Zayd's repentance is primed by the preceding forty-nine *maqāmas*, in which the reader has been trained not to take things at face value. Kennedy, *Recognition*, 303–6. By contrast, Katia Zakharia argues that the manner and frequency of Quranic citations in the *Ḥarīriyya* are part of an underlying, inexorable logic that leads to Abū Zayd's eventual repentance in *maqāma* # 50, a scene that she compares to al-Ḥallāj's (d. 309/922) apotheosis in martyrdom. Zakharia, "Les références coraniques," 286.

89. *HMC*, 102.

90. Ibn Qutayba, *ʿUyūn al-Akhbār*, 2:337.

91. *HMC*, 102.

92. The practice of rulers accepting petitions directly from their subjects is associated with the *maẓālim* sessions held by caliphs and other rulers to address injustices (*maẓālim*). Although it is claimed that this emerged in the Umayyad period, it seems likely to be formalized as a regular practice of rule in the Abbasid period. Nielsen, "Maẓālim." Rulers could also delegate the authority to third parties, who might or might not themselves be judges. Tillier, "*Qāḍīs*."

93. Ibn Qutayba, *ʿUyūn al-akhbār*, 2:337.

94. This reluctance to serve as a judge is something of a topos. For some Ḥanbalī examples, see M. Cook, *Commanding Right*, 123, 148. More generally, this trope has been discussed as part of a discourse on "the refused dignity" going back to Moses in the Book of Exodus. A. J. Wensinck observes that certain pious Muslims felt that the role of judge is part of the questionable sultanic authority. Wensinck, "Refused Dignity," 497–99.

95. M. Cook, *Commanding Right*, 3–7. Ibn Saʿd, *Kitāb al-Ṭabaqāt*, 9:374.

96. *HMC*, 102. The phrase *idhā tawallā* in Quran 2.205 is usually translated as "when he turns back" or something to that effect, but Abū Zayd is clearly using the term *tawallā* in the sense of "taking power," an interpretation that is attested in the exegetical tradition. Al-Rāzī, *Tafsīr*, 5:216–17.

97. S. Ahmed, *What Is Islam?*, 120, 345.

CHAPTER 7

1. For *majālis* generally, see Mauder, *Sultan's Salon*; Pfeifer, *Empire of Salon*; and Ali, *Arabic*.

2. Ibn Abī ʿUṣaybiʿa, *Literary History of Medicine*, §15.40.3.

3. Elias Muhanna suggests that the commentary-anthology emerged with the *Sarḥ al-ʿUyūn fī Sharḥ Risālat Ibn Zaydūn* of Ibn Nubāta (d. 768/1366). Muhanna, *World in a Book*, 51. Rowson identifies the seventh/thirteenth century and the earlier commentaries of al-Sharīshī and Ibn Abī al-Ḥadīd (d. 655–56/1257–58) as the beginning of digressive commentary on prose texts. Rowson, "Alexandrian Age," 109. On Mamlūk anthologies generally, see Bauer, "Literarische Anthologien."

4. Rowson, "Alexandrian Age," 109–10.

5. On the *ṭufaylī*, see Selove, Ḥikāyat Abī al-Qāsim; Selove and Turner, "Heretics and Party-crashers."

6. Mauder provides a typology of *majālis*. Mauder, *Sultan's Salon*, 63–72.

7. Samer Ali suggests that, in the context of a hierarchical society, "the *mujālasāt* offered a kind of intimacy and equality." Ali, *Arabic*, 47.

8. ʿAbd al-Ḥamīd notes the importance of mastering these fields for bureaucrats in his epistle to the bureaucrats. ʿAbd al-Ḥamīd, *ʿAbd al-Ḥamīd*, 283. As Helen Pfeifer puts it, the effortless conversation of the *majlis* "required years of education and practice" to acquire the proper *adab*, both in the sense of knowledge and behavior. Pfeifer, *Empire of Salon*, 134–35. On the ideal of encyclopedic education, see Muhanna, *World in a Book*, 92–93.

9. Heinrichs, review of *ʿAbbasid Belles-Lettres*, 130.

10. al-Tawḥīdī, *Kitāb al-Imtāʿ*, 1:104–43; Margoliouth, "Discussion"; Adamson and Key, "Philosophy of Language."

11. al-Tawḥīdī, *Kitāb al-Imtāʿ*, 1:70–96; van Gelder, *Anthology*, 195–207.

12. al-Tawḥīdī, *Kitāb al-Imtāʿ*, 2:130.

13. al-Maydanī, *Majmaʿ al-amthāl*, 1:206. The vizier refers to this proverb. Al-Tawḥīdī, *Kitāb al-Imtāʿ*, 1:28.

14. al-Tawḥīdī, *Kitāb al-Imtāʿ*, 2:104.

15. Ibid., 2:113.

16. Ibid., 2:115. Al-Tawḥīdī expresses his amazement that discussing these noble matters was possible in these constraining times, suggesting that there is some difficult relationship between discourse and writing: "*wa-l-ʿajab annahu yajrī ḥarf min hādhihi al-umūr al-sharīfa fī hādhihi al-awqāt al-ḍayyiqa*."

17. Ibid.

18. Ibn ʿAbd al-Barr, *Bahjat al-majālis*, 1:35–36.

19. Ibid., 1:36.

20. Luke Yarbrough, "Christian Shīʿī," 289.

21. Ibn ʿAbd al-Barr, *Bahjat al-majālis*, 1:568–73.

22. al-Ḥuṣrī, *Zahr al-ādāb*, 1:22. The words translated here as "elegantly chosen and its linkages well-formed (*muḥarrar al-naqd wa-muqaddar al-sard*)" are full of layered meaning. Just below the surface of this phrase is a metaphor that contrasts silken and chain-mail garments. Although *sard* in modern Arabic refers to narrative, it is here paired with *muqaddar*, which makes the phrase *muqaddar al-sard* an allusion to the Quranic command to the prophet David to "make long coats of mail and measure out its links (*wa-qaddir fī al-sard*)." Although *muḥarrar* here refers to something elegantly written or, because it is paired *naqd*, elegantly chosen, at the same time, it is redolent also of the term for silk (*ḥarīr*).

23. Miller, "Commentary and Text Organization," 56–57; Tuttle, "Expansion"; al-Ṣafadī, *Kitāb al-Ghayth al-musajjam*, 1:4.

24. al-Jarīrī, *Al-Jalīs al-ṣāliḥ*, 1:161–63. Similar phrases and logics can be found in al-Tanūkhī's (d. 384/994) *Nishwār al-muḥāḍara*. In his introduction, al-Tanūkhī explicitly rejects organizing his work into "separate chapters (*abwāban mubawwaba*)" or into "orders arrayed according to type (*anwāʿan murattaba*)." To do so, he suggests would make readers find the work "cold and tiresome," leading them to abandon it, since "mixing them together is more pleasing to the ear . . . and lighter to the heart and the mind." Al-Tanūkhī, *Nishwār al-muḥāḍara*, 1:12–13. As Samer Ali notes, the *majālis* "were a literary pretext that framed the majority of literary anthologies." Ali, *Arabic*, 18. On different strategies of mixing or segregating jest and earnest, see van Gelder, "Mixtures," 85–86.

25. al-Rāzī, *Tafsīr*, 7:2.

26. al-Ḥuṣrī, *Zahr al-ādāb*, 1:27.

27. Ibid.

28. al-Sharīshī, *Sharḥ* (Ibrāhīm), 1:6–7.

29. Ibid., 1:9.

30. Ibid., 1:70–71.

31. *HMC*, 46.

32. al-Panjdīhī, *Maghānī*, Suleymaniye MS Murad Molla, 193v. This hadith is not widely attested. Al-Suyūṭī, *al-Ziyādāt*, 785 (#1,000); al-ʿAsqalānī, *al-Talkhīṣ al-ḥabīr*, 3:308 (#1587).

33. al-Thaʿlabī, *Kitāb Qiṣaṣ al-anbiyāʾ*, 157–61.

34. al-Panjdīhī, *Maghānī*, Suleymaniye MS Murad Molla, 193v. This hadith about beautiful faces is included in al-Suyūṭī's *ikhtiṣār* of Ibn al-Jawzī's work on weak hadith. Al-Suyūṭī, *Kitāb al-Laʾālī*, 1:104.

35. al-Sharīshī, *Sharḥ* (Ibrāhīm), 1:376–83. It comes to just over three pages in the more compact Būlāq edition, which has fewer paragraph breaks than the more recent edition. Al-Sharīshī, *Sharḥ* (Būlāq), 1:146–49.

36. al-Sharīshī, *Sharḥ* (Ibrāhīm), 1:376.

37. Ibid., 378.

38. This may be the *Kitāb al-Wishāḥ* of Ibn Durayd (d. 321/934), which is preserved in an Escorial manuscript. See Kraemer, "Legajo-Studien," 267–73. Although selections from Ibn Durayd's book quoted by al-Suyūṭī are restricted to names of poets and the like, the material in the Escorial manuscript is much more varied. Al-Suyūṭī, *al-Muzhir*, 2:270–75; *GALS*, 1:174. On the other hand, this *Kitāb al-Wishāḥ* may also be an entirely different book by the same name.

39. The secondary literature on love and love poetry in Arabic is too extensive to be documented here. Among these are Chittick, "Love in Islamic Thought"; Giffen, *Theory of Profane Love Among the Arabs*; Algazi and Drory, "L'amour"; and Bell, *Love Theory in Later*

Hanbalite Islam. One may also find extensive discussion of both Persian and Arabic in Ingenito, *Beholding Beauty*.

40. *HMC*, 16–17.

41. al-Ṣafadī, *Nuṣrat al-thāʾir*, 61. Reading "*an taṣif al-shayʾ bi-l-madḥ thumma tadhummahu aw-bi-dhamm thumma tamdaḥahu*." The parallelism seems to demand the interpolation of "*bi-l-madḥ*," which is not present in the text of the edition.

42. al-Sharīshī, *Sharḥ* (Ibrāhīm), 1:154.

43. van Gelder, "Ibn Rashīq."

44. al-Sharīshī, *Sharḥ* (Ibrāhīm), 1:154. We find a similar sentiment quoted in Ibn Qutayba's *ʿUyūn al-akhbār*, in which his source states that "we the Arabs place some [speech] ahead and some behind. We add and omit, but we do not thereby intend to lie." Ibn Qutayba, *ʿUyūn al-akhbār*, 2:136. Quoted in the epigraph to chapter 2 in Borrut, *Entre mémoire et pouvoir*, 61.

45. al-Sharīshī, *Sharḥ* (Ibrāhīm), 1:154.

46. *HMC*, 19.

47. Ibid., 20.

48. al-Sharīshī, *Sharḥ* (Ibrāhīm), 1:170–72.

49. The minor differences between the two commentaries are interesting. Al-Panjdīhī includes a story about al-Buḥturī's love of a youth about whom he wrote his first poem, which al-Sharīshī omits, perhaps because al-Sharīshī deals extensively with poetry about youths elsewhere. In one instance, the two include different versions of the same story about al-Buḥturī and Abū al-ʿAnbas al-Ṣaymarī (d. 275/888), both of which are attributed to or drawn from Abū al-Faraj al-Iṣfahānī. Al-Panjdīhī's story is drawn from an *isnād* that includes al-Iṣfahānī, the author of *Kitāb al-Aghānī*. Al-Sharīshī replaces that story with a longer version attributed to al-Mubarrad, which can also be found in *Kitāb al-Aghānī*. Al-Iṣfahānī, *Kitāb al-Aghānī*, 21:40–41; al-Sharīshī, *Sharḥ* (Ibrāhīm), 1:92–94; al-Panjdīhī, *Maghānī*, Suleymaniye MS Murad Molla 1549, 67r–68r. Al-Sharīshī also adds al-Buḥturī's "testament (*waṣiyya*)," which can be found in both al-Ḥuṣrī's *Zahr al-ādāb* and Ibn Rashīq's *Al-ʿUmda*.

50. On the long-standing debate between the Rose and the Narcissus, see Heinrichs, "Rose Versus Narcissus."

51. *HMC*, 13.

52. al-Sharīshī, *Sharḥ* (Ibrāhīm), 1:103–10.

53. Ibid., 1:104. This is far from the only instance of cross-referencing in al-Sharīshī's commentary. In later volumes, he will pass over a topic pointing to earlier material, but he also points forward. See 1:107, 135.

54. Ibid., 1:124.

55. Ibid., 1:312.

56. Toral, "*ʿIqd al-Farīd*."

57. Yāqūt, *Muʿjam al-udabāʾ*, 464.

58. al-Sharīshī, *Sharḥ* (Ibrāhīm), 1:183.

59. Jacobi, "'Khayāl' Motif."

60. Although the Bulaq edition attributes this to al-Raḍī, the edition of Ibrāhīm corrects the text in the first instance (but not in the second) to say that it was al-Murtaḍā, having identified the poem in question in the Dīwān of al-Murtaḍā. Al-Sharīshī, *Sharḥ* (Būlāq), 1:257, and *Sharḥ* (Ibrāhīm), 2:230–31.

61. al-Ṣafadī, Kitāb al-Ghayth al-musajjam.

62. Tuttle, "Play and Display," 373, 377; Rashād, *Al-Ṣafadī wa-sharḥuhu*, 185–86; Talib, "Al-Ṣafadī, His Critics," 116–18.

63. Tuttle, "Play and Display"; al-Ṣafadī, *Ikhtirāʿ al-khurāʿ*.

64. *HMC*, 78.

65. Ibn al-Abbār, *Kitāb al-takmila*, 145.

66. *HMC*, 111.

67. al-Sharīshī, *Sharḥ* (Ibrāhīm), 1:124. Ibn Labbāl (or Lubbāl) is also said to be a commentator on the *Ḥarīriyya*, but he does not appear in al-Sharīshī's *isnād*s for the text, which is somewhat surprising because Ibn Labbāl is also from Sharīsh and most likely taught our commentator. Ibn Labbāl's commentary does not, however, appear to be extant. Benchrifa, *Ibn Lubbāl*, 56.

68. al-Sharīshī, *Sharḥ* (Ibrāhīm), 2:160. Chenery notes al-Sharīshī's critique of this *maqāma* in his introduction to his translation of it. Al-Ḥarīrī, *Assemblies* (Chenery), 1:186.

69. al-Sharīshī, *Sharḥ* (Ibrāhīm), 1:34. The way that al-Ḥarīrī introduces al-Hamadhānī's *maqāma*s in the *Ḥarīriyya*'s introduction is also noteworthy. He states that they were mentioned "in one of the gatherings of *adab* (*bi-baʿḍ andiyat al-adab*)." The term *nādī* (pl. *andiya*) is commonly deployed as a synonym for *majlis*. *HMC*, 4.

70. al-Sharīshī, *Sharḥ* (Ibrāhīm), 2:278–79.

71. al-Ḥarīrī, *Assemblies* (Chenery), 1:207. The question of imitation and originality is central to the analyses of Hämeen-Anttila, for example, where he notes that Ibn Mārī's *maqāma*s are "close imitations of al-Ḥarīrī, but unfortunately they seem to lack both the narrative joie de vivre of al-Hamadhānī and the linguistic mastery of al-Ḥarīrī." By contrast, Ibn Abī al-Khiṣāl, to whom we will return below, is described as one of "the most original of the Andalusian maqama writers." This question of originality and imitation is part of Hämeen-Anttila's broader concern with the presence or lack of "novelistic" features in the *maqāma*. Hämeen-Anttila, *Maqama*, 190, 245, 251. This tendency is a symptom of what might be called "novelism," which Clifford Siskin describes as the "habitual subordination of writing to the novel." Siskin, "Epilogue," 423.

72. al-Hamadhānī, *Maqāmāt* (Istanbul), 34–40.

73. Malti-Douglas, "*Maqāmāt* and *Adab*," 254.

74. For delaying the fulfillment of a promise in al-Hamadhānī, see, for example, *Al-maqāma al-Mawṣiliyya*, in which Abū al-Fatḥ promises to revive a dead man and manages to defer the fulfillment of that promise for some time until the townsfolk become angry. Al-Hamadhānī, *Maqāmāt* (Istanbul), 34–36.

75. *HMC*, 85. The term *nammām* is glossed in the lexicon *Lisān al-ʿArab* as "the one who does not hold fast and preserve stories," and it is linked to a term for a leaky waterskin (*julūd namma*), which suggests that it is doubly apt to call the vase a "spiller of secrets."

76. *Maqāma* #18 also contains several allusions to the Quran and particularly to the rewards of the people of paradise as compared to the punishment of those in hellfire, both in the present and in the Prophetic past, such as Thamūd and ʿĀd. See Cooperson's edition; *HMC*, 88.

77. Kennedy, *Recognition*, 303–6.

78. See the translation and study by James T. Monroe: Al-Saraqusṭī, *al-Maqāmāt al-Luzūmīyah*. Al-Saraqusṭī. The *isnād*s in these *maqāma*s include another fictional transmitter, who intervenes between the narrator and the author.

79. al-Ḥanafī, "*Maqāmāt*"; Stewart, "Maqāmāt of Aḥmad b. Abī Bakr."

80. Ibn al-Ṣayqal, *Al-Maqāmāt al-Zayniyya*; Zakharia, "Ibn al-Ṣayqal."

81. Pomerantz, "Play of Genre."

82. The lisp extends to the verb used to indicate that al-Hāris is narrating the story. It reads *ḥaddasa* for *ḥaddatha*, which Humphrey Davies renders as "Faid al-Hāwif ibn Hifām." Al-Shidyāq, *Leg over Leg*, ¶1.13.2.

83. Pomerantz, "*Maqāma* Collection," 638.

84. Geert Jan van Gelder reminds us that parody does not necessarily entail mockery. Van Gelder, "Forbidden Firebrands," 4.

85. The collection only survives in limited excerpts in an anthology of *adab*. ʿImād al-Dīn al-Iṣfahānī, *Kharīdat al-qaṣr*, 3.1:130. The editor of this volume observes in a footnote that the critique of al-Ḥarīrī is incorrect and overly critical.

86. Ibn al-ʿAṭṭār, *al-Maqāmāt al-Qurashiyya*, Suleymaniye MS Ayasofya 4297, 3v.

87. Ibid., 13v–16r.

88. Blankinship, "Al-Maʿarrī's Esteem," 263–64n67. Blankinship cites Franz Rosenthal's translation of Ibn Khaldūn here, which explains the term to mean that the "two vizierates" were those of the pen and the sword.

89. Hämeen-Anttila, *Maqama*, 247–53.

90. Ibn Abī al-Khiṣāl, *Rasāʾil*, 424.

91. Ibid., 426.

92. Abū Zayd is asked of his lineage in *maqāmas* #6, #22, and #25. He is often asked to explain himself or to explain his riddling and allusive speech (in *maqāmas* #8, 23, and 25, among others).

93. Ibn Abī al-Khiṣāl, *Rasāʾil*, 426.

94. Ibid., 422–23.

95. Ibn al-Abbār, *Kitāb al-takmila*, 136–37.

CONCLUSION

Epigraphs: Foucault, *Archaeology of Knowledge*, 10; Benjamin, "Task of the Translator," 15.

1. Foucault, *Archaeology of Knowledge*, 8.

2. For the term "Arabic Cosmopolis," which draws from the work of Sheldon Pollock on Sanskrit, see Ronit Ricci, Islam Translated, 4. For a review of the "cosmopolis scholarship" concerning Arabic, Persian, and Sanskrit, as well as a critical review its problems, see Field, "Poetry for Linguistic Description," 1955. The Ḥarīriyya's impact on the literatures of Persian, Hebrew, Syriac, and other languages is well beyond the scope of this book, but I provisionally opt for this untested terminology of the cosmopolis to emphasize that the world of readers cannot be limited to the Arab or Islamic worlds. For some examples, see Alagunfon, Classical Arabic. Behmardi, "Madira of Baghdad." Katsumata, "Style of the Maqāma." Mahmoud, "Multilingual Poetics."

3. Benjamin, "Task of the Translator," 15.

4. Cooperson, "Note on the Translation," xli.

5. Ibid., xxx. Cooperson also notes the existence of other interlinear translations.

6. al-Ḥarīrī, *Maqāmāt*, British Library MS Or7976, 2r–3v.

7. The seventeenth century, for example, has been identified as one in which there was a rise of "pamphlets" in the pre-print Ottoman world. Shafir, *Order and Disorder*, 19–23. The same century is also identified as one in which a more impersonal form of "deep reading" emerged. El-Rouayheb, *Islamic Intellectual History*, 97–128. On the problem of

"other revolutions" that trouble the modernity/premodernity binary, see Shafir, "Moral Revolutions," 622.

8. The translation was completed in Aleppo between AD 1213 and 1216 (AH 609–13). Lavi, "Rationale," 280. ʿAbd al-Laṭīf al-Baghdādī's first certificate of transmission of the *Ḥarīriyya* was in Aleppo on the twenty-fifth of Dhū al-Qaʿda 613 (March 5, 1217), and al-Ḥarīzī lived in Aleppo until his death in 622/1225.

9. Lavi, "Rationale," 281.

10. Schippers, "Hebrew *maqama*," 305.

11. al-Ḥarīzī, *"Taḥkemoni,"* 35.

12. Mallette, *Lives*, 183.

13. Mufti, *Forget English!*, 241–42.

Bibliography

Abbasi, Rushain. "Did Premodern Muslims Distinguish the Religious and Secular? The Dīn–Dunyā Binary in Medieval Islamic Thought." *Journal of Islamic Studies* 31, no. 2 (2020): 185–225.

———. "Islam and the Invention of Religion: A Study of Medieval Muslim Discourses on *Dīn*." *Studia Islamica* 116 (2021): 1–106.

ʿAbd al-Ḥamīd al-Kātib. *ʿAbd al-Ḥamīd al-kātib wa-mā tabaqqā min rasāʾilihi wa-rasāʾil Sālim Abī al-ʿAlāʾ*. Edited by Iḥsān ʿAbbās. ʿAmmān: Dār al-Shurūq, 1988.

ʿAbd al-Jabbār. *Tathbīt dalāʾil al-nubūwa*. Edited by ʿAbd al-Karīm ʿUthmān. Beirut: Dār al-ʿArabiyya, 1966.

ʿAbd al-Mutaʿāl al-Ṣaʿīdī. *Tārīkh al-iṣlāḥ fī al-Azhar wa-ṣafaḥāt min al-jihād fī al-iṣlāḥ*. Cairo: Maṭbaʿat al-Iʿtimād, 1943.

ʿAbd al-Qādir al-Qurashī. *Al-Jawāhir al-maḍiyya fī ṭabaqāt al-ḥanafiyya*. Edited by ʿAbd al-Fattāḥ Muḥammad al-Ḥalw. Cairo: Hajar, 1993.

ʿAbduh, Muḥammad. *Al-Aʿmāl al-Kāmila li-l-imām al-shaykh Muḥammad ʿAbduh*. Edited by Muḥammad ʿAmāra. Beirut: Dār al-Shurūq, 1993.

———. "*Khuṭbat al-Mufassir.*" In *Nahj al-Balāgha*, edited by Muḥammad ʿAbduh, 1: Beirut: al-Maṭbaʿa al-Adabiyya, 1885.

Abu Deeb, Kemal. *Al-Jurjānī's Theory of Poetic Imagery*. Warminster: Aris and Phillips, 1979.

Adamson, Peter Scott, and Alexander Key. "Philosophy of Language in the Medieval Arabic Tradition." In *Linguistic Content: New Essays in the History of the Philosophy of Language*, edited by Margaret Cameron and Robert Stainton, 74–99. Oxford: Oxford University Press, 2015.

Adang, Camilla. "Ibn Hazm on Homosexuality: A Case-Study of Zahiri Legal Methodology." *Al-Qantara* 24 (2003): 5–31.

Adang, Camilla, Maribel Fierro, and Sabine Schmidtke, eds. *Ibn Ḥazm of Cordoba: The Life and Works of a Controversial Thinker*. Leiden: Brill, 2012.

Ahmed, Asad Q. *Palimpsests of Themselves: Logic and Commentary in Postclassical Muslim South Asia*. Oakland: University of California Press, 2022.

Ahmed, Shahab. *What Is Islam? The Importance of Being Islamic*. Princeton, NJ: Princeton University Press, 2016.

al-Akhfash al-Aṣghar. *Kitāb al-Ikhtiyārayn*. Edited by Fakhr al-Dīn Qabāwa. Beirut: Muʾassasat al-Risāla, 1984.

Alagunfon, Sulaiman Adewale. *The Classical Arabic Maqāma in Yorubaland, Nigeria*. Leiden: Brill, 2025.

Alfaisal, Haifa S. "Liberty and the Literary: Coloniality and Nahdawist Comparative Criticism of Rūḥī Al-Khālidī's *History of the Science of Literature with the Franks, the Arabs, and Victor Hugo* (1904)." *Modern Language Quarterly* 77 (2016): 523–46.

———. "The Politics of Literary Value in Early Modernist Arabic Comparative Literary Criticism." *Journal of Arabic Literature* 50 (2019): 251–77.

Algazi, Gadi, and Rina Drory. "L'amour à la Cour des Abbasides: Un code de competénce social." *Annales* 55 (2000): 1255–82.

Ali, Samer M. *Arabic Literary Salons in the Islamic Middle Ages: Poetry, Public Performance, and the Presentation of the Past.* Notre Dame, IN: University of Notre Dame Pess, 2010.

Aljoumani, Said. "Ṣuwar al-ijāzāt al-manqūla fī al-makhṭūṭāt al-ʿArabiyya: Al-sabab wa-l-waẓīfa." *Journal of Islamic Manuscripts* 9 (2018): 72–100.

Aljoumani, Said, and Benedikt Reier. "The Documentary Depth of Hadith Transmission: Audition Attendance Lists." *Al-ʿUsur al-Wusta* 32 (2024): 142–64.

Allan, Michael. "How *Adab* Became Literary: Formalism, Orientalism, and the Institutions of World Literature." *Journal of Arabic Literature* 43 (2012): 172–96.

———. *In the Shadow of World Literature: Sites of Reading in Colonial Egypt.* Princeton, NJ: Princeton University Press, 2016.

al-Anbārī, Abu al-Khayr Salāma b. ʿAbd al-Bāqī. *Sharḥ Maqāmāt al-Ḥarīrī.* Suleymaniye MS Laleli, 1847.

Anonymous. Staatsbiliothek Berlin MS, Sprenger 1243.

Anderson, Benedict. *Imagined Communities: Reflections on the Origin and Spread of Nationalism.* Rev. ed. New York: Verso, 2006.

Antoon, Sinan. *The Poetics of the Obscene in Premodern Arabic Poetry: Ibn al-Ḥajjāj and* Sukhf. Basingstoke: Palgrave Macmillan, 2014.

Apter, Emily S. *Against World Literature: On the Politics of Untranslatability.* New York: Verso, 2013.

Arslan, C. Ceyhun. "Entanglements Between the Tanzimat and al-Nahḍah: Jurjī Zaydān Between Tārīkh ādāb al-lughah al-turkiyyah and Tārīkh ādāb al-lughah al-ʿarabiyyah." *Journal of Arabic Literature* 50 (2019): 298–324.

———. *The Ottoman Canon and the Construction of Arabic and Turkish Literatures.* Edinburgh: Edinburgh University Press, 2024.

Asad, Talal. *Formations of the Secular: Christianity, Islam, Modernity.* Stanford, CA: Stanford University Press, 2003.

———. "The Idea of an Anthropology of Islam." *Qui parle* 17 (2009): 1–30.

al-ʿAskarī, Abū Hilāl. *Jamharat al-amthāl.* Edited by Muḥammad Abū al-Faḍl Ibrāhīm and ʿAbd al-Majīd Qaṭāmish. Beirut: Dār al-Jīl, 1988.

———. *Kitāb al-Ṣināʿatayn al-kitāba wa-l-shiʿr.* Edited by ʿAlī Muḥammad al-Bajāwī. Cairo: ʿĪsā al-Bābī al-Ḥalabī, 1971.

———. *Al-Gharāʾib al-multaqaṭa min musnad al-firdaws al-musammā zahr al-firdaws.* Edited by al-ʿArbī al-Dāʾiz al-Firyāṭī. Dubai: Jamʿiyyat Dār al-Birr, 2018.

———. *Al-Talkhīṣ al-ḥabīr fī takhrīj aḥādīth al-Rāfiʿī al-kabīr.* Edited by Abū ʿĀṣim Ḥasan b. ʿAbbās. Cairo: Muʾassasat Qurṭuba, 1995.

al-ʿAsqalānī, Ibn Ḥajar. *Al-Fatḥ al-bārī bi-sharḥ Ṣaḥīḥ al-Bukhārī.* Edited by ʿAbd al-Qādir Shayba al-Ḥamad. Riyadh: Sulṭān b. ʿAbd al-ʿAzīz, 2001.

Auji, Hala. *Printing Arab Modernity: Book Culture and the American Press in Nineteenth-Century Beirut.* Leiden: Brill, 2016.

al-Baghdādī, ʿAbd al-Qādir b. ʿUmar. *Ḥāshiya ʿalā Sharḥ Bānat Suʿād li-bn Hishām li-Ibn Hishām.* Edited by Naẓīf Muḥarram Khawāja. Wiesbaden: Franz Steiner, 1980.

Bakhtin, Mikhail. *Rabelais and His World.* Translated by Hélène Iswolsky. Bloomington: Indiana University Press, 1984.

Bar-Itzhak, Chen. "Intellectual Captivity: Literary Theory, World Literature, and the Ethics of Interpretation." *Journal of World Literature* 5 (2020): 79–110.

Bauer, Thomas. "'Ayna hādhā min al-Mutanabbī!': Toward an Aesthetics of Mamluk Literature." *MSR* 17 (2013): 5–22.

———. *Die Kultur der Ambiguität*. Berlin: Verlag der Weltreligionen, 2011.

———. "In Search of 'Post-Classical Literature': A Review Essay." *MSR* 11 (2007): 137–67.

———. "Literarische Anthologien der Mamlukenzeit." In *Die Mamluken: Studien zu ihrer Geschichte und Kultur; Zum Gedenken an Ulrich Haarmann (1942–1999)*, edited by Stephan Conermann and Anja Pistor-Hatam, 71–122. Hamburg: EB-Verlag, 2003.

———. "Mamluk Literature: Misunderstandings and New Approaches." *MSR* 9 (2005): 105–32.

Beaumont, Daniel. "The Trickster and Rhetoric in the *Maqāmāt*." *Edebiyat* 5 (1994): 1–14.

Beecroft, Alexander. *An Ecology of World Literature: From Antiquity to the Present Day*. New York: Verso, 2015.

———. *Authorship and Cultural Identity in Early Greece and China: Patterns of Literary Circulation*. Cambridge: Cambridge University Press, 2010.

Beeston, A. F. L. Review of "Certificates of Transmission on a Manuscript of the *Maqāmāt* of Ḥarīrī (MS. Cairo, Adab 105)," by Pierre A. MacKay (*Transactions of the American Philosophical Society*, n.s., 61, no. 4 [1971]). *Journal of the Royal Asiatic Society* 105, no. 1 (1973): 56.

Behmardi, Vahid. "The Madira of Baghdad versus the Sikbaj of Nishapur: The Migration of a Maqama from Arabic to Persian." In *Poetry's Voice—Society's Norms: Forms of Interaction between Middle Eastern Writers and their Societies*, edited by Andreas Pflitsch and Barbara Winckler, 95–104. Wiesbaden: Reichert Verlag, 2006.

Bell, Joseph. *Love Theory in Later Hanbalite Islam*. Albany, NY: SUNY Press, 1979.

Benchrifa, Mohamed (Muḥammad b. Sharīfa). *Ibn Lubbāl al-Sharīshī*. Casablanca: Maṭbaʿat al-Najāḥ al-Jadīda, 1996.

Benjamin, Walter. "The Task of the Translator: An Introduction to the Translation of Baudelaire's *Tableaux Parisiens*." In *The Translation Studies Reader*, edited by Lawrence Venuti, 15–25. London: Routledge, 2000.

Bhattacharya, Baidik. *Colonialism, World Literature, and the Making of the Modern Culture of Letters*. Cambridge: Cambridge University Press, 2024.

Bhattacharya, Usree. "The Teaching of English in India." In *Oxford Research Encyclopedia of Education*.

Bin Tyeer, Sarah R. *The Qur'an and the Aesthetics of Premodern Arabic Prose*. London: Palgrave Macmillan, 2016.

Blankinship, Kevin. "Al-Maʿarrī's Anxious Menagerie: The Epistle of the Horse and the Mule." *Journal of Abbasid Studies* 8 (2021): 142–71.

———. "Al-Maʿarrī's Esteem in the Islamic West: A Preliminary Overview." *Al-Masāq* 31 (2019): 253–71.

Blankinship, Kevin, and Aglae Pizzone. "Self-Commentary as Defensive Strategy in the Works of John Tzetzes (d. 1180 C.E.) and Abū al-ʿAlāʾ al-Maʿarrī (d. 1057 C.E.)." *Philological Encounters* 8 (2022): 1–37.

Blecher, Joel. *Said the Prophet of God: Hadith Commentary Across a Millennium*. Oakland: University of California Press, 2018.

Bonadeo, Cecilia Martini. *ʿAbd al-Laṭīf al-Baġdādī's Philosophical Journey: From Aristotle's Metaphysics to the "Metaphysical Science."* Leiden: Brill, 2013.

Bonebakker, Seeger, A. "Nihil Obstat in Story Telling?" *Mededelingen der Koninklijke Nederlandse Akademie van Wetenschappen* 55 (1992): 289–307.

———. *Some Early Definitions of the Tawriya and Ṣafadī's Faḍḍ al-Xitām 'an at-Tawriya wa-'l-Istixdām*. The Hague: Mouton & Co, 1966.

———. "Some Medieval Views on Fantastic Stories." *Quaderni di Studi Arabi* 10 (1992): 21–43.

Booth, Wayne C. *A Rhetoric of Irony*. Chicago: University of Chicago Press, 1974.

Borrut, Antoine. *Entre mémoire et pouvoir: L'espace syrien sous les derniers Omeyyades et les premiers Abbassides (v. 72–193/692–809)*. Leiden: Brill, 2011.

Bosworth, Clifford Edmund. *The Mediaeval Islamic Underworld: The* Bānū Sāsān *in Arabic Society and Literature*. Leiden: Brill, 1976.

Bourdieu, Pierre. *Distinction: A Social Critique of the Judgement of Taste*. Cambridge, MA: Harvard University Press, 1984.

Brockelman, Carl. "al-Anbārī, Abū 'l-Barakāt." *EI2*.

———. *Geschichte der arabischen Litteratur: Supplementbänden*. (*GALS*) Leiden: Brill, 1937–42.

———. *Geschichte der arabischen Litteratur: Zweite den supplementbänden angepasste Auflage*. (*GAL*) Leiden: Brill, 1943–49.

Brown, Jonathan. *The Canonization of al-Bukhārī and Muslim: The Formation and Function of the Sunnī Ḥadīth Canon*. Leiden: Brill, 2007.

———. "Even If It's Not True It's True: Using Unreliable Hadīths in Sunni Islam." *Islamic Law and Society* 18 (2011): 1–52.

Bulliet, Richard, W. "The Age Structure of Medieval Islamic Education." In *Education and Learning in the Early Islamic World*, edited by Claude Gilliot, 39–52. London: Routledge, 2017.

Burak, Guy. "Evidentiary Truth Claims, Imperial Registers, and the Ottoman Archive: Contending Legal Views of Archival and Record-Keeping Practices in Ottoman Greater Syria (Seventeenth–Nineteenth Centuries)." *Bulletin of the School of Oriental and African Studies* 79 (2016): 233–54.

Burton, John. "Naskh." *EI2*.

Büssow, Johann. "Muḥammad 'Abduh: The Theology of Unity (Egypt, 1898)." In *Religious Dynamics Under the Impact of Imperialism and Colonialism: A Sourcebook*, edited by Björn Bentlage et al., 141–59. Leiden: Brill, 2017.

Carter, Michael G. *Sībawayhi*. London: I. B. Tauris, 2004.

Casanova, Pascale. *The World Republic of Letters*. Translated by M. B. Debevoise. Cambridge, MA: Harvard University Press, 2004.

Chakrabarty, Dipesh. "Postcoloniality and the Artifice of History: Who Speaks for 'Indian' Pasts?" *Representations* 37 (1992): 1–26.

Chamberlain, Michael. *Knowledge and Social Practice in Medieval Damascus, 1190–1350*. Cambridge: Cambridge University Press, 2002.

Chea, Pheng. *What Is a World? On Postcolonial Literature as World Literature*. Durham, NC: Duke University Press, 2016.

Cheikh-Moussa, Abdallah. "Avarice ou sophistique? Une lecture du *Livres des Avares* d'al-Ǧāḥiẓ (II)." *Bulletin d'Études Orientales* 51 (1999): 209–27.

Chenery, Thomas. Introduction to *The Assemblies of al Hariri: Translated from the Arabic with an Introduction and Notes Historical and Grammatical*. Vol. 1. London: Williams and Norgate, 1867.

Chiabotti, Francesco. "Yūsuf b. Ismāʿīl al-Nabahānī (m. 1932), adīb soufi au temps de la Réforme." In Adab *and Modernity: A "Civilizing Process"? (Sixteenth–Twenty-First Century)*, edited by Catherine Mayeur-Jaouen, 504–26. Leiden: Brill, 2019.

Chittick, William. "Love in Islamic Thought." *Religion Compass* 8, no. 7 (2014): 229–38.

Conrad, Lawrence I. "Seven and the *Tasbīʿ*: On the Implications of Numerical Symbolism for the Study of Medieval Islamic History." *Journal of the Economic and Social History of the Orient/Journal de L'histoire Economique et Sociale de l'Orient* 31 (1988): 42–73.

Cook, Deborah. "Foucault, Freud, and the Repressive Hypothesis." *Journal of the British Society for Phenomenology* 45 (2014): 148–61.

Cook, Michael. *Commanding Right and Forbidding Wrong in Islamic Thought*. Cambridge: Cambridge University Press, 2001.

Cooperson, Michael. "The Abbasid 'Golden Age': An Excavation." *Al-ʿUṣūr al-Wusṭā* 25 (2017): 41–65.

———. *Classical Arabic Biography: The Heirs of the Prophets in the Age of al-Ma'mun*. Cambridge: Cambridge University Press, 2000.

———. "Ibn Ḥanbal and Bishr al-Ḥāfī: A Case Study in Biographical Traditions." *Studia Islamica* 86 (1997): 71–101.

———. Introduction to *Impostures: Fifty Rogue's Tales Translated Fifty Ways*, by al-Ḥarīrī, New York: New York University Press, 2020.

———. "Note on the Translation." In *Impostures: Fifty Rogue's Tales Translated Fifty Ways*, by al-Ḥarīrī, xxxii–li. New York: New York University Press, 2020.

———. "Probability, Plausibility, and 'Spiritual Communication' in Classical Arabic Biography." In *On Fiction and* Adab *in Medieval Arabic Literature*, edited by Philip F. Kennedy, 69–84. Wiesbaden: Harrassowitz Verlag, 2005.

Damrosch, David. *What Is World Literature?* Princeton, NJ: Princeton University Press, 2003.

Davidson, Garrett A. *Carrying on the Tradition: A Social and Intellectual History of Hadith Transmission Across a Thousand Years*. Leiden: Brill, 2020.

Ḍayf, Shawqī. *Al-Maqāma*. Cairo: Dār al-Maʿārif, 1954.

Déroche, François. "Fakes and Islamic Manuscripts." In *Fakes and Forgeries of Written Artefacts from Ancient Mesopotamia to Modern China*, edited by Cécile Michel and Michael Friedrich, 89–100. Berlin: De Gruyter, 2020.

Deuchar, Hannah Scott. "Loan-Words: Economy, Equivalence, and Debt in the Arabic Translation Debates." *Comparative Literature Studies* 57 (2020): 187–209.

———. "'Nahda': Mapping a Keyword in Cultural Discourse." *Alif: Journal of Comparative Poetics* 37 (2017): 50–84.

———. Review of *Popular Fiction, Translation and the Nahda in Egypt*, by Samah Selim. *International Journal of Middle East Studies* 52 (2020): 567–69.

al-Dhahabī. *Siyar aʿlām al-nubalāʾ*. Edited by Shuʿayb Arnaʾūt et al. Beirut: Muʾassasat al-Risāla, 1996.

al-Dhahabī. *Tārīkh al-islām wa-wafayāt al-mashāhīr wa-l-aʿlām*. Edited by Bashshār ʿAwwād Maʿrūf. Beirut: Dār al-Gharb al-Islāmī, 2003.

Dozy, Reinhart. *Takmilat al-Maʿājim al-ʿArabiyya*. Translated by Muḥammad Salīm al-Nuʿaymī. Baghdad: Wazārat al-Thaqāfa wa-l-Iʿlām, 1980.

Dreher, Josef. "A Collection of Theological and Mystical Texts Describing the Prophet Muḥammad: The *Jawāhir al-biḥār* by Yūsuf b. Ismāʿīl al-Nabhānī." In *Sufism, Literary Production, and Printing in the Nineteenth Century*, edited by Rachida Chih, Catherine Mayeur-Jaouen, and Rüdiger Seeseman, 255–75. Leiden: Brill, 2015.

Drory, Rina. "*maqāma* (pl. *maqāmāt*)." In *Encyclopedia of Arabic Literature*, edited by Julie Scott Meisami and Paul Starkey. London: Routledge, 1998.

———. *Models and Contacts: Arabic Literature and Its Impact on Medieval Jewish Culture*. Leiden: Brill, 2000.

———. "Three Attempts to Legitimize Fiction in Classical Arabic Literature." *Jerusalem Studies in Arabic and Islam* 18 (1994): 146–64.

Elinson, Alexander. "Market Values, Holiday Mayhem and the Parody of Official Culture in Ibn al-Murābiʿ al-Azdī's 'Maqāma of the Feast.'" *La corónica: A Journal of Medieval Hispanic Languages, Literatures, and Cultures* 38 (2009): 139–61.

El-Leithy, Tamer. "Living Documents, Dying Archives: Towards a Historical Anthropology of Medieval Arabic Archives." *Al-Qantara* 32 (2011): 389–434.

El-Rouayheb, Khaled. *Before Homosexuality in the Arab-Islamic World, 1500–1800*. Chicago: University of Chicago Press, 2005.

———. *Islamic Intellectual History in the Seventeenth Century: Scholarly Currents in the Ottoman Empire and the Maghreb*. New York: Cambridge University Press, 2015.

Elshakry, Marwa. *Reading Darwin in Arabic, 1860–1950*. Chicago: University of Chicago Press, 2013.

El Shamsy, Ahmed. *Rediscovering the Islamic Classics: How Editors and Print Culture Transformed an Intellectual Tradition*. Princeton, NJ: Princeton University Press, 2022.

Enderwitz, Susanne. "Adab b) and Islamic Scholarship in the ʿAbbāsid Period." *EI3*.

al-Farghānī. *Muntahā al-madārik fī sharḥ tāʾiyyat Ibn al-Fāriḍ*. Beirut: Dār al-Kutub al-ʿIlmiyya, 2007.

Fieni, David. *Decadent Orientalisms: The Decay of Colonial Modernity*. New York: Fordham University Press, 2020.

Foucault, Michel. *The Archaeology of Knowledge*. Translated by A. M. Sheridan Smith. London: Routledge, 2002.

———. *The History of Sexuality: An Introduction*. Translated by Robert Hurley. Vol. 1. New York: Pantheon Books, 1978.

Freeman, Elizabeth. *Time Binds: Queer Temporalities, Queer Histories*. Durham, NC: Duke University Press, 2010.

Gacek, Adam. *Arabic Manuscripts: A Vademecum for Readers*. Leiden: Brill, 2009.

———. "The Copenhagen Manuscript of the Maqāmāt al-Ḥarīriyya, copied, illuminated, and glossed by the Mamluk litterateur Ṣalāḥ ad-Dīn aṣ-Ṣafadī." In *Writing and Writings: Investigations in Islamic Text and Script in Honour of Januarius Justus Witkam*, edited by Robert M. Kerr and Thomas Milo, 143–66. Cambridge: Archetype, 2010.

Gallagher, Catherine. "The Rise of Fictionality." In *History, Geography, and Culture*, vol. 1 of *The Novel*, edited by Franco Moretti, 336–63. Princeton, NJ: Princeton University Press, 2006.

Ganim, John M. "Medieval Literature as Monster: The Grotesque Before and After Bakhtin." *Exemplaria* 7 (1995): 27–40.

Garba, Tapji, and Sara-Maria Sorentino. "Slavery Is a Metaphor: A Critical Commentary on Eve Tuck and K. Wayne Yang's 'Decolonization Is Not a Metaphor.'" *Antipode* 52 (2020): 764–82.

George, Alain F. "The Illustrations of the *Maqāmāt* and the Shadow Play." *Muqarnas* 28 (2011): 1–42.

———. "Orality, Writing, and the Image in the *Maqāmāt*: Arabic Illustrated Books in Context." *Art History* 35 (2012): 10–37.

Gesink, Indira Falk. *Islamic Reform and Conservatism: Al-Azhar and the Evolution of Modern Sunni Islam*. London: I. B. Tauris, 2010.

Ghazal, Amal. "'Illiberal' Thought in the Liberal Age." In *Arabic Thought Beyond the Liberal Age: Towards an Intellectual History of the Nahda*, edited by Jens Hanssen and Max Weiss, 214–33. Cambridge: Cambridge University Press, 2016.

———. "Yūsuf al-Nabhānī: Poem of the Short 'R' in Defaming Innovation and Praising Esteemed Tradition (Lebanon, 1908/09)." In *Religious Dynamics Under the Impact of Imperialism and Colonialism: A Sourcebook*, edited by Björn Bentlage, Marion Eggert, and Hans Martin Krämer, 111–24. Leiden: Brill, 2017.

Giffen, Lois Anita. *Theory of Profane Love Among the Arabs: The Development of the Genre*. New York: New York University Press, 1971.

Goldziher, Ignaz. *Muslim Studies*. Edited by S. M. Stern. Translated by C. R. Barber and S. M. Stern. Vol. 2. Albany: State University of New York Press, 1966–71.

Grabar, Oleg. "Pictures or Commentaries: The Illustrations of the *Maqamat* of al-Hariri." In *Studies in Art and Literature of the Near East in Honor of Richard Ettinghausen*, edited by Peter J. Chelkowski, 85–104. New York: New York University Press, 1974.

Griffel, Frank. "Is There an Autograph of al-Ghazālī in MS Yale, Landberg 318?" In *Islam and Rationality: The Impact of al-Ghazālī, Papers Collected on His 900th Anniversary*, edited by Georges Tamer, 168–86. Leiden: Brill, 2015.

Grigoryan, Sona. *Neither Belief nor Unbelief: Intentional Ambivalence in al-Maʿarrī's "Luzūm."* Berlin: De Gruyter, 2023.

Gruendler, Beatrice. "ʿAbbāsid Praise Poetry in Light of Dramatic Discourse and Speech Act Theory." In *Understanding Near Eastern Literatures: A Spectrum of Interdisciplinary Approaches*, edited by Beatrice Gruendler and Verena Klemm, 157–69. Wiesbaden: Reichert, 2000.

———. "Early Arabic Philologists: Poetry's Friends or Foes?" In *World Philology*, edited by Sheldon Pollock, Benjamin A. Elman, and Ku-ming Kevin Chang, 92–113. Cambridge, MA: Harvard University Press, 2015.

———. *Medieval Arabic Praise Poetry: Ibn al-Rūmī and the Patron's Redemption*. London: Routledge, 2003.

———. "A Rat and Its Redactors: Silent Co-Authorship in *Kalīla wa-Dimna*." In *Les périples de Kalila et Dimna: Itinéraires de fables dans les arts et la littérature du monde islamique*, edited by Eloïse Brac de la Perrière, Aïda El Khiari, and Annie Vernay-Nouri, 3–42. Leiden: Brill, 2022.

Gully, Adrian. *The Culture of Letter-Writing in Pre-Modern Islamic Society*. Edinburgh: Edinburgh University Press, 2008.

Gündüz, Hacı Osman. "Ottoman-Era Arabic Literature: Overview of Select Secondary Scholarship." *Al-Abhath* 69 (2021): 107–22.

Haider, Najam. "Contesting Intoxication: Early Juristic Debates over the Lawfulness of Alcoholic Beverages." *Islamic Law and Society* 20 (2013): 48–89.

———. "On Lunatics and Loving Sons: A Textual Study of the Mamlūk Treatment of al-Ḥākim." *Journal of the Royal Asiatic Society* 18 (2008): 109–39.

———. *The Rebel and the Imām in Early Islam: Explorations in Muslim Historiography*. Cambridge: Cambridge University Press, 2019.

Haj, Samira. *Reconfiguring Islamic Tradition: Reform, Rationality, Modernity*. Stanford, CA: Stanford University Press, 2009.

Hallberg, Andreas. "Standard Language Ideology and Prescriptivism in the Arabic-speaking World." In *The Routledge Handbook of Linguistic Prescriptivism*, edited by Joan C. Beal, Morana Lukač, and Robin Straaijer, 287–303. London: Routledge, 2023.

al-Hamadhānī, Badīʿ al-Zamān. *Maqāmāt Abī al-Faḍl Badīʿ al-Zamān al-Hamadhānī*. Edited by Yūsuf al-Nabhānī. Istanbul: Maṭbaʿat al-Jawāʾib, 1881.

———. *Maqāmāt Badīʿ al-Zamān al-Hamadhānī*. Edited by Muḥammad ʿAbduh. Beirut: al-Maṭbaʿa al-Kāthūlīkiyya, 1889.

Hämeen-Anttila, Jaakko. "Marginalia Harīriana." *ZMDG* 11 (1997): 251–80.

———. *Maqama: A History of a Genre*. Wiesbaden: Harrassowitz, 2002.

———. "The *Maqāma* of the Lion." *Arabic and Middle Eastern Literature* 1 (1998): 141–52.

Hammond, Marlé. *Beyond Elegy: Classical Arabic Women's Poetry in Context*. Oxford: Oxford University Press, 2010.

al-Ḥanafī. "*Maqāmāt* al-Ḥanafī." In *Beiträge zur Maqamen-Litteratur*, edited by Oskar Rescher, 2–115. Istanbul: Maṭbaʿat Aḥmad Kāmil, 1914.

Harb, Lara. *Arabic Poetics: Aesthetic Experience in Classical Arabic Literature*. Cambridge: Cambridge University Press, 2020.

———. "Al-Jurjānī, ʿAbd al-Qāhir." *EI3*.

———. "Mimesis and Mythos in Aristotelian Arabic Poetics." *Comparative Literature* 76 (2024): 1–19.

al-Ḥarīrī. *The Assemblies of al Hariri*. Translated by Thomas Chenery. Vol. 1. London: Williams and Norgate, 1867.

———. *Durrat al-ghawwāṣ fī awhām al-khawāṣṣ wa-fī ākhirihi al-sharḥ li-Aḥmad Shihāb al-Dīn al-Khafājī*. Constantinople: Maṭbaʿat al-jawāʾib, 1882.

———. *Impostures: Fifty Rogue's Tales Translated Fifty Ways*. Translated by Michael Cooperson. New York: New York University Press, 2020.

———. *Kitāb al-Maqāmāt al-adabiyya*. Cairo: Dār al-Kutub al-ʿArabiyya al-Kubrā, 1912.

———. *Al-Maqāmāt*. *BNF* MS Arabe 7290.

———. *Al-Maqāmāt*. Danish Royal Library MS, Cod. Arab Add. 83.

———. *Maqāmāt*. British Library MS Or7976.

———. *Maqāmāt*. Princeton MS, Garrett 131Hq.

———. *Maqāmāt Abī Zayd al-Sarūjī*. Istanbul University MS, A4566.

al-Ḥarīzī, Judah. *The "Taḥkemoni" of Judah al-Ḥarizi: An English Translation*. Translated by Victor Emanuel Reichert. Jerusalem: R. H. Cohen's Press, 1965–73.

al-Ḥuṣrī, Abū Isḥāq Ibrāhīm b. ʿAlī. *Zahr al-ādāb wa-thamar al-albāb*. Edited by Ṣalāḥ al-Dīn al-Hawārī. Beirut: al-Maktaba al-ʿAṣriyya, 2001.

Heck, Paul. *The Construction of Knowledge in Islamic Civilization: Qudāma b. Jaʿfar and His "Kitāb al-kharāj wa-ṣināʿat al-kitāba."* Leiden: Brill, 2002.

Heinrichs, Wolfhart. Arabische Dichtung und griechische Poetik: Hazim Al-Qartağannis Grundlegung der Poetik mit Hilfe aristotelischer Begriffe. Beirut: Franz Steiner, 1969.

The Hand of the North Wind: Opinions on Metaphor and the Early Meaning of istiʿāra *in Arabic poetics*. Wiesbaden: Franz Steiner, 1977.

———. "Literary Theory: The Problem of Its Efficiency." In *Arabic Poetry: Theory and Development*, edited by G. E. von Grunebaum, 19–70. Wiesbaden: Otto Harrassowitz, 1973.

———. "Muwallad (2)." *EI2*.

———. Review of *ʿAbbasid Belles-Lettres*, vol. 2 of *The Cambridge History of Arabic Literature*, by J. Ashtiany, T. M. Johnstone, J. D. Latham, R. B. Serjeant, and G. R. Smith. *Al-ʿArabiyya* 26 (1993): 129–37.

———. "Rose Versus Narcissus: Observations on an Arabic Literary Debate." In *Dispute Poems and Dialogues in the Ancient and Mediaeval Near East: Forms and Types of Literary Debates in Semitic and Related Literatures*, edited by G. J. Reinink, and Herman L. J. Vanstiphout, 179–98. Leuven: Peeters, 1991.

Hermansen, Marcia K., and Bruce B. Lawrence. "Indo-Persian Tazkiras as Memorative Communications." In *Beyond Turk and Hindu: Rethinking Religious Identities in Islamicate South Asia*, edited by David Gilmartin and Bruce B. Lawrence, 149–75. Gainesville: University Press of Florida, 2000.

Hill, Peter. *Utopia and Civilization in the Arab Nahda*. Cambridge: Cambridge University Press, 2020.

Hirschfeld, Hartwig. Review of *The Maqāmāt of Badīʿ al-Zamān al-Hamadānī. Translated from the Arabic, with an introduction and notes, historical and grammatical, by W. J. Prendergast*. *Journal of the Royal Asiatic Society of Great Britain and Ireland* (April 1917): 409–11.

Hirschkind, Charles. *The Ethical Soundscape: Cassette Sermons and Islamic Counterpublics*. New York: Columbia University Press, 2006.

Hirschler, Konrad. "The Development of Arabic Multi-Text and Composite Manuscripts." In *The Emergence of Multi-Text Manuscripts*, edited by Alessandro Bausi, Michael Friedrich, and Marilena Maiaci, 275–303. Berlin: De Gruyter, 2019.

———. "From Archive to Archival Practices: Rethinking the Preservation of Mamluk Administrative Documents." *Journal of American Oriental Society* 136 (2016): 1–28.

———. *A Monument to Medieval Syrian Book Culture: The Library of Ibn ʿAbd al-Hādī*. Edinburgh: Edinburgh University Press, 2019.

———. *The Written Word in Medieval Arabic Lands: A Social and Cultural History of Reading Practices*. Edinburgh: Edinburgh University Press, 2012.

Holt, Elizabeth M. *Fictitious Capital: Silk, Cotton, and the Rise of the Arabic Novel*. New York: Fordham University Press, 2017.

Hourani, Albert. *Arabic Thought in the Liberal Age, 1798–1939*. Cambridge: Cambridge University Press, 1983.

Hudson, Leila. *Transforming Damascus: Space and Modernity in an Islamic City*. London: I. B. Tauris, 2008.

Hutcheon, Linda. *Irony's Edge: The Theory and Politics of Irony*. London: Routledge, 1994.

Ibn al-Abbār. *Kitāb al-takmila li-kitāb al-ṣila*. Algiers: al-Maṭbaʿa al-Sharqīya, 1919.

Ibn ʿAbd al-Barr. *Bahjat al-majālis wa-uns al-mujālis wa-shaḥdh al-dhāhin wa-l-hājis*. Edited by Muḥammad Mursī al-Khūlī. Beirut: Dār al-Kutub al-ʿIlmiyya, 1982.

Ibn ʿAbd Rabbih, *al-ʿIqd al-farīd*. Edited by Muḥammad Saʿīd al-ʿAryān. Cairo: Al-Maktaba al-Tijāriyya al-Kubrā, 1953.

Ibn Abī al-Khiṣāl. *Rasāʾil Ibn Abī al-Khiṣāl*. Edited by Muḥammad Riḍwān al-Dāya. Damascus: Dār al-Fikr, 1988.

Ibn Abī Uṣaybiʿa. *A Literary History of Medicine: The "Uyūn al-anbāʾ fī ṭabaqāt al-aṭibbā" of Ibn Abī Uṣaybiʿa*. Translated and edited by Emilie Savage-Smith, Simon Swain, and Geert Jan van Gelder. Leiden: Brill, 2020.

Ibn al-ʿAdīm. *Bughyat al-ṭalab fī taʾrīkh Ḥalab*. Edited by Suhayl Zakār. Beirut: Dār al-Fikr, 1985.

Ibn al-Anbārī. *Al-Inṣāf fī masāʾil al-khilāf bayn al-naḥwiyyīn al-Baṣriyyīn wa-l-Kūfiyyīn*. Edited by Gotthold Weil. Leiden: Brill, 1913.

———. Ibn al-Anbārī. *Nuzhat al-alibbāʾ fī ṭabaqāt al-udabāʾ*. Cairo: s.n., 1877.

———. *Nuzhat al-alibbāʾ fī ṭabaqāt al-udabāʾ*. Edited by Ibrāhīm al-Sāmirāʾī. Baghdad: Maṭbaʿat al-Maʿārif, 1959.

Ibn Aʿtham. *Kitāb al-Futūḥ*. Edited by Muḥammad Khān et al. Hyderabad: Dāʾirat al-Maʿārif al-ʿUthmāniyya, 1388–95/1968–75.

Ibn al-Athīr, Ḍiyāʾ al-Dīn. *Al-Mathal al-sāʾir fī adab al-kātib wa-l-shāʿir*. Edited by Aḥmad al-Ḥūfī and Badawī Ṭabāna. Cairo: Dār Nahḍat Miṣr li-l-Ṭabʿ wa-l-Nashr, n.d.

Ibn al-ʿAṭṭār, *al-Maqāmāt al-Qurashiyya*, Suleymaniye MS Ayasofya 4297.

Ibn Buṭlān. *Daʿwat al-Aṭibbāʾ*. Edited by ʿĀdil al-Bakrī. Baghdad: al-Majmaʿ al-ʿIlmī, 2002.

———. *The Doctors' Dinner Party*. Translated and edited by Philip F. Kennedy and Jeremy Farrell. New York: New York University Press, 2023.

Ibn al-Fāriḍ. *Al-Juzʾ al-awwal min sharḥ dīwān Ibn al-Fāriḍ wa-bi-hāmishihi Kashf al-wujūh al-ghurr li-maʿānī naẓm al-durr*. Cairo: al-Maṭbaʿa al-Azhariyya al-Miṣriyya, 1902.

Ibn Fāris. *Mutakhayyar al-Alfāẓ*. Edited by Hilāl Nājī. Baghdad: Maṭbaʿat al-Maʿārif, 1970.

Ibn Funduq, ʿAli ibn Zayd al-Bayhaqi. *Tārīkh-i Bayhaq*. Edited by Aḥmad Bahmanyār. Tehran: Furūqī, 1965.

Ibn al-Jawzī. *Al-Maqāmāt*. Suleymaniye MS, Nuruosmaniye 4271.

———. *Ibn al-Jawzī's Kitāb al-Quṣṣāṣ wa'l-Mudhakkirīn: Including a Critical Edition, Annotated Translation and Introduction*. Edited by Merlin L. Swartz. Beirut: Dār al-Mashriq, 1971.

Ibn Khallikān. *Wafayāt al-aʿyān wa-anbāʾ abnāʾ al-zamān*. Edited by Iḥsān ʿAbbās. Beirut: Dār Ṣādir, 1978.

Ibn al-Khashshāb. *Istidrākāt Ibn al-Khashshāb ʿalā Abī al-Qāsim Muḥammad b. al-Ḥarīrī wa-Intiṣār Ibn Barrī li-Ibn al-Ḥarīrī*. Suleymaniye MS, Fazil Ahmed Pasha 1203.

———. *Istidrākāt Ibn al-Khashshāb ʿalā Maqāmāt al-Ḥarīrī*. Edited by Samiya Ḥasanʿalyān. Beirut: al-ʿĀrif li-l-Maṭbūʿāt, 2021.

———. *Istidrākāt Ibn al-Khashshāb ʿalā Maqāmāt al-Ḥarīrī wa-intiṣār Ibn Barrī li-l-Ḥarīriyya*. Edited by al-Tajānī Saʿīd Maḥmūd. Beirut: Dār al-Kutub al-ʿIlmiyya, 2020.

———. *Naqd Ibn al-Khashshāb al-Baghdādī ʿalā al-Maqāmāt al-Ḥarīriyya*, Yale MS, Landberg 503.

———. "Risāla li-l-Imām Abī Muḥammad ʿAbd Allāh b. Aḥmad al-Maʿrūf bi-Ibn al-Khashshāb al-Baghdādī fī al-iʿtirāḍ ʿalā al-Ḥarīrī maʿa intiṣār Ibn Barrī li-l-Ḥarīrī." In *Kitāb Maqāmāt al-Ḥarīrī*. 1–36. Cairo: al-Maṭbaʿa al-Ḥusaynīya, 1929.

Ibn Khayr al-Ishbīlī. *Fahrasat Ibn Khayr al-Ishbīlī*. Tūnis: Dār al-Gharb al-Islāmī, 2009.

Ibn Manẓūr, *Lisān al-ʿArab*. Edited by ʿAbd Allāh ʿAlī al-Kabīr, Muḥammad Aḥmad Ḥasab Allāh, and Hāshim Muḥammad al-Shādhilī. Cairo: Dār al-Maʿārif, 1981.

Ibn al-Muqaffaʿ. *La version arabe de Kalîlah et Dimnah d'apres le plus ancien manuscrit arabe daté*. Edited by Louis Cheikho. Beirut: Imprimerie Catholique, 1905.

Ibn al-Nadīm. *Kitāb al-Fihrist*. Edited by Ayman Fuʾād Sayyid. London: Al-Furqān Islamic Heritage Foundation, 2014.

Ibn Nāqiyā. "Maqāmāt Ibn Nāqiyā." In *Beiträge zur Maqamen-Literatur*, edited by Oskar Rescher, 123–52. Istanbul: Maṭbaʿat Aḥmad Kāmil, 1914.

Ibn Qutayba. *Kitāb ʿUyūn al-akhbār*. Beirut: Dār al-Kitāb al-ʿArabī, 1925.

Ibn Rashīq. *Al-ʿUmda fī ṣināʿat al-shiʿr wa-naqdihi*. Edited by ʿAbd al-Wāḥid Shaʿlān. Cairo: Maktabat al-Khānjī, 2000.

Ibn Saʿd. *Kitāb al-Ṭabaqāt al-Kabīr*. Edited by ʿAlī Muḥammad ʿUmar. Cairo: Maktabat al-Khānjī, 2001.

Ibn al-Ṣayqal al-Jazarī. *Al-Maqāmāt al-Zayniyya*. Edited by ʿAbbās Muṣṭafā al-Ṣāliḥī. Amman: Dār al-Masīra, 1980.

Ibn Sīnā. *Al-Shifāʾ: Al-Manṭiq—al-Shiʿr*. Edited by ʿAbd al-Raḥmān Badawī. Cairo: al-Dār al-Miṣrīya li-l-Taʾlīf wa-l-Tarjama, 1966.

Ibn ʿUṣfūr al-Ishbīlī. *Ḍarāʾir al-shiʿr*. Edited by al-Sayyid Ibrāhīm Muḥammad. Cairo: Dār al-Andalus, 1980.

Ingenito, Domenico. *Beholding Beauty: Saʿdī of Shiraz and the Aesthetics of Desire in Medieval Persian Poetry*. Leiden: Brill, 2021.

al-Iṣfahānī, Abū al-Faraj. *Kitāb al-Aghānī*. Edited by Iḥsān ʿAbbās. Beirut: Dār Ṣādir, 2008.

al-Iṣfahānī, ʿImād al-Dīn. *Kharīdat al-qaṣr wa-jarīdat ahl al-ʿaṣr: Qiṣm al-ʿIrāq*. Edited by Muḥammad Bahja al-Atharī and Jamīl Saʿīd. Baghdad: al-Majmaʿ al-ʿIlmī al-ʿIrāqī, 1955–80.

Jackson, Sherman A. *The Islamic Secular*. Oxford: Oxford University Press, 2024.

Jacobi, Renate. "The 'Khayāl' Motif in Early Arabic Poetry." *Oriens* 32 (1990): 50–64.

Jaques, R. Kevin. "The Other Rabīʿ: Biographical Traditions and the Development of Early Shāfiʿī Authority." *Islamic Law and Society* 14 (2007): 143–79.

al-Jarīrī, al-Muʿāfā b. Zakariyyā al-Nahrawānī. *Al-Jalīs al-ṣāliḥ al-kāfī wa-l-anīs al-nāṣiḥ al-shāfī*. Edited by Muḥammad Mursī al-Khūlī. Beirut: ʿĀlam al-Kutub, 1993.

Jayyusi, Salma. "Response to Thomas Bauer, Review of *Arabic Literature in the Post-Classical Period*, edited by Roger Allen and D. S. Richards." *MSR* 12 (2008): 193–207.

Johnson, Rebecca C. *Stranger Fictions: A History of the Novel in Arabic Translation*. Ithaca, NY: Cornell University Press, 2021.

Jones, Alan. *Marāthī and Ṣuʿlūk Poems*. Vol. 1 of *Early Arabic Poetry*. Oxford: Oxford University Press, 1992.

Jones, William. *Poems, Consisting Chiefly of Translations from the Asiatick Tongues*. Edited by Rudolf Beck. Augsburg: Universität Augsburg, 2009. Originally published 1772.

al-Jurjānī, ʿAbd al-Qāhir. *Kitāb Asrār al-balāgha*. Edited by Helmut Ritter. Istanbul: Maṭbaʿat Wazārat al-Maʿārif, 1954.

———. *Kitāb Dalāʾil al-iʿjāz*. Edited by Maḥmūd and Muḥammad Shākir. Cairo: Maktabat al-Khānjī, 1984.

al-Jurjānī, Muḥammad b. ʿAlī b. Muḥammad. *Al-Ishārāt wa-l-tanbīhāt fī ʿilm al-balāgha*. Edited by ʿAbd al-Qādir Ḥusayn. Cairo: Maktabat al-Ādāb, 1997.

al-Kalāʿī, Abū al-Qāsim Muḥammad b. ʿAbd al-Ghafūr. *Iḥkām ṣanʿat al-kalām*. Edited by Muḥammad Riḍwān al-Dāya. Beirut: Dār al-Thaqāfa, 1966.

Karamustafa, Ahmet T. *God's Unruly Friends: Dervish Groups in the Islamic Later Middle Period, 1200–1550*. Salt Lake City: University of Utah Press, 1994.

Kateman, Ammeke. *Muḥammad ʿAbduh and His Interlocutors: Conceptualizing Religion in a Globalizing World*. Leiden: Brill, 2019.

———. "Tellings of an Encounter: A Meeting Between Muḥammad ʿAbduh, Herbert Spencer and Wilfrid Blunt (1903)." *Philological Encounters* 3 (2018): 105–28.

Katsumata, Naoya. "The Style of the *Maqāma*: Arabic, Persian, Hebrew, Syriac." *Middle Eastern Literatures* 5 (2002): 117–37.

Katz, Marion Holmes. "The Multiplicity of the Pre-Modern Islamic Tradition." *Political Theology* 23 (2022): 679–84.

———. *Wives and Work: Islamic Law and Ethics Before Modernity*. New York: Columbia University Press, 2022.

Kāẓim, Nādir. *Al-Maqāmāt wa-l-talaqqī: Baḥt fī anmāṭ al-talaqqī li-Maqāmāt al-Hamadhānī fī al-naqd al-ʿArabī al-Ḥadīt*. Beirut: Al-Muʾassasa al-ʿArabiyya li-l-Dirāsāt wa-l-Nashr, 2003.

Keegan, Matthew L. "Before and After *Kalīla wa-Dimna*: An Introduction to the Special Issue on Animals, *Adab*, and Fictivity." *Journal of Abbasid Studies* 8 (2021): 1–11.

———. "Commentarial Acts and Hermeneutical Dramas: The Ethics of Reading al-Ḥarīrī's *Maqāmāt*." PhD diss., New York University, 2017.

———. "Commentators, Collators, and Copyists: Interpreting Manuscript Variation in the Exordium of al-Ḥarīrī's *Maqāmāt*." In *Arabic Humanities, Islamic Thought: Essays in Honor of Everett K. Rowson*, edited by Joseph E. Lowry and Shawkat M. Toorawa, 295–316. Leiden: Brill, 2017.

———. "Digressions in the Islamic Archive: Al-Ḥarīrī's *Maqāmāt* and the Forgotten Commentary of al-Panǧdīhī (d. 584/1188)." *Intellectual History of the Islamicate World* 10 (2021): 82–118.

———. "'Elsewhere Lies Its Meaning': The Vagaries of *Kalīla and Dimna*'s Reception." *Poetica* 52 (2021): 13–40.

———. "al-Muṭarrizī." *EI3*.

———. "Rethinking Poetry as (Anti-Crusader) Propaganda: Licentiousness and Cross-Confessional Patronage in the *Ḫarīdat al-qaṣr*." *Intellectual History of the Islamicate World* 11 (2022): 24–58.

———. "Al-Tawḥīdī, Fictionality, and the Mediatedness of Narrative." *postmedieval* 13 (2022): 331–49.

———. "Throwing the Reins to the Reader: Hierarchy, Jurjānian Poetics, and al-Muṭarrizī's Commentary on the *Maqāmāt*." *Journal of Abbasid Studies* 5 (2018): 105–45.

Kennedy, Philip F. *Recognition in the Arabic Narrative Tradition: Discovery, Deliverance, and Delusion*. Edinburgh: Edinburgh University Press, 2016.

Kia, Mana. *Persianate Selves: Memories of Place and Origin Before Nationalism*. Stanford: Stanford University Press, 2020.

Kilito, Abdelfettah. *Al-Adab wa-l-gharāba*. Casablanca: Dār Tūbqāl, 2013.

———. *Arabs and the Art of Storytelling: A Strange Familiarity*. Syracuse, NY: Syracuse University Press, 2014.

———. *Al-Ghāʾib: Dirāsa fī maqāma li-l-Ḥarīrī*. Casablanca: Dār Tūbqāl, 2007.

———. *Lan tatakallam lughatī*. Beirut: Dār al-Ṭalīʿa, 2002.

———. *Les séances: Récits et codes culturels chez Hamadhânî et Harîrî*. Paris: Sindbad, 1983.

———. *Al-Maqāmāt: Al-Sard wa-l-Ansāq wa-l-Thaqāfa*. Translated by ʿAbd al-Kabīr al-Sharqāwī. Casablanca: Dār Tūbqāl, 2001.

———. *Thou Shalt Not Speak My Language*. Syracuse, NY: Syracuse University Press, 2017.

Klein, Yaron. "Between Public and Private: An Examination of Ḥisba Literature." *Harvard Middle Eastern and Islamic Review* 7 (2006): 41–62.

Kraemer, Jörg. "Legajo-Studien zur altarabischen Philologie." *ZMDG* 110 (1960): 252–300.

Larkin, Margaret. "Abū l-ʿAlāʾ al-Maʿarrī's *Muʿjiz Aḥmad* and the Limits of Poetic Commentary." *Oriens* 41 (2013): 479–97.

———. *The Theology of Meaning: ʿAbd al-Qāhir al-Jurjānī's Theory of Discourse*. New Haven, CT: American Oriental Society, 1995.

Lavi, Abraham. "The Rationale of al-Ḥarīzī in Biblicizing the Maqāmāt of al-Ḥarīrī." 74 (1984): 280–93.

Lawrence, Jonathan. "It's All Just Poetry: Writing ʿUmar ibn Abī Rabīʿah's Life." *Journal of Arabic Literature* 52 (2021): 321–50.

Leder, Stefan. "Conventions of Fictional Narration in Learned Literature." In *Storytelling in the Framework of Non-Fictional Arabic Literature*, edited by Stefan Leder, 34–60. Wiesbaden: Harrassowitz Verlag, 1998.

———. "The Use of Composite Form in the Making." In *On Fiction and Adab in Medieval Arabic Literature*, edited by Philip F. Kennedy, 125–48. Wiesbaden: Harrassowitz Verlag, 2005.

Leemhuis, Frederik. "Readings of the Qurʾān." In *Encyclopaedia of the Qurʾān*, edited by Jane Dammen McAuliffe. Accessed online August 17, 2022. https://referenceworks.brill.com/view/db/eqo.

Leezenberg, Michiel. "'A Rare Pearl Passed from Hand to Hand': Cosmpolitan Orders and Pre-Modern Forms of Literary Domination." *Journal of World Literature* 5 (2020): 253–77.

Lindermann, Colinda. "A Shared Set of Solecisms: The Mamlūk and Ottoman Reception of al-Ḥarīrī's *Durrat al-ghawwāṣ*." *Philological Encounters* 4 (2019): 55–79.

Livingston, Daisy. "The Paperwork of a Mamluk *Muqtaʿ*: Documentary Life Cycles, Archival Spaces, and the Importance of Documents Lying Around." *Al-ʿUsur al-Wusta* 28 (2020): 346–75.

———. *Zajr al-nābiḥ: Muqtaṭafāt*. Edited by Amjad Ṭarābulsī. Damascus: Majmaʿ al-Lugha al-ʿArabiyya, 1982.

al-Maʿarrī, Abū al-ʿAlāʾ. *Shurūḥ Saqṭ al-Zand*. Edited by Ṭāhā Ḥusayn et al. Cairo: al-Hayʾa al-Miṣriyya al-ʿĀmma li-l-Kitāb, 1986.

Macaulay, Thomas Babington. "Minute by the Hon'ble T. B. Macaulay, dated the 2nd February 1835." In *Selections from Educational Records, Part I: 1781–1839*, edited by H. Sharp, 107–17. Calcutta: Superintendent of Government Printing, 1920.

MacKay, Pierre A. "Certificates of Transmission on a Manuscript of the *Maqāmāt* of Ḥarīrī (MS. Cairo, Adab 105)." *Transactions of the American Philosophical Society*, n.s., 61, no. 4 (1971): 1–81.

Mackintosh-Smith, Tim. Introduction to *A Physician on the Nile: A Description of Egypt and Journal of the Famine Years*, by Muwaffaq al-Dīn ʿAbd al-Laṭīf al-Baghdādī, xxi–xlvii. Translated and edited by Tim Mackintosh-Smith. New York: New York University Press, 2021.

Madelung, Wilfred. Review of *Abū ʿUbaid al-Qāsim b. Sallām's K. al-nāsikh wa-l-mansūkh (MS. Istanbul, Topkapi, Ahmet III A 143)*, edited with a commentary by John Burton. *Journal of Near Eastern Studies* 50 (1991): 228–30.

Mahmood, Saba. *Religious Difference in a Secular Age: A Minority Report*. Princeton, NJ: Princeton University Press, 2015.

Mahmoud, Alaaeldin. "Multilingual Poetics in Arabic and Persian *Maqāmāt*: Between *al-Taṣannuʿ* and *Sabk*." *Postmedieval* 15 (2004): 657–86.

Majid, Anouar. "Can the Postcolonial Critic Speak? Orientalism and the Rushdie Affair." *Cultural Critique* 32 (1995): 5–42.

Mallette, Karla. *Lives of the Great Languages: Arabic and Latin in the Medieval Mediterranean*. Chicago: University of Chicago Press, 2021.

———. "Orientalism and the Nineteenth-Century Nationalist: Michele Amari, Ernest Renan, and 1848." *Romanic Review* 96, no. 2 (2005): 233–52.

Malti-Douglas, Fedwa. "Controversy and Its Effects in the Biographical Tradition of al-Khaṭīb al-Baghdādī." *Studia Islamica* 46 (1977): 115–31.

———. "Dreams, the Blind, and the Semiotics of the Biographical Notice." *Studia Islamica* 51 (1980): 137–62.

———. "Maqāmāt and Adab: 'Al-Maqāma al-Maḍīriyya' of al-Hamadhānī." *Journal of the American Oriental Society* 105 (1985): 247–58.

Margoliouth, D. S. "IV. The Discussion Between Abu Bishr Matta and Abu Sa'id al-Sirafi on the Merits of Logic and Grammar." *Journal of the Royal Asiatic Society of Great Britain and Ireland* (January 1905): 79–129.

Margoliouth, D. S., and Charles Pellat. "al-Ḥarīrī." *EI2*.

Marlow, Louise. *Hierarchy and Egalitarianism in Islamic Thought*. Cambridge: Cambridge University Press, 2002.

Marx, Karl, and Friedrich Engels. *The Communist Manifesto: With an Introduction and Notes by Gareth Stedman Jones* (London: Penguin Books, 2002).

Marzolph, Ulrich. "The Literary Genre of 'Oriental Miscellany.'" In *Le répertoire narratif arabe médiéval: Transmission et ouverture; Actes du colloque international, Université de Liège, 15–17 septembre 2005*, edited by Frédéric Bauden, Aboubakr Chraïbi, and Antonella Ghersetti, 309–19. Paris: Droz S. A., 2008.

Mattar, Karim. *Specters of World Literature: Orientalism, Modernity, and the Novel in the Middle East*. Edinburgh: Edinburgh University Press, 2020.

Mauder, Christian. *In the Sultan's Salon: Learning, Religion, and Rulership in the Mamluk Court of Qāsniṣawh al-Ghawrī (r. 1501–1516)*. Leiden: Brill, 2021.

al-Maydanī. *Majmaʿ al-amthāl*. Tehran: al-Maʿārif wa-l-Thaqāfa, 1987.

McLaren, Andrew G. "Dating Ibn Aʿtham's History: Of Persian Manuscripts, Obscure Biographies, and Incomplete *Isnāds*." *Al-ʿUṣūr al-Wusṭā* 30 (2022): 183–234.

———. "Ibn Aʿtham's History: Transmission and Translation in Islamicate Written Culture, 290–873/902–1468." PhD diss., Columbia University, 2021.

Meisami, Julie Scott. "Masʿūdī and the Reign of al-Amīn: Narrative and Meaning in Medieval Muslim Historiography." In *On Fiction and* Adab *in Medieval Arabic Literature*, edited by Philip F. Kennedy, 149–232. Weisbaden: Harrassowitz Verlag, 2005.

———. *Persian Historiography to the End of the Twelfth Century*. Edinburgh: Edinburgh University Press, 1999.

———. *Structure and Meaning in Medieval Arabic and Persian Poetry: Orient Pearls*. London: Routledge, 2003.

Messick, Brinkley. *The Calligraphic State: Textual Domination and History in a Muslim Society*. Berkeley: University of California Press, 1993.

Miller, Jeannie. "Commentary and Text Organization in al-Jāḥiẓ's *Book of Animals*." In *Practices of Commentary: Medieval Traditions and Transmissions*, edited by Amanda Goodman and Suzanne Conklin Akbari, 55–86. Leeds: ARC Humanities Press, 2023.

Mīrkhānd. *Tārīkh-i Rawḍat al-ṣafā*. Edited by Riḍā Qulī Khān Hidāyat. Tehran: Markaz-i Khayyām Pīrūz, 1959.

Miskawayh. *Tajārib al-Umam wa-Taʿāqub al-Himam*. Edited by Sayyid Kisrawī Ḥasan. Beirut: Dār al-Kutub al-ʿIlmiyya, 2002.

Monroe, James T. *The Art of Badīʿ al-Zamān al-Hamadhānī as Picaresque Narrative*. Beirut: American University of Beirut, 1983.

Montgomery, James E. "Al-Jāḥiẓ's *Kitāb al-Bayān wa al-Tabyīn*." In *Writing and Representation in Medieval Islam: Muslim Horizons*, edited by Julia Bray, 91–152. London: Routledge, 2006.

al-Mufaḍḍal, Abū al-ʿAbbās. *Dīwān al-Mufaḍḍalīyāt*. Edited by Charles James Lyall. Beirut: Maṭbaʿat al-Ābāʾ al-Yasūʿiyyīn, 1920.

Mufti, Aamir. *Forget English! Orientalisms and World Literatures*. Cambridge, MA: Harvard University Press, 2016.

———. "Orientalism and the Institution of World Literatures." *Critical Inquiry* 36 (2010): 458–93.

Muhanna, Elias. *The World in a Book: Al-Nuwayri and the Islamic Encyclopedic Tradition*. Princeton, NJ: Princeton University Press, 2018.

Murtāḍ, ʿAbd al-Mālik. *Fann al-maqāmāt fī al-adab al-ʿArabī*. Tunis: al-Dār al-Tūnisiyya li-l-Nashr, 1988.

al-Musawi, Muhsin J. *The Medieval Islamic Republic of Letters: Arabic Knowledge Construction*. Notre Dame, IN: University of Notre Dame, 2015.

al-Muṭarrizī, Burhān al-Dīn Abū al-Fatḥ. *Al-Īḍāḥ fī sharḥ Maqāmāt Abī al-Qāsim al-Ḥarīrī*. Princeton MS Garrett no. 574Y.

———. *Al-Īḍāḥ fī sharḥ Maqāmāt al-Ḥarīrī*. Suleymaniye MS Nuruosmaniye 4061.

———. *Al-Īḍāḥ fī sharḥ Maqāmāt al-Ḥarīrī*. Suleymaniye MS Haci Selim Aga 973.

———. *Al-Īḍāḥ fī sharḥ Maqāmāt al-Ḥarīrī*. Edited by Khūrshīd Ḥasan. Lahore: University of the Punjab, 2005.

Myrne, Pernilla. *Female Sexuality in the Early Medieval Islamic World: Gender and Sex in Arabic Literature*. London: I. B. Tauris, 2020.

Nakissa, Aria. "An Epistemic Shift in Islamic Law: Educational Reform at al-Azhar and Dār al-ʿUlūm." *Islamic Law and Society* 21 (2014): 209–51.

Nasser, Shady Hekmat. *The Transmission of the Variant Readings of the Qur'ān: The Problem of* Tawātur *and the Emergence of* Shawādhdh. Leiden: Brill, 2013.

Neuwirth, Angelika. "Adab Standing Trial—Whose Norms Should Rule Society? The Case of al-Ḥarīrī's 'al-Maqāmah al-Ramliyyah.'" In *Myths, Historical Archetypes, and Symbolic Figures in Arabic Literature: Towards a New Hermeneutic Approach; Proceedings of the International Symposium in Beirut, June 25th–June 30th, 1996*, edited by Angelika Neuwirth, Birgit Embalo, Sebastian Gunter, and Maher Jarrar, 205–24. Beirut: Orient-Institut, 1996.

———."Al-Ḥarīrī's Travel in Search of Distraction: al-Riḥla fī ṭalabi l-istiṭrāf." *Annali di Ca'Foscari: Rivista della Facoltà di Lingue e Letterature straniere dell'Università di Ca'Foscari* 48 (2009): 35–50.

———. "*Ayyu ḥajarin ʿalā man ansha'a mulaḥan?* Al-Ḥarīrī's Plea for the Legitimacy of Playful Transgressions of Social Norms." In *Humor in der Arabischen Kultur*, edited by Georges Tamer, 241–54. Berlin: De Gruyter, 2009.

———. "Woman's Wit and Juridical Discourse: A 'Forensic *maqāma*' by the Classical Arabic Scholar al-Ḥarīrī." *Figurationen* 6 (2005): 23–36.

Nicholson, Reynold A. *Studies in Islamic Mysticism*. Cambridge: Cambridge University Press, 1921.

Nielsen, J. S. "Maẓālim." *EI2*.

Norman, York A. "Disputing the 'Iron Circle': Renan, Afghani, and Kemal on Islam, Science, and Modernity." *Journal of World History* 22 (2011): 693–714.

O'Kane, Bernard. "Text and Paintings in the al-Wāṣiṭī *Maqāmāt*." *Ars Orientalis* 42 (2012): 41–55.

Olivieri, Simona. "*Kitāb al-ʾInṣāf*: Analysis of the Linguistic Debate and the Relations Among Grammarians." PhD diss., Sapienza University of Rome, 2016.

Orfali, Bilal. "A Sketch Map of Arabic Poetry Anthologies up to the Fall of Baghdad." *Journal of Arabic Literature* 43 (2012): 29–59.

Orfali, Bilal, and Maurice Pomerantz. *The "Maqāmāt" of Badīʿ al-Zamān al-Hamadhānī*. Wiesbaden: Reichert, 2022.

Orlemanski, Julie. "Who Has Fiction? Modernity, Fictionality, and the Middle Ages." *New Literary History* 50 (2019): 145–70.

Owens, Jonathan. "The Grammatical Tradition and Arabic Language Teaching: A View from Here." In *Investigating Arabic: Current Parameters in Analysis and Learning*, edited by Alaa Elgibali, 101–16. Leiden: Brill, 2004.

Pagani, Samuela. "The Reality and Image of the Prophet According to the Theologian and Poet ʿAbd al-Ghanī al-Nābulusī." In *The Presence of the Prophet in Early Modern and Contemporary Islam*, 501–34. Leiden: Brill, 2021.

Paige, Nicholas D. *Before Fiction: The Ancien Régime of the Novel*. Philadelphia: University of Pennsylvania Press, 2011.

al-Panjdīhī. *Maghānī al-muqāmāt fī maʿānī al-Maqāmāt*. Suleymaniye MS Hamidiye 1195.

———. *Maghānī al-muqāmāt fī maʿānī al-Maqāmāt*. Suleymaniye MS Murad Molla 1549.

———. *Maghānī al-muqāmāt fī maʿānī al-Maqāmāt*. Beyazid MS V2611.

Patel, Abdulrazzak. *The Arab Nahḍah: The Making of the Intellectual and Humanist Movement*. Edinburgh, Edinburgh University Press, 2013.

Pellat, Charles. *Le milieu baṣrien et la formation de Ǧāḥiẓ*. Paris: Libraire d'Amérique et d'Orient Adrien-Maisonneuve, 1953.

Pfeifer, Helen. *Empire of Salons: Conquest and Community in the Early Modern Ottoman Lands*. Princeton, NJ: Princeton University Press, 2022.

Pollock, Sheldon. "Philology in Three Dimensions." *postmedieval* 5 (2014): 398–413.

Pomerantz, Maurice. "A *Maqāma* Collection by a Mamlūk Historian: *Al-Maqāmāt al-Ǧalāliyya* by al-Ḥasan b. Abī Muḥammad al-Ṣafadī (*fl.* First Quarter of the 8th/14th c.)." *Arabica* 61 (2014): 631–63.

———. "The Play of Genre: A *Maqāma* of 'Ease After Hardship' from the Eighth/Fourteenth Century and Its Literary Context." In *The Heritage of Arabo-Islamic Learning: Studies in Honor of Wadad Kadi*, edited by Maurice A. Pomerantz and Aram A. Shahin, 461–82. Leiden: Brill, 2015.

Post, Arjan. "A Taymiyyan Sufi's Refutation of the Akbarian School: ʿImād al-Dīn Aḥmad al-Wāsiṭī's (d. 711/1311) *Lawāmiʿ al-Istirshād*." In *Egypt and Syria in the Fatimid, Ayyubid, and Mamluk Eras*, edited by K. D'Hulster, G. Schallenbergh, and J. Van Steenbergen, 309–25. Leuven: Peeters, 2019.

Preston, Thomas. Preface to *"Makamat" or Rhetorical Anecdotes of Al Hariri of Basra Translated from the Arabic, with Annotations*, viii–xv. Translated by Thomas Preston. London: Oriental Translation Fund, 1850.

Pritchett, Frances W. "Orient Pearls Unstrung: The Quest for Unity in the Ghazal." *Edebiyat* 4 (1993): 119–35.

al-Qāḍī, Wadād. "Badīʿ al-Zamān al-Hamadhānī and His Social and Political Vision." In *Literary Heritage of Classical Islam: Arabic and Islamic Studies in Honor of James A. Bellamy*, edited by Mustansir Mir, 197–223. Princeton, NJ: Darwin Press, 1993.

———. "*Maqāmāt Badīʿ al-Zamān al-Hamadhānī Taqniyyat al-Qināʿ wa-Marāmīhā al-Fanniyya wa-l-Fikriyya*." In *al-Ruʾyā wa-l-ʿIbāra: Dirāsāt fī al-Adab wa-l-Fikr wa-l-Tārīkh*. 461–82. Edited by Bilal Orfali. Beirut: Dār al-Mashriq, 2015.

al-Qashānī [or al-Kashānī]. *Kashf al-wujūh al-ghurr li-maʿānī naẓm al-durr: Sharḥ tāʾiyyat Ibn al-Fāriḍ*. Edited by Aḥmad Farīd al-Mazyadī. Beirut: Dār al-Kutub al-ʿIlmiyya, 2005.

al-Qazwīnī, ʿAlī b. Abī al-Qāsim. *Kitāb al-Mughnī fī sharḥ al-maqāmāt al-Ḥarīriyya*. Suleymaniye MS Esad Efendi 2819.

al-Qifṭī. *Inbāḥ al-ruwāt ʿalā anbāh al-nuḥāt*. Edited by Muḥammad Abū al-Faḍl Ibrāhīm. Cairo: Dār al-Fikr al-ʿArabī, 1986.

al-Qifṭī. *Inbāh al-ruwāt ʿalā anbāh al-nuḥāt*. Suleymaniye MS Feyzullah 1382.

al-Qurashī, ʿAbd al-Qādir. *Al-Jawāhir al-maḍiyya fī ṭabaqāt al-Ḥanafiyya*. Edited by ʿAbd al-Fattāḥ Muḥammad al-Ḥalw. Cairo: Hajar, 1993.

Qureshi, Jawad Anwar. "Ibn ʿArabi and the Akbarī Tradition." In *Routledge Handbook on Sufism*, 89–102. London: Routledge, 2020.

Qutbuddin, Tahera. "*Nahj al-balāgha*." *EI3*.

Rashād, Nabīl Muḥammad. *Al-Ṣafadī wa-sharḥuhu ʿalā Lāmiyyat al-ʿAjam: Dirāsa taḥlīliyya*. Cairo: Maktabat al-Adab, 2007.

Rassi, Salam. "Scribal and Commentary Traditions at the Dawn of Print: The Manuscripts of the Near Eastern School of Theology as an Archive of the Early *Nahḍa*." *Philological Encounters* 6 (2021): 402–37.

al-Rāzī, Fakhr al-Dīn. *Tafsīr Fakhr al-Dīn al-Rāzī al-mushtahir bi-l-tafsīr al-kabīr wa-mafātīḥ al-ghayb*. Beirut: Dār al-Fikr, 1981.

Renan, Ernest. *De la part des peuples Sémitiques dans l'histoire de la civilisation: Discours d'ouverture du cours de langues Hébraïque, Chaldaïque et Syriaque, au Collége de France*. Paris: Mechel Lévy Frères, 1862.

———. *L'Islamisme et la Science: Conférence faite a la Sorbonne le 29 Mars 1883*. Paris: Calmann Lévy, 1883.

———. "Les séances de Hariri." In *Essais de morale et de critique*, 287–302. Paris: Michel Lévy Frères, 1859.

Ricci, Ronit. *Islam Translated: Literature, Conversion, and the Arabic Cosmopolis of South and Southeast Asia*. Chicago: University of Chicago Press, 2011.

Richardson, Kristina. "Tracing a Gypsy Mixed Language Through Medieval and Early Modern Arabic and Persian Literature." *Der Islam* 94 (2017): 115–57.

Ritter, Helmut. "Autographs in Turkish Libraries." *Oriens* 6 (1953): 63–90.

Roberts, Deborah H. "Translation and the 'Surreptitious Classic': Obscenity and Translatability." In *Translation and the Classic: Identity as Change in the History of Culture*, edited by Alexandra Lianeri and Vanda Zajko, 279–311. Oxford: Oxford University Press, 2008.

Rosen, Tova. "The Beard as Spectacle and Scandal in a Thirteenth-Century Hebrew *Maqāma*." *Intellectual History of the Islamicate World* 10 (2021): 138–61.

Rosenthal, Franz. *The Technique and Approach of Muslim Scholarship*. Rome: Analecta orientalia, 1947.

Rowson, Everett K. "An Alexandrian Age in Fourteenth-Century Damascus: Twin Commentaries on Two Celebrated Arabic Epistles." *MSR* 7 (2003): 97–110.

Roxburgh, David J. "In Pursuit of Shadows: Al-Hariri's *Maqāmāt*." *Muqarnas Online* 30 (2013): 171–212.

Rustow, Marina. *The Lost Archive: Traces of a Caliphate in a Cairo Synagogue*. Princeton, NJ: Princeton University Press, 2020.

Sacy, Silvestre de. "Avertissement." In *Les séances de Hariri publiées en arabe avec un commentaire choisi*, edited by Silvestre de Sacy, iii–x. Paris: Imprimerie Royale, 1822.

———. *Chrestomathie arabe, ou extraits de divers écrivains arabes*. Paris: L'Impreimerie Impériale, 1806.

Saʿdī Shīrāzī. *The Gulistán (Rose Garden) of Shekh Sadí of Shíráz: A New Edition Carefully Collated with Original MSS*. Edited by E. B. Eastwick. Hertford: Stephen Austin, 1850.

al-Ṣafadī, Khalīl b. Aybak. *Ikhtirāʿ al-khurāʿ*. Edited by Fārūq Islīm. Damascus: Ittiḥād al-Kuttāb al-ʿArab, 2000.

———. *Kitāb al-Ghayth al-musajjam fī sharḥ Lāmiyyat al-ʿAjam*. Cairo: al-Maṭbaʿa al-Azhariyya, 1887–88.

———. *Kitāb al-Wāfī bi-l-wafayāt*. Edited by Helmut Ritter et al. Beirut: Orient-Institut, 1991–2004.

———. *Nuṣrat al-thāʾir ʿalā al-mathal al-sāʾir*. Edited by Muḥammad ʿAlī Sulṭān. Damascus: Majmaʿ al-Lugha al-ʿArabīya, 1971.

Said, Edward W. *Orientalism*. New York: Pantheon Books, 1978.

Sajdi, Dana. "Decline, Its Discontents and Ottoman Cultural History: By Way of Introduction." In *Ottoman Tulips, Ottoman Coffee: Leisure and Lifestyle in the Eighteenth Century*, edited by Dana Sajdi, 1–40. London: Tauris, 2007.

Saleh, Walid A. "Preliminary Remarks on the Historiography of *tafsīr* in Arabic: A History of the Book Approach." *Journal of Qurʾanic Studies* 12 (2010): 6–40.

al-Saraqusṭī, *al-Maqāmāt al-Luzūmīyah by Abū l-Ṭāhir Muḥammad ibn Yūsuf al-Tamīmī al-Saraqusṭī Ibn al-Aštarkūwī (d. 538/1143)*, translated by James T. Monroe, 1–110. Leiden: Brill, 2002.

Savant, Sarah Bowen, and Majid Montazer Mahdi. "The History of Iranian Cities Through Their Books: What Ms. Köprülü 01589 Tells Us About 8th/14th Century Shiraz." *Eurasian Studies* 16 (2018): 430–64.

Sayeed, Asma. *Women and the Transmission of Religious Knowledge in Islam*. Cambridge: Cambridge University Press, 2015.

Schaefer, Karl R. "The Material Nature of Block Printed Amulets: What Makes Them Amulets?" In *Amulets and Talismans of the Middle East and North Africa in Context*, 180–208. Leiden: Brill, 2022.

Schippers, Ari. "The Hebrew *maqama*." In *Maqama: A History of a Genre*, edited by Jaakko Hämeen-Anttila, 302–26. Wiesbaden: Harrassowitz, 2002.

Schwartz, Kathryn. "Meaningful Mediums: A Material and Intellectual History of Manuscript and Print Production in Nineteenth-Century Ottoman Cairo." PhD diss., Harvard University, 2015.

Selim, Samah. *The Novel and the Rural Imaginary in Egypt, 1880–1985*. London: Routledge, 2004.

Sellheim, R. "al-Tibrīzī." *EI2*.

Selove, Emily. *Ḥikāyat Abī al-Qāsim*: A Literary Banquet. Edinburgh: Edinburgh University Press, 2016.

Selove, Emily and John Turner. "Heretics and Party-Crashers: Al-Khaṭīb al-Baghdādī's *Kitāb al-Taṭfīl*." *Journal of Abbasid Studies* 6 (2019): 106–22.

Serjeant, R. B. Review of "Certificates of Transmission on a Manuscript of the *Maqāmāt* of Ḥarīrī (MS. Cairo, Adab 105)," by Pierre A. MacKay (*Transactions of the American Philosophical Society*, n.s., 61, no. 4 [1971]). *Bulletin of the School of Oriental and African Studies* 35 (1972): 197.

Seydi, Masoumeh, and Maxim Romanov. *Al-Ṯurayyā Project: A Gazetteer and a Geospatial Model of the Early Islamic World*. (Based on Georgette Cornu's *Atlas du monde arabo-*

islamique à l'époque classique: IXe–Xe siècles, Leiden: Brill, 1983.) https://althurayya.github.io/, 2022–.

Shafir, Nir. "Moral Revolutions: The Politics of Piety in the Ottoman Empire Reimagined." *Comparative Studies in Society and History* 61 (2019): 595–623.

al-Sharīshī, Aḥmad b. ʿAbd al-Muʾmin. *Sharḥ Maqāmāt al-Ḥarīrī*. Edited by Muḥammad Abū al-Faḍl Ibrāhīm. Beirut: al-Maktaba al-ʿAṣriyya, 1992.

———. *Sharḥ al-Maqāmāt al-Ḥarīriyya*. Cairo: Būlāq, 1868.

———. *Sharḥ Maqāmāt al-Ḥarīrī (Mukhtaṣar)*. Leiden University MS Ar. 5804.

———. *Sharḥ Maqāmāt al-Ḥarīrī (Mutawaṣṣit)*. Leiden University MS Or. 470.

Sharlet, Jocelyn. *Patronage and Poetry in the Islamic World*. London: I. B. Tauris, 2011.

———. "The Thought That Counts: Gift Exchange Poetry by Kushājim, al-Ṣanawbarī and al-Sarī al-Raffāʾ." *Middle Eastern Literatures* 14 (2011): 235–70.

———. "Tokens of Resentment: Medieval Arabic Narratives About Gift Exchange and Social Conflict." *Journal of Arabic and Islamic Studies* 11 (2011): 62–100.

al-Shidyāq. *Leg over Leg, or, The Turtle in the Tree, Concerning the Fāriyāq, What Manner of Creature Might He Be (Kitāb al-Sāq ʿalā al-Sāq fī mā huwa al-Fāriyāq)*. Translated and edited by Humphrey T. Davies. New York: New York University Press, 2013.

Sijpesteijn, Petra. *Shaping a Muslim State: The World of a Mid-Eighth-Century Egyptian Official*. Oxford: Oxford University Press, 2013.

Siskin, Clifford. "Epilogue: The Rise of Novelism." In *Cultural Institutions of the Novel*, edited by Deidre Lynch and William B. Warner, 423–40. Durham, NC: Duke University Press, 1996.

Smoor, Pieter. "The Delirious Sword of Maʿarri: An Annotated Version of His Luzumiyya in the Rhyme-Form 'Nun Maksura Mushaddada.'" In *Festschrift Ewald Wagner zum 65. Geburtstag*, edited by Wolfhart Heinrichs and Gregor Schoeler, 381–424. Beirut: Franz Steiner, 1994.

Sperl, Stefan. *Mannerism in Arabic Poetry: A Structural Analysis of Selected Texts (3rd Century AH/9th Century AD–5th Century AH/11th Century AD)*. Cambridge: Cambridge University Press, 1989.

Stephan, Johannes. "Modalities of Fictionality in the Arabic Tradition: *Kalīla wa-Dimna*'s Readers from the Third/Ninth to the Sixth/Twelfth Century." *Journal of Abbasid Studies* 9 (2022): 8–39.

Stern, S. M. "Some Noteworthy Manuscripts of the Poems of Abu'l-ʿAlāʾ al-Maʿarrī." *Oriens* 7 (1954): 322–47.

Stetkevych, Jaroslav. "Arabic Poetry and Assorted Poetics." In *Islamic Studies: A Tradition and Its Problems*, edited by Malcolm. H. Kerr, 103–23. Malibu, CA: Undena Publications, 1980.

Stetkevych, Suzanne Pinckney. "Irony, Archeology, and the Rule of Rhyme: Two Readings of the *Ṭasmu* Luzūmiyya of Abū l-ʿAlāʾ al-Maʿarrī." *Journal of American Oriental Society* 138 (2018): 507–32.

Stewart, Devin J. "ʿĪsā b. Hišām's Shiism and Religious Polemic in the *Maqāmāt* of Badīʿ al-Zamān al-Hamaḏānī (d. 398/1008)." *Intellectual History of the Islamicate World* 10 (2022): 11–81.

———. "The *Maqāma*." In *Arabic Literature in the Post-Classical Period*, edited by Roger Allen and D. S. Richards, 145–58. Cambridge History of Arabic Literature. Cambridge: Cambridge University Press, 2006.

———. "The *Maqāmāt* of Aḥmad b. Abī Bakr b. Aḥmad al-Rāzī al-Ḥanafī and the Ideology of the Counter-Crusade in Twelfth-Century Syria." *Middle Eastern Literatures* 11 (2008): 211–32.

———. "Of Rhetoric, Reason, and Revelation: Ibn al-Jawzī's *Maqāmāt* as an Anti-Parody and *Sefer Taḥkemoni* of Yehudah al-Ḥarīzī." *Middle Eastern Literatures* 19 (2016): 206–33.

———. "Professional Literary Mendicancy in the Letters and *Maqāmāt* of Badīʿ al-Zamān al-Hamadhānī." In *Writers and Rulers: Perspectives on Their Relationship from Abbasid to Safavid Times*, edited by Beatrice Gruendler and Louise Marlow, 39–48. Wiesbaden: Reichert Verlag, 2004.

———. "Rhythmical Anxiety: Notes on Abū al-ʿAlāʾ al-Maʿarrī's *al-Fuṣūl wa-l-Ghayāt* and Its Reception." In *The Qurʾan and* Adab*: The Shaping of Literary Traditions in Classical Islam*, edited by Nuha al-Shaar. Oxford: Oxford University Press, 2017.

al-Subkī, Tāj al-Dīn. *Al-Ṭabaqāt al-Shāfiʿiyya al-kubrā*. Edited by Maḥmūd Muḥammad Ṭanāḥī and ʿAbd al-Fattāḥ Muḥammad al-Ḥulw. Cairo: Dār Iḥyāʾ al-Kutub al-ʿArabiyya, 1964–1976.

Suleiman, Yasir. *The Arabic Grammatical Tradition: A Study in* taʿlīl. Edinburgh: Edinburgh University Press, 1999.

al-Suyūṭī. *Kitāb al-Laʾāliʾ al-maṣnūʿa fī al-aḥādīth al-maṣnūʿa*. Edited by Abū ʿAbd al-Raḥmān Ṣalāḥ. Beirut: Dār al-Kutub al-ʿIlmiyya 1996.

———. *Al-Muzhir fī ʿulūm al-lugha wa-anwāʿihā*. Cairo: Maṭbaʿat al-Saʿāda, 1907.

———. *Al-Ziyādāt ʿalā al-mawḍūʿāt wa-yusammā dhayl al-laʾāliʾ al-maṣnūʿa*. Edited by Rāmiz Khālid Ḥājj Ḥasan. Riyadh: Maktabat al-Maʿārif, 2010.

al-Ṭabarī. *Annales quos scripsit Abu Djafar Mohammed Ibn Djarir at-Tabari*. Edited by M. J. de Goeje. Ludg. Bat.: E. J. Brill, 1879–1901.

———. *Tafsīr al-Ṭabarī: Jāmiʿ al-bayān ʿan taʾwīl āy al-Qurʾān*. Edited by ʿAbd Allāh b. ʿAbd al-Muḥsin al-Turkī. Cairo: Hajr, 2001.

Tageldin, Shaden M. *Disarming Words: Empire and the Seductions of Translation in Egypt*. Oakland: University of California Press, 2011.

———. "Hugo, Translated: The Measures of Modernity in Muḥammad Rūḥī al-Khālidī's Poetics of Comparative Literature." *Publications of the Modern Language Association of America* 138 (2023): 616–38.

al-Ṭahṭāwī. *An Imam in Paris: Account of a Stay in France by an Egyptian Cleric (1826–1831)*. Translated by Daniel L Newman. London: Saqi, 2012.

———. *Takhlīṣ al-ibrīz fī talkhīṣ Bārīz*. Cairo: Hindāwī, 2011.

Talib, Adam. *How Do You Say "Epigram" in Arabic?: Literary History at the Limits of Comparison*. Leiden: Brill, 2018.

———. "Al-Ṣafadī, His Critics, and the Drag of Philological Time." *Philological Encounters* 4 (2019): 109–34.

al-Tanūkhī. *Nishwār al-muḥāḍara wa-akhbār al-mudhākara*. Edited by ʿAbbūd al-Shāljī. Beirut: Dār Ṣādir, 1971–73.

al-Ṭarābulsī, Amjad. "*al-Muqaddima*." In *Zajr al-nābiḥ: Muqtaṭafāt*. Edited by Amjad Ṭarābulsī. Damascus: Majmaʿ al-Lugha al-ʿArabiyya, 1982.

al-Tawḥīdī. *Kitāb al-Imtāʿ wa-l-Muʾānasa*. Edited by Aḥmad Amīn and Aḥmad al-Zayn. Cairo: Dār Maktabat al-Ḥayāt, 1953.

al-Thaʿlabī, Abū Isḥāq. *Al-Kashf wa-l-Bayān*. Edited by Abū Muḥammad b. ʿĀshūr. Beirut: Dār Iḥyāʾ al-Turāth al-ʿArabī, 2002.

———. *Kitāb Qiṣaṣ al-anbiyāʾ al-musammā bi-l-ʿarāʾis*. Cairo: al-Maṭbaʿa al-ʿĀmira al-Sharafiyya, 1905–6.

Thaver, Tehseen. "Encountering Ambiguity: Muʿtazilī and Twelver Shīʿī Approaches to the Qur'an's Ambiguous Verses." *Journal of Qur'anic Studies* 18 (2016): 91–115.

al-Tibrīzī, Abū Zakariyyā. *Sharḥ al-qaṣāʾid al-sabʿ maʿa al-muḍāf ilayhi*. Suleymaniye MS, Ayasofya 4095.

Tillier, Mathieu. "*Qāḍī*s and the Political Use of the Maẓālim Jurisdiction Under the ʿAbbāsids." In *Public Violence in Islamic Societies: Power, Discipline, and the Construction of the Public Sphere, 7th–19th Centuries CE*, edited by Christian Lange and Maribel Fierro, 42–66. Edinburgh: Edinburgh University Press, 2009.

Toorawa, Shawkat. "The Autobiography of ʿAbd al-Laṭīf al-Baġdādī (1162–1231)." In *Interpreting the Self: Autobiography in the Arabic Literary Tradition*, edited by Dwight F. Reynolds, 156–64. Berkeley: University of California Press, 2001.

———. "A Portrait of ʿAbd al-Laṭīf al-Baġdādī's Education and Instruction." In *Law and Education in Medieval Islam: Studies in Memory of Professor G. Makdisi*, edited by Joseph Lowry, Devin Stewart, and Shawkat Toorawa, 91–109. Oxford: E. J. W. Gibb Memorial Trust, 2004.

Toral, Isabel. "The *ʿIqd al-farīd* by Ibn ʿAbd Rabbih: The Birth of a Classic." In *Approaches to the Study of Pre-Modern Arabic Anthologies*, edited by Bilal Orfali and Nadia Maria El Cheikh, 3–20. Leiden: Brill, 2021.

Toral-Niehoff, Isabel. "'Fact and Fiction' in der mittelalterlichen arabischen Literatur: Anmerkungen zu einer Debatte." In *Faktuales und fiktionales Erzählen: Inderdisziplinäre Perspektiven*, edited by Monika Fludernik, Nicole Falkenhayer, and Julian Steiner, 59–76. Würzburg: Ergon-Verlag, 2015.

Tuck, Eve, and K. Wayne Yang. "Decolonization Is Not a Metaphor." *Tabula Rasa* 38 (2021): 61–111.

Tuttle, Kelly. "Expansion and Digression: A Study in Mamluk Literary Commentary." PhD diss., University of Pennsylvania, 2013.

———. "Play and Display: Al-Ṣafadī's *Invention of Absurdity*." *postmedieval* 4 (2013): 364–78.

al-ʿUkbarī, ʿAbd Allāh b. al-Ḥusayn. *Sharḥ al-alfāẓ al-lughawiyya min al-Maqāmāt al-Ḥarīrīya*. Edited by Nāṣir Ḥusayn ʿAlī. Damascus: Dār Saʿd al-Dīn, 2005.

Vajda, Georges. "The Oral Transmission of Knowledge in Traditional Islam." In *Education and Learning in the Early Islamic World*, edited by Claude Gilliot, 163–72. London: Routledge, 2017.

van Ess, Josef. *Im Halbschatten: Der Orientalist Hellmut Ritter (1892–1971)*. Wiesbaden: Harrassowitz Verlag, 2013.

van Gelder, Geert Jan. *Beyond the Line: Classical Arabic Literary Critics on the Coherence and Unity of the Poem*. Leiden: Brill, 1982.

———. *Classical Arabic Literature: A Library of Arabic Literature Anthology*. New York: New York University Press, 2013.

———. "Forbidden Firebrands: Frivolous *Iqtibās* (Quotation from the Qurʾān) According to the Medieval Arab Critics." *Quaderni di Studi Arabi* 20/21 (2002–2003): 3–16.

———. "Good Times, Bad Times: Opinions on Fasād az-Zamān, 'The Corruption of Time.'" In *Inḥiṭāṭ–The Decline Paradigm: Its Influence and Persistence in the Writing of Arab Cultural History*, edited by Syrinx von Hees, 111–30. Würzburg: Ergon Verlag, 2017.

———. "Ibn Rashīq." *EI3*.

———. "Mixtures of Jest and Earnest in Classical Arabic Literature, Part I." *Journal of Arabic Literature* 23 (1992): 83–108.

———. "Mixtures of Jest and Earnest in Classical Arabic Literature, Part II." *Journal of Arabic Literature* 23 (1992): 169–190.

———. Review of *Sheherazade Through the Looking Glass: The Metamorphosis of the "Thousand and One Nights,"* by Eva Sallis. *Journal of the Royal Asiatic Society* 10 (2000): 230–32.

Veracini, Lorenzo. "Colonialist and Decolonial Metaphors." *Law Text Culture* 26 (2022): 21–35.

Vishanoff, David R. *The Formation of Islamic Hermeneutics: How Sunni Legal Theorists Imagined a Revealed Law.* New Haven, CT: American Oriental Society, 2011.

von Grunebaum, Gustave E. *Medieval Islam: A Study in Cultural Orientation.* Chicago: University of Chicago Press, 1946.

———. *A Tenth-Century Document of Arabic Literary Theory and Criticism: The Sections on Poetry of al-Bāqillānī's "Iʿjāz al-Qurʾān."* Translated by Gustave E. Von Grunebaum. Chicago: University of Chicago Press, 1950.

von Hees, Syrinx, ed. Inḥiṭāṭ—*The Decline Paradigm: Its Influence and Persistence in the Writing of Arab Cultural History.* Würzburg: Ergon Verlag, 2017.

Wagner, Ewald. Review of "Certificates of Transmission on a Manuscript of the *Maqāmāt* of Ḥarīrī," by Pierre A. MacKay (*Transactions of the American Philosophical Society*, n.s., 61, no. 4 [1971]). *ZMDG* 123 (1973): 406–7.

al-Wansharīsī, Aḥmad b. Yaḥyā. *Al-Miʿyār al-muʿrib wa-l-jāmiʿ al-mughrib ʿan fatāwā ahl Ifrīqiyya wa-l-Andalus wa-l-Maghrib.* Edited by Muḥammad Ḥajjī. Rabat: Wizārat al-Awqāf wa-l-Shuʾūn al-Islāmiyya li-l-Mamlaka al-Maghribiyya, 1981–83.

Ware, Rudolph T. *The Walking Qur'an: Islamic Education, Embodied Knowledge, and History in West Africa.* Chapel Hill: University of North Carolina Press, 2014.

al-Wāsiṭī. *Sharḥ Maqāmāt al-Ḥarīrī.* Princeton MS Garrett 2908Y.

Weipert, Reinhard. "al-Aṣmaʿī." *EI3.*

Weiss, Bernard G. *The Search for God's Law: Islamic Jurisprudence in the Writings of Sayf al-Din al-Amidi.* Salt Lake City: University of Utah Press, 1992.

Wensinck, A. J. "ʿAmr b. al-ʿĀṣ." *EI2.*

———. "The Refused Dignity." In *A Volume of Oriental Studies Presented to Edward G. Browne . . . on His 60th Birthday (7 February 1922).* Edited by T. W. Arnold and Reynold A. Nicholson, 491–99. Cambridge: Cambridge University Press, 1922.

Wenzel, Jennifer. *The Disposition of Nature: Environmental Crisis and World Literature.* New York: Fordham University Press, 2019.

Witkam, Jan Just. "The Human Element Between Text and Reader: The *ijāza* in Arabic Manuscripts." In *Education and Learning in the Early Islamic World*, edited by Claude Gilliot, 149–62. London: Routledge, 2017.

Yāqūt al-Ḥamawī al-Rūmī. *Muʿjam al-buldān.* Beirut: Dār Ṣādir, 1977.

———. *Muʿjam al-udabāʾ: Irshād al-Arīb ilā Maʿrifat al-Adīb.* Edited by Iḥsān ʿAbbās. Beirut: Dār al-Gharb al-Islāmī, 1993.

Yarbrough, Luke. "A Christian Shīʿī, and Other Curious Confreres: Ibn ʿAbd al-Barr of Córdoba on Getting Along with Unbelievers." *Al-Masāq* 30 (2018): 284–303.

al-Yāzijī. *Epistola critica Nasifi al-iazigi Berytensis ad De Sacyum.* Leipzig: German Oriental Society, 1848.

Zadeh, Travis. "'Fire Cannot Harm It': Mediation, Temptation and the Charismatic Power of the Qur'an." *Journal of Qur'anic Studies* 10 (2008): 50–72.

Zakharia, Katia. *Abū Zayd al-Sarūǧī, imposteur et mystique: Relire les Maqāmāt d'al-Ḥarīrī*. Damascus: Institut Français d'Études Arabes, 2000.

———. "Ibn al-Ṣayqal al-Jazarī, auteur de *maqāmāt*." *Synergies: Monde Arabe* 6 (2009) 73–90.

———. "Norme et fiction dans la genèse des *Maqâmât* d'al-Harîrî." *Bulletin d'Études Orientales* 46 (1994): 217–31.

———. "Les références coraniques dans les *Maqāmāt* d'Al-Ḥarīrī: Éléments d'une lecture sémiologique." *Arabica* 34 (1987): 275–86.

Zaydān, Jurjī. *Tārīkh Ādāb al-Lugha al-ʿArabiyya*. Cairo: Hindāwī, 2013.

Zeeman, Nicolette. "Imaginative Theory." In *Middle English*, edited by Paul Strohm, 222–40. Oxford Twenty-First Century Approaches to Literature. Oxford: Oxford University Press, 2007.

Index

Page numbers in **bold** refer to illustrations.

Acknowledgments

This project began many years ago, and I have accumulated many debts in the process, most of which will likely go unpaid. Everett K. Rowson, my doctoral adviser, has shared his generous support, thoughtful conversation, and encyclopedic knowledge with me over the years. I wish to express my gratitude to my teachers, advisers, and mentors including Michael Allan, Joel Blecher, Michael Cooperson, Beatrice Gruendler, Anouar El-Haitami, Marion Katz, Philip Kennedy, Tamer El-Leithy, James Montgomery, Bilal Orfali, Maurice Pomerantz, and Shawkat Toorawa. They have generously offered their time and insight in ways that shaped this project. The members of Michael Cook's Holberg Seminar gave helpful feedback on some of the original dissertation chapters. Although this book began as a dissertation, I have completely rewritten it over the past several years, and I was lucky to have friends and colleagues who were willing to read my drafts, convey crucial feedback, and provide miraculous aid acquiring manuscripts. Those tireless readers and intercessors include Tom Abi Samra, C. Ceyhun Arslan, Guy Burak, Hannah Scott Deuchar, Hacı Osman Gündüz, Lara Harb, Konrad Hirschler, Karim Malak, Christian Mauder, Benedict Reier, Guy Ron-Gilboa, Emily Sun, Chloe Wheeler, and my editor Jenny Tan. The excellent copyediting of Karen Carroll also came to the rescue more times than I wish to admit in print. Thank you to the Princeton Islamic Studies Colloquium workshop at Princeton University and to Lara Harb and her students for workshopping Chapters 5 and 7. The erudite anonymous reviewers gave me a lot to think about and some wise counsel, which I tried to heed as much as I could.

I have received the support of several institutions and grants over the course of this project, including New York University, American University of Sharjah, Barnard College, and the Institute for Advanced Study. I have learned so much from my colleagues and students at these institutions, and I am especially thankful to the advice of my Institute colleagues in the final stages of this project, in particular Garrett Davidson, Rana Mikati, and

SherAli K. Tareen. I also received postdoctoral support from the Anonym-Classic project at Freie Universität Berlin, which received funding from the European Research Council (ERC) under the European Union's Horizon 2020 research and innovation programme under grant agreement No. 742 635. This publication was made possible in part through the support of a grant from Templeton Religion Trust. The opinions expressed in this publication are those of the authors and do not, however, necessarily reflect the views of Templeton Religion Trust. Thanks are also due to Brill Publishers for permission to reuse some previously published material. Finally, I express my gratitude for the generous help of librarians and libraries across the world, especially the Süleymaniye Kütüphanesi, the Leiden University Library, the Bibliothèque Nationale de France, the British Library, the Princeton University Firestone Library, the Dār al-Kutub al-Miṣriyya in Cairo, and the Staatsbibliothek zu Berlin.

Andrew McLaren and Sarah Savant deserve special thanks for reading through the entire book manuscript and offering thorough feedback that addressed both minute details and big picture questions. Andrew has also been letting me talk and text at him for several years now while I was working through my inchoate ideas for this project and many others. Several years ago in Cairo, my cousin Ferdinand Evaldsson offered me a spare room while I offered him my occasional services as an Arabic translator, and I have enjoyed our conversations about religion, art, and politics ever since. For his consultations about the artwork for this book, I offer my humble gratitude. I am a better scholar and a better person than I might otherwise be thanks to Elias G. Saba, my friend and colleague who has provided advice and encouragement on this and other projects for over fifteen years. And to the many, many other people not mentioned here who gave me feedback, advice, pushback, and probing questions over the years at conferences and workshops, please know that it was valued. The errors and oversights are, of course, my own responsibility.

The people closest to me have shaped my life and, by extension, made this project possible. My parents and brother were my first teachers, and they have supported me and taught me so much over the years. The many members of the Alvarez-Jones-Keegan clan have embraced me with open arms and brought immense joy into my life. As for Perla, my brilliant and marvelous wife, she has lived with this project since the very beginning. She has offered her advice and her keen eye to drafts of my work going back to the dissertation. More than that, she has been a comrade and companion in the fight for justice amid causes that seem lost. She has made every success sweeter and every burden lighter. This book is dedicated to her.

www.ingramcontent.com/pod-product-compliance
Lightning Source LLC
Chambersburg PA
CBHW030258100426
42812CB00002B/481
* 9 7 8 1 5 1 2 8 2 8 8 7 0 *